Copts in Context

Studies in Comparative Religion
Frederick M. Denny, Series Editor

COPTS IN CONTEXT

Negotiating Identity, Tradition, and Modernity

Edited by
Nelly van Doorn-Harder

The University of South Carolina Press

© 2017 University of South Carolina

Published by the University of South Carolina Press
Columbia, South Carolina 29208

www.sc.edu/uscpress

Manufactured in the United States of America

24 23 22 21 20 19 18 17
10 9 8 7 6 5 4 3 2 1

Library of Congress Cataloging-in-Publication Data
can be found at http://catalog.loc.gov/

ISBN: 978-1-61117-784-8 (hardcover)
ISBN: 978-1-61117-785-5 (ebook)

CONTENTS

List of Illustrations • vii

Series Editor's Preface • ix

Preface • xi

Note on Transliteration • xiii

Introduction: Creating and Maintaining Tradition in Modernity • 1

Part 1: Identity in Transition

The Copts in the January Revolution of 2011 • 21
Sebastian Elsässer

The Undesirables of Egypt: A Story of Persecution and Defiance • 34
Mariz Tadros

Examining the Role of Media in Coptic Studies • 52
Angie Heo

Father Samaan and the Charismatic Trend within the Coptic Church • 66
Gaétan du Roy

Transmitting Coptic Musical Heritage • 80
Séverine Gabry-Thienpont

Part 2: Challenges of the Diaspora

Singing Strategic Multiculturalism: The Discursive Politics of Song in Coptic-Canadian Protests • 93
Carolyn M. Ramzy

Coptic Migrant Churches: Transnationalism and the Negotiation of Different Roles • 107
Ghada Botros

Strategies of Adaptation for Survival: The Introduction of Converts
to the Coptic Orthodox Community in the Greater Toronto Area • 124
Rachel Loewen

Belonging to the Church Community: From Childhood Years Onward • 134
Nora Stene

Part 3: Tradition

The Revival of the Coptic Language and the Formation
of Coptic Ethnoreligious Identity in Modern Egypt • 151
Hiroko Miyokawa

Reading the Church's Story: The "'Amr-Benjamin Paradigm"
and Its Echoes in *The History of the Patriarchs of Alexandria* • 157
Mark Swanson

The Evolution of Lent in Alexandria and the
Alleged Reforms of Patriarch Demetrius • 169
Maged S. A. Mikhail

The Perfect Monk: Ideals of Masculinity in the Monastery of Shenoute • 181
Caroline T. Schroeder

The Paradox of Monasticism: The Transformation of
Ascetic Ideals from the Fourth to the Seventh Century • 194
Karel C. Innemée

Reconsidering the Emerging Monastic Desertscape • 205
Darlene L. Brooks Hedstrom

Notes • 219

Selected Bibliography • 267

Contributors • 275

Index • 279

ILLUSTRATIONS

Fig. 1. Words of encouragement from Pope Tawadros, early 2013 • 2

Fig. 2. Recent icon of Saint Dimayana and her forty virgins • 5

Fig. 3. Portrait of Saint and Pope Kyrillos VI • 10

Fig. 4. Poster to commemorate Pope Shenouda's fiftieth anniversary as a monk • 12

Fig. 5. Icon of the Archangel Gabriel • 58

Fig. 6. Icon painting of the Virgin Mary, by Ishaq Rufa'il Girgis • 60

Fig. 7. Flyer for Magued Tawfik's hagiographic films • 61

Fig. 8. Poster of the six martyrs of the Nag Hammadi shootings • 63

Fig. 9. "Stick method" to teach the *Halleluia* • 87

Fig. 10. Egyptian Coptic-Canadians protest the 2010 Nag Hammadi killings • 94

Fig. 11. Taratil CD dispensing machine • 98

Fig. 12. Cover/masthead from *'Ayn Shams* magazine, no. 1 • 153

Fig. 13. Survey map of the surroundings of the Monastery of Saint Macarius • 202

Fig. 14. Structure 25, preliminary reconstruction • 203

SERIES EDITOR'S PREFACE

This remarkable book provides contemporary readers and scholars around the world with a delightful and rewarding journey through the complex and generally lesser known dimension of Egyptian religious history: Coptic Christianity. Professor van Doorn-Harder and her superb contributors themselves represent a rich diversity of scholarly and cultural contexts and together have indeed enabled us to learn about "Copts in diverse *contexts*." The contexts in which Coptic Christians have lived, loved, believed and survived through long and often challenging eras, contexts and regions are described and explained. as the subtitle proclaims, by "Negotiating Identity, Tradition, and Modernity."

Copts in Context will provide an exciting product in the popular market of historical studies of lesser known but intriguing subjects. If I were still a full-time religious studies professor of history of religions and Islamic studies, with a considerable amount of field research in Egypt, I would immediately design a course using this book and encourage colleagues in history, theology, anthropology, and sociology to use it as well. Professors and their students will be thrilled to learn about Copts in Egyptian history down to the present, not only as they have lived and believed but also as they are living in significant growing "migrant churches" in the contemporary world well beyond Egypt, such as in Canada. Christian readers from any denomination will be introduced to contemporary Coptic sacred music including hymns.

Frederick Mathewson Denny

PREFACE

This book is the culmination of several years of research and collaboration that started in September 2008 with a panel during the International Congress for Coptic Studies. During this panel papers were read that covered topics related to challenges and opportunities scholars faced when studying the contemporary Coptic Orthodox Church of Egypt, the indigenous church of that nation. One of the panel's conclusions was that in the Coptic context it is impossible to divorce history and ancient tradition from the modern period, even from current-day events.

Two years later several of us met again in September (17–19, 2010) during a three-day international meeting at Wake Forest University. This time the theme of the meeting included historical matters. Using the working title "The Future of Coptic Studies: Theories, Methodologies, and Subjects," the goal was to assess how various developments within the field of Coptic studies informed studies within the different time periods. Coptic studies covers a timespan of nearly two thousand years, starting as a subcategory of pharaonic, early Christian, and other studies on antiquity. Most of its practitioners, such as textual scholars, archaeologists, and art historians, have studied the pre-Islamic period. Research on Egypt's Christian heritage after the seventh century, the time of the Arab-Muslim invasion, only began to develop during the past thirty years, so there remains much to say about the modern era and how early history continues to inform current events.

While preparing a book based on the conference, on January 25, 2011, the Arab Spring reached Egypt. With several of the authors living in Egypt and/or being involved in these events, the book had to be put on hold. When two years later their minds could turn to academia again and the revised chapters started to arrive at my computer, it became clear that the focus of the book had shifted from research trends to elements of Coptic identity. In spite of these academic considerations, the ultimate goal of the book remains to provide a bird's-eye view of topics that present the Coptic historic and contemporary experience to a wider audience.

Among the many readers, the three anonymous peer reviewers provided invaluable suggestions toward reaching this goal and strengthening the content of this book. I express my deep appreciation to them as well as to Kari Vogt and Magda Kamel, who took the time to read most of the chapters, and I thank Maged S. A. Mikhail and Mark Swanson for carefully reading my introduction. I also thank the students at Wake Forest University, who over the years helped me with the editorial work:

Lindsey Mullen, Martha Fulton, Meagan Lankford, Chris Iskander, John Iskander, John James, and Keith Menhinick. They read through the manuscript and came up with useful ideas about how to make the book accessible to the classroom.

The generous grants that paid for the international conference came from Dr. Kline Harrison's Office for Global Affairs, the Religion Department, and the Department of Philosophy at Wake Forest University. I thank the colleagues and students from the WFU School of Divinity for organizing a reception in honor of Bishop Serapion, the Coptic bishop of Los Angeles, Southern California, and Hawai'i. This meeting would not have been so successful had it not been for the bishop's keynote speech, his support, and his presence. And, of course, I will always remain grateful to the members of the Coptic community in Winston Salem, North Carolina, who, under the leadership of Mrs. Laurice Iskander, provided us with meals and places to stay.

This book would furthermore not have been possible without the help of colleagues who participated in the conference as moderators and respondents: Stephen Boyd, Linda Bridges, Michaelle Browers, Mary Foskett, Simeon Ilesanmi, Ronald Neal, Lynn Neal, Gail O'Day, Tanisha Ramachandran, Neal Walls, and Charles Wilkin. I also thank David Morgan from Duke University and Vincent Cornell from Emory University for their brilliant responses to some of the panels.

Above all, I would like to thank the participants at the different meetings and the authors who provided material for this book. Some of them are presenting brand-new material, while others have revisited earlier research. All of them went the extra mile to represent a community that has lived, for too long, at the outer edges of World Christianity.

I also need to mention the good advice and encouragement given by many colleagues: Christian Chaillot, Gawdat Gabra, Magdi Guirguis, Laure Guirguis, Vivian Ibrahim, Levi Klempner, Helen Moussa, Michael Saad, Hani Takla and Jason Zaborowski. I thank them all.

Finally, I thank James Denton and Linda Fogle at the University of South Carolina Press for their patience and for not losing faith in this project.

NOTE ON TRANSLITERATION

The essays in this book are the result of research performed within various disciplines, and the sources used range from interviews and websites in Arabic and English and other languages to published materials and manuscripts in Arabic, Greek, and Coptic. Depending on the discipline and source materials, Arabic words are represented in a variety of ways, ranging from the scientific transliteration of standard Arabic, including diacritical marks, to the representation without diacritical marks of words and names as pronounced in contemporary everyday conversation. Rather than trying to impose an artificial uniformity on the collection, the decisions of each individual author have been respected. For the most part, though, the use of diacritical marks has been limited to bibliographical references to books and articles in Arabic, or to citations of sources with such marks in the title, for example: Gabry-Thienpont, Séverine. "*Tarânîm* et *madîh:* chants liturgiques coptes ou chansons populaires égyptiennes?"

Complete references to sources quoted are provided within the notes to each essay. The bibliography at the end of this volume includes selected titles of books and articles that are of relevance to studying the Coptic Orthodox Church throughout the various time periods discussed in this book.

INTRODUCTION
Creating and Maintaining Tradition in Modernity

The year 2013 will be imprinted on Coptic memory for centuries to come.[1] During the chaotic last days of the regime of Mohamed Morsi (2011–2012), the president elected after the Arab Spring revolution of January 26, 2011, two events happened that shocked both Christian and Muslim Egyptians to the core.[2] In April the Coptic cathedral, the heart of Coptic faith, culture, and life, was openly attacked by an angry mob throwing firebombs and rocks into the building.[3] While still reeling from this event, the army forced President Morsi out of office.[4] Mid-August, in what appeared to be acts of retaliation and frustration following the police raid that killed more than one thousand Muslim Brotherhood members and supporters at Rabia al-Adawiya Square,[5] mobs damaged or fully destroyed nearly one hundred churches, schools, libraries, and other Christian institutions.[6] Destruction on this scale had not happened since the time of the Bahri Mamluks (1250–1382): a period remembered as "a grievous one for the Coptic Christian community."[7]

Coptic Orthodox places were not the only ones attacked; Protestant and Catholic property went up in flames as well. However, for the Orthodox Copts, the original Christians of Egypt, it was not just material property that vanished, but their sacred history and geography as well. This geography, firmly rooted in Egyptian soil, follows the itinerary of the Holy Family. It is situated on ground that absorbed the blood of the early martyrs and is marked by places where saints once lived and the Holy Virgin is believed to have appeared.[8]

The material losses were least important in the attack on one of the largest cathedrals in Africa; roofs can be repaired, walls rebuilt. Instead, it was the symbolic significance of these losses that was most affecting. To the Orthodox Copts the cathedral is the center of their faith and heritage. Named after Saint Mark the Apostle, it represents the history of their Church[9] and community indigenous to Egypt and traces its origins to the arrival of the Apostle Mark in Alexandria, sometime between the years 42 and 62 C.E. The Church's current pope, Tawadros II (2012–), is the 118th in a line of nearly uninterrupted succession starting with Saint Mark.[10] Large parts of Coptic history remain unknown; however, the little we do know, especially after the Arab invasion of 641 C.E., depends on the lives of the popes. They guided the believers in their faith, often embodied the struggles of the entire community, and served as their official representatives to the ruling governments.

Fig. 1. Words of encouragement from Pope Tawadros sent early 2013 in the midst of the chaos of the revolution. "Always include the word *kyrie eleison* [Lord have mercy] in your prayers these days and continuously remember that it moved the Mokattam. I am certain that God's promise is ever present and He will protect our country." Photograph by the author. Used with the permission of the Coptic Orthodox Church.

For most of their existence the Copts and their popes remained unknown outside Egypt. In part thanks to the aftermath of the Arab Spring, increased ecumenical relationships, and modern media, Pope Tawadros has become a familiar presence around the globe. For example, the ceremonies of his election and enthronement, for the first time in history, could be watched live on TV.[11]

Pope Tawadros's public speeches in the aftermath of the August attacks also brought to the attention of the world the particularities of Coptic theology that insist on nonviolence. Throughout history Copts have seldom retaliated or fought back, instead stressing the spiritual benefits of suffering, even martyrdom.[12] Tawadros II did not divert from this policy when he told a United States delegation that "the price of freedom is precious and burning churches is part of the price we offer to our country with patience and love."[13] The pope gained high praise from Copts inside and outside Egypt when he announced that, instead of filing official complaints about the harm done, his community would offer the burnt churches as a sacrificial offering, a *qorban,* to the nation of Egypt. However, some activist groups of young Copts have critiqued the pope for not condemning what happened in Rabia Square and for not standing up to defend civil liberties.[14] Although in the eyes of many their points are well taken, most observers would concede that the pope showed a sense of prudence and practicality in a complex situation: it was next to impossible to identify individual culprits from among the attacking mobs. Instead, he tried to underscore the Coptic sense of nationalism and belonging. Even when unwelcome, invisible, or living in diaspora, for many Copts, Egypt remains the homeland.

Copticness—Creating and Embodying a Metanarrative: On Being a Copt

The essays in this book have been organized with the theme of Coptic identity as the guiding principle. By itself a concept too general to define, broadly speaking, *identity* refers to the self-understanding of a certain group, its sense of belonging, and the commonalities and connections between and among its members.[15] It is the conglomerate of particular cultures and practices developed and constructed over time that includes the group's values, traditions, idioms and peculiarities.

As is the case with other population groups, the answer to the question "Who is a Copt?" is complex. On a theological level it refers to those who are baptized into the Coptic Orthodox Church and are allowed to participate in all its sacraments. Ethnically, it is an Orthodox Christian from Egypt. Culturally, according to the Coptic scholar Mariz Tadros, many Coptic authors "describe the basis of their identity as being a common ancient Egyptian heritage, which is based in turn on notions of historical roots in the land and ties to the civilization, to a heritage dating back thousands of years."[16] The everyday language for Copts in Egypt, however, is Arabic. Being part of the Arabic-speaking world has oriented many Copts toward the Middle East. For example, the strong support of Pope Shenouda (1971–2012) for Arab causes, such as the Palestinian right to Jerusalem, gained him the unofficial title Pope of the Arabs.[17] Yet for many Copts this affiliation remains problematic, since Arab identity is intertwined with Islamic heritage. Moreover, increasing numbers of Copts living outside of Egypt grow up never speaking a word of Arabic.

The original meaning of the word Copt is "Egyptian." It derives from *Qibt*, the Arabic translation of the Greek word for Egypt, *Aigyptos*.[18] Originally all Egyptians were referred to as Copts, but over time the word became synonymous with Egyptian Christians. It remains difficult to know exactly how many Copts live in Egypt, with estimates ranging from 5 to 10 percent of the population.[19]

The Copts have never governed Egypt. When Christianity first spread they were ruled by the Byzantine Empire, which in 641 C.E. was replaced by the Arab invasion. Their language, Coptic, the spoken language of ancient Egypt, was never used as the official administrative and literary language; instead, Greek and later Arabic were used.[20] Although in numbers one could define Copts as a minority, they understand themselves to be fully Egyptian. As a result they have always rejected the classification "minority."

However, scholars such as Jurgen Habermas have observed that it is vital for minorities in pluralistic societies to have the ability to disagree with the principles of the majority within a constitutional framework.[21] For the Copts it has not yet been possible to arrive at such a level of full participation. Coptic concerns and demands have never truly been part of the national discussion in Egypt, which constitutionally privileges the Arab, Islamic identity. The position of the Copts is looked upon as "the Coptic question" or problem. The term used in Arabic is the *Coptic File* (*al-millaf al-qibti*), a term that conveys the idea that the condition of the Copts is not really central to the national interests and can be filed away if needed.

While the 2011 revolution seemed to have created new platforms for the Copts to have their voices heard, the options quickly dwindled when incidences of sectarian violence increased. From co-revolutionaries at Tahrir Square, by August 2013 Copts had become scapegoats for the heavy-handedness on the part of army and security forces. Several essays in this book discuss how different Coptic groups negotiated the opening and closing of the window of opportunities for emancipation and participation. The Maspero events especially brought home the limits of Coptic agency.

Sebastian Elsässer's essay details the road that a Coptic activist group, the Maspero Youth Movement, walked, from initial euphoria to despair on October 9, 2011, when their peaceful protest against the destruction of a church in Aswan ended in a massacre at the hands of military and police forces.[22] These events exposed some of the persistent and recurring questions about identity, exclusion, and belonging that have been central to the Coptic community throughout the twentieth century[23]; they struck Coptic sensibilities to the core, setting Coptic media ablaze and triggering, among other things, the public demonstrations laden with symbolism in Canada that are described in Carolyn M. Ramzy's esssay.

Copts experience exclusion, materially or symbolically, in many influential sectors of society. A few exceptions aside, access to the highest levels of power has been out of reach for most of their existence. Although influence on the state apparatus escapes them, several Coptic families have focused on marshalling financial and other resources that provide leverage in times of need, while the community often uses its symbolic resources in the struggle for influence.[24] Rallying around Church and community for many Copts continues to be one of the main strategies for participating in the public realm of Egypt.

Copts not only share a deep sense of belonging with the rest of Egyptians, but they also have many social, cultural, and economic similarities with the Muslim population.[25] At the same time, Copts rely on their own discursive and symbolic resources to draw the boundary lines that set them apart as a group in its own right.[26] These efforts of constructing, re-constructing, and strengthening a uniquely Coptic identity create subtle boundaries in orientation and standards that accumulate into a set of markers that observers of the Coptic Church have identified as "Copticness."[27]

For example, dress has increasingly become a marker of identity. Copts have their own media such as newspapers, journals, and private television stations. They affirm Christian identity via a small cross tattooed on the right wrist which can be hidden or not, by wearing crosses, and by displaying pictures of their favorite saints such as Saint George, the Roman soldier, and Saint Dimyana who is always

Fig. 2. A recent icon of Saint Dimayana and her forty virgins. Photograph by the author. Used with the permission of the Coptic Orthodox Church.

surrounded by a community of forty virgins; all are remembered as martyrs who refused to worship Roman gods. Since his death in 1971, the picture of the saintly pope Kyrillos VI, who was canonized in June 2013, is also present in nearly every Coptic pocket, handbag, car, or house.

Naturally, processes of both inclusion and exclusion are simultaneously required for specific Coptic identity markers to emerge within the process of constructing and deconstructing boundaries.[28] Scholars such as Simon Harrison have observed that when the similarities between groups are close this boundary-making process intensifies.[29] While the most obvious distinction between the Orthodox Copts and other Egyptians seems to be religious, they also differentiate themselves from other Christian denominations such as Protestants, Roman Catholics, and more evangelical movements that seem to encroach on certain areas of their Church. Some Orthodox Copts, for example, attend their own church to partake of the sacraments while attending Protestant churches for other types of worship services. The essay by Gaétan du Roy deals with such new trends in Coptic worship. One of the main markers of difference between the Orthodox Copts and other denominations is that the Coptic Orthodox Church is indigenous to Egypt while the Catholic, Protestant, and other Orthodox denominations were introduced from the outside.

Although Copticness might be considered to be the hallmark of the Coptic Orthodox Christians in Egypt, Copts residing in the diaspora and other non-Egyptian Copts share in this identity as well. Until the 1960s the Coptic Church was present only in Egypt, the Sudan, and Ethiopia, but today Coptic communities reside all around the world.[30] More than five hundred churches governed by twenty-six bishops have been opened in diaspora. As a result, Copts, by birth, marriage, or conversion, living as far away as Australia and Hong Kong, share Egypt as the religious, cultural, and symbolic center of their church.

Coptic communities, in spite of their vast geographical distances from one another, continue to define themselves in reference to their shared Church rules, history, and traditions. Nora Stene's essay analyzes how participating in the sacramental and congregational life in Coptic churches in Cairo and London inserts children into the fabric of the community and endows them with a strong sense of belonging. Furthermore, in Egypt, as well as in diaspora, Coptic memories about the foundational events in their Church as transmitted through the ages set them apart from their environment. Copts feel connected with all of their forebears and are interested in every aspect of their history, from the archaeological evidence of monasteries and churches, to texts, art, and other markers and makers of Coptic history, including martyrs, monks, saints, nuns, popes, and bishops.

Since the beginning of the twentieth century Copts have been active in rediscovering, preserving, and transmitting their history and tradition. Across the diaspora, initiatives such as the Saint Shenouda the Archimandrite Coptic Society in Los Angeles, California, and the Canadian Society for Coptic Studies (CSCS) have been launched to preserve and study Coptic history.[31] Journals such as *Le Monde Copte, Coptologia, Coptica*, and the *Journal of the Canadian Society for Coptic Studies* (JCSCS) showcase research that often comes from the hands of Coptic scholars who engaged in Coptic studies while working full time as city comptrollers, medical doctors, or engineers.[32]

Until recently Copts were mostly interested in ancient, pre-Islamic history. For many Copts foundational events, modern or ancient, are inextricably intertwined. Ancient debates, practices, and cultural expressions are reappropriated and placed into contemporary contexts. Stories of survival and miraculous rescue that happened hundreds of years ago are told as if they happened yesterday and the narrator herself had been present. Thus, in order to understand the repository of Coptic culture, tradition, and values, one has to understand some of the formative moments in Coptic Orthodox history.

Emerging Identities: The Early Centuries

Current expressions of Coptic self-understanding and identity were shaped under the influence of transformative moments and symbols in the history of the Coptic Orthodox Church that have become the foundation for collective memories, religious practices, the material landscape, and the soundscape.[33] Furthermore, the Coptic horizon has always been shifting from the city to the desert and back. This was the case in the early centuries when the monastic movement was in its infancy and remains the case today as Coptic bishops and the pope are elected from among the monks.

During the first three centuries C.E. there was no separate Coptic identity, only the Egyptian identity. Christians were all part of the universal Church. It was around the fourth century that a distinctly Coptic Church, along with a religious as well as a national identity came into being.[34] Until that time Alexandria was the intellectual and philosophical center of the Christian world. As far as we know, the title of pope (papa/father) was first used in the third century for the archbishop of Alexandria.[35] Illustrious theologians such as Clement (ca. 150–215 C.E.) and Origen (ca. 185–234/235 C.E.) were connected to the Catechetical School of Alexandria, a leading center of theological learning in the ancient Christian world. Reflecting its cosmopolitan character was the fact that most of the church leaders wrote in Greek, while Coptic was the language of the laypeople.

Until the fourth century there were intermittent periods of persecution by Roman emperors who tried to eradicate Christianity. None is remembered as vividly as the time of Diocletian, whose persecutions were so relentless that his reign (284–305 C.E.) is remembered as the Era of the Martyrs. The Coptic calendar starts on the day that he began his reign on August 29, 284.

Egyptian Church leaders took center stage in formative theological debates such as those surrounding the nature of Christ. Before becoming the twentieth Coptic pope in 328, the famous Athanasius of Alexandria helped formulate the original version of the Nicene Creed (325 C.E.). When by 313 C.E. Christianity became a legal religion of the empire, the number of Egyptians who moved into the desert in search of peace and quiet multiplied. Although he spent a lifetime in the eastern Egyptian desert, far from civilization, Saint Anthony (ca. 251–356 C.E.) became well known as the founder of eremitic monastic life.

Christianity spread, steadily replacing the pharaonic and Roman religions. When Dioscorus became the pope of Alexandria (444–454 C.E.), he ruled a strong and healthy church. That same century, in the year 451, during the Council of Chalcedon, the beginning of a rift appeared between the Coptic Church and the rest of Christendom. The theological quarrel concerned Christ's divinity and humanity. In this very technical debate both theological camps believed in the one person of Jesus Christ, who was both perfect God and perfect man, but disagreed vehemently as to which theological terminology should be used. Chalcedonian theologians favored the use of the formula "in two natures" while the Copts and Syrians favored a definition that identified Jesus as "of two natures." Adding fuel to the subsequent debates and polemic between the two camps is the fact that *nature* (Greek *phusis*) had several definitions. The political quarrel also concerned the primacy of Rome and Constantinople vis-à-vis Alexandria. The quarrel affected the Copts on their own ground when, following the split the emperor placed a rival Melkite, or pro-Chalcedonian pope, in Alexandria, dividing Egypt's Christians.

Most of the history before and after the Arab conquest of Egypt (641 C.E.) has not been written in Coptic. After gaining prominence in the third century with Bible translations for the native Egyptians,[36] written Coptic reached its zenith during the fourth/fifth century with the prolific writings of Saint Shenoute the Archimandrite. Writings in the Coptic language were mostly religious and often produced by monks. All clergy needed knowledge of Coptic, as it was and continues to be used as the liturgical language.[37]

Coptic collective memory is based on a certain interpretation of history that, according to the Coptic scholar Samuel Moawad, was perceived as serving "the salvation plan of God for mankind" and "depended more on people than on events."[38] Much of Coptic ecclesiastical and official history is transmitted via the collection of chronicles called *The History of the Patriarchs,* the enduring influence of which is discussed by Mark Swanson in his essay. The genres of martyrdom, biography, encomium, and, later, apocalyptic tales served as influential sources that reflected Coptic suffering while highlighting individuals who upheld the true dogma and persisted in their faith.

An event based on *The History of the Patriarchs* that features in several of this book's essays is that of the miracle of the Muqattam Mountain. It dates from the time of Fatimid caliph Al-Mu'iz and the 62nd patriarch, Patriarch Afrahām ibn Zurʿah (975–978). During a public debate the caliph challenged the Coptic community to prove the truth of the Bible verse Matthew 20:17, that faith like a mustard seed can move a mountain.[39] Through the intervention of the devout one-eyed tanner Samaan, in cooperation with the Virgin Mary, the patriarch, and the entire community, the mountain moved and disaster to the Coptic community was averted. The story continues to inspire Coptic imagination in numerous ways and has gained renewed attention with the building of the large church complex and pilgrimage center named after Samaan.

Medieval Strategies

Issues of identity became central to the Copts on account of the split following the Council of Chalcedon in 451 C.E. and the Arab conquest of Egypt in 641 C.E. Accusations of heresy from other Christians affected Coptic writings, as did Muslim views on Christians as polytheists. Copts wrote their history to demonstrate Christian steadfastness and the virtues of their community and, as the essays by Mark Swanson and Maged S. A. Mikhail show, to highlight the legitimacy and faithfulness of their Church and its leadership.

From the fourteenth to the seventeenth centuries, the Coptic community was reduced by more than half, and Copts became a minority in their own land.[40] Apart from diseases such as the plague, the most important reason for this demographic shift was conversion to Islam. During the Fatimid period (969–1171), Christians were anxious about the influence of Islam and imagined an ever-Islamizing and Arabizing world.[41] Especially during the Mamluk period (1250–1517), many Copts converted to Islam out of economic necessity or in response to other pressures.[42] Febe Armanios's research has showed how, after the Ottomans conquered Egypt in 1517, religious rituals and pious expressions helped the Copts forge a specific Coptic identity, not only vis-à-vis the Muslim environment but also when facing foreign Catholic missionaries. Sermons describing the vices of others conveyed the ideals of Coptic morality, faith, race, and nation.[43] By the late seventeenth century Copts had started to define the outlines of their moral ethics and religious boundaries by regularizing religious rituals and dogmas via expressions of art, iconography, and architecture, as well as through the creation of new manuscripts.[44]

The Premodern Period: Rediscovering Tradition

The nineteenth century was a time of profound change for the Copts. Egypt emancipated from the Ottoman Empire, becoming an independent nation, while in 1856 the Copts were emancipated from the so-called dhimmi status, the status of being secondary to Muslims, and were made full citizens. These developments concurrently opened new vistas; by the middle of the century schools opened throughout the country, printed media developed, and Egyptians rediscovered their history and heritage.

It was also a time of challenges for the Copts. Protestant Western missionaries tried to convert them by opening schools. Young Copts educated in these schools started to question their Church's rituals and dogmas, and Coptic clergy had to take proactive measures to cope with these new mindsets.[45] The reforming pope Kyrillos IV (1854–1861) set the tone for future Coptic strategies in redefining boundaries: he created a new future by reaching back into the past. Inspired by Western educational models, he opened schools where Copts could learn new sciences and languages. One of his most innovative decisions was to teach the Coptic language for the first time in centuries to all Copts, not just to the clergy.[46]

Profound transitions continued during the first decades of the twentieth century. Educated in the new schools, Copts rose to positions of prominence. They engaged in Egypt's national movement and resisted British colonial power. As the educational level of lay Copts surpassed that of the clergy, the Coptic community council, the Majlis al-Milli, the council made up of laymen to take part in the Church's administration of community affairs, increased in prominence and influence. Under Pope Kyrillos VI this balance of power shifted back to the members of the clergy, who have held onto it ever since.

Individual Copts designed new strategies that helped the community rediscover its roots; in 1902 the Coptic Museum opened and became a landmark in preserving and rediscovering Coptic artistic legacy. Newfound Coptic awareness of the pharaonic heritage led to a growing interest in studying the Church's history and intensified study of the Coptic language.[47] Individuals such as Iqladiyus Labib (1868–1918), whose work Hiroko Miyokawa discusses in the tenth essay, advanced the study of Coptic language. Using the Sunday school models from the Protestant missions, visionary educator saint and archdeacon Habib Guirguis (1876–1951) created new curricula that allowed Copts to transmit their faith to children and youth.[48] During this period Coptic identity became redefined as an enduring national identity that considered all Egyptians to be descendants of the ancient Egyptians, the pharaohs.[49] In her research on new media Elizabeth Iskander found

Fig. 3. A portrait of Saint and Pope Kyrillos VI (r. 1959–1971), hanging in the Church of the Virgin Mary in Zamalek, Cairo. Photograph by the author. Used with the permission of the Coptic Orthodox Church.

that these narratives of the pharaonic roots are more present than ever among Copts in Egypt as well as in the diaspora.[50]

In the years following Coptic lay leaders remained actively engaged in creating and facilitating various forms of cultural and religious education. By the 1950s these efforts yielded a growing number of Coptic youth who were well versed in Coptic theology and culture and held leadership positions in their local churches.

They were pressing against the doors of a Church hierarchy that could not yet imagine how to accommodate this new generation.

Saint and Pope Kyrillos VI (1959–1971): Reinventing Tradition

When Kyrillos VI (1959–1971) became the 116th Coptic pope, he found a critical mass of young men and women eager to enter full-time Church service. His monastic and other reform initiatives opened the doors for these Copts, many of whom rose to high levels of Church leadership. They used their positions to continue and launch educational and pastoral initiatives that strengthened the Church and touched upon the whole of Coptic life at home as well as in church. From cradle to grave they defined Coptic identity, in the process drawing clear boundaries between their Church and the rest of society.

Building on the existing blocks of Coptic revival, the Sunday school programs, and the keen interest in Coptic history, Pope Kyrillos added a dimension of monasticism and a deep respect for saints and martyrs. The recovery of these sources of Coptic spirituality led to a religious renaissance and helped the Copts navigate the chaos of President Gamal Abdel Nasser's regime (1956–1970), when nationalization programs took away large parts of their wealth and broke the influence that powerful lay Copts had held on Church affairs for the previous half a century. Strengthening the monasteries meant raising the spiritual level of the Church's clerical leadership and also inspired active lay involvement. Concomitant with renewed interest in the spiritual legacies of the monastic life, interest in monastic settlements, practices, and writings skyrocketed. Monks started to reclaim the desert, rebuild the ruins of old monastic places, and, by the 1980s, teamed up with scholars of Coptic language, archaeologists, art historians, and preservation specialists to recover the ruins of ancient monasteries and uncover frescos that had been hidden by soot, dirt, and paint or plaster for centuries.[51]

In cooperation with President Nasser, who provided the required permits, Pope Kyrillos oversaw the building and restoration of numerous churches. In 1968 one of the most prominent Coptic landmarks opened: Saint Mark's Cathedral in Cairo became the largest cathedral and papal residence in Africa. Accompanying these building activities were projects aimed at preserving the Coptic liturgical music and reviving the art of iconography.

The Higher Institute of Coptic Studies (ICS), founded in 1954, served as main center for such activities. Its first president was the cofounder and Coptic scholar Aziz S. Atiya (1898–1988). He gained enduring fame by editing *The Coptic Encyclopedia* (1991), which was the first attempt to bring together the disparate fields of Coptic knowledge.[52] The Coptic musicologist Ragheb Moftah (1898–2001) headed the music and hymn department at ICS where he recorded the Coptic Orthodox Liturgy of Saint Basil.[53] Moftah recreated the "pure" Coptic musical heritage from old recordings of liturgical hymnody called *alhan,* which in his understanding was linked to the ancient Egyptian heritage. According to the ethnomusicologist Carolyn M. Ramzy, these liturgical soundscapes were considered to be the most

Fig. 4. A large poster to commemorate Pope Shenouda's (1971–2012) fiftieth anniversary as a monk (1954–2004). The picture evokes memories of his early days when he lived alone in a cave in the desert. Photograph by the author.

authentic representation of Coptic identity. Performing them meant preserving the authenticity of Copticness.[54] In the art department of ICS, Isaac Fanous (1919–2007) created a new genre of Coptic iconography that finds its roots in the pharaonic legacy as well as in the art of the early Coptic era.[55] The liturgical music and icons produced at ICS are now being used and imitated in churches in Egypt as well as across the world wherever Copts live in diaspora.

Pope Shenouda III (1971–2012): Expanding Tradition

Pope Shenouda III (1971–2012) solidified the Church's education and oversaw its growth outside Egypt.[56] He also positioned himself as the Church's main political spokesperson vis-à-vis the government—a situation that many young Copts strongly criticized toward the end of his reign.

During his long reign Coptic studies, both in and outside Egypt, flourished because of his continued interest in education. Expressions of material, visual, and auditory culture expanded as individual Copts added their artistic imaginations to the existing works. For example, in 1975 four musicians created the David Ensemble that performs Coptic hymns from a tradition believed to be "the natural continuation of the pharaonic hymns."⁵⁷ And the well-known mother superior, Mother Irini (1936–2006) of the Convent of Abu Saifein in Cairo, inserted an entire register of gendered themes into Coptic iconography by highlighting the role of women in Coptic history in the icons she commissioned for the new chapels within her convent.⁵⁸

Pope Shenouda was a prolific writer and preacher whose theological teachings guided the believers in questions arising from the manifold challenges of contemporary life. With his faith firmly grounded in the Alexandrian patristic theology, his main arguments were drawn from the Bible.⁵⁹ Maintaining and defining the Coptic Orthodox faith is the central theme in Pope Shenouda's writing. It is also a goal in the ecumenical dialogues that multiplied during his tenure. The decisions of the Holy Synod, the body that consists of all the bishops and is chaired by the pope, equally reflect strategies to define the boundaries of the Coptic Orthodox faith. For example, starting in 1996 the synod produced official statements condemning Protestant attempts to convert the Copts.⁶⁰ At the same time, as Gaétan du Roy describes in his essay on the churches at the Muqattam, Copts are experimenting with charismatic and other models of worship inspired by Protestant churches. These trends show keen interest in the narratives of healing and experimenting with alternative styles of prayer, worship, and preaching. As a result, drawing the line "between us and them" in some cases has become increasingly challenging.

During the time of Pope Shenouda there was also an explosion of Coptic media. Through the production of DVDs, images, journals, newspapers, TV channels, and online spaces, opportunities increased for Copts to interact with one another across the world. Such processes create new discourses and bonds of solidarity, as well as a renewed sense of belonging, especially for Copts in diaspora.⁶¹

This Book

Until quite recently, edited volumes about the Copts mostly covered topics of antiquity with only incidental entries on the modern or contemporary time period tucked in the back.⁶² In fact, up to two decades ago study of the Copts seemed limited to the time before the Arab invasion.⁶³ This situation has changed as scholars, Coptic and not Coptic, have become interested in areas such as developments in the diaspora, religious education, the role of children, Coptic media, and Coptic participation in Egyptian society and politics. As the present volume shows, these new interests have resulted in a range of interdisciplinary approaches; ethnomusicologists, sociologists, anthropologists, historians, historians of religion, and political scientists are now taking note of the Copts. At the same time studies of the ancient, medieval, and early modern periods are equally connecting disparate fields of study and using ever-widening interdisciplinary lenses. To reflect these changes the essays in this volume connect the present with the past and the past with the present. Starting with contemporary issues we work back to topics that belong to the ancient past yet remain vital in Coptic memory and understanding of culture and tradition.

The essays in this book are grouped into main parts: "Identity in Transition," "Challenges of the Diaspora," and "Tradition." The first part covers developments during the past fifty years, with several essays on the Arab Spring events. The second part concerns Copts in diaspora. The third part, on tradition, recaptures aspects of Coptic history that continue to influence and inspire contemporary trends in Coptic thinking. The role of the patriarchs and monasticism especially stand out in this part.

Several topics are not represented, although they are vital for our understanding of the Coptic community. Topics on which little has been written include gender within the Coptic context, the role and authority of the popes, the role of individual bishops, and the work of individual theologians such as Matta el-Miskin (1919–2006), the former abbot of the Monastery of Saint Macarius.[64] While this book features four essays on Copts in Canada and London, research into Coptic communities in diaspora has only just begun; there is much room for further work on Copts in the various Western countries, in Africa, and in South America.

The materials have been put together with more than students of Coptic studies in mind. Each essay provides a wealth of information for students as well as for the general reader who is interested in non-Western expressions of Christianity, the Middle East, minority studies, religious studies in general, or in interfaith engagements between Muslims and Christians.

The Essays

Identity in Transition

The first four essays are directly or indirectly connected to the Arab Spring events and depict the various ways in which Coptic identity is not static but in transition. Sebastian Elsässer's essay places some Coptic protest actions during the 2011 revolution in the context of developments during the Mubarak era (1981–2011). Via a chronology of events, he provides insights into a new movement within the Church that is unwilling blindly to obey the Coptic leadership as he charts the work of young activists and their relationship to the Church. Resisting threats of violence against the Copts from Salafi Muslims, the army, and the police, the youth strove for Coptic emancipation within the wider framework of the revolution.

Mariz Tadros's essay analyzes the triple predicament of the Zabbalin, garbage collectors who moved from the countryside to Cairo, where they face poverty, religious discrimination, and displacement. Inspired by the revolution, they staged a peaceful protest that turned into an incident of severe sectarian violence.

Angie Heo details how new media technologies transform religious rituals and specific relationships, such as that between the individual believer and the saints. Media also changes the way Copts connect with each other around the world. Ranging from DVDs to TV stations launched in Egypt and in the diaspora, these media influence the religious worldviews of Copts and allow those living outside Egypt to follow closely the events in the motherland.[65] Sectarian violence can now be witnessed around the world, even, in certain circumstances, in real time. Within days of the event, for example, the attack on the cathedral could be watched on the Internet via video clips collected by Copts inside and outside Egypt.[66]

Gaétan Du Roy's contribution analyzes one of the charismatic movements that are growing within the Coptic Orthodox Church. The Muqattam megachurch led by the charismatic priest Father Samaan challenges traditional views and methods of healing and intercession while at the same time deeply connecting with Coptic practices.

In the fifth essay in this section Séverine Gabry-Thienpont discusses some of the initiatives Copts have undertaken to document their liturgical hymnody and devotional songs that are believed to resemble the chants Egyptians sung during the time of the pharaohs. She furthermore provides insight into current attempts to standardize this music that was traditionally transmitted via oral and auditory means. In the twenty-first century this method no longer works, and Copts have designed pedagogical devices that help the communities in and outside Egypt to reproduce these melodies correctly.

Challenges of the Diaspora

Three essays concern some of the manifold challenges Copts face in the lands of migration. Copts started to leave Egypt during the 1960s following the 1952 Nasser revolution when the Coptic gentry lost large parts of its wealth and Nasser's pan-Arab ideology prioritized Egypt's Islamic heritage (with the premise that Arab nations were unified by language and history).[67] Never before had Copts left their homeland in such numbers, but this time those who had the financial resources and necessary education emigrated in droves. These expatriate communities have become vital resources for the Church and have left significant imprints on its international activities and self-image.[68]

The Church in Cairo upholds the official stance that Copts abroad should not interfere in Egypt's politics. However, Carolyn M. Ramzy's essay illustrates that depending on their locale, Coptic groups in diaspora might choose to ignore this directive. Her ethnomusicological analysis of the folk songs that are popular among certain Coptic Canadians reveals how some of them express their discontent with the situation in Egypt in ways that could potentially be problematic for the Church back home. At the same time her essay underscores the crucial role played by the Coptic musical tradition as a vehicle for expressing grief and identity.

Ghada Botros's essay shows how the churches in diaspora function as the first safety nets for immigrants while simultaneously balancing the needs of young Copts who were born outside Egypt. Providing assistance with finding work and housing, churches also serve as homes away from home. As Copts become successful as professionals and in business, they provide the funds to build new churches and community centers.

About the same time that emigration movements started, missionary activities were launched in sub-Saharan Africa that led to the creation of more than sixty new Coptic churches, monasteries, hospitals, and other community services in various countries. In Egypt, Islamic law allows only proselytizing activities carried out by Muslims. Therefore, since the seventh century the Coptic Church could only sustain its growth by birth. Not experiencing such restrictions in the West, Copts in North America have started to launch special ministries for non-Coptic youth and families. Rachel Loewen studies the brand-new role of the Coptic Orthodox Church as a missionary church in Toronto.

The essays by Ghada Botros and Rachel Loewen both examine the Church's challenges in attracting the youth and preparing children to become lifelong members. Nora Stene looks into the formation of children as they participate in and reflect on the Church's sacraments.[69] She elaborates on the importance of taking children seriously as religious actors as they learn the particular Coptic idioms. Her essay poses pertinent questions about how to train, teach, and inspire children and youth to become the actors who create and maintain the future Coptic community.

Tradition

The third part of the present book concerns the recapturing of Coptic history and tradition. It starts with a short essay by Hiroko Miyokawa that details the strategies employed by Iqladius Labib to revive the Coptic language. Pope Kyrillos IV was the first pope in the early modern period to open Coptic lessons to students outside the ranks of the clergy. As the pope he had the authority and power to initiate this change that was revolutionary at the time.[70] The Coptic Orthodox pope holds a crucial position in the Church. Yet in spite of their importance, for most of Coptic history we know little about these leaders. The main source remains the influential work entitled the *The History of the Patriarchs of Alexandria*, a work written over the course of several centuries. The essay by Mark Swanson shows how this text has long shaped the knowledge and perceptions of the Coptic community and of its popes, and the history they made or witnessed.[71]

Maged S. A. Mikhail's chapter parses the provenance of the traditions surrounding the Lenten reforms of Patriarch Demetrius (d. 232). He details the various claims surrounding the authority of the textual traditions about this reform and shows how ritual practices based on a certain understanding of the traditions influenced Coptic identity.[72] Furthermore, he demonstrates that much of what we know about the earliest centuries has reached us via Arabic texts that, in spite of their centrality, have often been neglected in Coptic studies.[73]

Monks who perfected the Christian faith while fighting demons in the desert are just as actively remembered as the Coptic popes who defended the faith (initially from heresy and later from Muslim powers). Monasticism along with its ideals, goals, and realities remains a central theme in Coptic religious life and imagination. The Coptic pope and his bishops all started their clerical careers as monks and continue to withdraw into the desert for spiritual renewal during times of crisis. At an early age Coptic children learn about the lives of monks and nuns. In Sunday school they hear stories about the heroes of the desert such as Saint Anthony, Saint Shenoute of Atrib, and Saint Mary the Egyptian. Archaeological digs in early monastic settlements continue to reveal information about the history and daily life of Coptic monks. New readings of old texts yield information about the monastic life that contradicts myths and conventional traditions. Interest in the enduring connection between the early desert fathers and mothers and the history of the Church, as well as interest in their lives and teachings, has become stronger than ever. So it seems fitting that the last three essays address new findings related to this vital part of Coptic religion and culture.

Shenoute of Atrib (ca. 348–466 C.E.), the abbot of the White Monastery, remains one of the prime symbols of Coptic identity. He became part of Church history when, together with Archbishop Cyril of Alexandria, in 431 C.E. he attended the Council of Ephesus. Mostly known as a monastic and Church leader, his writings became part of the Coptic literary legacy. Using textual materials, Caroline T. Schroeder analyzes how Shenoute's ideals on emotional discourse, paternity, genealogies, and legacies, while considered paragons of Coptic identity, in fact, derived from biblical as well as Hellenistic expectations for men's roles, such as those of fathers and sons.

Karel C. Innemée revisits the contradictions and tensions that arose when the monks who lived in independent communities had to comply with the desires of the official Church hierarchy. Having set out to live their lives away from the world, which included the Church hierarchy, they often found themselves ordained priests and bishops against their will. Today the pope, bishops, and monks who work as priests still wistfully remember their time in the monastery; indeed Pope Shenouda III (1971–2012) used to refer to the time he lived as a hermit as the most beautiful days of his life. Innemée discusses how new archaeological evidence shows that, much earlier than was thought before, monks had to compromise their ideals of seclusion as their small-scale settlements turned into densely populated "monastic suburbia."

Darlene L. Brooks Hedstrom closes the book with an essay that addresses the way narrow interpretations of what many scholars declared to be monastic dwellings, paired with the prejudiced lens through which monks and nuns were understood as fanatic and illiterate, influenced the results of archaeological findings. Only by broadening the theoretical lenses will it be possible to understand more about the monastics who left family and possessions behind to move into the desert. Instead of reinforcing the idea of a minority within a minority, new findings should reveal the living reality of monastics and the strategies they used to communicate their religious ideals to the outside world.

Preservation is vital to the Coptic community, and attention to this important issue is increasing. For example, in December 2014 Pope Tawadros organized a conference at the Institute of Coptic Studies that focused on "the applications of modern technology for documentation and conservation of Coptic heritage."[74]

Taken together, the essays in this volume show how dealing with the tradition reaffirms as well as changes Coptic identity. While it was never static to begin with, now Copts living across the globe create new opportunities and new expressions of what it means to belong and to be a member of the Coptic Orthodox Church. There is the Egyptian Copt who can trace his or her family back to the pharaohs, and the Canadian Coptic convert, yet the faith of each of them remains anchored in Egypt, where the pope's seat is at Africa's largest church, the Coptic cathedral in Cairo.

PART 1

IDENTITY IN TRANSITION

THE COPTS IN THE JANUARY REVOLUTION OF 2011

Sebastian Elsässer

Copts experienced the popular uprising against the regime of Hosni Mubarak and the following turbulent period in many different ways, much like their Muslim compatriots. The emotions of the Coptic community ranged from elation and hope to puzzlement, consternation, and anxiety. Some were actively engaged, while others looked away and focused on their daily lives. The most significant, innovative effect of the January revolution on the Coptic community was the rise of a revolutionary current specific to the Copts, a current whose focus was not on merely *participating* in the revolution, but also on *appropriating* it for the cause of Coptic emancipation. For a brief period it succeeded not only in breaking the long-standing pattern of political restraint among the Copts, but also in its strategy of direct public and popular action that articulated community-related concerns and grievances, such as legal and administrative discrimination and the lack of public recognition of Coptic identity and culture.

This current did not remain unchallenged from either side. The Muslim majority was still reluctant to recognize the legitimacy of Coptic grievances, while the influential clergy of the Coptic Orthodox Church continued to advocate and pursue different ways of political action. Together with increasing public attention to sectarian conflict, the Coptic question was high on the political agenda in the months after the fall of Mubarak, thereby revealing problems in Muslim-Christian coexistence with unprecedented clarity. While these problems remained continuously on a high level throughout 2012 and 2013, the postrevolutionary initiatives to address them were pushed to the sidelines by the political power struggles that saw the rise of the Muslim Brotherhood throughout 2012, its subsequent fall, and the return of the army in 2013.

The Coptic Question in the Mubarak Era

Coptic attitudes toward the Mubarak regime had been deeply ambiguous. Many were convinced that the Mubarak regime was not ideal but still better than the alternative possibilities, the worst being Islamist rule. However, such pragmatic considerations seldom concealed the broad sense of disappointment, alienation, and marginalization that beset many Copts as they reflected on their situation and their status in Egyptian society and politics. This general disillusionment was the result not only of personal experiences of discrimination, but also of a discourse of withheld rights and unfulfilled promises (amounting to persecution, according to some) that left a deep impact on the Church and community and inescapably shaped people's worldview and political consciousness, whether they were personally subject to difficulties or not. Coptic concerns and grievances were based on several related issues, which can be analytically separated into six main aspects: (1) the communal or sectarian character of Egyptian society; (2) struggles over national identity; (3) the problematic institutional relationship between the Egyptian state and the religious communities; (4) the vicissitudes of legal pluralism; (5) the political marginalization of the Copts; and (6) the negative effects of authoritarian rule.

First, the processes of nation-building and social modernization fundamentally changed Egyptian society in many ways over the twentieth century, but they did not diminish the social role of the religious communities. Even at times when religion was socially and politically receding, communal religious life remained important for large parts of the population. The low rate of intermarriage is an indication of the continuing importance of sectarian boundaries.[1] During the last two generations, the impact of religious revivalism, among Muslims as well as Copts, has increased social separation among the middle and lower strata of society. A substantial majority of the present Coptic population was socialized primarily by the Church and the religious community, which determines their view of society and the world.[2] The radicalization of a distinct religious and ethnic identity among Copts corresponds with the increasing Islamization of the social environment.

Second, even though Egyptian nationalist discourse and practice has consistently attempted to mend sectarian divisions, articulations of Egyptian identity have remained vague and shifting. Most of them have tended toward a more or less eclectic combination of Egyptian, Arab, and Islamic nationalism. Copts have historically found different ways of inscribing their own communal identity and tradition into nationalist discourses. With the gradual rise of an Islamic reading of national history and identity—its strongest impact has been since the 1970s—this had become increasingly difficult. Approaches that treat Egypt's long Christian legacy as largely insignificant have consequently had a growing impact on education and the state-controlled media.[3] Feeling alienated, a growing number of Copts have adopted radical counternarratives, which went as far as rejecting the Arabic and Islamic identity of Egypt altogether, thereby widening the chasm.[4] Even the moderate majority of Christian voices have stressed the urgent need for toning down Islamic references in education, as well as restricting aggressive Islamic *daʿwa* (religious propaganda), and assuring an adequate presence of Christian religious content in the state media.

Third, there is a constitutional and institutional imbalance: Islam has been the Egyptian state religion since the first modern constitution of 1923, which means that it has been fostered, as well as intensively controlled. Although Egyptian constitutions have guaranteed the freedom of religion, they have remained conspicuously silent on the precise status of Christianity and the Christian churches. In practice they enjoyed freedom of worship and a great degree of internal autonomy. However, they were also mostly excluded from government funding and other forms of official support. While separation from the state was not necessarily a drawback for the churches—many Muslims, especially those with Islamist leanings, complained about intrusive and often high-handed government supervision of the Islamic sphere—it had the effect of excluding Christians from any role in government policies concerning religion.

Fourth, an essential aspect of legal, social, and political communalism in modern Egypt has been the preservation of a plurality of family law codes for the different religious communities.[5] However, Islam stands above the other religions as Shari'a is considered the governing law in matters concerning family and personal status. This obviously implies discrimination against Christians and Christian religion: A Christian man cannot marry a Muslim woman, and the state authorities do not recognize conversion from Islam to Christianity. However, as the Coptic Orthodox clergy always made it a priority to defend the holy sacrament of marriage and its own central role in regulating family issues against secular intrusions, they have acquiesced with the existing legal system and rejected civil marriage. As Muslim religious authorities were equally disinclined to changing the system, it was preserved with all its contradictions and gray zones. While this may conform to the prevalence of communal orientation and conservative religious values in Egyptian society, it has deprived the Egyptian state of nonpartisan and mutually acceptable legal norms by which to arbitrate the increasingly frequent conflicts over conversion and interreligious relationships.[6]

Fifth, after a period of successful political integration under the leadership of lay notables in the 1920s, Coptic engagement in national politics declined, especially after the 1952 "revolution." The post-1952 Republican regime was dominated by an almost exclusively Muslim military clique, even though, at least in its Nasserite phase, it displayed a strong public commitment to the equality of all citizens. The drift to a sectarian logic was gradual; it first became evident in the late 1970s, when the leadership of the Coptic Orthodox Church assumed the role of speaking for the Coptic population to the state in the face of the Islamizing policies of President Anwar Sadat. Rather than counterbalancing this trend by promoting Coptic participation, the regime of Hosni Mubarak surreptitiously strengthened political sectarianism. In practice this meant that negotiations of critical issues between the Church and the regime took place behind closed doors, coupled with polite exchange of formalities in public. This approach aimed at creating an appearance of national unity while keeping the vexing issues of discrimination, marginalization, and religious violence out of the public eye. In hindsight problems were concealed and solutions delayed, while social and religious tensions were boiling under the surface and erupting more frequently during the last decade of Mubarak's rule. A large part of the Coptic population accepted the political role of the Church leadership and respected Patriarch Shenouda III (in office 1971–2012) for his struggle to defend Coptic rights and interests. However, neither were they satisfied with the concessions the Church was able to extract from the regime, nor had they given up on aspirations of genuine political participation.

And, finally, authoritarian rule under Mubarak and his predecessors had consequences for Muslims and Christians alike. Among its corollaries were the nontransparency of political decision making, widespread human-rights violations, administrative inefficiency, arbitrariness, and corruption. Bad governance exacerbated the existing legal, institutional, and social tensions. It created an environment in which religious discrimination based on individual prejudice could proceed virtually unchecked, often under the pretext of secretive "security" practices.[7] In case of sensitive issues, for example, church building or religiously motivated violence, Copts often complained that state authorities, including the weak judiciary, were apparently more eager to appease Muslim extremists than to safeguard the legal rights of the victims. It is important to note that the lack of basic rights was not a unique experience to the Copts in a system in which legal claims against the state and others could only be enforced with the help of patronage and bribery.

Copts in the Uprising against the Mubarak Regime

Several of these aspects demonstrate that the Coptic question was not of recent making but was still in many ways symptomatic for the state of Egypt under the late Mubarak regime. In spite of the impact of the Internet and press liberalization since the mid-1990s, vital public debates made little difference to the stagnant political process. The regime's typical approach was to deny the existence of problems or conceal them behind nationalist rhetoric. Political action was usually erratic and evidently served the ultimate purpose of stabilizing the regime. Frustration and indignation over this state of affairs were not confined to the Copts. In the shockwave caused by the Alexandria terrorist attack on January 1, 2011, even Muslim Egyptians who did not sympathize with Coptic demands became concerned about the impact of the government's mismanagement of sectarian tensions on society and on Egypt's reputation in the world.

Thus it was not surprising that Muslim-Christian coexistence and the challenge of sectarian strife became important themes in the uprising against the Mubarak regime and remained on the public agenda during the following months.[8] The symbolism of national unity and religious tolerance that characterized the demonstrations was certainly magnified by the media coverage. It was nevertheless a faithful reflection of the general spirit of the Tahrir movement. There was a consensus that political, social, and religious contradictions had to be temporarily set apart in a united struggle against the regime, based on the common demands of freedom, dignity, and social justice. Regardless of actual Coptic participation, the movement embraced the theme of national unity and claimed to represent all Egyptians, Muslims as well as Christians. In fact, during the first week of the uprising, during its most violent days, from January 25 ("the Day of Rage") until January 28 ("the Friday of Rage"), Coptic presence was limited. An indication of this fact was that, from these events to February 2 and 3 (the so-called Battle of the Camel) more than eight hundred people were killed in Cairo and other Egyptian cities, and only fourteen of them were Christians.[9] Faithful to their quietist political stance, the Coptic Orthodox clergy had explicitly cautioned their flock against participating in the Day of Rage protests. Some reportedly organized special services and activities to keep the Coptic youth off the streets.[10] It is interesting that skepticism also prevailed among Coptic activists, chiefly sparked by the fear that an uprising against the regime might lead to chaos and provide an opportunity for Islamists to seize power.[11] Most were convinced that a popular movement against Mubarak would be dominated by the Muslim Brotherhood, and many changed their attitude toward the revolution when this was not the case.

However, when Christians did take to the streets to participate in sit-ins from the very beginning, they were uplifted by an overwhelming sense of solidarity. "When [we] were in the square, we were incredibly happy," remembered a Christian protester. "We thought that there wouldn't be any more discrimination against Copts, that life will finally be good and fair."[12] Building human chains around praying Muslims was one way for Christians to participate in creating interreligious solidarity. Beyond Tahrir square, Muslims and Christians jointly formed popular committees and militias to protect their neighborhoods. Despite the security breakdown following January 28, there were no significant transgressions against churches in the period before March 2011.[13]

When things settled down in Tahrir square, during the second week of protests, Christians became visible in the public prayer rituals.[14] It is interesting that Christian protesters—similar to the secular Muslims who led the movement—did not object to the widespread use of religious slogans and symbols as instruments of resistance:[15] "Prayer is a basic element of Egyptian identity. We were all happy to see our Muslim compatriots lined up for prayer, in order to call on God and ask Him to grant our rights. . . . And when we were singing our Christian hymns (tarānīm), they stood next to us and listened to us. Often, I heard them join in with our 'Amen' so that God might protect our fatherland Egypt."[16]

Roughly speaking, there were three different groups of Christian protesters: (1) members and supporters of leftist and liberal parties and youth movements, human-rights and civil-society activists; (2) Coptic activists, people who primarily and exclusively engaged in the defense of Coptic rights and interests; and (3) non-affiliated people, many of whom had never engaged in any sort of activism before.

Priests who came to Tahrir square came independent from their respective churches, but the largest part of the Coptic-Orthodox clergy refrained from visible revolutionary engagement. This was not just an expression of hesitation and political caution in uncertain times; it also signaled a deep-seated skepticism toward "street politics" in general, which did not go away after Mubarak had been forced out of office. If the church leadership had a consistent political stance in the transitional period, it was that order should be maintained at all costs. Frequent and pertinacious demonstrations and sit-ins were considered "outside the bounds of the freedom of expression" and "damaging to Egypt's reputation." The logic of the

Church leadership was that, when "the patience of the rulers is wearing thin," the people should go home rather than risk a confrontation.[17] Even though the official political approach of the Coptic Orthodox Church remained unchanged, this did not prevent the emergence of a Coptic youth movement, recruited from the ranks of the church-going youth who embraced a tactic of civil disobedience. The formation of this movement was predicated not only on the new sense of freedom after the fall of Mubarak, but also on one of the more negative corollaries of the revolution: the renewed eruption of sectarian tensions.

Sectarian Incidents in the Transition Period

The transition period after the fall of Mubarak was a time of general unrest and uncertainty. Many people's lives were even more difficult than before owing to crime and economic depression. While the ruling military council, the political parties, and the revolutionary youth were quarrelling over a roadmap for the transition process, social groups started voicing their own demands toward the state. Among these were not only professional networks but also religious and ethnic groups such as the Copts, the Nubians, and the Bedouins from Sinai. The weak transitional government, consisting of the military council and the cabinet of Essam Sharaf (in office from March 3 until November 24, 2011), faced an avalanche of issues that it was ill-equipped to deal with. It negotiated, made concessions, formed commissions for further study of important issues, and also used repression to curb the revolutionary impatience of parts of the population.

The sudden security vacuum facilitated the escalation of sectarian tensions, which in turn created situations that the army, stepping in for a police in disarray, was not trained to deal with. The population no longer afraid of the police and state security and the increasing availability of weapons further complicated the situation. Social forces with conflicting views of Coptic issues such as Coptic activists on the one side and radical Islamists on the other side were emboldened to mobilize publicly in order to draw attention to their causes and influence government policies.

Conflicts revolved around the same issues that had already proven to be explosive over the last decade, for example, interreligious love affairs and religious conversion. In the deeply conservative environment of villages and migrant-dominated lower-class areas in the city, such incidents constituted a double violation of social boundaries, as defined by religion (Islam) and patriarchal codes. Consequently, the male relatives of women involved usually felt obliged to seek revenge (*tha'r*) for reasons of shame, while the religious component typically mobilized mobs of angry young men. When not mediated promptly, this lethal combination could result in a spiral of violence and destruction. Similar conflicts were triggered by disputes over the construction and renovation of churches.

All the major sectarian incidents in the transitional period fit into this pattern. For example, at the roots of the Sul/Atfih (governorate of Giza) incident on March 4, 2011, was allegedly a love affair between a Christian man and a Muslim woman, which led to brawl within her extended family that turned into a deadly shoot-out; one young man was killed. After his funeral a crowd of people attacked the village church. When the police and the army finally intervened, the church had already been pillaged and burned. Some Christians fled the village, but there were no human casualties. A new secondary threat emerged in the aftermath of this incident on March 7, 2011, when Muslims and Christians clashed in spontaneous and disorderly protests near the garbage collectors' quarter of Mansheyet Nasser, leaving at least thirteen people dead and 140 injured. The army was present but unable to control the escalating street fights.

Another incident was triggered by the confusing story of a married Coptic woman from Upper Egypt who had, according to her own account, run away with her Muslim lover. Upon finding her, the family had locked her away in a church facility in Imbaba, a lower-class neighborhood of Cairo. Church sources later denied that the woman was held against her will in the church. However, on May 7, 2011, the Muslim "husband" appeared in front of the church supported by a group of Salafi Muslims. Within hours, more than two thousand Salafis and local inhabitants had gathered. Inside the sanctuary hundreds of Christian activists attempted to defend the church. The police tried to calm the situation with the help of local Salafi shaykhs. When shots rang a battle broke out that raged for hours. Security forces looked on, unwilling to risk their own safety. Another church in the same neighborhood was also torched and burned. There were twelve casualties on both sides and many injuries.

Imbaba was not the first sectarian incident in which Salafis—adherents of an especially rigid and puritan trend within Egyptian Islam—were involved. Even before the revolution parts of the Salafi movement seemed increasingly eager to seek confrontation with Christians and especially with the Coptic Orthodox Church—mainly over issues of conversion. In doing so they portrayed themselves as part of a global Islamic struggle against Christian mission (*tanṣīr*) and Westernization.[18] In March and April 2011 Salafis gathered in Alexandria and Cairo (some even in front of the Coptic cathedral in Abbasiyya), calling on the government to "put Pope Shenouda on trial" and to "search churches and monasteries for imprisoned women."[19] The increasing assertiveness of the Salafi movement was not limited to Coptic issues and was widely discussed in the Egyptian public arena.[20]

The Emergence of the Coptic Youth Movement

Alarm over the Salafi threat was strong among Copts and increased people's desire to act. Following the Sul incident, thousands flocked to the sit-in organized by Coptic activists at Maspero – the strip of the Corniche Road in front of the National Radio and Television Building (5–12 March). It is significant that this was the first Coptic mass demonstration ever in central Cairo. A demonstration against the Imbaba incident led to a renewed sit-in at Maspero (8–20 May), in which thousands of people participated. Through these sit-ins and the larger movement they set off what is known as the Maspero Youth Movement (*ḥarakat shabāb Masbīrū*), which reshaped Coptic activism.

This mobilization of the Coptic masses was the work of unknown young activists who seized the revolutionary opportunity. It was neither initiated nor led by any of the familiar faces of Coptic political action such as clergy, Coptic rights activists, and would-be political leaders such as Nagib Gibra'il and the USA-based Michael Meunier. A look at the key persons and their political record reveals, however, that this movement did not appear in a vacuum but resulted from a process of cross-fertilization between religiously motivated church activism and the oppositional liberal and leftist activism. The church or community side contributed the popular issues and networks the movement thrived on, but the political strategy and discourse were unthinkable without the imprint of oppositional and revolutionary politics.

While in the 2000s outbreaks of anger and frustration had become more frequent, especially among lower-class Copts, this had not led to sustained political mobilization or self-empowerment. People continued to regard the clergy as their intercessors with the authorities. Demonstrations, held within church compounds, not in front of state buildings, aimed at pushing bishops or the patriarch to press demands with the government. Some Coptic intellectuals and activists who had carved out a presence in the media pressed the same demands, but they were incapable of connecting with the people on the ground.

A community leader with a political agenda was Father Mityas Nasr (Minqarius), a propagator of pharaonic-Egyptian culture and defender of Coptic identity whose service as a parish priest in the garbage collectors' community of Ezbet el Nakhl had earned him a dedicated following far beyond his neighborhood. In 2004, with the help of young volunteers, he launched a magazine called *al-Katiba al-Tibiyya* (the "Theban Legion," a reference to a group of early Coptic martyrs) that soon circulated in churches all over Egypt.[21] The style and content of the magazine were provocative from the beginning; almost every issue opened with a story about crimes and injustices against the Copts. Importantly, the fight for the preservation of Coptic-Egyptian identity and the defense of Coptic rights, including the struggle against conversion, was combined with vitriolic criticism against the government. While this approach was not new in itself—it had been dominating the discourse of expatriate activists for decades—few had ever been courageous or reckless enough to propagate it openly inside Egypt.[22]

In an important step towards political activism, in the summer of 2009 some members of the circle around Mityas Nasr and the *Katiba* magazine joined the opposition and civil society activist Hani Elgezery, to set up the Copts for Egypt movement (*Aqbāṭ min ajl Miṣr*).[23] As its first public act, the group called for a "Coptic strike" on September 11, 2009, the New Year's Day of the Ancient Egyptian, or Coptic, calendar. As a sign of protest against the failure of the government to protect Christians against attacks on churches and Copts, Copts should abstain from joyful activities and only walk the streets dressed in black. Even though the call was not observed widely, it was hotly debated in the media. Church representatives and many in the public criticized it as sectarian and destructive.[24]

The novel approach of Copts for Egypt, apart from the intentional breaking of public taboos, was that the group adopted the political strategies of the opposition:

demonstrations, vigils, and strikes, as well as extensive use of social media.[25] The rising anger among young Copts in the face of incidents such as the Nag Hammadi shootings on Coptic Christmas Eve, January 6, 2010 (seven dead), and the January 1, 2011, bombing of the al-Qiddisayn church in Alexandria (twenty-one casualties) increased the support base for radical action. The new type of advocacy was fully applied on November 23 and 24 during the religious riots in the 'Umraniyya neighborhood on the outskirts of Giza where fierce protests occurred when local authorities declared a newly constructed church illegal. A sit-in of dozens of young Copts inside the building was dissolved during a brutal nighttime raid. The next day thousands of local Copts and activists from other parts of the Greater Cairo area marched to the governorate in the center of Giza and engaged in street fights with the police. In the end two people died, forty were injured, and more than 250 were arrested. Another example of the new attitude of resistance could be witnessed at the funeral service for the victims of the Alexandria terror attack on January 2, 2011. The mourners chanted slogans demanding the dismissal of the governor and booed loudly when Bishop Yu'annis, the representative of the sick patriarch, read a telegram of condolence from President Mubarak. Politicians who had come to the funeral were threatened and had to be rushed to safety.[26]

Coptic protest, however, while growing, remained largely spontaneous, lacking leadership and a clear agenda. There were also disagreements between those who wanted to escalate the fight against the regime and those who urged a more cautious strategy. A radical group called the Coptic Youth Front (*jabhat al-shabāb al-qibṭī*), an offshoot of the *Katiba* magazine and Copts for Egypt activist circles, joined the revolution from the beginning. The Tahrir experience made the Coptic activists part of the revolutionary youth, guaranteeing considerable support from within this movement. Most important, it taught them how to organize large-scale demonstrations and sit-ins, knowledge that allowed for a whole new level of mobilization and endurance.

The character and aim of the Maspero sit-ins was twofold. First, they were meant to signal a forceful Coptic presence in postrevolutionary Egypt and inscribe the claims of recognition and equality on the general revolutionary agenda. Affirming Coptic dignity and identity were crucial. Many participants—especially those from the lower classes—expressed these aspirations in a strongly religious idiom by carrying wooden crosses, Coptic icons, or banners with prayers or pious slogans written on them. The discourse of the leaders, while using the secular language of democracy, religious freedom, and human rights, was also filled with religious references. Most of the leaders were members of the educated middle strata of densely populated Cairo quarters such as Shubra, 'Ayn Shams, Matariyya, and Imbaba. Some older and more-established intellectuals and activists, for example, the lawyer Amir Ramzi, emerged as the movement's public spokesmen. Together they represented the middle of society, the "silent majority" that had never engaged in politics or even expressed their opinions in public. For many involved this was an act of emancipation in itself.

In a more narrow sense the leaders used the sit-ins to raise specific demands and pressure the government, a strategy that was remarkably successful in the short run. While some of the demands were directly related to the sectarian incidents that triggered the protests, typically calling for proper investigations, prosecution of Muslim attackers, compensation of the victims, and return to the status quo ante, others even addressed further-reaching issues.[27] The transitional government, eager to appease the Coptic demonstrators, made significant concessions that marked a clear departure from the ways of the Mubarak era. The churches in Sul and Imbaba were both rebuilt by the military within a few weeks. Some local Salafi sheikhs involved in the Imbaba incident were brought to court. To end the sit-in after the Imbaba incident, the government further vowed to draw up a unified law for the construction of places of worship that would make building and renovating churches easier, as well as another law against religious discrimination and incitement. It promised to take up investigations concerning the fate of a number of Coptic women who had disappeared.[28]

While the Maspero and other popular movements reveled in the effectiveness of street action, the military council became increasingly impatient about what it perceived to be "disorder." After an attack on a church in the village of al-Marinab (district Edfu, governorate Aswan) on September 30, 2011, things turned catastrophic.[29] In several television appearances the governor of Aswan, General Mustafa al-Sayyid, rejected any criticism against the security forces and his own person and accused the church of violating building regulations and deceiving the authorities.[30] Enraged about this apparent return to the "old ways" of lies and indifference, Coptic and human-rights activists called for the governor's removal.

On Sunday, October 9, a large security force with units of military police stopped a Coptic protest march in downtown Cairo. An ill-conceived attempt to disperse the crowd and to prevent another sit-in turned into an orgy of violence. Twenty-seven protesters died. They were shot or run over by tanks; one soldier was also killed. In the hours of chaos the reaction of the military and state television was erratic and bordered on open sectarian incitement.

Only when denial of the atrocities was no longer possible, the military council apologized to the families of the victims for the "tragedy" that had happened. Later, a military court tried and sentenced three soldiers for their role in the massacre, but three Coptic protesters were also sentenced for allegedly stealing firearms from the armed forces during the turmoil.[31] In the immediate aftermath the role of the military was strongly condemned by Coptic activists and the revolutionary youth who portrayed the massacre as intentional.[32] Funeral processions resounded with calls for the removal of Field Marshal Mohammed Hussein Tantawi, the head of the military council. Among the Maspero victims was twenty-year-old Mina Daniel, a well-known Tahrir "veteran" who embodied the strong ties between the new Coptic street activism and the revolutionary youth.[33] The Maspero massacre was a serious blow for the Coptic youth movement. Disputes among the leadership and shock and despair among the support base destroyed much of the organizational growth and mobilization that had been achieved from March to October 2011. The unsuccessful confrontation with the army undermined the appeal of the Coptic revolutionary current as an alternative and more successful way of defending Coptic rights.

The State, Politics, and Coptic Concerns after the Revolution

The Coptic sit-ins showed how pressure from the street could force political authorities to take Coptic concerns seriously—as long as they were in principle willing to respond to popular demands. A case in point was the treatment of religious tension and religious violence. The quick reconstruction of the destroyed churches in Sul, Imbaba, and al-Marinab by the army was a sign that the transitional government recognized its responsibility to uphold the basic rights of Coptic citizens, especially in the sensitive area of religious worship.

Changes in the political treatment of Coptic concerns were remarkable during the tenure of the administration of Essam Abdel-Aziz Sharaf (March–November 2011). In May 2011, following the Imbaba incident, the prime minister created a Commission of National Justice composed of senior representatives from civil society and the human-rights community. This was the first time that an Egyptian government acknowledged explicitly that measures had to be taken against the discrimination and harassment of Copts and other religious minorities. The commission was given the assignment to devise a "Unified Law for the Construction of Places of Worship" (*al-qānūn al-muwaḥḥad li-binā' dūr al-'ibāda*) and to draw up a law against religious discrimination and incitement.[34] A draft of the "Unified Law" was presented to the public on May 31 and discussed extensively. However, its promulgation was delayed as the Coptic Orthodox Church and some Islamic institutions announced reservations concerning several clauses In October 2011, a week after the Maspero massacre, the cabinet promulgated the promised antidiscrimination law. The "Unified Law," however, disappeared from the political agenda. Other controversial and sensitive issues, for example, conversion, family law, religious education, and media policies, remained completely unaddressed before the Commission of National Justice ceased to function with the demise of the Sharaf administration.

In another step taken by the transitional government representatives of the revolutionary youth, including the Maspero Youth, were invited to join a subcommission that was to function as an early-warning system against sectarian violence. Although this measure did not attract much public attention, it was even more significant than the widely debated laws, because it was an attempt to tackle religious tension at its roots and gave an official voice to the younger generation.[35]

The revolutionary youth demonstrated that the initiative of concerned citizens and civil society organizations could be crucial in defusing tensions on the ground. If the security apparatus no longer would reduce its interference in sectarian tensions, then religious, social, and political actors could play a bigger role in shaping peaceful coexistence. However, given the conflicting religious agendas in Egyptian society, this aim could not be realized without controversy. For instance, Christians were less than enthused about the prominent role that the well-known Salafi sheikh Muhammad Hassan was allowed to play in dissuading the local Muslim youth from violence and celebrating a public conciliation ceremony after the Sul incident.[36] Nevertheless, this reconciliation approach was certainly a serious attempt to give some substance to mediation, an instrument that had been distorted and abused by Mubarak's security apparatus.

The Copts and Transitional Politics

Within a global perspective, the limits of change concerning the treatment of Coptic issues were identical with the general limits of revolutionary politics. Large sectors of the state were relatively immune to change and continued to operate in the same ways as before, even if some of the leading actors had changed. By the end of 2011 the revolutionary momentum was over and the political struggle focused on who from among the strongest political players would get to govern Egypt.

It soon became clear that most Copts continued to see their political future not in any sort of sectarian political formation but in the model of integration represented by the Wafd Party of the 1920s and 1930s. Among the many new parties formed after the revolution, there was not a single one with an open or hidden sectarian Coptic orientation. However, this does not mean that there was no political mobilization on the basis of Coptic identity.

Beyond diverging political and intellectual horizons and different attitudes toward the revolution, there was a very broad consensus among educated Copts on the priority of defending the secular/civil state (*dawla madaniyya*) against Islamization. Islamist forces, for example, the Muslim Brotherhood's Freedom and Justice Party (FJP), were actually trying to attract Copts and were ready to accept them as members and even as candidates. Coptic support would enhance their desired image of open-mindedness and religious tolerance. The scholar and intellectual Rafiq Habib, a Coptic Protestant who had a long record of cooperation with the Islamist movement, became one of FJP's vice presidents. Nevertheless, considering the increased polarization between secular and Islamic forces, Islamic parties were unable to attract a significant number of Copts, whether as voters or as members and allies.

The natural political home of the Copts remained the nonreligious or secular current, which was represented in the November 2011–January 2012 elections by the lists of the Wafd Party, the Egyptian Bloc (*al-kutla al-miṣriyya*), and the Revolution Continues Alliance (*al-thawra mustamirra*). The Free Egyptians (*al-miṣriyyūn al-aḥrār*) Party, arguably the strongest member of the Egyptian Bloc, was a business-friendly party funded by the Coptic tycoon Nagib Sawiris.[37] Coptic participation in all secular parties and movements was lively. Only their meager results in the face of the Islamist landslide—the Muslim Brotherhood list won about 45 percent of the seats and the Salafi Nur Party another 25 percent—were responsible for the fact that elected Coptic representation in Parliament remained very low (six out of 498).

The parliamentary elections were only a transitory moment in the post-Mubarak political landscape. The presidential elections of May and June 2012 witnessed the reemergence of the status quo–oriented political current that united behind Mubarak's last prime minister Ahmad Shafiq, a tendency that was attractive to many Copts thanks to its strong enmity with the Muslim Brotherhood.

However, contrary to a view held especially within the Islamist camp, Shafiq did not owe his near victory against Muslim Brotherhood candidate Mohamed Morsi to the Coptic vote but to his very solid showing in most of the populous Delta provinces, in which Copts only make up around 1 percent of the population. Further research needs to be done to analyze Coptic political attitudes and voting behavior.

The continuing absence of an effective representation of Coptic laymen in general politics favored the reemergence of the Church leadership in this arena.[38] The aging patriarch Shenouda III had played an entirely passive role in the events of the year 2011. After his death on March 17, 2012, he was succeeded by Tawadros II (born 1952) on November 18, 2012. Tawadros supported the decision of the Egyptian churches on November 17, 2012, to withdraw their representatives from the Constituent Assembly, thus taking an important step toward siding with the growing anti-Muslim Brotherhood coalition.[39] In a move enthusiastically welcomed within the Coptic community, which was almost unanimously opposed to the rule of the Muslim Brotherhood and its allies and participated widely in anti-Muslim Brotherhood demonstrations, Tawadros also gave the Coptic Orthodox Church's blessing to the coup by the minister of defense General Abd al-Fattah al-Sisi against President Mohamed Morsi on July 3, 2013.

Conclusion

The fall of the Mubarak regime has had a noticeable impact on the Coptic community and the treatment of the Coptic question in Egyptian politics and society. Especially in its first months, it created an unprecedented opening; public pressure on the state to find reasonable solutions increased manifold, partly on account of a remarkable upsurge in Coptic political activism. However, other developments were a reason for pessimism to most Copts.

Amid general security problems, sectarian violence increased. Islamist actors, no longer excluded from politics, were on the rise and achieved a triumphant victory in Egypt's first free elections. Copts reacted in different ways to the Islamist challenge. Parts of the population were gripped by emotions of fear, panic, and resignation, which found their expression in reports about a wave of emigration.[40] The opposite reaction to the perceived Islamist threat was the increasing mobilization of Coptic youth, which also coincided with an increasing militancy (understood defensively). A growing number of Copts shed their political passivity, many of them to join the new liberal and secular parties that were set up after the revolution. To them and to a large part of the community, the election results were sobering and the continuing threat of sectarian strife disheartening. Faced with the scenario of the entrenchment of Islamist dominance in politics, many came to despair of the idea of a democratic transition and became increasingly supportive of the reestablishment of (non-Islamist) authoritarian rule.

THE UNDESIRABLES OF EGYPT
A Story of Persecution and Defiance
Mariz Tadros

This essay captures the trajectory of a distinct community in Egyptian society that has historically suffered from persecution as a consequence of the intersection of three identity markers—religion, profession, and class: the garbage collectors, commonly known as the Zabbalin. The story of the Zabbalin, who are for the most part Coptic Christians, speaks of the enmeshment of religious persecution, bad governance, and the devastating impact of neoliberalism on local livelihoods. In these regards it is important to consider three overlapping arguments associated with religious persecution, exclusionary politics, and development and resistance and subversion.

The first postulation is that the Zabbalin represent a case study of a most acute pattern of the *collective* persecution of a group on the basis of their religious identity across several decades. However, the dynamics of their persecution represent a microcosm of broader political and societal patterns of religious discrimination against the Christian minority in Egypt. When the livelihoods of the garbage collectors raising pigs were eliminated by a decree issued by President Hosni Mubarak to cull the pigs, this action was cloaked in arguments that drew on "scientific evidence," "national security," and "citizen wellbeing." In reality, the decision was underpinned by religious prejudice and the workings of a regime deploying religion for its own political ends. Similarly, religious discrimination against the broader Coptic citizenry is often cloaked in discourses that seek to deny the religious underpinnings of the problem, presenting them as manufactured by foreign conspiracies or provoked by parties keen to undermine the national security of the country.

Moreover, the nature of the interface between the political system and Coptic citizens can also be seen in the predicament of the Zabbalin. Under Mubarak they were tolerated but then subjected to the most intense assault on their livelihoods, bringing the animosity toward the regime to new levels. After the January 2011 revolution the Zabbalin sought to express their voices by collective action in the public space, like many other citizens, and they became subject to violent assaults, which had increased against Christians in general. With the coming to power of

Mohamed Morsi, they had high expectations that their role in building a new Egypt (via waste management) would be recognized, but again they were disappointed by the poor governance policies and exclusionary politics toward Copts. Like many Copts, they celebrated the ousting of Morsi from power and have sought to rebuild their lives, though the future remains opaque.

The second argument relates to the complex configuration of power relations that influence the positioning of the Zabbalin in Egypt. The intensifying impact of persecution on the Zabbalin is also exacerbated by class dynamics within the Coptic community. As we shall see, when the decision to cull the pigs was announced, the top echelons of the Coptic Orthodox Church did nothing to engage in policy dialogue with the government on behalf of the Zabbalin, even though, in other incidents where citizens were discriminated against on the basis of their religious affiliation, the Coptic leadership had intervened with the authorities. It is evident that the Zabbalin have suffered social marginalization because of the nature of their profession as the garbage collectors. Moreover, within the Zabbalin community there are variations in the degree of marginalization, with the wealthier strata being less vulnerable to socioeconomic exclusion than the poorer members. The latter have also been exploited by the wealthier members, deepening their exclusion.

The story of the marginalization of the Zabbalin is also one of bad governance issuing exclusionary development policies. The Egyptian government had caused a huge blow to the livelihoods of the Zabbalin when it contracted foreign companies to handle Egypt's waste-management portfolio. The outcome was the replacement of a functioning and ecologically sound waste-management system with a highly ineffective one that is disconnected from the local dynamics of how citizens engage with garbage in Egypt and which has wiped out local subsistence livelihoods—congruent with broader critiques of the impact of neoliberal policies on the poor.

Finally, the story of the Zabbalin is also one of agency and resistance. Resistance has taken many forms, including the subversion of the decision to cull every single pig by hiding some, open resistance by protesting against the assault on Christians in March 2011, and symbolic expressions of defiance by cursing those who have dispossessed and marginalized them.

This essay is based on primary data collecting in 2009 and 2011. Interviews were conducted with garbage collectors who had lost their livelihoods to the cull in all three settlements and with individuals and families who were affected by the mob assault in March 2011. This research was complemented with secondary data analysis from 2009 to 2013. The data sought to capture the contending narratives of various stakeholders involved at different junctures: government representatives, the wealthy and poor garbage collectors, NGO board members and practitioners, and Church leaders.

Background

The Zabbalin communities are most heavily concentrated in Cairo (where there is the most garbage) and are almost all Christians who migrated from Upper Egypt in the past century. The neglect of Upper Egypt under the centralized government of Gamal Abdel Nasser in the 1950s, which pursued an intensive industrialization policy, led to an increase in the number of poor landless peasants who migrated to Cairo in search of work. The narratives of the first garbage collectors to settle in Cairo from other areas, whether from Ezbet el Nakhl (north of Cairo), Mansheyet Nasser, Muqattam (south of Cairo), or Ard el Lewa (central Cairo) are almost the same. They all came in search of work to Cairo, where they met with former inhabitants of the Al Wahat Oasis who settled in Cairo and were engaged in garbage-related work. There in Cairo the new migrants were introduced to the garbage-collection profession. Subsequently, they were introduced to the idea of breeding pigs in order to expand their work from garbage collection to garbage sorting. Once the immigrants had settled, other members of the family migrated to Cairo. Extended families belonging to the same tribe settled in close proximity to each other.

The Zabbalin have a long tradition of using pigs to consume the organic waste that is collected, which allows them to extract valuable recyclable material from the garbage to be sold. This system allowed the Zabbalin to deal with a large amount of waste in a cost-effective way. According to the Coptic activist Marie Assaad, Zabbalin recycled more than 90 percent of all garbage, thus doing the environment a favor by minimizing the waste that needed to be dumped, buried, or burned.

The largest Zabbalin community in Mansheyet Nasser, is situated in the Muqattam mountains, once on the outskirts of the city, now very much part of it. Mansheyet Nasser is part of the Cairo governorate. The community is estimated to be about thirty thousand people. The second-largest community is based in Ard el Lewa, a haphazard squatter settlement sandwiched between Dokki and Mohandessin, two of the city's upper-class and upper-middle-class suburbs, and Bulaq el Dakrour, another squatter settlement. The population of Ard el Lewa is estimated to be about seven thousand people. The community is partly governed by the Giza governorate, and partly by the 6th of October Governorate. The third site was the garbage collectors' community in Ezbet el Nakhl, a highly populated urban squatter and slum settlement north of Cairo. The community is part of the Qalubiyya Governorate. In all three settlements the majority of the garbage collectors belong to Egypt's 10-percent Christian minority. While all three communities are part of Greater Cairo, their affiliation to different governorates is significant in that they are subject to different governors' policies which may vary greatly.

Intermarriage was the custom, and the social norms and traditions of the original rural community were maintained. Their experience was one of dispossession. They settled in obscure areas out of the eye of the government or on the fringes of the city (Muqattam and Ezbet el Nakhl). As the population of the city increased, their settlement sites became attractive to the new governor and they would be evicted, moving to a new settlement until the same circumstance occurred. In most instances the difficulty in obtaining formal ownership of the land obstructed their access to infrastructure. Many Zabbalin recount at least four different relocations before settling in their present community. For example, a migrant who would eventually work in the garbage profession might arrive at Imbaba, then relocate to Arab el Tawayla before moving to Arab el Hessn, and finally settling at Ezbet el Nakhl. Many of the Zabbalin at Ard el Lewa tell a similar story: "The government evicted us from one place to another. They say we are polluters of the environment. We arrived at Imbaba, then moved to Ain el Seera, then to Hodn el Gabal (Batn el Baqqara), and then Mazalak Ard el Lewa, where again, the government came to level us with the bulldozers, so they went to Shafi and then were evicted to Ard el Lewa." With each move the families would move their pigs and belongings and establish a new pigsty with an adjoining area for the storage of garbage and for living (sometimes using the same area).

There are hierarchies in the profession: on the bottom rung are the garbage scavengers who wander the streets of Cairo with their donkey carts in search of any recyclable materials thrown in garbage bins or on the sides of the roads. Slightly better off are the garbage collectors who collect the garbage from the residential homes. The fees paid to the garbage collectors are a pittance, often amounting to less than LE5 (less than 50 pence) a month per residential home. The richer the district where the collectors work, the greater the prospects for earning a livelihood from garbage collections, because the garbage will be rich in recyclable material, which is where the real opportunity for income generation lies. Garbage collectors collecting garbage from urban centers of Upper Egyptian towns or from the villages tend to be the poorest because of the limited recyclable material. Garbage collectors based in Muqattam and Ezbet el Nakhl tend to be better off because of their collection of garbage from the upper-class districts of Cairo. Garbage collectors who exclusively rely on the collection of garbage without owning pigsties have fewer income-generating prospects. The collected garbage is transferred to the garbage collectors who run pigsties.

The pigs, which consume the equivalent of their weight (a ninety-kilogram pig would consume ninety kilograms of organic waste) every day, relieve the Zabbalin in a cost-efficient ways of the need to process an enormous amount of garbage. While the men are responsible for gathering the waste from locations around the city, the women are tasked with taking care of the pigs. After the pigs have removed the organic waste from the garbage, it is left to the women to complete the most tedious, and hazardous, job of all: sorting the remaining garbage in their homes.

The wealthiest members of the garbage collectors' community are those who have well-established recycling industries, which are both capital and machine-intensive, with several paid laborers. They sell raw recycled carton, metals, plastic, and other elements to exporters to China and elsewhere. They were the least likely to be affected by the culling of the pigs. Running a pigsty, however, did not necessarily generate a good income for the Zabbalin. In Ard el Lewa, Israe'eel Ayad, a wealthy tycoon in the garbage industry, owned shares in both the pigs and the pigsties, leaving the Zabbalin raising pigs with minimal profit, a scenario very much reminiscent of the feudal order. In addition, very few recycling industries were established in that community, further limiting the Zabbalin's ability to generate additional income.

Social and political exclusion have meant that health and educational opportunities have been often compromised. Those better off in Ezbet el Nakhl and Ard el Lewa, and virtually all the inhabitants of Muqattam, have a work area separate from the living area. The poorer garbage collectors often use the space for garbage sorting as the space for living as well. Women in Ard el Lewa talk about giving birth in the pigsties amid the pigs and garbage. Yet the narrative of the garbage collectors who have owned pigsties is neither about the hardship of their lives nor about the daily exposure to hazard. It is not their livelihood that is a source of agony, but the persecution of them by the government.

In 2002 the Egyptian authorities contracted private international companies to assist in the disposal of garbage in the main governorates of Cairo and Alexandria. (Their efficiency and scale of operation have recently been questioned.)[1] In 2002 the Giza Governorate signed an agreement with two private companies (one Spanish and one Italian) to collect the three thousand tons of garbage produced daily by the governorate and dispose of it.[2] That same year the garbage collectors protested that their role was being totally neglected in the contractual agreements, and they opposed being governed by the Italian company. A spokesman from the company said, "I don't know what all the fuss is about; we are ready to accept the experienced labor in our business, but we are against the old fashioned non-environmental technique of garbage collection."[3] But the fact is that the Zabbalin have, over decades, developed a largely unregulated and informal system of garbage collection, sorting, and recycling, which is provided in return for a small fee.

The Swine Flu Saga

In early May 2009 the Egyptian government announced that it planned to cull all of the nation's estimated three hundred thousand pigs. This action was necessary, the government stated, in order to control the spread of so-called swine flu,[4] which was declared a "public health emergency of international concern" by the WHO. The decision to cull the pigs, approved by Parliament, was taken to protect the country from the pandemic even though there had not been a single confirmed case of H_1N_1 influenza in the country.

One well-established communal response to epidemics is to blame a scapegoat, most often a marginalized social group with little or no power.[5] At the outset of the H_1N_1 outbreak, for example, Mexicans were vilified, and there were voices in the United States calling for the closure of the border between the two countries.[6] In the case of Egypt, when reports emerged about an international outbreak of swine flu, public attention immediately focused on Egypt's pig population. The undesirability of the pigs extended to three levels. The first level was the stigma of the pigs themselves: in Islam the pig is seen as an unclean animal, and there are clear injunctions in the Koran prohibiting Muslims from breeding or eating pigs. The second is the religious undesirability of the social group raising the pigs: the garbage collectors are overwhelmingly members of the indigenous Coptic Christian minority, who number roughly 10 percent of the population. The third is the social undesirability of a group whose profession is associated with garbage disposal. The Zabbalin have thus been triply marginalized by virtue of their religion and, by both Muslims and Christians, by virtue of their profession.

The narrative conveyed by the government and public opinion in the media and on the street casting pigs and their breeders as responsible for swine flu became hegemonic. It assumed a hegemonic nature in that all contending narratives were sidelined and opposition voices muted. Alternative narratives formulated by those who were sceptical about the logic of the mainstream narrative were either absent or vigorously marginalized. Those who have attempted to voice an alternative narrative include a few outspoken critics of the culling policy who wrote in the press, the garbage collectors themselves, whose narrative was largely ignored, and the Christian Copts living in the diaspora, who deplored the sectarian nature of the culling.

The Public Narrative: The Lives of the Pigs or the Lives of Egyptians?

The fact that the H1N1 was commonly referred to as swine flu meant that from the outset rumors linked pigs with the pandemic; in this the WHO's regional office is not entirely free from blame. The personnel there were aware that the Arab-Muslim context in which they operated would be extremely sensitive to anything swine-related. Yet there was no regional agenda implemented to inform governments and the public about the nature of H1N1, namely the lack of risk of swine-to-human transmission. When the government narrative developed into one revolving around pigs, the WHO did not respond sensitively or decisively to these regional concerns. When the WHO finally made an international appeal against naming the H1N1 swine flu, the association of the pandemic with pigs had already become entrenched both in Egypt and in the Middle East more generally.

On the Egyptian national front the immediate question became: If the flu is transmitted by swine, what about Egypt's pig population? The government initially proposed to relocate the pigsties from urban centres to a satellite city in the desert. Presidential decree no. 238, issued in 2008, had already set aside 238 feddans (roughly the equivalent of the same number of acres) of desert land on the outskirts of 15th of May City for garbage sorting and recycling. The Ministry of Agriculture saw things differently. They argued that an immediate relocation was not possible, since resettling all these pigsties would be a lengthy process because of missing infrastructure. From this point onward it was clear that if various government ministries were deliberating between culling and resettling, the former looked increasingly attractive. Opposition to relocation came from another circle as well: The residents of the 15th of May City protested to the local governor that they did not want the garbage collectors to settle in their city, arguing that they would be a source of pollution and rubbish.[7]

During the parliamentary discussions that took place on the April 28, 2009, the growing consensus was that pigs were responsible for the transmission of the

H1N1, as well as of many other viruses, and they must be killed immediately. Any delay was considered to be a risk to the health of Egyptian citizens. The religious inferences were striking. How can pigs be bred in the land of Al-Azhar in the first place?, asked one MP.[8] Hussein Ibrahim, an MP with the Muslim Brotherhood, asked whether the pigs have "special immunity," which is why they should be spared the culling, while poultry were not spared when the avian flu struck in Egypt. The implication of these questions, as one of the Coptic MPs, Ibtessam Habib, pointed out, is that the government was reluctant to take action against the pigs because of their association with Christians.[9] The comment was sufficiently inflammatory to propel the handful of Coptic MPs in the 554-member Parliament to react. Another Coptic Christian MP, Georgette Kaleeny, made two interesting points. The first was that few Christians eat pork and that she personally does not, and, second, that most of those who own pigsties are Muslims. Although factually incorrect, these ideas were used to support the mainstream narrative about the culling of the pigs as having nothing to do with Christians. Coptic M.P. Ibtessam Habib also spoke about there being nothing in the Bible to support the eating of pork.[10]

Kaleeny made pleas that, in case of slaughter of the pigs, the garbage collectors need to be adequately compensated and provided with alternative employment. Yet any attempt at making the livelihoods of the garbage collectors central to the debates was shunned: The matter was considered inconsequential, because the lives of Egyptians were at risk. Besides, many argued, that "if we culled a million poultry in the avian flu crisis, what is the problem with culling the pigs for a disease far worse?" Others asked, "What will happen if we live another fifteen years without pigs?"[11] As one critic pointed out, MPs representing the NDP (the ruling National Democratic Party) and the Muslim Brotherhood were united against common enemies, both religion and health.[12] In addition to the vilification of pigs, attention turned to the Zabbalin. An MP from the Muslim Brotherhood, Akram el Sha'er, called for all the garbage collectors in the country to be given a health check-up to ensure that they were not transmitters of the virus.[13] Exactly the same demands were made by the ruling party MPs: Magdy Allam, a member of the ruling party, called for a strict separation of the garbage collectors and the residents in order to prevent the spread of the disease, especially since the former mingled with pigs.

The hegemonic narrative that developed sheds light on how H1N1 was understood and interpreted. The first element of this narrative was its religious character; the second was the use of science to legitimize the religious stance; and the third was a critique of the pig itself and the conditions in which it was raised. Each is briefly discussed below.

Sitting on a Sectarian Volcano

The government was keen to stress publicly that the culling of the pigs was nonsectarian. Many prominent Islamist thinkers, such as Ihsan Abd el Kodous, a writer and active member of the press syndicate, objected to the compensation being given to those whose pigs were be culled. He pointed to Egypt's status as a Muslim country under Shari'a law, which prohibits the breeding or consumption of pigs in its territory.

The renowned Muslim writer Ibrahim Issa, editor in chief of the prominent opposition newspaper *Al-Distour*, was among the few critics who challenged both the government and the prevailing public opinion in favor of the culling. He sharply criticized the sectarian basis for the policy, pointing to the coalition between the ruling party and the Muslim Brotherhood "in an Islamic campaign against the pigs," which he interpreted as a "humorous exaggeration in line with the religious hypocrisy prevailing in our lives in Egypt."[14] He argued that the hysterical, panic-stricken mood in the country was an exceptional response to a health issue and must be understood in those exceptional terms. Why, he asked, did the people react so dramatically to the threat of H1N1, when the same people did not rise in anger against the contamination of their drinking water with sewage, the contamination of food, the rising rates of kidney and liver disease, or the air pollution that has inflicted large numbers of children with respiratory disease? The cause of this unexpected obsession with the health risks of H1N1, Issa suggested, was that "Muslims deliberately or spontaneously found this an opportunity to despise the Copts, since the pig is forbidden in the Muslim religion and a symbol of filth in populist thought: Hence Coptic Christians were transformed into a source of infection (and harm)—since they come into contact with pigs and eat pork, as opposed to Muslims who have no dealings with pigs."[15] What the reaction to H1N1 also revealed, wrote Issa, was that the Copts act as if they consider themselves a second-class minority and not as citizens with equal rights. As a result of their own awareness of their diminished status, he argued, they neither defended their right to eat pork nor to breed pigs nor did they seek to correct the mistaken association between pigs and the H1N1, he argued.

Certainly the position adopted by the leadership of the Coptic Orthodox Church, the spiritual representative of the Coptic community in Egypt,[16] strongly supported Issa's scathing critique of the Christians' response to the crisis. Despite the refutations, the government must have been concerned about the impact that the culling might have on the Christian Zabbalin because the minister of health paid the Zabbalin's spiritual leader, Pope Shenouda, a visit. Following the visit, Pope Shenouda made several remarks, quoted in the press, emphasizing that the majority of Egyptians do not eat pork and that those who do tend to be either Westerners or local Christians who associate with them.[17] In his weekly sermon he warned parishioners not to go to places where pigs were raised. The implications of his statements are far-reaching. First, by making reference to the pork-eating Westerners, he reinforced a sense of Egyptian unity and attempted to disassociate Copts from the rest of the Christians. Second, the warning to avoid places where pigs are bred strengthens the myth that it is pigs who communicate the disease to humans and further ostracizes the garbage collectors who associate with them. The only Copts to express opposition to the culling of the pigs on account of the sectarian nature of the charge were those now living outside Egypt in the diaspora who have long lobbied against religious discrimination in their home country. Their protests were met with the conventional response that such claims of religious discrimination are inspired by a Western imperialist agenda in line with the former British colonialist policy of divide and rule.[18] In the narrative the evidence that the culling of the pigs is not sectarian is that both the Coptic Orthodox Church leadership and the Coptic MPs endorsed the decision.[19]

The intensity of the sectarian sentiment in the Egyptian street was far greater than it was in Parliament or the media. Marie Assaad recounts that in the period preceding the decision to cull the pigs, "Egypt was sitting on a sectarian volcano about to erupt in the most violent way. People were saying 'the Christians are going to kill us. This is part of the West's plan to eradicate Muslims. We have to kill the pigs before they kill us." Assaad said that the garbage collectors' had legitimate reason to fear a mob taking things into their hands and attacking them.

However, counterarguments suggest that, while the narrative may have been sectarian, the government's adoption of a pig-culling policy was in fact more a result of poor governance than religious discrimination. The government's record in handling natural and man-made disasters and, in particular, health issues such as avian influenza certainly indicates poorly established and implemented policy responses that are lacking in transparency and accountability. The institutional processes for engaging with crises are characterized by a top-down, inconsistent, and sporadic implementation of policy, with no regard for the sociocultural context in which that policy is applied.[20] No doubt, the government's responses to the H1N1, which, along with the culling, included the closing of schools and universities for a month, strict medical surveillance in airports, and quarantine of identified cases in hospital, are symptomatic of these long-standing institutional dynamics which are themselves not necessarily motivated by sectarian concerns. Nevertheless, the actual implementation of the culling, as described below, suggests sectarian underpinnings in three ways: the inhumane manner of killing the pigs; the unjust compensation received by the Zabbalin; and the persecution to which they were subjected.

"There are pigs living in our midst!"

Revulsion, horror, and condemnation characterized the public responses. The lack of sanitary hygiene was very much part of a narrative of naming and shaming all the Zabbalin communities.[21] Government officials also contributed to the vilification of the Zabbalin. For example, the minister of health, Hatem El Gabally, speaking to both the upper and lower houses of Parliament, advised on a series of measures to protect against H1N1 (such as hand-washing and "keeping away from pigs and *those who are in contact with them*" (emphasis added).[22] The Zabbalin, it was also argued, had formed powerful mafias that had earlier resisted the implementation of the relocation orders issued by the government. Their concern for their livelihoods came at the expense of the welfare of Egyptians.

The use of the term *ticking bomb* to refer to the harsh, filthy conditions in which the Zabbalin lived was reminiscent of the language that was used in the

1990s when the government and progovernment press suddenly "discovered" the squatter settlements and shanty towns from which many of the Islamist militants who undertook terrorist operations came. Then, too, there was much descriptive focus on how "those people" lived and how it was "unacceptable" to continue to allow them to live in such conditions. The narrative decrying the conditions in which the Zabbalin live is revealing: Certainly the garbage sorting process occurs in close proximity to the pigsties where the organic food is disbursed to the pigs. The piled-up garbage bags waiting to be sorted do smell. However, the situation in many squatter settlements is not much better. Further, it is not that the Zabbalin are socially disposed to living with garbage; there is a clear economic dimension to this. The wealthier garbage collectors were able to separate the garbage sorting operations from their residential homes; the poorer Zabbalin had no option but to use the same space for breeding pigs, housing donkeys, and storing and sorting the garbage, as well as working, cooking, sleeping, and raising children (in particular in Ard el Lewa and Ezbet el Nakhl). There have, however, been successful cases of engagement with garbage collectors to encourage them to keep work and home spaces separate. The separation of livelihood and living spaces in the Zabbalin community of Torah el Maadi is a case in point. The intervention there was successful because land titles were given to the garbage collectors; measures were instituted to ensure the security of the private pigsties and access to infrastructure (water, electricity, and so on). In other words practical incentives associated with maintaining their livelihoods catalyzed a process of social change in lifestyle. As of this writing, the government has not provided the garbage collectors with secure land titles for any proposed settlement.

It seems the fact that the Zabbalin breed pigs is the qualifying differentiating factor. Deeming it a national security issue and calling for the physical intervention of the security forces, the government elevated the issue of the pigs to a level where disputing the logic of these claims and policies would be tantamount to an act of national treason. It also meant that the "price" to be paid—as many as three hundred thousand—seemed inconsequential in comparison to the stated goal of saving the Egyptian people.[23]

The Garbage Collectors' Narrative: "They came upon us as if we were criminals"

One of the most striking features of the way in which the mainstream narrative in favor of culling the pigs became hegemonic is the absence of alternative narratives before, during, or after the decision was implemented. It might have been expected, for example, that some human-rights based narrative would develop, emphasizing the human-rights abuses, social stigmatization, and loss of livelihood that the Zabbalin have suffered. It might also have been expected that the development NGOs working among the Zabbalin would voice their concerns. Both responses were conspicuously absent. The human-rights proponents, social activists, and development practitioners did not claim a narrative of their own. For the human-rights activists, it is possible that their failure to advocate on behalf of the Zabbalin was political: They may have feared that they would antagonize everyone by speaking on behalf of a despised group. As for the development NGOs, they chose backdoor strategies of seeking to negotiate better terms for the Zabbalin; because they only worked in one community (Mansheyet Nasser in Muqattam), Zabbalin elsewhere did not even have a party to mediate their interests. The Zabbalin tell a very different narrative from the mainstream one, and it is one that has gone largely unheard and unremarked.

The story of the day the pigs were confiscated remains largely untold. The press and media were not allowed in the areas. In Muqattam the youth formed a human shield to prevent the authorities from entering the area and tried individually to prevent them from entering their pigsties. Confrontations with the police ensued, and eyewitnesses from the Zabbalin said tear gas and rubber bullets were used to disperse the youth. The entire area was cordoned off by security forces with military vehicles. The Zabbalin believe the heavy militarized security forces and the arrest of many youth were intended to intimidate people from opposing the authorities. In Ezbet el Nakhl and Ard el Lewa the majority of the Zabbalin did not show any opposition to the confiscation of their pigs "because we saw on television what happened to our brothers in Muqattam and we did not want it to happen to us," as one pointed out. It is rare for images of police brutality (which is prevalent) to be broadcast on national television; however, perhaps the images of the garbage collectors being arrested were meant to act as a warning to garbage collectors in other communities against forming opposition. The stories are familiar: Those who objected to the compensation or to the way the security barged into their homes were threatened, beaten, and sometimes arrested. None of the communities knew when the security forces would arrive, a fact that was probably purposely kept secret in order to prevent the pigs being smuggled to another venue.

The scale of the operation was immense. National and local security forces, accompanied by members of the local council and veterinarians from the Ministry of Agriculture took control of the area, often advancing with large trucks and bulldozers to remove the pigs and raze the pigsties. They often stormed into houses with full force. "They attacked us as if we were criminals," said one garbage collector from Ard el Lewa. The culling of the pigs went on for more than two months and, while the government claimed that the country became free of the animals, there is no way to verify whether this is the case.

Following Parliament's decision to cull the pigs, a presidential decree was issued recommending that the pigs be slaughtered according to agreed-upon standards rather than being simply killed. By slaughtering the pigs the garbage collectors would then be able to sell the meat. But while many pigs belonging to the garbage collectors of Mansheyet Nasser were slaughtered, those belonging to Ard el Lewa and Ezbet el Nakhl were not. The experience of the garbage collectors from both communities is strikingly similar. In the case of the pigs bred in Ard el Lewa some of the Zabbalin followed the government trucks to see where they would be taken: "They took them alive and put them in a pit in the mountain and poured acid over them, covered them with sand and left them to die. It was a really barbarous way to treat them," reported one member of the Zabbalin. In Ezbet el Nakhl the Zabbalin tell a similar story: "They lifted the pigs on trucks and they sprayed acid on them, then two men would hit the pigs with a heavy rod on their heads and then they would take the pigs to a burial place and cover them with acid. . . . I witnessed this myself."

These eyewitness accounts from the garbage collectors are corroborated by a journalist's filming of the entire process. (The video was later uploaded to YouTube.)[24] The journalist, affiliated with the independent newspaper *Al-Masry al Youm*, was severely reprimanded by the governor of al Qalubbiyya. Even after the video became public, however, there were no calls to hold the government accountable, nor were there protests about the inhumanity of the way the cull was carried out. What protest there was came from international animal-rights activists.

They Have Taken Away Our Livelihoods

When the culling of the pigs was announced and implemented, the financial concerns of the Zabbalin were brushed aside. The government announced that it would compensate them. In line with the government's long history of granting compensation to politically and socially marginalized people (in particular the poor), the compensation given to the garbage collectors was less than what was announced. For the Zabbalin the evident injustice of the compensation is beside the point. Many know what good it does to be given compensation when you have lost your livelihood. Selling pork was only a marginal income-generating activity for most Zabbalin, who sold their pigs only in order to pay for exceptional expenses, such as marriage or illness. The day-to-day survival of the Zabbalin and their families relied on their ability to extract recyclable material from the garbage which could then be sold to others in the recycling chain. The mainstream narrative completely ignored the complex dynamics of the garbage collecting and recycling arrangements that the Zabbalin had built up over time. As a result the government and the media completely underestimated the scope of the devastation brought upon the Zabbalin, as well as the long-term implications for garbage collection in Egypt as a whole. Culling the pigs was the single greatest disincentive to collecting garbage that the government could have provided. The pigs, which consumed daily the equivalent of their weight, enabled the Zabbalin to process in a cost-efficient way an enormous amount of garbage every day. Without the pigs, the entire recycling process was undermined.

The organic waste generated by the sorting process (and once consumed on-site by the pigs) now needs to be transferred to the government garbage dump. There are three main obstacles to this. First, the poor garbage collectors who do not own trucks need to hire them; second, even those who do own a vehicle must pay garbage-dump fees; and third, when the Zabbalin transfer the garbage after it has been sorted, they risk incurring enormous fines from the traffic authorities for "polluting the environment." The last is a particularly acute problem for the Zabbalin of Ezbet el Nakhl.

As a survival strategy some Zabbalin hurriedly sort out the garbage in front of the residential homes at dawn, taking away only the recyclable material and leaving the organic waste there. Yet the men are not as experienced and efficient at sorting the garbage as the women, who can no longer partake in the process since they cannot do the sorting in the streets. The result for the Zabbalin is that instead of sixteen to eighteen members of a household working in the garbage industry, there is room for only one or two. The full implications of the changes in the garbage-collecting industry on gender relations as a result of the cull need to be more thoroughly examined. What are the consequences of women now being excluded from this livelihood? What are the implications of women now pressing the men "to go out and find a job to feed the family"?

Alternative-livelihood options for the Zabbalin are currently obscure. Some of the Zabbalin are now raising goats instead of pigs. Yet, according to long-time champion of the Zabbalin Laila Iskander, goats cannot replace pigs in eating organic waste because they consume far less. The second most popular alternative adopted by the Zabbalin who have lost their pigsties is to work in different stages along the recycling chain. After much lobbying on the part of Laila Iskander, the Zaballin were given license in 2011 to form a union, but a great deal of collective mobilization will be required to ensure the kind of participation that would translate into power.

"Let them rot in their own garbage"

Following the stigmatization and culling of the pigs, many Zabbalin decided to leave the trade. "Let them [the residents] rot in their own garbage," one explained. In many residential quarters the stigmatization predated culling. Many of the Zabbalin in Muqattam, Ezbet el Nakhl, and Ard el Lewa tell a similar story. "Suddenly from the beginning of the health scare regarding the 'swine flu' at the end of April 2009, people began to treat them like a disease. People told us not to go up to their apartments to pick up the garbage; instead they would throw their garbage from the balconies or windows so we don't contaminate them," said one garbage collector bitterly. Such experiences may have been particularly painful in the light of the many years of contact between the residents and the Zabbalin, sometimes across generations. In Ard el Lewa one garbage collector said that at the time of the hysterical media campaign about H1N1, the local health clinic refused to treat his nephew "because we are infected as we breed pigs." In another Zabbalin community children were expelled from school and told never to return because they were carriers of disease. Many garbage collectors left the profession following the cull. Others returned after the residents saw the accumulating piles of garbage and begged them to return.

The prediction of a garbage disaster that the Zabbalin had so confidently articulated became a reality only a few months after the culling. By September, Cairo's streets and alleys and even motorways were piling up with garbage. Egypt's twenty-six governorates produce twenty-five thousand tons of garbage daily, with

Cairo, not surprisingly, providing the heaviest load: from twelve thousand to fifteen thousand tons a day. Giza is the next largest producer, dispensing three thousand tons daily, while the Alexandria and Qualubiya Governorates offer up another two thousand tons each. Included in this solid waste is medical, construction, and demolition garbage.[25] In both wealthy and poor residential quarters, near schools and hospitals, literal mountains of garbage piled up; empty spots in the middle of residential areas were converted into informal garbage dumps. As of September 2016 the situation had not changed substantially, and the level of garbage in the streets, in front of schools, and in residential areas was conspicuously high.

Open Resistance

Although the Zabbalin have been politically excluded, their response has not always been one of political complacency. The local Coptic church in Muqattam, a highly influential institution in the lives of ordinary garbage collectors, has in the person of Father Samaan discouraged its followers from protesting or adopting any politically confrontational tactics expressing their discontent. This, in addition to the weakness of collective action due to internal fragmentation, has undermined the Zaballin's ability to amplify their voices in demanding their rights. However, members of the Zaballin community have risen in protest on several occasions. In 2002, when their livelihoods were displaced by the private companies, they held several protests. They protested again in 2009 in response to the culling of the pigs and then again in March 2011 in the aftermath of the revolution after the torching of the church in Afteeh. The latter was particularly bloody, as described below.

On March 8, 2011, around midday a group of 150 to 300 garbage collectors living on top of the Muqattam hills in the Zabbalin settlement called Mansheyet Nasr went down to the autostrade, the highway linking north and south Cairo, to hold a stand-in against the burning of the church in Sol and in solidarity with other protestors who had congregated in Maspero. Some placards said "No to destroying churches"; others read "Muslim, Christian one hand." As people assembled on the road, commuters began to complain that the protestors were blocking traffic, and a fight broke out. Rumors quickly spread in the surrounding neighborhoods of Sayyida 'Aisha and Khalifa that the Christian garbage collectors were on their way to burn the Sayyida 'Aisha mosque. Thugs armed with guns and knives and joined by many residents of the surrounding areas set upon the Zabbalin with Molotov cocktails and knives; they also burned the garbage-collection trucks. In response the youth threw bricks, stones, and glass to defend those approaching their settlement. Meanwhile, many witnesses said that the local sheikh in the Sayeda Zeynab mosque was inciting people to go "save your fellow Muslims from the Christians. . . . The Christians are killing the Muslims"; "Go to jihad."

About 4:45 P.M., according to witnesses, the army arrived with two tanks. "They started firing in the air to dissipate the crowd. . . . Nobody was budging. The two tanks then headed toward the entrance of Muqattam," said one of the witnesses, adding that he was surprised that the tanks went in the direction of

Muqattam. He thought that the army would have assigned a tank at Sayeda Aisha and another at the Muqattam in order to separate the crowds.

Several witnesses to whom the researcher spoke were injured in the twelve hours that followed—not only from the attacks by the residents of Sayeda Aisha, but from the army's actions as well. According to several witnesses, the army began to shoot live bullets haphazardly at the garbage collectors. Among those whom I interviewed in April 2011, some had caught bullets through their thighs, backs, and stomachs while they were trying to save the injured.

The fighting continued until approximately 3:00 A.M., with witnesses saying that the people from Sayeda Aisha and surrounding areas were attacking from behind the army tanks. During this period some of the residents reached Mansheyet Nasr, property was looted and burned, some women were assaulted, and houses were destroyed. Some of the Muslim residents of Mansheyet Nasr came to the defense of their Christian neighbors; one Muslim man died while seeking to defend his Christian neighbor against the violence. Some witnesses noted that the houses and property were not burned randomly; only the Christian ones were targeted. (Christian households in Muqattam could be recognized by the religious pictures they hang.)

The crowds, according to witnesses, blocked the fire engine from entering the area and did not let the ambulance through. Residents, both Muslim and Christian, came to the rescue of the injured by driving them in their private vehicles to nearby hospitals or to the medical clinic up in Mansheyet Nasser. By dawn ten members of the garbage collectors were dead (nine Christians and one Muslim) and about 150 were injured, some sustaining lifelong disabilities.

Having learned from experience that often the victims are framed as villains, some of the members of the Zabbalin community, such as the lawyer Maged Adel, set about documenting the events visually, interviewing the injured, and collecting evidence (such as the bullet shells, bullets, and so on). Regrettably, the mainstream official narrative represented the garbage collectors as the instigators of the violence.

A formal complaint was filed at the general prosecutor's office against the assault on the garbage collectors by the army and the residents of the surrounding areas. As of September 2016 no action from the general prosecutor had been taken. Compensation was sought for the injured and for the families of the deceased. Forty injured persons applied for compensation and managed, after a long struggle, to obtain their entitlements.

The situation was far more complex with regard to the deceased. In order for them to be given state compensation, they would have to be recognized as martyrs of the revolution. According to Maged Adel, the criteria for recognition as a martyr is that the person must have died while protesting in the general squares or in front of the police stations in the period between January and March. The government refused to recognize the garbage collectors who were protesting at the autostrade as martyrs, because they did not fulfill these conditions. In contrast, the Coptic protestors who died at Maspero, together with those who died in the clashes downtown, were recognized as martyrs by a special decree from the prime minister. Why the government would recognize the protestors who died at Maspero and not those who died at the autostrade has much to do with advocacy, voice and power. Human-rights organizations, many political activists, and the youth revolutionaries spoke out vociferously against the massacre at Maspero; the matter was given much media attention and was widely debated. In contrast, there was hardly any advocacy or lobbying on behalf of the garbage collectors, nor did the matter receive any media attention or public visibility. The Coptic Orthodox Church leadership made no public claim on their behalf either. Maged Adel sought a special decree from the prime minister to have the garbage collectors acquire the same status of martyrs as those who died in Maspero, but it took more than a year for their status as martyrs to be recognized. For these ten families the struggle to have their deceased recognized as martyrs was not primarily driven by financial compensation (although many are in a dire economic situation) but by the quest for public recognition that their loved ones were killed because the state failed to protect them while they exercised the most basic rights, that of expressing their voice peacefully.

From an Invisible Existence to Survival in the Shadows

The political situation in Egypt after the January 25, 2011, revolution was characterized by a sense of political chaos, a breakdown in the security system, both in terms of police protection of the citizenry and in the enforcement of the rule of law. This security laxity led to the emergence of all kinds of practices, including organized criminal activity that targeted individuals and communities for economic exploitation and citizens taking advantage of the security blind eye to engage in all kinds of encroachments, such as building or upgrading property illegally. The garbage collectors were in a precarious situation. They could follow suit and openly reconstruct their pigsties and raise pigs again, taking advantage of the general state of lawlessness. However, their particular identity and profession made them vulnerable to a new power whose ascendency was experienced informally in the immediate aftermath of the revolution, well before they assumed political office: the Islamists. In terms of formal political power, the Muslim Brotherhood won a majority of seats in Parliament in January 2012, and their candidate, Mohamed Morsi, won the presidency in June 2012. However, informally in the streets various Islamist forces of different shadows (Brothers, Salafis, Gama'at Islamiyya, Jihadi groups) had sought to assume the role of community policing. The garbage collectors would have incurred the wrath of the ultraradical Islamists for daring to violate the precepts of Islam by raising pigs. The fact that they are a despised group would have increased their vulnerability. However, some garbage collectors began to raise a small number of pigs, secretly, sometimes on the roofs of their homes or in their backyards.

At the heart of Mohamed Morsi's presidential platform was promising Egyptians within one hundred days in office a cleaner environment, especially with respect to garbage collection. After President Morsi's first one hundred days in office, it became clear that the government had no intention of integrating the Zabbalin into any of its major clean-up plans (which other than the planting of trees in a couple of suburbs were not visible to the average citizen).

Like the majority of Copts, the garbage collectors endorsed the revolution against the Muslim Brotherhood government in June 2013. The increasing attacks from pro-Morsi factions on Christians, their property, their churches, and faith-based organizations sent shock waves throughout the community and deepened the garbage collectors' suspicion that citizenship rights would be mediated by religion.[26] However, the garbage collectors' fortunes seemed to take a turn for the better with the takeover of the new transitional government, thanks to the appointment of Laila Iskander, their long-time champion, as the minister of environmental affairs. During her tenure she encouraged the garbage collectors to form companies so that they would have a legal status. Iskander then liaised with the myriad of authorities in order for companies to receive contracts, which meant that workers would have a legal status, and the government issued uniforms and released equipment to help them in their work. During the transition government fourteen companies led by the garbage collectors began working a pilot scheme in Dokki, a suburb in west Cairo; and many more had formed partnerships with local authorities in different parts of the city. The question is whether this is a honeymoon period precipitated by serendipity—the appointment of Laila Iskander—or whether the appointment of future ministers will see the adoption of a reversed policy. If the quality of waste management improves in these districts where the garbage collectors' companies are undertaking pilot projects, this may convince officials that there is political gain to be made by pursuing Iskander's path. However, such a trajectory may be challenged if future officials find more lucrative deals to be made with other players in the waste-management industry, both domestic and foreign. In essence, the quality of Egypt's governance, accountability to its citizenry, and will to pursue an inclusive democratic path can be measured by how it treats its garbage collectors' communities.

The contracts with the foreign companies assigned with waste management will expire in 2017. The contracts were signed behind closed doors under Mubarak's administration, and subsequent governments were reluctant to cancel the contracts out of fear that this action might have legal consequences and cost millions in compensation. However, once the contracts terminate in 2017 there will be a real litmus test of whether two revolutions have changed the political scene in Egypt and whether the authorities will act on the basis that recognizing the economic role of the garbage collectors is intimately connected to the quality of the citizens' environment and key to the country's pathway to sustainable development.

Conclusion

In narrating the story of the Zaballin in Egypt, both society and state are implicated in the systematic marginalization and persecution of this group. Society has stigmatized the garbage collectors because of their association with pigs and because of their lowly socioeconomic status. The fact that the majority are Christian has further subjected them to persecution on a religious basis. Human-rights and advocacy groups have failed to acknowledge and defend them. The highest echelons of the Coptic Orthodox Church leadership have ignored them and, in the instance of H1N1, have served as a complicit party in their repression. The Coptic Orthodox Church leadership, represented by the late Pope Shenouda, was also able to gain political brownie points; by supporting the cull they were able to appear to take a "patriotic" stance in relation to the H1N1 saga. Given the marginalization of the Zabbalin within the Christian minority, the Church could do so at no major internal political cost As for the state, not only has it failed to provide a modicum of rights accorded to other citizens; it has also actively persecuted them, under Mubarak's and post-Mubarak regimes alike. The Zabbalin were among the first targets of the Supreme Council of Armed Force (SCAF's) live bullets against the Egyptian citizenry. Yet the Zabbalin have exercised their agency in various forms of resistance and subversion of the status quo. They have protested, performed sit-ins, and gone on strike.

The Zabbalin are not a homogenous group. The community is economically stratified in a way that has undermined the possibility of effective collective action. Certainly, none of the wealthy entrepreneurs and business tycoons of Mansheyet Nasser were in the protests or in the vicinity when the garbage collectors were attacked in March 2011. Moreover, their economic enterprises were minimally affected by the slaughtering of the pigs in 2009, since their livelihoods were diversified, and many relied on predominantly capital-intensive recycling industries. Further, their economic status had gained them social capital with the government, which they were able to mobilize in order to minimize government harassment.

The most effective mode of protest that the garbage collectors could initiate to reclaim their rights would be to organize a nationwide strike, whereby all the garbage collectors' communities would desist from collecting the rubbish for one week. The country would be brought to a standstill. Yet the possibility of organizing such a strike is severely undermined by the internal hierarchies in the Zabbalin community; those with economic and political clout are blocking any unified action that could potentially undermine their own vested interests in the status quo.

Yet no matter how geographically, socially, and politically excluded the Zabbalin community appears to be, they are still part of a wider polity, one which, even if it applies a targeted form of discrimination against them, is not immune from a rebound effect. From a socioeconomic viewpoint, the residents of Cairo are the main losers behind the culling policy; since 2009 Egyptian citizens have fully experienced the Zaballin's curse cum prophecy "Let them rot in their own garbage." Egyptian citizens' prospects of living in an environment free of garbage and associated hazards is intrinsically tied to the fate of the Zaballin, since the latter have proven so far to be the most capable of dealing with waste management in an ecologically sound and culturally appropriate manner. How the Egyptian government treats its garbage collectors' community in the future is one proxy of (a) whether it recognizes the rights of those who are marginalized on the basis of religion and class and (b) the quality of its governance policy.

EXAMINING THE ROLE OF MEDIA IN COPTIC STUDIES

Angie Heo

Media and Contemporary Coptic Studies

In the sanctuaries of Coptic Orthodox churches throughout Egypt, a multimedia environment of holy worship immerses Copts in icons and glowing candles, relics and swirling incense. Today these centuries-old forms of saintly media intermingle with newer technologies of print iconography, portrait photos, and, in some places, flickering television monitors that broadcast the Divine Liturgy live. In recent decades the explosive advent of mass media has given rise to new possibilities and practices. In wealthier, heavily attended churches one might discover a team of media experts dedicated to video and audio recording of sermons, feast days, weddings, baptisms, and other ritual events. For those in search of more domestic options for veneration and prayer, replicas of these media serve them well. One Coptic woman from Beni Suef, for instance, created her own private niche of print icons, photos, miniature statues, and vials of oil in a corner of her room, which she called "my church at home."

Coptic Christians have gained attention as the barometer of Egypt's democratic future, as many scholars of contemporary Copts have importantly pointed out. Much of the attention has come during the post-Mubarak transition, which includes both the ascendance of the Muslim Brotherhood in statist politics in 2011 and the military's ousting of President Mohamed Morsi in 2013. Identified as the largest of Egypt's "religious minorities," Copts, along with the hotly debated issues surrounding their integration into the social and national fabric, make up what has been nicknamed the Coptic File (*al-milaff al-qibti*). Part of understanding these issues requires studying the role that religion currently plays in the cultural aspects of Coptic belonging and everyday life. The widespread growth and regulation of religious discourses, values, and practices, among Muslims and Christians alike, suggest that religious traditions and their development in the modern world are central factors in the making of Egypt's social and political future. To answer questions about the nature of Coptic exclusion and integration, it is thus increasingly important to ask questions about how Coptic Christianity itself shapes a topography of lived interaction and participation.

Media technologies contribute significantly to the religious world of today's Copts, as the ethnographic scenes at the beginning of this essay attest. In addition to generating new religious practices in churches and homes, media introduce sociopolitical circuits of communication and activity. The pivotal advance of satellite television in the last five to ten years and its uses among Copts in Egypt and the diaspora abroad have created unprecedented networks of transnational production, distribution, and reception. More generally speaking, the role of media has spurred interest among scholars of the Arab Middle East who seek a better grasp of how social movements and revolutionary politics amid youth are organized and mobilized. New forms of social media, such as facebook and mobile phones (offering texting and image transfer), for example, have famously enabled crowds to organize strategically against efforts of the Egyptian police to erect blockades and prevent further protests in Tahrir Square in January 2011. Months later the Egyptian military's use of state television during Coptic demonstrations in Maspero was an important reminder that uses of media are not intrinsically liberating. In this instance media were a part of the military industrial complex as the military called to the viewing audience to "protect the army from the Copts." The politics of Coptic belonging, therefore, turn upon the ways in which media shape the community writ large, offering prospects for the inclusion of Copts in national-level politics, while also subjecting them to new types of vulnerability and violence.

I identify as an anthropologist of religion and media, with a focus on the convergence of Coptic Christian practices of intercession with the spread of modern mass media. From 2004 to 2014 I conducted fieldwork among Copts throughout various regions in Egypt, mostly focusing on greater Cairo. I join a growing community of ethnographers, sociologists, and historians who wish to understand how media technologies transform religious practices and how deep histories of religion offer varied contexts for modern media use and development. In what follows I propose some directions for examining the role of media in church revival, traditional practices of ritual memory, and mass political movements with national consequences.

The Modernity of Revival

One of the most celebrated events in the historiography of modern Copts is the revival of the Coptic Orthodox Church from the late-nineteenth century onward. This "renaissance" or "reawakening" (*al-nahda*) is characterized by the comprehensive integration of the laypeople into the participatory structures of the Church. Beginning in the late 1950s with the initiative of Pope Kyrillos VI (1959–1971), new roles and positions were created such as lay deaconesses (*al-mukarrasat*) for women, with a burgeoning generation of modern-minded professionals joining the ranks of monastic and pastoral leadership.[1] Under the governance of Pope Shenouda III (1971–2012), educational and social-service programs continued to mushroom from Upper Egypt to the Delta, and the number of churches and monasteries continued to swell. Such institutional structures rendered Coptic

Christianity essential to community sustenance and the Church integral to its self-representation. The political consequences of expanding the lay basis of church reform thus entailed the strengthening of clerical authority itself—what the sociologist Dina el-Khawaga accurately captures in her phrase "the clericalized laity."[2]

Without a doubt the proliferation of modern media in Egypt has enabled the Coptic revival and the increasing impact of lay collaboration in religious life. Anyone familiar with the history of Coptic education knows that the reforming efforts of Pope Kyrillos IV (1854–1861), known as Abu Islah (Father of Reform), led him to import a printing press from abroad. While some Copts used print media toward anticolonial and nationalist ends, be it through journalism or education, others used it to develop and distribute religious curricula on a mass scale. In the early 1900s seminary institutions were founded in Cairo, Alexandria, and Asyut, and, by 1918, the much esteemed Habib Guirguis was beginning to launch what has become known as the Sunday School Movement. Across churches in Egypt today, youth and families continue to be involved in an active program of classes, prayer groups, and meetings that aim at educating Copts about the traditions and rites of Coptic Orthodoxy.

A recent phenomenon of media recruitment in religious education in the Coptic Orthodox Church is the postgraduate program offered to lay people. For Copts with vocational or baccalaureate degrees seeking to serve the church with more theological training, the Coptic seminaries have opened up their enrollment beyond regular candidates for priesthood. As of 2006 there are six governorates equipped with a clerical college (*al-Kulliya al-Iklirikiya*): in Cairo ('Abbasiyya), Qalyubiya (Shubra al-Kheima), Tanta, Munufiyya, Port Said, and Asyut. For instance, the clerical college in Shubra al-Kheima, where I attended classes as a guest student, was founded in 1988. The college offers a four-year program of classes in the evenings, with approximately two hundred students enrolling each year.[3] The curriculum varies from college to college. Using print texts authored by the late Pope Shenouda, and leading Coptic theologians, such as Father 'Abdal-Masih al-Basit of Musturud and the late Bishop Yu'annis of Gharbiyya, students delve into the following subject areas, among many others: doctrinal theology, liturgy, church history, hymnody, apologetics, and comparative theology, and languages such as Coptic, Hebrew, and English. At the time when I was in Shubra al-Khaima (2006–2007), the diocese was also developing a small television recording studio named Copt SAT on the premises, under the auspices of Bishop Murqus and Bishop Daniel, which has since discontinued.

Libraries of print tracts and audio recordings are also to be found on the shelves of living rooms and bedrooms in Coptic homes. Alongside stickers and framed images of favorite saints plastered on doors and walls, popular books and sermons make their way into the minds and hearts of their owners. Pamphlets of saintly vitae, which include collected testimonies of miracles, are reminders of what virtues require cultivation. Slim paperback tracts by the late Pope Shenouda including "Questions of the People" deliver answers to practical questions of everyday living, based on his famous Wednesday-night exchanges with an audience of hundreds of Copts. Cassettes and CDs might include his popular sermon series on

Songs of Solomon, along with less well known ones elaborating such biblical parables as that of the Samaritan woman.

Any student of Coptic Christianity familiar with the media worlds of Egypt at large is also familiar with the efflorescence of Christian satellite TV channels in the last decade or so. For about thirty Egyptian pounds or around four U.S. dollars a month (if the cables are not pirated or split among families, which makes costs commonly cheaper), satellite television is fairly affordable and viewed in the vast majority of homes. Most notably, the area includes centers in Upper Egypt such as Minia and Asyut where, in the humorous words of Bishop Butrus of Aghapy TV, "Copts watch TV all day and night." With the advent of new channels catering to Christian audiences in the Arab world, Copts have begun to watch more religiously oriented programs, previously unavailable to them on state television. These channels include al-HayatTV, launched in 2003 with headquarters in Cyprus, and SAT 7, launched in 1996, also in Cyprus, with a branch based in Muqattam, Cairo. The former is notorious for broadcasting the inflammatory views of Coptic priest Father Zakareya Boutros who regularly denounced Islam and the teachings of the Qur'an on his talk show. Since 2010 his program "Al-Haqiqa" ("The Truth") has been discontinued. Some Copts hypothesize that the Egyptian government had a hand in terminating its production.

In addition to interdenominational TV shows produced abroad, the Coptic Orthodox Church has also furnished the Coptic public with its own satellite channels. As of 2013 there are three channels dedicated to Orthodox-specific programming: Aghapy TV founded in 2005, Coptic TV (CTV) in 2007, and MeSAT in 2012. With recording studios in Heliopolis, the director of Aghapy TV is Bishop Boutrus. In its inception Aghapy TV was established in part because of the lack of Christian religious programming (compared to Islamic) on state television networks. Initially, both its financial administration and broadcasting facilities through Telestar were based in Los Angeles. With a cost of roughly twenty thousand USD per month to run, the network was exclusively supported through donations and volunteers. Compared to Aghapy TV, CTV enjoys significantly more financial leverage and resources at hand, since it is privately owned and funded by the Coptic pharmaceuticals entrepreneur Tharwat Bassily. CTV is headquartered in an industrial district of Salam City in Egypt where it is managed by its director Wagdy Sabry. Unlike Aghapy, CTV is fully equipped with a professional team of editors, animation and graphic designers, accountants, and anchors. With its headquarters in the Cathedral of Saint Mark in al-'Abbasiyya, MeSAT was founded by Pope Shenouda toward the end of his papal tenure.

Among Copts, Aghapy TV and CTV are especially popular, and both have been invited to join NileSAT, the Egyptian state satellite network. CTV has since joined NileSAT which increases its viewership among Egyptians. Like al-Hayat TV and SAT 7, CTV's programs are also available through live streaming online. According to institutional regulations, all the Coptic Orthodox channels must obtain permission from the Church before running their contents, but cases of censorship are rare. For the most part Aghapy TV and CTV feature the same or similar programming: daily recordings of masses and feast days at well-known churches and the patriarchate, daily lessons from liturgy, youth chorale performances, sermons and Bible studies, and children's animation series bought from CBN (Christian Broadcasting Network, USA) and dubbed into Arabic. During certain events of importance for the entire Church, such as Pope Shenouda's death in 2012 or the funeral for the Alexandrian martyrs in 2011 (the twenty-three victims of a church bombing), both channels provide live coverage of ongoing events of relevance for their viewers. Official church positions on internal conflicts are also aired. For example, in the thick of scandalous contest, when a figure named Max Michel proclaimed himself pope of the Church of Saint Athanasios in 2005, Bishops Mousa and Bishoy challenged his claims in a program on Aghapy TV "Where Is the Truth" (*Aina al-Haqiqa*)?

Aside from church-related activity, Coptic channels hold a range of positions regarding their role in promoting Coptic politics. In my interviews administrators at Aghapy TV adamantly voiced to me that their programs are exclusively "religious" and have no concern with the political affairs of Copts.[4] CTV is less clear-cut on this matter. Following the Maspero massacre of 2011 (see below), for instance, CTV interviewed detainees and families of those arrested, publicizing the political conditions of Coptic participants in the aftermath of military violence. In the fragile months following President Morsi's election, CTV had also experienced some regulatory pressures. In January 2013 one of its key anchors, Dina ʿAbdel-Karim, known for her outspoken style against Islam, mysteriously left the station, with rumors within the Coptic community that she was forced to leave. For the diaspora abroad, new media outlets are more politically active. In 2009 Father Bishoy al-Antony, who had formerly worked with Aghapy TV, launched an American-based, all-English-language station named Christian Youth Channel (CYC), targeting Coptic youth in the United States, Canada, Australia, and Europe.[5] Like Aghapy TV, it is funded through donations and covers church teachings, sermons, and religious rituals. Unlike Aghapy TV, it features explicit opinions voiced by members of both the diaspora and bishops within Egypt on sensitive topics, such as elections, human rights, and religious discrimination.

Developments in media technologies, from mass print and audio to television and Internet, have thus comprehensively shaped the making of the Coptic community in Egypt and abroad. The education of the laypeople and their participation in the Church takes varied forms. As CTV's Wagdy Sabry explained to me, "Copts can now listen to church hymns at home, experience the holy masses, and feel closer to leaders whom they cannot see in person easily."[6] At the same time the content of Coptic media is also an index of different freedoms and pressures and the extent to which Copts can either differ from the Church and/or express views that oppose the state.

Technologies of Ritual Memory

In the growing scholarship on religion and media, ethnographers and historians have engaged in theoretical discussions on how to define the terms *religion* and *media* and how to specify their relationship. Two important points have already been made. First, media technologies exceed the instrumental realm of religion. This is to suggest that the study of media does not merely concern how religious leaders and movements strategically "make use" of TV, film, and radio in order to advance their aims. Instead, it must also address the ways in which media often transform the contents and structure of ritual practices such as prayer and performance, as well as the ways they cultivate new bodily sensibilities and new arenas of social and political engagement. Second, the distinction between religion and media is an unstable one, prompting some scholars to characterize "religion as media."[7] For example, rather than considering, on the one hand, culture and religion as the humanistic realms of ritual and memory, and on the other, technology as the means of their reproduction, the anthropologist William Mazzarella has called for thinking about religion and technology in an "intermedium" relationship.[8] Religious practices are not only mediated, but also intrinsically mediational.

The proposed challenge, then, is to study how media technologies transform the mediating operations of religion itself. Such operations include processes of divine transmission and memory, forms of perception and circulation—all definitive of belonging to church and community, at various distances and through different skills and activities. In Coptic Egypt a rich crucible of rituals and traditions invites consideration of the ways in which uses of media shape Coptic Christian practices of religion and vice versa.

The veneration of holy saints, such as Pope Kyrillos IV or Saint Menas the Wonderworker, is one such long-standing practice of religious mediation and memory. As guardians who serve as models of holy living and heavenly patrons who tend to everyday needs and desires on earth, saints are figures of "intercession" (*shafa'at al-qiddisin*). Intercession involves the remembrance of saintly lives and virtues by enlisting the mental and bodily faculties of imagination. The collective memory of saints thus mediates relations between the authoritative origins, the lived present, and the envisioned future. In the words of the esteemed Matthew the Poor, the late abbot of the Monastery of Saint Macarius in Wadi Natrun, those who are able to imagine with "profound sensory perception" can "easily receive images of previously living persons and impress them on their own lives."[9] For many social historians and anthropologists, the task at hand is to specify with empirical detail how memories of saints and spiritual biographies are crafted through practices of narrating and imagining their lives of virtue. Acts of intercession, as ritual acts of prayer and petition, establish links that mediate between the past and present, the heavenly and the earthly.

As old Coptic Cairo currently attests, the material settings of saint veneration are thick with images of late antiquity and the medieval period, such as portrait icons and other palpable likenesses. Those icons anointed with the Church's holy oil are more than ornamental decorations; they serve as consecrated passage points for receiving blessings. In the past some icons were also ritual offerings in dedication to families seeking remembrance of a saint or angel in heaven. As technologies of imagination, they are age-old images that have historically shaped the sensory techniques and properties of intercession.

Fig. 5. Icon of the Archangel Gabriel dedicated to a family and located in the Church of the Archangel Gabriel in Abdin, downtown Cairo. Photograph by the author. Used with the permission of the Coptic Orthodox Church.

Icons are arguably embedded in a larger network of bodily and spiritual images, including visionary experience. Dreams and visions are popular topics of narrative interpretation among both Copts and Muslims in Egypt today. According to the abbess of the Convent of Amir Tadrus in Harat al-Rum (in what is now known as Islamic Cairo), icons help identify saints so that people recognize who they are when they appear in dreams and visions. In our conversation about heavenly bodies, she explained to me that saints visit people with "resurrected bodies of light" which resemble the bodily forms they had on earth. In my fieldwork I have additionally encountered Copts, and stories of Copts, who have dreamt of anonymous saints and then used icons to figure out the names and missing faces of these characters. The divine injunction "Do not be afraid" when one beholds heavenly apparitions is perhaps most tested when bodily capacities for seeing strange, unfamiliar images lead to bodily encounters with the unknown. In this way the inner memory of holy persons of the envisioned past is thus mediated by external props of saintly identity which are commonly available and publicly accessible. To the extent that memory is grounded in repetition and recognition, locating saints within personal visions also means participating in broader visual contexts of veneration.

An account of this visual context requires an account of the influence of mass media on the collective memory of sainthood cults. Perhaps the most mass-reproduced image is that of the Virgin Mary as Miraculous Mary or Our Lady of the Miraculous Medal, the worldwide representation of the Virgin in fluid robes, with hands outstretched and head crowned with a halo. This world-renowned image, known among Copts as *al-manzar al-tagalli* ("the transfigurational vision"), is originally a Catholic one believed to capture the nineteenth-century vision of the Virgin to the French nun Saint Catherine Labouré. In any given shrine it is often reproduced through framed print poster icons and miniature laminated stickers, placed next to iconographic depictions of martyrs and saints of the third and fourth centuries. Such standardization of Marian recognition is the outcome of the spatial and temporal abstraction of the Marian image from its original site of appearance (Saint Catherine Labouré's vision) and its technological reproducibility via print and photography. In other words the mass-mediated forms of saintly figures impact the ways in which they are known across globalizing contexts of Christianity through historical periods and geographical regions.

The public and collective memory of the Marian apparitions in Egypt is likewise influenced by visual technologies of regularity. Quoting one eyewitness, "the Lady Virgin comes in the language in which we understand her." As she gestured to a mural portrait that her husband had painted for one church in Giza (see fig. 6), one friend elaborated: "The Virgin appeared exactly like that in al-Warraq." While for some observers such as I, the similarity between his mural portrait and the Miraculous Mary is self-evident, for this Coptic witness of various Marian apparitions, the similarity lies between public events of her perceptible appearance in Egypt. The key issue is what standards and conventions define the laws of

Fig. 6. Icon painting of the Virgin Mary located in the Church of St. George in al-Monib, Giza. Painting by Ishaq Rufa'il Girgis, Photograph by the author. Used with the permission of the Coptic Orthodox Church.

similarity—what Peirceans might refer to as the "symbolic" aspects of iconization. Mass mediation is therefore constitutively part of the ritual mediation of memory.

Technologies of video and DVD play a major role in popularizing the lives of Coptic saints in Egypt and abroad. From 1988 to 2013 the film director Magued Tawfik produced more than forty-three films depicting the biographies of martyrs and heroes (see fig. 7), as well as those of historical figures and leaders of the Coptic Orthodox Church. One of his most recent films features the late Pope Shenouda. These films are primarily educational, tutoring viewers on the background and trials of saints such as Saint Ana Simon and Saint George of the fourth century and contemporary wonderworkers such as 'Abdel-Masih al-Manahri and Mother Irini (1936–2006), the former mother superior of the Convent of Abu Seifein. The costs of production have multiplied over the years: Tawfik's first film on Saint Bishop

Examining the Role of Media in Coptic Studies

Fig. 7. Advertisement flyer for Magued Tawfik's hagiographic films. Photograph by the author. Used with the permission of the Coptic Orthodox Church.

Abram cost 1,800 pounds compared to the more than 20,000 pounds he raised for each of his latest films. Funded by churches and monasteries, they are watched throughout Upper Egypt and the diaspora community in Australia, Canada, and the United States. He is considered a pioneer of the Coptic genre of hagiographic film. Each of his films must be approved by both the Coptic Orthodox Church and the Egyptian Ministry of Culture. In an effort to reach a broader swath of viewing audiences, Tawfik has added English subtitles to a select number of films and even translated some of them into sign language for the deaf.

On some occasions his work has introduced new cinematic conditions for sensory and technical interaction with saintly pasts. In many of his movies, such as those featuring Saint Marina and Saint Abanub of the glorious era of martyrs, the priests of local churches recount the history of their images at popular shrines of their protagonists. Toward the end of these films they offer instructive examples of how pilgrims and parishioners interact with the bodily relics and icons, recording acts of veneration on site. In interviews conducted in 2006 and 2013, Tawfik described to me the feedback he has received from viewers, conveyed through letters and phone calls. In addition to expressing gratitude for making movies that depict the lives of Coptic heroes, some viewers have reported other responses to the films. For example, one woman described how she experienced a dream-vision of the Virgin after watching a video. A man described how a viewer afflicted with demons and evil spirits screamed while seeing the fictional character of Saint George on the screen, experiencing a virtual exorcism. Another described how his failing eye was healed after he placed it on the cinematic image of Saint Marina's relics. Such videographic presences suggest that mass media both extend and transform conditions for remembering the power of saints, when bodily images in shrines and churches are not readily available to sight and touch.

In my view as an ethnographer of media, the question to ask is not whether or not these miracles really happened, but what histories and cultures of media are offered in these novel contexts of cinematic interaction. After all, against technologically determinist lines of thought, there is nothing intrinsic in mass print, photography, and television that structures universal modes of engagement. Various forms of media, such as print icons and video hagiography, transform the circulation and reproduction of ritual memory, and, at the same time, long-standing rituals of sensory mediation and saintly interaction forge emergent uses and potentials availed in technology.

Mass Politics and Violence

New Year's Day 2011 sparked the beginning of a tumultuous year of violence for all Egyptians but in particular for the Coptic community. After the bombing of the Church of the Saints in Alexandria which left twenty-three dead and the exhilarating defeat of the Mubarak regime in Tahrir, Copts faced heightened risks of vulnerability and attack. Within weeks of Mubarak's downfall, mass protests in Mansheyet Nasser and sectarian scandals in Sul, south of Helwan, led to street riots, killings, and subsequent demands for accountability against "hidden hands" of violence. The fresh memory of martyrs proliferated through visual paraphernalia, with posters featuring photos of them, crowned and named, hanging in shops and stores (see fig. 8). These contents and contexts of death differed from the ancient narratives of the *Holy Synaxarium* (book with the lives of the saints), heightening the injustice of attacks, rather than the 'holy lives and deaths' of the newly interpolated martyrs.

The politics of media and mobilization has gained interest among analysts worldwide, especially in the wake of the Arab uprisings. There is no doubt that media also played a significant role in advancing revolutionary activity against state authoritarianism and generating spaces for Coptic secularist politics outside the regulatory purview of the Coptic Orthodox Church. For example, the sociologist of media Elizabeth Iskander has examined how popular blogs, facebook profiles, and online forums disseminated discourses of critical dissent among Copts from 2005 to 2010.[10] As a social institution, mass media establishes networks of communication, which coordinate scales and speeds of political action. Studying the relationship between mass media and mass politics has thus become more critical for understanding how Copts seek political recognition through unprecedented means and from different audiences, both national and international. These methods of seeking response and redress through mass mobilization have in turn, at times, resulted in mass-mediated forms of violence.

Examining the Role of Media in Coptic Studies

Fig. 8. Poster of the six martyrs of the Nag Hammadi shootings on January 7, 2010. The poster is hung in a corner of a Coptic bookstore in Shubra. Photograph by the author. Used with the permission of the Coptic Orthodox Church.

Leading up to the Tahrir protests, new organizations for Coptic activism, such as the Maspero Youth Union (*Ittihad Shabab Masbiro*), utilized media outlets to galvanize mass demonstrations and protests. Since its founding, the union has strategically indulged in political cultures of spectatorship and accountability in order to advance publicly its causes. In nearly all of its marches demonstrations began in Shubra to gather Christian protestors and ended symbolically in front of the state TV headquarters at Maspero, neighboring Tahrir. According to one of its founders, Rami Kamil, the TV building was selected in part on account of the biased reporting of media against the interests of Copts.[11] It is notable that, before 2009, Copts had primarily staged demonstrations and protests on church grounds, mostly within the territory of the Coptic Orthodox patriarchate. Since the Nag Hammadi killings in 2010 and the Alexandrian bombing of 2011, Copts had congregated at the Maspero TV building for demonstrations. This shift in the location of antistate activism indicated efforts of a younger generation of Egyptians to carve out a secularist grounds for Coptic politics. Furthermore, the Maspero Youth Union's appeal to national TV coverage suggests that their audience of address was not so much the clergy who had previously represented their political interests, but the Egyptian public writ large. Mass-mediated protests thereby contributed to political shifts from religious modes of representation to more secularist ones.

The Maspero massacre of October 9, 2011, resulted in twenty-seven deaths and more than three hundred wounded. On that evening the Maspero Youth Union had organized a demonstration in response to acts of violence and government corruption involving a church building in al-Marinab, a village in Aswan. On Bloody Sunday, as the fateful day is now remembered, the demonstrations ended in a gruesome confrontation lasting throughout the night and involving the military, the protesting youth, unknown thugs, and spectators. In the aftermath of the shock, the following day there began a series of accusations against the military and police arrests, as well as a show of public mourning and sympathy. As recently as 2013, the Union continued to attract a critical mass of both Coptic and Muslim youth, which grew after the spectacularly violent events of the Maspero massacre.

One of the critical issues in understanding the Maspero incident is how media technologies, such as the television and Internet, enabled acts of violence at new speeds and in new forms. Shooting live coverage of the protests and confrontations between military and youth, state channels announced news of Copts attacking soldiers at the Maspero building. One well-known anchor, Rasha Magdy, went further and evoked images from the October 1973 war, calling upon viewers to "defend the army" against Coptic attacks. Within hours of these announcements, Christian satellite TV channels, frequently watched by Copts through Internet streaming, simultaneously broadcast footage of military tanks trammeling demonstrators. According to one eyewitness, both Muslims from the surrounding neighborhood in Bulaq and Christians from as far away as Upper Egypt were mobilized to fight as a result of these contending footages. By issuing reports and commands in real time, the divided circulation of news generated crowds of sectarian unrest on the streets. The Maspero massacre introduced orders of mass violence in which feedback loops of information generated new acts of violence uploaded for viewing once again.

Beyond events in Maspero, mass media networks also advance the transnational production of Coptic Christian activism. In particular, the communities in diaspora have offered a particular political audience for the plight of Copts in postrevolution Egypt. Copts on both ends have learned to broadcast conditions of sectarian tension and discrimination by uploading photos captured on mobile phones. Understanding how media organizes movements toward political action is thus necessary for understanding how Coptic Christians create their identity as an international sociopolitical entity. Increasingly, humanitarian groups also promote various strategies of documenting and publicizing acts of violence in order to appeal for justice and responsibility, both within Egypt and abroad. As these trends continue during the next years of fragile transition and state building, one topic of research in Coptic studies will be the examination of media use among Coptic activists for developing politics of their own making.

Conclusion

In this brief survey we have examined the role of media in the social, religious, and political realms of Coptic livelihood. These three different angles toward studying media all demonstrate how technologies create new types of Coptic belonging, vulnerability, and activity, while simultaneously transforming realms of religion and politics.

Research on Coptic Christianity in contemporary contexts richly benefits from approaches that bring together practices of ancient tradition with the current technological advancements that sustain and transform them. For ethnographers of media, the study of systems and practices of mediation is essential for contextualizing the function and status of modern media within longer histories of creativity, memory, and suffering. It is my hope that this essay advances us in this direction by opening up avenues for innovative future work in Coptic studies.

FATHER SAMAAN AND THE CHARISMATIC TREND WITHIN THE COPTIC CHURCH
Gaétan du Roy

The scene takes place late at night in Father Samaan's office after the weekly Thursday evening church service. The priest's office is crowded with a group of young people and several believers who try to get his *baraka* (blessing). Father suddenly raises his voice to calm the laughter and discussions: "*Khalas ya gama'a da mish kalam basit!*" ("Silence! These are important words!") Indeed, the television set in front of the priest's desk has begun broadcasting a program that presents Father Samaan himself narrating how, when he was sixteen, he fell asleep about midnight and began dreaming. In the dream he was wearing a white *galabeyya*, the traditional Egyptian garment, with a black spot where his heart would be. Farahat, as he was called at that time, decided to buy some paint to cover the stain. After leaving the house he met an imposing man dressed in white. Beside him, a woman was standing, also dressed in white. As he approached, Farahat realized that the man was radiating a pure, almost blinding beauty. The man asked him what he wanted. Farahat explained that he wanted to buy some paint.

Why?

Because I have a black mark I want to get rid of—my *galabeyya* looks terrible.

Fine. But I don't sell [paint]. After a moment of silence:

All right, I will wipe it away from you—but on one condition.

What's that?, Farahat asked.

Don't get dirty again.

The man placed his hand on the spot and it disappeared.[1]

Father Samaan is currently one of the best-known priests in Cairo. His life is a success story of evangelical preaching, and his biography is peppered with hagiographic tales, miracles, and divine calls.[2] This essay focuses on the various strategies that have led to Father Samaan's fame as a Charismatic preacher and healer, visible in the enormous churches built under his guidance that are carved in the rocks of the Muqattam Mountain. Also important are the connections between Father Samaan and Egyptian Evangelical Protestants, for whom the Muqattam church served as the megachurch that was symbolic of the unity of the Church, understood as the unity of all Christians.

Father Samaan's history and work highlight the ways in which forms of ecumenism and varieties of religious experience appeared during the reign of Pope

Shenouda (1971–2012).³ This movement was deeply influenced by American Protestant Evangelicalism and Pentecostalism, as can be seen in public exorcisms, a traditional practice within the Coptic Orthodox Church which this movement has infused with other meanings; in the focus on redemption and conversion (understood as a real individual encounter with Jesus Christ); and in the strong links between Samaan and Evangelicals, both Egyptian and foreign.⁴

Charismatic Trends within the Coptic Orthodox Church

By *Charismatic Copts* I mean the emerging tendency within the Coptic Orthodox Church that can be compared to the Charismatic Catholic Movement that emerged in the United States by the end of the 1960s. This movement was deeply influenced by Protestant Evangelical thinking and instigated a revival within the Roman Catholic Church.⁵ The term *charismatic* also stresses the importance of Father Samaan's charisma, taken here in the biblical sense as a power given by the Holy Spirit and also referring to Max Weber's theory of charisma as a type of authority.⁶ In order to understand this Charismatic Movement it has to be placed within the context of trends of globalization and their impact on religion. As Olivier Roy has argued, forces of deculturation and deterritorialization are typical of the globalization of religions.⁷ For Samaan's church, the deculturation process can be seen in the focus on Jesus Christ rather than on the traditional Coptic intercessors. This is a soft change that does not include the radical rupture that Pentecostals propose, for example in Latin America, where conversion entails a complete change of life.⁸ Furthermore, we can affirm that more and more Christians refuse to be Copts only in the nominal sense, belonging to a parish and subject to their priest's authority; instead they want to affirm their religious choices, for example, through daily personal devotions. Deterritorialization can be seen in the networks which link Muqattam to other churches in the West, networks including Christian satellite channels and the Internet. This new global horizon of meaning lays emphasis on the Christian identity more than on the Coptic one. This horizon emerged precisely through the new media and created new patterns giving meaning to Egyptian experiences. In the 1960s a new "communal self-awareness,"⁹ akin to Benedict Anderson's "imagined community" emerged, centered on a rediscovery of tradition with the Church as an "organizing point"¹⁰ of reality.¹¹ This identification is still powerful and represents the perspective of the majority of the Copts.¹² However, the community imagined by Charismatic Copts offers new forms of identification as it seems to refer to the Church as the community of all the Christians of Egypt and possibly to Christianity worldwide.

Egyptian Evangelicals and Charismatic Copts were greatly influenced by Father Matta el-Miskin (1919–2006), one of the leaders of the renewal movement within the Coptic Orthodox Church in the 1940s, which was called the Sunday School Movement.¹³ The well-known monk, along with other important leaders including the future bishop of ecumenical and social affairs, Samuel, Bishop of Ecumenical and Social Services (1962–81), and the future Pope Shenouda belonged to the first generation of well-educated members of the laity who wanted to reform and improve their Church. Matta el-Miskin, who later on became the abbott of the Monastery of Saint Macarius, proposed a new articulation between the faithful and God, between the Coptic identity and the Christian one. For example, he encouraged the Coptic Orthodox Church to open itself to the other Christian denominations. This ecumenical openness was original and largely compatible with Protestant perspectives. As Dina el-Khawaga puts it, referring "to the founding fathers and to the original roots of Christianity," it "left little space for the separation between Monophysites, Orthodox and Catholics."[14] Moreover Matta el-Miskin taught that "theology is not a theory, not even a thought; it is a living and personal truth, located permanently within the person of the Redeemer."[15]

Brigitte Voile has called the 1960s "la décennie charismatique," the Charismatic decade.[16] This time period was marked by the reign of Pope Kyrillos VI, who was at the same time an institutional reformer and a great saint, particularly venerated among the Copts. The period also witnessed apparitions of the Virgin in Zeitoun in 1968 and myriad miracles and healings. Since then, the Coptic community has seen an outpouring of miracles of all kinds, due, most of the time, to the intercession of a saint, the Virgin Mary, or even a living saint. At the same time, throughout Egypt, Muslims and Christians have been practicing their faith in an increasingly public way.

Shenouda III, who became pope in 1971, continued the work of institutionalization launched by Pope Kyrillos VI and extended the hold of the clergy on the faithful; the number of priests increased dramatically, and the churches became the center of life for many Copts. Egyptian Christians, who earlier had not been particularly involved in the Church, became active members of their parishes. In an attempt to bring the entire Coptic community under Church control, Pope Shenouda put into place several strategies that led to a level of uniformity within the lay community. For example, he incorporated all those working for the Church, such as the members of the Church's community council, into its hierarchy by ordaining them at a certain clerical rank, such as that of deacon.[17] The pope also tried to give a new impetus to the process of organizing and containing collective public religious passions. After the outpouring of miracles during the 1960s the clergy tried to channel these new devotional expressions. In other words, Pope Shenouda tried to consolidate the clergy's control on Coptic piety in order to fight against the excesses of popular or folk religiosity.[18]

The Charismatic Movement was born in this same context and was clearly influenced by it, but it stressed other aspects of the faith and religious practice. Devotion was to be more focused on a direct relation with Jesus Christ and far less on the intercession of the Virgin or the saints, usually called double intercession. Although intercession remains very important for the majority of Copts, there is evidence for a progressive shift through the Charismatic Movement toward a more direct, individual relation with God. Once again Matta el-Miskin's influence can be pointed out. He expressed in a 1967 book his skepticism about the excessive recourse to Virgin Mary's intercession as he wrote: "The Orthodox Church doesn't believe it is possible for anybody to be an intermediary between God and the people except Jesus the Messiah."[19] This Charismatic Movement became well known and attracted the interest of many believers at the end of the 1990s and especially during the 2000s, even if those who were attracted did not accept all the Charismatic ideas and practices. This version of the Christian faith is appealing to a new generation that is well educated, individualistic, and well versed in new technologies. The new media landscape in Egypt during the 2000s greatly influenced this new generation, especially the new satellite channels that allowed access to a broad range of religious discourses inside as well as outside Egypt. While the Coptic Orthodox patriarchate launched two channels (Aghaby in 2005 and CTV in 2007), another was created to serve as a platform for Charismatic Coptic preachers as well as Protestant Evangelical pastors. These programs and religious talk shows were instrumental in creating a new transnational Christian horizon of meaning. For the first time Copts could hear, through Father Zakareya Boutros, direct attacks against Islam on al-Haya channel and testimonies from Muslims converted to Christianity.[20] It gave the impression that Western Christians were standing up against Islam together with them.

Father Samaan's spiritual project can be seen as an attempt to extend Christianity's glow in Egypt and to demonstrate the strength of the Christian faith in its ability to recruit Coptic, as well as Muslim, souls for the Lord. In this regard and in connection with all the visions Samaan had about his mission and the role God has given him, this movement might be described as a kind of millenarianism fed on eschatological prophecies.[21] It must be noted that millenarianism is not primarily about the end of time, but about God's kingdom settling on earth before the end of the world. More precisely, Egyptian Charismatics can be defined as postmillenarianists, which means they are focused on the idea that "the kingdom of God is already here, in the construction phase, and that the bulk of the fighting against forces of darkness has to be done by Christians, not by Jesus when he will come back."[22] The idea emerging from these prophetic visions seems to be that a new momentum will be given to Christianity in Egypt, that a period of conversion to Christianity is about to begin in Egypt. Father Samaan often says that the Zabbalin are an example for all Egyptians. According to the priest, these poor people, who work as garbage collectors, repented of their sins to become good Christians and, as such, they are a model to follow to return to the "true religion." This Charismatic movement, which is focusing on an ecumenical form of Christianity rather than on the Coptic Orthodox Church, did not please Pope Shenouda, who was a vigilant custodian of the community's boundaries.[23] He regularly attacked this trend as a result, for example, by excommunicating Charismatic Coptic leaders such as Father Daniel, a monk who attracted many followers through his sermons and healings.

Father Samaan's Youth

Father Samaan, as can be seen when he tells his story on satellite TV, considers himself guided by God. All the faithful who attend his church know the story well. Father Samaan, formerly called Farahat, was born in 1941 in Mit Ya'ish, a small village in the Delta near the town of Mansura. The son of a modest landowner, he was the youngest of six children. At the age of six, the bishop of Daqahleyya ordained him a deacon.[24] Over the years, while studying at the government school, he drifted away from religion. Then, at sixteen he heard a voice asking him about the direction his life was taking: "But then suddenly he saw himself in a picture projected on to the wall in front of him. It was as if God was running a complete cine-film of his life. 'These are all the things you have done, from when you first knew sin up to this moment.'"[25]

Frightened, he grabbed the first book he saw: *Prayers of the Saints*. "The first thing he read really hit him between the eyes. People, it said, 'are heartless and cruel and never do right' (Romans 3.10)." And also, "we are 'less than a puff of air' (Psalms 51.5)." The confession "'I have sinned and done wrong since the day I was born' (Psalms 51.5)"[26] seemed to sum up his life. Yet the next verse he read—"But to all who received him, who believed in his name, he gave power to become children of God"—gave hope (John 1:12). A year later Farahat heard a voice telling him to burn his favorite book with worldly love songs and sing hymns instead. He felt the urge to talk about Jesus to those around him and became a preacher. He crisscrossed the country visiting the smallest hamlets and knocked on doors to proclaim the word of God. This itinerant preaching was possible because of the new phenomenon of rural ministries that had been launched in 1957 by the future Bishop Samuel (then still called Father Makari) in collaboration with Father Boulos Boulos who was a parish priest in Damanhur in the Delta.[27] The idea was to reach out to villages that had no church, while at the same time addressing people's social needs. This was an ecumenical enterprise, and Copts often teamed up with Protestants.[28]

During the same period Khalas al-Nufus (the Society for the Salvation of the Souls), an ecumenical organization that still exists, had started to operate in the countryside. Its goal was "the predication through the Bible, which means to reach the people through redemption and the return to God."[29] One of these missionaries reached Farahat's village during the 1960s and convinced him to move to Cairo to work for the Khalas al-Nufus printing press.[30] About the same time, he began to work for the *al-Gumhurreya* newspaper. It was then that a colleague suggested to him that he go preach in a neighborhood (not yet Muqattam) located on the outskirts of Cairo. According to John Waters, Farahat realized at that time that he had a gift for exorcism.[31] It is likely that during this period he also met Father Zakareya Boutros for the first time. In 1969 Zakareya Boutros had become the priest of a church in Heliopolis, and he invited Farahat to become one of his assistants.[32] Nowadays, as mentioned above, Father Zakareya has become a controversial televangelist whose famous attacks on Islam can be watched on the satellite channel al-Hayat and on his own channel al-Fadi, which was launched to facilitate the conversion of Muslims. Father Zakareya was forced to leave Egypt in 1989 after being accused of baptizing Muslims. He currently resides in the West.

According to his son-in-law Samuel Labib Maher, in spite of his closeness to Khalas al-Nufus, Farahat remained Orthodox. Nowadays, his connection to the association is still sensitive and has led to accusations that he is a former Protestant and has followed Evangelical practices. From 1976 until his ordination in 1978, Farahat was working for the patriarchal newspaper *al-Kirazah*, which might be understood as a way for him to get closer to the Orthodox Church at the time when he was probably thinking of becoming a priest.

Called to Muqattam

Meanwhile the future Father Samaan formed a relationship with the Zabbalin, a people whose job is garbage collection and waste management.[33] This story is the best-known part of his biography. It circulates orally and in writing. More recently, it has been the subject of a movie. It goes as follows. In the early 1970s Farahat was living in Shubra. The young man regularly met with the trash collector who worked in his neighborhood. The latter insisted for two years that Farahat visit the Zabbalin community. In 1974 Farahat received a call from God ordering him to respond to the invitation. He attempted to make the cumbersome journey to the area by bus but gave up and turned around, he remembered, "as Jonah" had done. "But the divine inner voice repeated its demand to get off the bus and go to the Zarayib,[34] as he was told before."[35] When he finally arrived in the neighborhood, he was "overwhelmed by a strange feeling that God wanted to do something there! But what it was he did not know. So he asked the trash collectors to take him to a quiet place to pray. They took him to the highest place in this area where he found a cave under an imposing rock that was later to become part of the monastery of St. Samaan the Tanner."[36]

He continued praying at the same place every Sunday for three weeks. The third Sunday he implored God to show him the way, and the miracle occurred. A strong wind carried a sheet of paper with a verse from the Acts of the Apostles: "One night the Lord said to Paul: 'Do not be afraid; keep on speaking, do not be silent. For I am with you, and no-one is going to attack and harm you, because I have many people in this city" (Acts 18: 9–10).[37] When he met with Pope Shenouda to convey his story, the pope said, "It is not a piece of paper, it's a heavenly message [*firman samawi*]."[38] Father Samaan realized that God had spoken to him through scripture. The rest of the story covers the construction of the first church, which later became the monastery.

Converting Souls

Father Samaan did not settle in the area right away but commuted to Muqattam to preach the word of God. It was not the Zabbalin's worldly needs that concerned him first; he wanted to save their souls.[39] In fact, his ultimate goal was not to help the poor of this district physically but spiritually. According to the well-known story, when Father Samaan began his ministry in the area those living in Muqattam were all "nominal Christians" who knew neither God nor the Bible. They were unaware of their own religion, and some Zabbalin told me that some prayed on mats, "like Muslims." A stereotypical story accounting for the miserable state of

Christians in the area before the coming of Father Samaan tells of alcoholics and drug addicts hanging out in the coffee shops. Fist fights were frequent. The area's inhabitants were portrayed as crude and rough Sa'idis (men from Upper Egypt).[40] Evidence of the pervasiveness of this image was a skit performed by young boys before a spiritual meeting in the Saint Samaan monastery in which stereotypical Sa'idis from Upper Egypt portrayed those with bad habits and the sins about which Father Samaan was concerned.[41] The story was about two fathers, one good and one bad. The good one listened to his children, took them on his lap, looked at them, and taught them right from wrong. The other one was absent and paid little attention to his two sons. When grown up, his children chased after girls and visited pornographic websites. The bad father, a rough Sa'idi, was dressed in the traditional dress of a *galabeyya*, while the good father was wearing a shirt and trousers.

Apart from his role as spiritual leader, Father Samaan regularly served as mediator between developmental organizations at Muqattam and in the community of the garbage collectors. External donors were delighted to have someone who could play the role of "chief of the Zabbalin," and, most important, someone who remained outside the clans and interests of the neighborhood.[42] Naturally, this position strengthened the priest's influence inside the community. To give a striking example, when Environmental Quality International, a consulting firm funded by the World Bank, decided to provide five recycling machines, the criteria for those receiving the equipment were to have access to sufficient electricity, to work in the business of recycled plastic, and to have the approval of Father Samaan.[43] Furthermore, Father Samaan entertained good relations with President Hosni Mubarak's representatives in the area and became an indispensable interlocutor for the National Democratic Party. For example, Ibrahim Suleyman, Mansheyet Nasser's member of Parliament and minister of housing, was instrumental in building the road that provided access to the monastery in the early 1990s.[44]

Father Samaan has also been a tireless builder. The churches he has built account for a significant part of his reputation. His first church was built shortly after he settled in the area. The pope even donated money for the church's roof.[45] Literacy classes were offered, patterned after Protestant teaching methods that use the Bible as main text. "We did all through the Bible," remembers the priest's wife.[46] Two American Protestants and a young Egyptian who now heads an NGO in the district were the first teachers. Father Samaan attracted many people to his adventures. He accepted all the foreign aid he could get to advance his projects.

The Miracle of the Mountain

When one traces the life of the priest in chronological order, one ends up with a succession of stories that probably did not evolve in the neat sequence that is currently presented. The story of Father Samaan's calling would not have been possible without the well-known legend of the moving of the Muqattam Mountain. Father Samaan appropriated this ancient miracle story and developed it for the benefit of his spiritual project and for the creation of an uncommon place of worship. It is said that in the tenth century the caliph al-Mu'izz challenged the Coptic patriarch Abraham to prove that the biblical saying that faith can move mountains was true; if he failed, Christians would be killed. Abraham asked the caliph to allow him three days of fasting and prayer. On the third day he saw the Virgin in a dream who told him to meet a blind tanner called Samaan. It was through the tanner, who led a virtuous life, that God accomplished the moving of Muqattam Mountain. Later on, according to the story, the caliph secretly converted into Christianity.[47]

Father Samaan "reinvented" Saint Samaan, giving his name to a church for the first time in Coptic history.[48] He also published the first hagiography of Saint Samaan in 1987.[49] Over time, as he reinvented the saint and the miracle of Muqattam, the priest was inventing himself as well; his life became interwoven with this tradition. In 1991 the relics of Saint Samaan were discovered and placed in the church that bears his name, bestowing a type of "homologation by the tradition" on this church, since relics are a central element of devotion to the saints in the Coptic religious tradition. When in 1993 the second edition of the saint's hagiography appeared, it included the narrative of the discovery of the relics, as well as the story of Father Samaan's divine call and mission among the Zabbalin. The priest's story was further highlighted in a movie on the miracle of the mountain that came out in 1995.

The more impressive part of the reinvention of the miracle was the building in the early 1990s of a huge complex at the heart of the mountain called "the Monastery" (although no monks live there), which was said to have been moved. Today the complex has seven churches and hosts funerals, baptisms, and numerous prayer meetings. In spite of the name, there is no monastery at the complex. However, the name refers to the monastic traditions of hermits who lived in the desert. More recently the caves have served as backdrop for religious TV programs and video clips. The pictures hanging in Father Samaan's reception room show him dressed in a *galabeyya* whitened by the dust of working, serving as constant reminder of the glorious epic of the monastery's construction.[50] Each year new floors are added to the buildings in order to accommodate the growing number of visitors.

Scenes from the Bible and the life of Saint Samaan, including representations of the miracle of the mountain, are carved in the monastery's rock walls. These decorations are the work of the Polish artist Mario, who has witnessed the constant expansion of the site for nearly twenty years. Over the course of those years the representation of the saint has become standardized. Nowadays his image is available on stickers, posters, and keychains.

Charismatic Religiosity

Currently Father Samaan is best known for his public exorcisms. In recent years the phenomenon has become increasingly successful, generating press articles and reviews, as well as severe criticism from the Coptic Church hierarchy, including Anba Bishoy, who used to be the right hand of Pope Shenouda.[51] His critics have regularly forced the priest to suspend these practices, which resume when things calm down.

However, he is not the only one practicing exorcisms. Father Makari Younan, the priest of the Murquseya al-Qadima church, which until the 1960s served as the patriarchal cathedral, provides similar services on a weekly basis.[52] Both priests are spiritual sons of the controversial Father Zakareya Boutros. The sermons and exorcisms of Father Samaan usually take place during megameetings at the monastery on Thursday. On these nights minibuses bring streams of Christians who come to listen to his sermons, to acquire the *baraka* of the place, and to have picnics. Local residents dress in their Sunday best. During this time adolescent boys and girls can freely meet, as the open space permits flirting from a distance.

The service is held in the main church carved into the rock that seats several thousand. Before the sermon a choir intones a series of religious songs, an "unorthodox" kind of Christian pop music. Many songs are composed by Mahir Fayezz, a popular Coptic singer.[53] It is remarkable that the songs one hears in the meetings of the Protestant church in Qasr al-Dubbara or at meetings of Khalas al-Nufus are the same as those sung at Muqattam. Father Samaan appears at the end of the songs to give a sermon that may last up to one hour. It is broadcast live on Sat 7, a Christian satellite channel.[54] Father Samaan's preaching is guided by questions of sin and redemption. His appeals to those present to give themselves to Jesus Christ are reminiscent of Charismatic and Pentecostal gatherings. The nontraditional songs and the stress on redemption have resulted in accusations that he follows a "Protestant" style.[55] His close cooperation with Protestants does not help to diminish this impression. For example, in 2005 the gathering of *al-salla al-ʿalami* (The World Prayer)[56] was held at the monastery. Bishop Bishoy severely criticized Father Samaan's invitation to Christians of all denominations to come and pray together, and he was forbidden to hold any such meetings in the future.[57] Another event that has led to similar criticism was a "prayer for Egypt," also called "the return to God" (*al ruguʿ ila Allah*), which was organized after the revolution, on 11/11/2011, by the monastery and the Qasr al-Dubbara Evangelical Church.[58] Father Samaan dismissed the criticisms by calling himself "religious but not an extremist" and open to all Christians.

Another part of his ministry, which earns him criticism as well as fame, are his public exorcisms. Usually after the sermon has ended, those who are sick or are thought to be possessed by evil spirits gather to seek healing or exorcism. The two terms seem to be interchangeable. For an "easy" case Father Samaan puts his cross on the forehead of the afflicted while reciting a prayer, sprinkles her with holy water, and blows on her face to release her from the spirit or heal the affliction she has. At times his wrestling with the spirit is so intense that the person thought to be possessed faints. At that moment Father Samaan can ask the spirit(s), "How many are you?" Depending on the case, a distorted voice answers "Two or three" or more. Then Father Samaan asks the possessed to lift one leg several times, and at the third time he orders the spirits to leave the body via the foot.[59] Once the afflicted gets up, apparently fully recovered, the audience applauds. The entire ritual is accompanied by music. Depending on the gravity of the situation, tunes vary from Christian pop music to Coptic chants.

Most of the people coming for exorcism are from the lower strata of the society. Muslims come to seek healing as well—a fact that is a great source of pride for the church and attests to Father Samaan's strength.[60] *Strength* is the word that comes up most often in the context of exorcisms. For the Copts who feel threatened by Islam, Muslim seekers are a sign of the superiority of the Coptic religion.[61] It seems that Muslims who come for exorcism ascribe a certain power to Coptic priests who traditionally are considered specialists in this area of healing.[62] Copts are convinced that true healing can only be accomplished by converting to Christianity.[63] Although never admitted openly, this sentiment shines through in an evangelical biography of Zakareya Boutros: "Zakaria's practice was to beseech God to heal the sick, if in each case it was God's will. He simultaneously encouraged the exercise of faith by the afflicted person, if it was possible, as well as in those who had accompanied that person to the meetings. He always asked those involved whether or not they really believed Christ could in fact still heal today. Only if the answer was in the affirmative did he proceed."[64]

The novelty of the meetings lies in how these exorcisms take place. They are now staged before a large audience and are broadcast via television and YouTube. They have become public spectacles for the whole world to see. They are now closely associated with a proselyte project, a metaphor of the (supposed) ongoing reconversion of Egypt to Christianity.

Healing by itself can be considered a miracle. Furthermore there is some testimony of individuals who have been brought back to life. Only these are clearly identified as *mu'gizat*, miracles, and singled out as extraordinary cases. One story tells of a young boy who crushed his head by a falling on a rock. His chances for survival were practically nonexistent. After Father Samaan prayed for his healing, the boy lived. Another story tells about a young girl who drowned. After Father Samaan and all of the Muqattam community prayed, she regained life.[65]

A New Way of Being Christian

This charismatic type of ministry is attracting Copts in growing numbers, probably for a variety of reasons. Some are attracted by the emotional worship; some may have grown weary of the "endless" Coptic masses (about three hours); and others appreciate the idea of direct contact with God, because they find the Coptic priests authoritarian and sometimes even rude. Moreover, some Copts also enjoy the possibility of experiencing different atmospheres in worship: on the one hand alternation between joy and pain during the charismatic meetings, on the other hand contemplation and prayer during traditional Coptic ceremonies. Some of these believers exhibit eclectic patterns of religious consumerism. They prefer one church for the singing, another one for the sermons, regardless of the church's denomination. Many attend Protestant as well as Orthodox meetings. They reject the strong traditionalism of some of the Coptic priests whom they consider to be closed-minded (*maqfulin*). Many of them also reject the denominational divisions among Christians. For example, when a young Orthodox Copt who works in an international company was asked if he was Coptic Orthodox, he replied, "I'm a Christian."

A young student I met in Muqattam, but who lives in Zeitoun (a lower-middle class suburb), confessed that she liked to go to Qasr al-Dubbara and appreciated Father Makari because he has a "special relationship with God." She studied in Protestant Sunday schools for ten years and applied for a place in the evangelization program of a Coptic Orthodox church while attending similar training sessions organized by American Evangelicals. Yet, she considered her main affiliation to be with the Coptic Orthodox Church, saying "*andi intima*" (I have an affiliation). In spite of her openness she feels isolated because she is convinced that she is the only one within her Coptic parish who has this point of view. On the opposite end of the spectrum are the faithful of the Muqattam monastery who are used to this ecumenical atmosphere. One young volunteer devoted to Father Samaan is embarrassed by the existence of strong links between the monastery and the Evangelicals of the Qasr al-Dubbara church. Observing the Orthodox tradition, he feels "that it is better if everyone prays in their own church." He finds it offensive to hear members of the Evangelical church say, "We should make them forget all their old traditions." But whenever he expresses this point of view, the other volunteers in Muqattam call him an extremist. Although this brief overview is based on a limited set of samples, the pattern seems consistent enough to show that some Copts are in search of emotional worship and want to experiment with new ways of belonging to their religious community. If they do not feel comfortable in their parish or in their denomination they go to other places that can offer them something else.

Most of the people coming from outside Muqattam to attend Samaan's meetings have experienced a change in their religious life. They have become more intent on practicing their religion or had a real encounter with Jesus. Those who claim to have had a born-again experience insist that, before converting, they had been bad. Some had a vision of the Virgin Mary and related this experience in detail.[66] This type of religiosity is strongly influenced by Protestant and Catholic missionaries who replace the veneration of saints with a more personal relationship to Jesus and/or Mary.[67] The difference is that the Charismatic Movement encourages building a relationship with Jesus directly.

Although we still lack sufficient evidence, we may tentatively argue that the Charismatic trend has initiated a shift in beliefs among Copts, particularly with regard to the role of the intercession of saints. Moreover, this movement is also a reformist one in the sense that it has led to the rejection of the overabundance of the miraculous to focus more on miracles of the New Testament, such as healings. There is a noticeable difference between Father Samaan's performance and charismatic powers and the other types of miracles that began to spread in the 1960s.[68] Father Samaan himself seems to be skeptical about icons exuding oil and manifestations of the Virgin. While I was asking a servant in the Muqattam church if the anniversary of Saint Samaan was going to transform into a *mouled* (popular pilgrimage) he instantly replied, "*mafish qiddisin,*" "there are no saints" or "there is no such thing as saints." He explained then that, of course, they exist but that miracles do not come from saints but from God. As this example shows, the Charismatic Copts do not reject saints or tradition in general, but insist on the fact that everything comes directly from God, which could be seen as a weakening of the role of intercessors. In brief, they articulate tradition and worship differently.

What is interesting regarding Samaan's religious strategies is that he has promoted at the same time the charismatic worship that we have described, as well as the traditional Coptic Orthodox teachings in the Sunday schools. There the garbage collectors learned the Coptic tradition and were taught that they live in a world populated by saints who can act and have an impact on their lives. It seems as if he is running different religious programs at the same time. One is slightly elitist and attracts mostly young men who attend the prayer meetings on a regular basis; the other is the normal Coptic religious program, traditional and centered on liturgy. But both programs interweave, and we cannot easily distinguish one from the other. What we are witnessing in Muqattam and elsewhere can be described as a syncretic process.[69] While the believers remain rooted in the Coptic Orthodox tradition (which is not a fixed entity itself), they import elements from the new Evangelical trends. This is a process of negotiation; Father Samaan's allegiance to the Coptic Church hierarchy remains undisputable as is evident in the presence of an imposing statue of Pope Shenouda that stands at the entrance of the church of Saint Samaan and keeps a watchful eye on the congregation. In the process of homologation by tradition, the act of exorcism is placed within the Coptic tradition: "Coptic priests have always practiced exorcisms." And during the joint meeting with the Protestant community from the Qasr al-Dubbara church, Protestant songs alternated Coptic hymns and the meeting closed with a Coptic Mass. Although they are shaping a different spiritual project, the Coptic Charismatics remain grounded in the Coptic Charismatic decade.[70] During the 1960s the pedagogy of intercession responded to the needs of a new urban middle class; nowadays the Charismatic Copts are proposing a new layout between faith and religious practice suitable for the new generation of Christians.

Authority and Visions

While participating in a trend that has become popular with young Copts, Father Samaan belongs to the "old generation" of charismatic preachers. He is strict and deals with the church community in an authoritarian manner. For example, the young men from Muqattam who attend the weekly youth meetings are totally devoted to Samaan, who is for them at once their priest, a kind of father, and a leader for those who are also servants in the church. A younger Charismatic priest such as Andrawus Iskander, who holds weekly meetings in Muqattam, is much less paternalistic than Father Samaan. The relationship he has with his followers is egalitarian and friendly, which might be explained by the fact that most of them are from the Egyptian upper-middle class. Father Samaan was not in favor of the revolution at all, and he even organized a pro-Mubarak demonstration at the entrance of Mansheyet Nasser during the uprising. Father Andrawus and the Evangelicals of Qasr al-Dubbara, in contrast, were committed to the revolution, which they interpreted as an answer to their prayers.[71] There is probably a generational divide at work here, with the older Evangelicals and Father Samaan reject any rebellion against authority.[72] As Samaan said in an interview, defying an authority is against the teachings of the Bible.[73] The new generation holds a more optimistic view that combines Evangelical forms of worship with political commitment.[74] Father Samaan has no political discourse to share; all his sermons deal with the necessity of perpetual redemption.[75]

What these two generations do share is a kind of millenarianism. Father Samaan is guided by dreams and visions that he shares with his audiences.[76] In one of his dreams "the mountain opened, and I saw a very strong light. But most important is that the mountain had disappeared. The horizon had opened. And the glory of God appeared. I am not the master of dreams, so why did God send me this dream? It is because the Lord will shine the glory of God in Egypt."[77] Father Samaan likes to share a dream he had a long time ago: He was sitting on a desk and saw all Egyptians pass by before his eyes. Sameh Maurice, the pastor of the Qasr al-Dubbara church, has similar visions: "Forty years ago God spoke to me when I was a child. He told me that he would visit Egypt, and that it would be a glorious visit. And I heard other people to whom God spoke. I listened to the elderly and to the youth; I listened to bishops, priests and monks." After relating this vision, he added that God had spoken again, a week earlier, to tell him that his coming was near.[78] These visions are based on the biblical quotations about Egypt, "*Mubarak Sha'bi Misr*"—"Blessed be Egypt my people"—and the sanctification of the land of Egypt by the sojourn of the Holy Family. Egypt in this perspective has a special mission in spreading Christianity. Even the revolution seems to be taken as a sign that something is about to happen in Egypt, that Christianity is about to expand and gain many followers.[79]

Conclusion

Finally, one could ask the question: what about the Zabbalin? They are at the heart of Samaan's spiritual project, but the main target of this new discourse seems to be the upper-middle class. The Zabbalin's place in this movement is ambivalent. Their "redemption" is a perfect metaphor for change through religion. For example, Ibrahim Abdel-Sayed, the director of the film about Father Samaan's life, considers the physical as well as spiritual changes within the garbage collectors' community as the work of the Holy Spirit, ignoring any intervention by the World Bank, Oxfam, or Sister Emmanuelle (1908-2008), the famous French nun who worked over two decades with the garbage collectors. The Muqattam area has become a living metaphor for the power of religion and the Holy Spirit to bring change. All the ingredients are there: the garbage collectors were dirty, now they are clean; they were ignorant, now they are attending university; they were almost pagans, now they are good Christians. The theme has some affinities with prosperity theology. Furthermore, those who come to be exorcised are often people from the lower class, to such an extent that this staging of a struggle against Evil might also be seen as a struggle against backwardness and popular habits.

It is impossible to know what proportion of Egyptian Christians feels attracted to these types of religious expression. They still seem to be a minority, but the new generation of preachers has already adopted similar practices. They deliver a more optimistic message that is congenial to younger generations. It makes the faithful feel less guilty and encourages them to become socially active. However, the Charismatics still need to find compromises between their desire to convert Muslims and their will to participate in the construction of a secular political scene.

After the revolution Samaan was challenged for his authoritarianism and his links to some of the cronies of the ancient regime, but he managed to preserve his independence, even playing an important role during the 2011–2012 legislative elections in Muqattam.[80] In 2013, however, the new pope, Tawadros II (2012–), decided to appoint a bishop, Bishop Aba Nub, to the Muqattam area to supervise Father Samaan. In 2014 the new bishop banned what he called "Protestant songs" from the monastery. He also suspended one of Samaan's assistant priests. It seems that the precarious balance built between Pope Shenouda and the priest of the Zabbalin will no longer be accepted by the new patriarch. Although the new pope is more open-minded than his predecessor, allowing Samaan to exercise the autonomy he has long enjoyed does not fit his vision for the future of the Coptic Orthodox Church.

TRANSMITTING COPTIC MUSICAL HERITAGE

Séverine Gabry-Thienpont

This essay discusses the process of incorporating Coptic liturgical music into the Coptic cultural heritage. Music, as an aesthetic production and a social manifestation, has become one of the main cultural markers that allow us to understand the Coptic community today. The goal of this essay is to show how Coptic music practices have been linked to the construction of Coptic identity since the nineteenth century, with two guiding questions: How is Coptic music heritage transmitted, and how does it strengthen the idea of a Coptic "tradition"?

Copts actively participate in church services where music plays a central liturgical role. Coptic liturgical music is characterized by a capella monodic songs chanted by men, particularly by the priests, deacons, and cantors, although some responsorial songs include parts sung by the whole assembly. The only instrumental accompaniments are cymbals and triangles.

Apart from liturgical songs, Coptic music also includes the *taranim* (singular *tarnima*): canticles sung outside worship.[1] Singing, whether of *taranim* or of hymns, is central in the daily routine of the community. Liturgical songs and *taranim* are performed, musically arranged, and recorded, as well as produced and broadcast by Coptic independent labels and sold at churches and monasteries. In addition, recordings provide church members with the opportunity to learn songs in tandem with the weekly teachings at the Sunday schools. In these Sunday schools lessons are provided at various levels, for the youngest to the oldest church members, and are considered to be of great importance for memorizing the liturgical songs as well as the *taranim*. Liturgical and nonliturgical forms of music are thus inherent expressions of Coptic identity as they support the traditional character of the church. Coptic music, whether it is via liturgical hymns or *taranim*, allows Copts to identify with their past and community.

Preservation of "Tradition": Musical Transcription of Coptic Liturgical Songs

Safeguarding the Coptic liturgical heritage is an initiative that began in the late nineteenth century and intensified considerably throughout the twentieth century until now.² This new attention to the components of Coptic culture coincided with interest in Egypt's pharaonic heritage in the mid-1800s and the founding of the Coptic Museum in Cairo in 1910. This museum presented the visual and material aspects of the history of the first centuries of Christianity for the first time.

During the past sixty years all Coptic melodies have been systematically recorded and cataloged. The first and most prominent of the Coptic scholars to engage in this process was Ragheb Moftah (1898–2001), who dedicated his life to Coptic music and its preservation. He is the primary author of the article on Coptic music in *The Coptic Encyclopedia*,³ one of the authors of *A Transcription of the Complete Liturgy of St Basil* (a major work in descriptive notation of Coptic music),⁴ as well as the author of numerous articles.⁵ Until 2001 he held the Coptic Music Chair at the Institute of Coptic Studies, created in 1954. The studio built to support this chair produced many recordings, which made Moftah the most important protagonist in the preservation of Coptic musical heritage. Under his guidance music became one of the main vehicles for transmitting Coptic culture. This work is continued today at the Institute of Coptic Studies by Michael Ghattas, professor of music. In cooperation with Raimund Vogels from the German Center for World Music in Hannover, Ghattas works on preserving the sound archives at the Coptic institute.

Before the advent of recording, musical transcription was the main tool to safeguard Coptic music and to preserve this sound heritage without the slightest modification. However, for the Copts, transcription of liturgical singing was never a goal in itself, because their transmission had always been carried out orally. Only around the end of the nineteenth century did Copts become interested in leaving an enduring trace of their liturgical music. The transcription of music that belongs to an oral tradition is complex and leaves ample opportunity for improvisation. Differences between the various transcribers have thus appeared, depending on the type of notation. Opinions differ as to how to fix this ornamental music, which provokes numerous debates among the transcribers about the quality of the different transcriptions.

Western scholars may have tackled the musical transcriptions questions before the Copts, but this does not mean that the Egyptian Christians never outlined any kind of notation. For example, during the twentieth century Copts such as Ragheb Moftah and George Kyrillos developed a method of scoring their songs on staves. While for Copts this method seems to be new, in fact, from early Greek manuscripts we know that the so-called ekphonetic notation did exist in the past. However, the research in this field concerning Egypt is only just beginning, and scholars hope that one day this type of notation will be discovered in Coptic manuscripts as well.⁶

Ekphonetic comes from the Greek *ekphonesis*, which means "to read aloud and solemnly." It is a notation system, which appeared around the eighth century as a tool for the cantors to remember the prosody inflections, ornaments, and melismas. The signs are a mnemonic device on which one reads one or a few words, but they do not specify any interval or value of the note. The article on Coptic music in the *Coptic Encyclopedia* mentions two manuscripts in Greek found in Egypt that use a type of old notation.⁷ The first one is dated three centuries before the Christianization of Egypt and shows the oldest presumed tracks of musical notation (Zenon,

Cairo Museum, n°59533); the second one is a fragment of a hymn, which is dated from the third century C.E. (from the Oxyrhynchos papyrus 1786, discovered by Bernard P. Grenfell and Arthur S. Hunt).[8] This last example may be the oldest track of any Christian (but not specially Coptic) musical notation.[9]

The first source of transcription of this music on staves dates from the German Jesuit priest Athanasius Kircher (1602–1680),[10] with a short notation of four staves in a neumatic style.[11] Then, in 1826, Guillaume André Villoteau (1759–1839) published another short example that he wrote during the Napoleonic French Egyptian Campaign (1798–1801).[12] The Jesuit fathers Jules Blin and Louis Badet,[13] in 1888 and 1899 respectively, continued this task with the goal of codifying Catholic Coptic music for its use in the Catholic Coptic Seminary, which opened in 1879. They both played a significant role in transmitting transcription models to the Coptic community in general (both Orthodox and Catholic). In the preface of their transcription books they emphasized the need to preserve the Coptic musical heritage, which has a history that dates back thousands of years and has been kept intact since pharaonic times. However, no evidence that can support this claim has ever been provided.[14] Since then, many attempts at transcription have been made using different forms. For example, a Hungarian musicologist, Ilona Borsai (1925–1982), opted for a descriptive notation of Coptic singing which allowed her to compare it with other types of Egyptian music.[15] While Borsai was studying Coptic music, her aim was to trace Egyptian music back to its origins by determining musical constants inherent in the different types of music played in Egypt. In her view transcription in ethnomusicology serves to consider variations, the relations between these variations, and to determine the main part of the melody. This approach allowed her to undertake a study of the cultural connections between some of the songs.[16] Using these comparative studies, Borsai discovered that some tunes used in Coptic liturgical music are also used in the popular melodies sung by Egyptian peasants. This similarity between the music of the Copts and that of the peasants is a recurring topic in scholarly discourse and an important field of future research.[17]

Borsai's work not only allows us to establish Coptic music as an age-old tradition but also helps us clearly to identify possible new musical practices. In the end all these practices are part of an effort to protect a musical heritage specific to the Coptic Christians. Thus the music serves as a vehicle to represent the unique nature of the Copts when compared to other Egyptians. As a result, when retrieving their cultural heritage, Copts have made the transmission of Coptic music one of their main objectives.

Coptic Music Transmission Development

The focus on Coptic music started during the second half of the nineteenth century under the papacy of Kyrillos IV, who, during his short term as pope (1854–1861), launched a comprehensive program of educational reforms. Coptic music and liturgical language were both touched by this reform, as was the general education of young Copts, both lay and (future) clergy. To assure high quality education, Pope

Kyrillos V (1874–1927) launched the Coptic Charity Society in 1881 and opened the first Coptic theological seminary in 1893.[18] Gradually, yet rapidly, religious and community teaching developed.

An important step in strengthening Coptic religious education was the creation of the Coptic Sunday School Movement in 1918 by Habib Guirguis,[19] a well-known composer of *taranim*.[20] Sunday schools first appeared in England in the late eighteenth century and were intended to provide children with a solid religious education. These schools served as a sort of extension of the church specially reserved for children. The Coptic Sunday school program remained essentially similar to that of the Protestants, with its emphasis on two major activities: the study of biblical stories and the study of music, both liturgical as well as paraliturgical. While teaching, whether in Cairo, Upper, or Middle Egypt, might involve different learning methods, it all aimed at passing down Coptic Orthodox knowledge to the younger generations and reinforcing a sense of communal belonging.

About the same time proper transmission of Coptic hymns became a serious issue in the preservation of Coptic music. The actions undertaken in the twentieth century thus reveal a gradual institutionalization of the transmission of these songs, supporting a unification of both musical practices and musical material. Present policy remains to make the songs uniform by standardizing their structures, ornamentation, and timbre. These processes are gradually being set in place with the help of cantors who have themselves been trained within the framework of this policy in rigorously established study programs.

The Didymus Institute for Blind Cantors

The Didymus Institute, the leading center for the teaching of Coptic song, provides a full study course allowing youth to become titular cantors in the Coptic Orthodox Church. The name of Didymus has been given to this institute as a tribute to the fourth-century theologian and music theorist Didymus the Blind (ca. 313–398), who is considered "the last great head of the catechetical school of Alexandria."[21]

Traditionally, Coptic cantors were chosen from among the blind. Nowadays, in spite of the name of the institute, the majority of pupils are no longer legally blind. Improved sanitary conditions in Egypt throughout the twentieth century have led to an improvement in individual health. While more than one hundred years ago many children went blind because of eye infections, this is no longer the case today. The blind are, nonetheless, still considered excellent cantors. Having lost one sense, they are presumed to be able to develop others, such as memory and voice, more easily.

Young men accepted into this institute benefit from a full education in which teaching is directly linked to religious practice. The first institute opened in Cairo in 1893. The second institute, located inside Deir el-Muharraq (the Muharraq Monastery), near Asyut, opened in 1977, at the same time as the seminary that is located inside the monastery. It yielded its first graduates in 1983.

Deir el-Muharraq dates back to the fourth century and appears to be the most ancient religious site in Egypt dedicated to the Virgin Mary. According to Coptic tradition, the founder of the communal monastic life, Saint Pachomius (died in the fourth century) or his disciples built the monastery on the spot where the Holy Family was believed to have stayed during their time in Egypt.[22]

At the Didymus Institute, about sixty-five students are taught by five "masters," or *moᶜallemin*, under the management of Father Misa'il, a monk at the monastery. Eligible students should be between fifteen and twenty-two years old, preferably having finished high school. This rule is in line with the policies of Pope Shenouda III (1971–2012), who strongly encouraged deacons to have at least a high school education, and mirrors policies of the monasteries, where monks now also are required to have a high school diploma or, preferably, a college degree.

However, some blind youth find themselves in monasteries after having been abandoned by their families. In these particular cases the academic standard is not taken into account and Father Misa'il accepts them without a formal education. For these young people, blind or not, the institute is a real opportunity to advance through a career in the Church, as its diploma will provide them with a certain social status and a fixed income.

The institute never advertises, but students learn about it from their priest or the cantor in their parish who will encourage them to become cantors if they have a beautiful voice. Selection criteria are strict: students need to have a good voice (*helw*) acceptable for church services (*sot kanassi*). To obtain admittance they take an oral exam and provide information about their families and themselves. Upon graduation, Father Misa'il places the cantors in churches using his wide network of Coptic priests and bishops. The occasional student will find work abroad, as in the case of Moᶜallem Salwad, who is presently cantor in the Coptic Church of the Holy Sepulcher in Jerusalem. He was trained at Deir el-Muharraq and has been living in the Holy Land since the end of the 1990s.

The selection of teachers (*mudarrisin*) is likewise rigorous. Preferably they hold a school diploma and have proven their pedagogical skills. Furthermore, they must have studied at one of the two Didymus Institutes. Personality is also considered, as the teacher needs to be capable of wielding authority and being strict. Finally, he must be of a pleasant nature (*mahlim*). Father Misa'il attaches great importance to the ability of the teacher to live as part of a group. Indeed, during the week most of the *mudarrisin* live at the institute alongside the students. Teachers also model the future cantors' role in the Eucharistic service and demonstrate what their actions mean for the services.

The Curriculum

The training at the Didymus Institute at Deir el-Muharraq takes six years. During these six years young men study hymns and pay special attention to all that relates to the smooth unfolding of the liturgical aspects. They attend lessons on the history of the Coptic Orthodox Church, from ancient times until the Arab period, which includes the preaching of Saint Mark, the study of the different ecumenical councils and the Byzantine era, as well as lessons in the theology of traditions (*taqsis.*)

Political questions related to Islam remain untouched. They also attend lessons on Coptic language and biblical exegesis, as well as the study of the psalmodies. The psalms must be memorized, with special care given to the seventy-one present in the *Agbeyya*, the book of the liturgical hours. They also memorize the texts of the *Agbeyya* prayers, in addition to the vespers texts (ᶜ*Ashiyya*) and the ones of the Mass (*el-Quddas*). Father Misa'il teaches all different levels the same *alhan*, or melodies, so that students can sing them together, especially during the church services. Blind students receive lessons in braille from a cantor who is himself blind. According to Father Misa'il, well before the current methods developed in the eighteenth century, Saint Didymus invented an early form of braille. Having lost his sight as a small boy, he taught himself to write by scratching letters on stones.

The Organization of Lessons and Premises

The organization of lessons throughout the day does not follow a fixed timetable; instead, the masters organize them from week to week. Generally, the morning is spent with singing lessons, and the students follow other lessons in the afternoon, from 4:00 to 7:00 P.M. These are taught by five monks from Deir el-Muharraq. Father Misa'il teaches only melodies. If the students have no lessons in the morning, they can stay in the dormitory. The only moment when they are all truly together is during the meals in the refectory. Certain students are in charge of cooking and others must do the washing up.

The institute has reasonably spacious facilities. One building holds the dormitory, Father Misa'il's office, the kitchen, and the refectory. Another building, an extension of the first, holds the classrooms. These are rather bare and dusty, equipped with wooden benches and, in some cases, blackboards. The whitewashed walls are covered with graffiti. Because there are sixty-five students in total, split into five levels, they cannot all have lessons at the same time. Out of the five levels, only four can work in the morning, as there are only four classrooms.

Father Misa'il and the other voice teachers do not consider the use of musical transcription to be useful. Transmission is always done orally. Father Misa'il himself cannot read notation and the students have absolutely no ability to read music. The transcriptions of Ragheb Moftah (1998) are not understood here; however, such work is held in high esteem and even seen as necessary. The use of cymbals is not taught either, and from the teachers' point of view, there is no reason that it should be. The rhythm is always the same, whatever the song. Ornamentation of the rhythm can occur, but the basic rhythmic structure remains the same. In fact, during the lessons the use of cymbals is forbidden, as this rhythmic presence is not deemed useful. Some would go so far as to suggest that using cymbals is a form of vanity that Coptic melodies can do well without. On the occasion of certain feasts of the saints, especially during the pilgrimages to other monasteries, some monks display undeniable rhythmic qualities and play the cymbals with great skill. However, this action can be criticized by others who hold that a sober execution is the key element in the "correct" performance of liturgical singing. Moreover, rather than being seen as a demonstrations of faith, feverish rhythms are judged to be indecent and inappropriate by many people within the Church. As for the Didymus Institute, playing cymbals is considered a distraction that prevents solid memorization of the songs. This, however, does not stop students from happily beating out the rhythm on tables or benches when mastering songs during lessons. The teachers may express disapproval but will still not prohibit them from starting again a few minutes later. While discipline is applied during lessons, this phenomenon does not seem to be taken as seriously as the official position of Father Misa'il might lead one to believe.

The doors and windows of the classrooms are rarely closed. A joyful cacophony fills the corridors until one of the teachers decides to close the door for a little bit of calm during the lesson. To this day the institute is short of teachers for singing lessons. Occasionally, a particularly excellent student may lead a lesson. At present the five cantors do not all work at the same time, but have various other obligations aside from their work as teachers in the institute.

As mentioned above, hymns are all learned orally. With the help of the teachers, supported by the *Khulaji,* the Coptic missal, and the *khidmat al-shammas,* the deacon service book, the students first learn to pronounce correctly the text in Coptic. Then the teachers have them repeat the melody with the text. Tapes are not used during the teaching but listening again to recordings outside the lessons is common. Students record themselves on their mobile phones or other devices and often leave their recorders on the teacher's table. Not all students have such gadgets, but, on average, in a class of about fifteen students, there will be four or five such devices, with more used in upper level classes. Oral transmission remains the main tool of learning, as originally this school was dedicated to blind young men. Some students still take a few notes on texts inside their liturgical book in order to have mnemonic references. They count and note precisely, for example, the number of times a vowel is repeated and call this *el-hazzat,* coming from the term *el-hazza,* the vibration. Nowadays, audio tapes, CDs, and mp3 files allow the dissemination of reference models. This way the believers can follow the ideal models and improve their interpretation of liturgical hymns. The transmission needs to be accurate to prove that it has never changed. Coming as close as possible to perfection, the precise performance trumps melodic fluidity.

In order to maintain this type of perfection among the Coptic lay audience and facilitate memorizing songs, several strategies of learning have been developed during the past decades. One of them, what I call stick notation, consists of a type of musical notation in the form of lines. According to performers, this technique has existed for thirty or forty years. I first became aware of it when doing fieldwork in Cairo, in 2007 in the district of Shubra that has a large Coptic population.[23]

A "Musical Script" with Sticks: A Learning Device

After witnessing stick notation in Shubra, but before understanding that this notation was actually known in many parishes, I was surprised to see that a similar

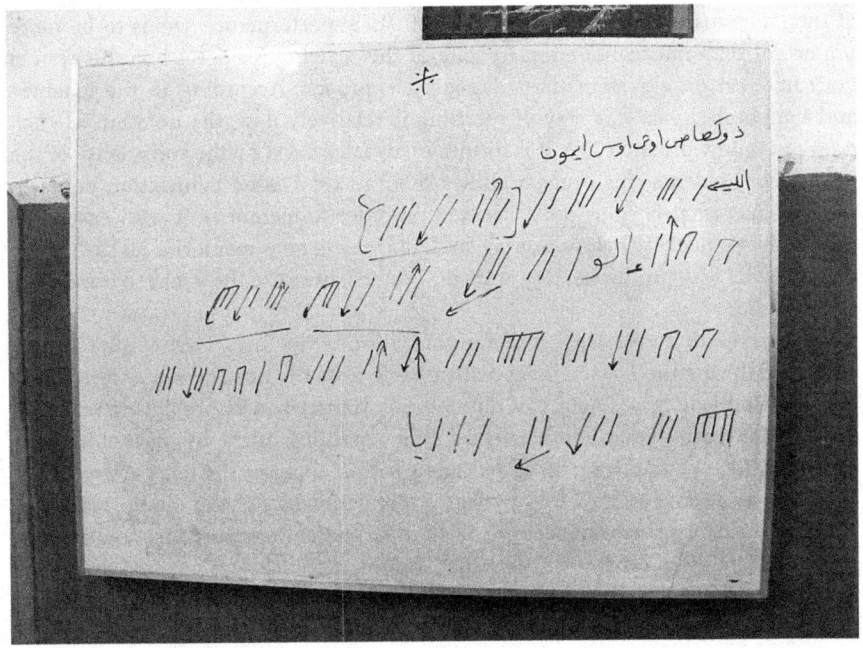

Fig. 9. "Stick method" to teach the *Halleluia* that is chanted at the beginning of Psalm 151. Photograph taken by the author at Deir el-Muharraq. Used with the permission of the Coptic Orthodox Church.

technique was being used in the hamlet of Zarabi, a village belonging to the Deir el-Muharraq. There all the farmers are Copts and, for the most part, Orthodox. In one of the other villages, Manchieh, many families are Coptic Orthodox as well as Catholic. Correct performance of Coptic liturgical songs is a priority, for both Catholic and Orthodox believers. In the church of Zarabi the young *shammas* (deacons) learn the liturgical hymns using a huge screen that projects the musical "sticks." This notation does not adopt any staves but consists of lines of different sizes that allow the believers to follow the liturgical text. Similar to the method used in Shubra, this projection allows students to memorize the songs with ease. For example, during the songs with some *hazzat*[24]—that is to say with long sentences in *tempo giusto*—the projector shows a series of lines or arrows carefully enumerated. In addition to this visual help, the priest counts the number of vowels on his fingers.

Although this system does not adopt any officially accepted code, it is increasingly used all over Egypt and within the diaspora. It is a mnemonic technique, which permits the memorization of the liturgical songs—which brings to mind the use of the ekphonetic notation. It represents a new way of singing Coptic hymns that is transmitted via various media so that the faithful, to perfect themselves in the execution of the Coptic hymns, can follow these examples. As was the case at the Didymus Institute, a type of mathematical performance seems to be more important than musical fluency. In spite of this striving for precision, the system does not rest on a systematic pedagogical approach. According to the teachers and the pupils, since this way of teaching is relatively new, the notation as such does not follow precise rules. It is intuitive, casual, guided by the spirituality of the music. For students this process allows them to establish a connection between the text and what is "musically" written, in order to memorize it with ease. This approach is especially helpful for lay students who cannot memorize all the Coptic melodies the way professional cantors do. Instead, they use the sticks to remember the melodies.

However, there is a logic in the organization of the lines. First of all, they are only used during the *hazzat*. Indeed on syllabic texts the lines do not appear at all; only the Coptic letters (sometimes phonetically transcribed in Arabic) are recorded and their intensity must be memorized. The beginning of the hymn is thus transcribed in its textual form and, as soon as a *hazzat* appears, the lines are recorded to understand the direction, the rhythm, and the intensity of this singing exercise.

Some musical performances are more sober than others, and this notation can accommodate these different approaches. In fact, the sticks are adapted according to the needs of the audience: The representation will be more detailed for young and inexperienced students than for adults, who learned these melodies in childhood. We have to consider that the meaning of these sticks is not universal. In some cases, for example, if sticks go up, it does not automatically mean that the melody is rising. Indeed, sometimes, teachers write arrows or wavy lines that might refer to some ornaments or to the hymn character (if it is sad or joyful). If a word glorifies God, then the movement is rising. The issue of this notation is such that it influences our understanding of this music, of its conception (time, durations, melodies, ornamentations), and of its transmission (role, significance of the teacher personality since there are no strict rules, and so forth). That is why, beyond the musicological aspect, it is crucial to understand the sociological and cognitive impact of this practice. As we are only starting to understand these musical processes, much research remains to be done in this field.

Sunday Schools and the Didymus Institute: Issues of Transmission Standardization

Transmitting the Coptic musical heritage takes a central place in the everyday life of the Coptic community. As we have seen during the past century, several initiatives to register Coptic music have been launched in order to preserve this intangible heritage; however, oral tradition (*taqalid*) is still considered to be the most reliable and faithful means of preservation. To the question, How do we know which practices existed centuries ago? the Copts would answer: Thanks to the transmission of the *taqalid*.

However, a look at the various events during the twentieth century leads us to think about the different steps involved in creating transmission. Since the very start of the twentieth century, the Sunday schools have given birth to a real consciousness of musical practices in Coptic worship. The goal remains to rally new generations around a shared practice, while increasing the number of active members of the Church. Thus, the institutionalization of this oral transmission through sound training supervised by clergy highlights the importance of a unified system. One of the strategies to create a unified system for learning hymns is consistent, controlled training of future clergy, cantors, and music teachers. For example, at the Didymus Institute the curriculum was established by Pope Shenouda III himself and is followed by all teachers. As a result curricula have been uniform, broadcast nationally and, more recently, internationally and then adapted to the needs of particular Coptic students. This uniformity of practice and transmission has made Coptic liturgy a symbol of uniqueness. By extension, this liturgy has become a major symbol for the Coptic community globally that continues to strengthen the Coptic identity today.

PART 2
CHALLENGES OF THE DIASPORA

SINGING STRATEGIC MULTICULTURALISM
The Discursive Politics of Song in Coptic-Canadian Protests

Carolyn M. Ramzy

I need thee oh Lord, I need thee
Oh bless me my Lord, I come to thee

Oh might God of Ages, oh be thou near
When the tempest rages, I need not fear

The demonstration began with two voices singing into a speakerphone. Two young Coptic Orthodox Christians were singing a translated Arabic devotional song known as a *tartila* (pl. *taratil*), galvanizing the throngs behind them in the freezing weather of a typical Toronto winter. They were abruptly interrupted by another voice giving directions in a mix of Arabic and English: "OK everyone, we are going to need to cross the street across the Eaton Center; then we are going to take a left. In front of us will be the crosses like a procession in the church and the coffins.... We are going to keep Eaton on our right and go towards Yonge [street]. The police will escort us." Before he was finished, the young man next to me cleared his throat in preparation. He was carrying a crumpled piece of paper with another *tartila*, this time in Arabic: "*Allah Huwa Alladhi Lana*" translated "God, Who is For Us."

God, who is for us, will never leave us
He will give us peace and protect us, always watching us

The march continued with a flurry of *taratil* and Coptic liturgical hymns known as *alhan* as a parade of demonstrators was escorted through Toronto's downtown core. Demonstrators were marching behind six empty coffins representing the victims of the rising sectarian violence in Egypt; this time the Nag Hammadi Christmas Eve clash of January 2010 that left six Coptic youth and one Muslim police officer dead. Photos of the victims' smiling faces posted on the front of the caskets brought the dead all the more closer.[1] Beneath Toronto's skyscrapers

Fig. 10. Egyptian Coptic-Canadians protest the 2010 Nag Hammadi killings in front of Ontario's Legislative Building in downtown Toronto. Photograph by the author, January 23, 2010.

the scene eerily mirrored funeral marches back home, when church congregations followed grieving families from church to grave, comforting one another with song. However, in this familiar mass procession, some male deacons wore their liturgical vestments, or *tuniyas,* over their winter coats, with their crossed sashes turned over to the recognized color of mourning, blue. Others were holding tall processional crosses usually reserved for canonical church services, such as the Easter or Christmas liturgies. Rather than the usual white and gold festive drapes, picture of the dead dangled from the crosses. While their white dress, blue sashes, and processional crosses are common in church contexts, they stood out in the public space as overt and intentional disclosures. As the deacons moved closer to the Ontario Legislative Building in Queens Park, funerary *alhan* of "Kyrie Eleison [Lord, have mercy]" and *taratil* gave way to angry chants, while accented English piled onto seamlessly enunciated shouts by the youth. Some demonstrators, who were born and raised in Canada, had never been to Egypt, nor could they speak in colloquial Egyptian Arabic. They seemed to yell out all the more passionately.

It is no doubt that sectarian tensions in Egypt had been on the rise long before the Nag Hammadi incident. Almost exactly a year later, more than twenty Coptic Christians also lost their lives in the New Year's Eve bombing of the Two Saints Orthodox Church of Alexandria.[2] After the January 25 revolution, when the

Security of Armed Forces (SCAF) took over Egypt, church burnings, demolitions, and interreligious clashes continued to dot the news, crescendoing into the story of one of bloodiest confrontations between demonstrators and the military on October 9, 2011. In what is now infamously known as Masbahit Masbiru, or the Maspero Massacre, images and Internet videos show army tanks running over protestors demonstrating in front of the Maspero Radio and Television Building.[3] After almost every incident Coptic-Canadians hit the streets. Toronto, today's site of the greatest influx of Coptic immigrants to Canada, witnessed the most prolific number of mass demonstrations, prayer meetings, and public political rallies.[4] Together with Canadian government officials, Coptic-Canadian activists publicly condemned these killings as "cowardly and inhumane acts of terrorism" and organized a delegation of political officials and clergy to travel to Ottawa and raise their concerns to the Canadian Parliament.[5] During many of these rallies, in between speeches by members of Parliament (MPs) or prayers by clergy, demonstrators almost always sang. They sang both Arabic *taratil* and their English translations, as well as church liturgical *alhan* in the antiquated Coptic language.

This essay concerns Coptic immigrant soundscapes of dissent. More specifically, it addresses the discursive politics of devotional musics such as *taratil* and *alhan* and their integral roles in Coptic-Canadian discourses of identity politics, shifting state allegiances, and transnational links to Egypt during a time of rising security concerns and sectarian tension. While Copts in Egypt have to wrestle with what Webb Keane calls the "hazards of representation" and the broader sense of invisibility in a Muslim majority nation, Copts in Canada do not.[6] Instead, they relish in a more open albeit tenuous disclosure welcomed by the state-initiated enterprise of Canadian multiculturalism. This essay explores how Coptic-Canadians strategically engage official discourses of diversity and difference to challenge an Islamic hegemony as they otherwise would not be able to do at home. Yet, as the sociologist Himani Bannerji argues, Canadian multiculturalist discourses themselves are embedded with orientalized and racialized undertones that legitimize a "colonial imperialist/racist ranking criteria" and arranges people in relations to an established Anglo-Canadian ethnic core culture. "The ethics and aesthetics of 'whiteness,'" she continues, "define and construct the 'multi' culture of Canada's others."[7] Not only do these discourses diffuse communities into monolithic and separate traditional enclaves; they also further insulate them from one another, creating divisive social relations as communities increasingly focus on symbols of religion, cultural difference, and so-called tradition. As Coptic-Canadians protest to the backdrop of Coptic liturgical *alhan* and devotional *taratil*, even undertaking a funeral march through downtown Toronto, how are they embedded in these larger discourses of power, containment, and state management, both in Canada and back home? In turn, how are they situating themselves most advantageously in these political narratives to address sectarian violence in Egypt and to highlight Keane's notion of the desire for visibility, not just to be seen, but also to be heard? This study is based on and draws on ethnographic research in the Greater Toronto Area.

Singing Home into Place: Translocating a Coptic Egypt to a Canadian Landscape

I began my research with Toronto's Coptic Orthodox community in 2005, investigating *taratil*, the most prevalent devotional genre outside of liturgical worship contexts.[8] While scholars have given attention to the Coptic hymnody of *alhan* as performed in Egypt,[9] very little has been written about the growing Coptic diaspora abroad. I was particularly interested in how newly arrived immigrants performed *taratil* to assuage their homesickness. As they sang, immigrants recalled and recreated an idealized home away from home. More important, they also created new social networks to replace the ones they left behind in Egypt.[10] In the northeast end of Toronto I worked at Saint Mark's Coptic Orthodox Church of Scarborough, the oldest church in North America.[11] Though services began as early as the 1960s in private residences, Saint Mark's officially opened its doors in 1978.[12] A plethora of other Orthodox churches soon followed in the Greater Toronto Area. What is today the looming building of the Coptic Canadian Center started out in the suburbs of Mississauga as the Saint Mary and Saint Athanasius Church in 1982. Additionally, the church towers of Saint George and Saint Rueiss Coptic Orthodox Church, built in 1995, stand high in a North York industrial park, even claiming a nearby warehouse as an expansion to its growing population. Today, these churches are each large cathedrals to their own, tending to smaller satellite communities around them.[13] Saint Mark's current expansion project, dubbed Saint Mark's Coptic Canadian Village, a compound of two new churches to seat a total of 3,700 parishioners, a community center, school, senior home, museum, daycare, office building, and even a theater, reveals that, unlike Coptic Churches in Egypt, Coptic-Canadian congregations are free to build as many churches as they wish. While building a church in Egypt is fraught with tension, because of issues ranging from the near impossibility of gaining building permits to what Anthony Shenoda calls an "architectural war" of the Islamically dominated horizon, where minarets tower over churches.[14] Copts in Canada seem to be compensating for these past repressions. And, as new church towers are built higher than the ones before, it almost seems as if communities are outbidding one another to be the first visible on the Canadian landscape.

Nowadays the census on the total number of Coptic Orthodox churches in Canada varies. The Coptic Orthodox Patriarchate Archdiocese of North America lists thirty churches, with twenty of them in the province of Ontario, while an aggregate of church and community lists compiled from various online directories lists the number as closer to fifty-one.[15] According to the latest Canadian census, released in 2011, there are 73,250 self-identified Egyptian Canadians living in Canada, while the *Encyclopedia of Canada's Peoples* asserts that the majority of these immigrants are Coptic Orthodox Christians.[16] Large and growing church communities in Toronto and beyond testify to these large numbers. Disenchanted with President Gamal Abdel Nasser's socialist policies and the slowly deteriorating economy of their newly independent state, many of these immigrants began arriving in Canada as early as the 1950s. Historically, many come from the land-owning and elite classes. Beginning in the 1970s, many Coptic immigrants began to cite religion as a primary reason for their departure, fearing the rising tide of Islamic conservatism under President Anwar Sadat's overt mix of religion and politics as the self-professed "believing president."

Also it was during this time that immigration policies both in the United States and Canada changed, welcoming professional and educated classes to the country and favoring those with initial family ties in the diaspora. By the 1990s immigrants came largely from the middle class and listed not only the worsening economic crisis under President Hosni Mubarak, but also a growing religiosity that further polarized Egyptian Christians and Muslims.[17] After the January 25, 2011, revolution, with the Security of Armed Forces' blatant targeting of Coptic Christians and other minorities and the country on the brink of economic collapse, many feared a major exodus in the form of immigration. The election of a Muslim Brotherhood candidate, Mohamed Morsi, only fueled sectarian tensions further. Though President Abdel Fattah al-Sisi brings a tenuous sense of security, new immigrants continue to arrive.[18] They bring with them not only the latest news, popular culture, and Egyptian slang, but a distinct devotional music culture as well.

Coptic Immigrant Music Culture

It is the first thing that greets parishioners as they walk in through the old entrance of Saint Mary and Saint Athanasius church in Mississauga's Coptic Canadian Center: a *taratil* CD dispensing machine. As sounds of the Coptic liturgy and *alhan* emanate overhead, intermingling with Arabic conversation, English snippets, and whoops of children, congregation members can take parts of this sonorous soundscape home for less than five Canadian dollars.[19] The machine dispenses Arabic *taratil*, their English translations, sermons, and the recorded liturgies of favorite priests. While the sight may be amusing to some, it is not a surprise to others. Rather, the machine allows continuous access to church materials beyond the limited operation hours of the volunteer-run bookstores in a church bustling with activities beyond Sunday's worship services. The *taratil*-dispensing machine also highlights Coptic devotional music's importance to what the anthropologist Thomas Turino recognizes as integral to the processes of personal and social integration that make people whole.[20] In other words Coptic music culture is a rich lens through which to understand a Coptic crafting of self, from moments of official induction to the church through child baptisms to weddings, and, finally, funerary liturgies. All of these celebrations are at the heart of forming and rebuilding new transplanted communities. Most, if not all, of these significant rites of passage are sung in official services. Even in death, one's existence is believed to continue in song, as people's spirits are thought to find their rest in an eternal state of *tasbih*, or musical praise of God in heaven. Between official liturgical services, other devotional musics fill the gap; Arabic *taratil* and *mada'ih*, or praise songs to a saint, contribute to linking Copts to a long genealogy of saints and martyrs

Fig. 11. *Taratil* CD dispensing machine; Saint Mary and Saint Athanasius Church of Mississauga and the Coptic Canadian Center. Photograph courtesy of Marcus Zacharia; January 22, 2012. Used with the permission of the Coptic Orthodox Church.

and crafting these holy figures into pious musical subjects outside of the church worship contexts.

Copts enjoy various genres of popular music as well. However, with the rising religiosity sweeping through Egypt, Copts have become more religious, merging many elements of their secular life into the sacred and bringing this combination with them to their new home.[21] Nothing is more evident than when Sunday school teachers and interlocutors make it a point to emphasize the spiritual benefits of *taratil* over *aghani*, secular songs and their dubious and illicit texts of "worldly" love. In Egypt *taratil* themselves have merged into the popular music industry, complete with touring ensembles, rising stars, and music videos, all which make their way to the diaspora via Christian satellite television and the Internet. Coptic-Canadians can even purchase and download their favorite *taratil* as ringtones for their cell phones, just as Copts do in Egypt.[22] Groups such as the Better Life Team, a mixed denominational group who soared to fame with their blending of Western popular music, Coptic liturgical, and Egyptian folk and popular idioms, have even toured in the United States and Canada, making Toronto one of their regular stops. In the North American Coptic diaspora, congregations have also formed their own ensembles. Though almost every church can boast its own local choirs, two of the most popular ensembles come from the Mississauga community just outside of Toronto: the Lady of Light Choir (whose name is the borrowed and translated name of the popular choir in Egypt *Chorale Umm al Nur*) and the Heritage of the Coptic Orthodox Church Choir (HCOC).

Along with the music itself, it is conversations about *taratil* and *alhan*—discussions over what is considered canonical, what is sacred or secular, what is Egyptian, and how much is too much Western influence—that reveal the negotiations around contemporary Coptic hyphenated identities and transnational links to Egypt. But as *taratil* and *alhan* are "put into discourse," sung and interwoven through prayer and everyday dialogue, they also disclose various technologies of power that Coptic communities engage, maneuver, and, in turn, create themselves. As Michel Foucault writes, such discourses of power can illuminate "the most tenuous and individual modes of behavior" that inspire more conversation and eventually institutionalize them as knowledge. In other words *taratil* and *alhan* are pedagogical songs, teaching congregants about social relationships and spiritual hierarchies, as well as about their cultural history as Egyptians.[23] This is especially evident in how Coptic clerics and scholars, borrowing from Western orientalist narratives, have canonized *alhan* as an unchanging oral genre directly inherited from the pharaohs.

As early as the seventeenth century, Copts were racialized by Western academic discourses that have fetishized them as the "true" and "modern sons of the pharaohs," thus focusing attention on Coptic *alhan* as more "authentic" living links to an ancient Egyptian past. In turn, despite their soaring popularity, *taratil* have been regarded as noncanonical on account of their missionary affiliations and the use of Arabic, the language of the Muslim other.[24] Coptic scholars and members of the church hierarchy, aware of their special place in the Western gaze, have slowly begun to borrow and produce similar narratives themselves. In discussing and performing the Orthodox hymnology, songs and hymns have become conduits of discussions surrounding community indigeneity, legitimacy, and power in a Muslim majority context, thus imbuing song with what Saba Mahmood has called the performative "politics of piety."[25]

The Discursive Politics of Unity: Coptic-Canadian Churches Negotiate Egyptian Nationalism

Father Marcos Marcos, who arrived in Montreal in 1964, was the first Orthodox priest to serve in Canada. He recounts that Copts were so eager to hear an Orthodox liturgy that, upon his arrival, they drove him straight to a rented hall to begin his services without any rest. There, he stayed up through the night, reviewing *alhan* with parishioners until worship the next morning. The same happened in his next stop in Ottawa, and again when he made his final stop in Toronto. There established Saint Mark's Coptic Orthodox Church in the suburb of Scarborough, which became the first church of its kind in all of North America. It is no coincidence that Saint Mark's church shares its name with Father Marcos. Rather, this pairing is intentional, pointing both to the Apostle Mark, who introduced Christianity to Egypt sometime between 50 and 62 C.E. and to the first priest to serve in the diaspora. Furthermore, many Orthodox churches built in new cities and the clergy assigned to them take that name as homage to the saint.²⁶ Just as Saint Mark was believed to have brought the light of Christianity to Egypt, so too did these diasporic churches bring the light to a new homeland in the hope of a reverse evangelism.²⁷ Besides exhibiting these evangelical undertones, this shared naming not only signaled a continued Orthodox genealogy that would translocate from one locale to another; it also revealed fierce allegiance to the mother church in Egypt and to the seat of the Coptic Pope of Alexandria, otherwise known as the Holy See of Saint Mark. Father Marcos Marcos and Saint Mark's church would set the precedent for the political role of Coptic diasporic churches, with their discursive use of an Egyptian *al-whida al-wataniya*, or national unity, as well a Canadian multiculturalism to negotiate complex transnational politics.

In his book *The Journey of the Coptic Orthodox Church to North American in Forty Years, 1964–2004,* Father Marcos goes to great lengths detailing that, as a connected extension, "the diasporic church shares the pains and the joys of the mother church." As immigrants, he continues, Copts strive to be "loyal ambassadors to Egypt, especially in a foreign land."²⁸ He lists a number of early trials that attest to this pledge, including a public stance taken in the city's leading newspaper, the *Toronto Daily Star.* In November 1969 an Egyptian Christian journalist named Fekry Aziz claimed that sectarian tensions were so tense under President Gamal Abdel Nasser that Copts wanted to establish their own Christian state within Egypt's borders.²⁹ Father Marcos readily published a scathing response on behalf of the Coptic Orthodox Church in North America that "vigorously declares that both [Christians and Muslims] are living harmoniously," echoing the official discourse of the Egyptian state. He also made sure to mention Nasser's contribution of half a million Egyptian pounds to build the new Coptic patriarchate in Cairo the previous year.³⁰ Father Marcos also emphasized the official letters that the diasporic church sent to protest incidents of sectarian violence, such as the al-Khanka church burning in a small Delta village in 1972.³¹ His letter about the incident to President Anwar Sadat, though critical, echoed Pope Shenouda's tenuous diplomacy used back in Egypt. While he stressed his appreciation for Sadat's attention to national unity, he also warned him that flaring sectarian violence could only harm images of "*watanna*"—"our homeland" of Egypt abroad. As staunch nationalists, he wrote, this was the last thing that Coptic-Canadians wanted.³²

Perhaps one of Father Marcos's most influential decisions came when he decided to part ways with the Coptic Association of America (CAA), a U.S.-based Coptic lobby group officially formed in 1964. Beginning in the 1970s and continuing through the mid-1980s, there emerged two streams of Coptic political engagements in North America. Nonprofit organizations such as CAA were especially active, with political rallies for Coptic religious and civic rights in Egypt. As they grew in strength, the historian Mariz Tadros points out that they represented an autonomous but powerful voice often incongruent with official Church discourse.³³ Clergy such as Father Marcos, and, in turn, congregants in Orthodox immigrant churches opted to follow a unified stance with the mother church in Egypt. As Tadros asserts, following a rocky relationship between Pope Shenouda and President

Sadat that ended in the pope's house arrest in 1981, Shenouda agreed to an informal entente with Sadat's successor, Hosni Mubarak. In exchange for a nonconfrontational policy toward sectarian incidents, Shenouda was released from house arrest in 1985; he resumed an open line of communication with the president and formed greater collaborations with state security in Church matters. Groups such as the CAA were openly critical, both of the Egyptian government and, later, of Pope Shenouda's cooperation with the state. While it was CAA who officially sponsored Father Marcos Marcos to serve abroad, there emerged a rift between his service and the organization's objectives, some of which took on overtly political slants. Marcos's official separation came in 1964 when he traveled to Canada and based his ministry in Toronto. This rift between Church and civilian organizations modeled the way in which future immigrant churches would politically engage with events in Egypt.

Following Pope Shenouda's nonconfrontational stance and entente with the state, Father Marcos outlined four major points of participation during sectarian-related hardship in Egypt. The first was solidarity through prayer with the Egyptian Church and emphasis on *al-wihda al wataniya*, or national unity. Second, as members of the Canadian Council of Churches and the National Council of Churches in the U.S.A., immigrant Orthodox churches would petition interdenominational church communities to participate in the "potent power of collective prayer." Third, immigrant churches would forward letters to the Egyptian president through the proper channels of their ambassadors both in the United States and in Canada. Finally, the churches agreed to deplore aggressive political demonstrations and to ask their congregations not to participate in order to avoid incidents such as the humiliation of Sadat by Coptic lobbyists during his U.S. visit in 1980.[34] When the first major episode of violence struck in January 2000, it was prayer and their accompanying devotional soundscapes that became key to church-sanctioned demonstrations of dissent.

On January 15, 2000, thousands of Coptic-Canadians gathered in the Saint George and Saint Rueiss Coptic Orthodox Church for a requiem service to mourn the twenty-one Christians who died in the Kosheh village in the small Upper Egyptian governorate of Sohag.[35] Between funerary *alhan*, Father Marcos gave an English-language sermon and comforted the parishioners: "We pray because we believe in the power of prayer."[36] He reminded them of the hagiographic story of Samaan, a humble tanner who, with the "faith of a mustard seed" (Matthew 17:20), moved the Muqattam Mountain on the outskirts of Cairo. Accompanied by the sung sounds of prayer, he reminded them, Samaan defied the tenth-century Arab caliph and protected the Orthodox community. The caliph was so moved by the forces of the people's piety that he granted them permission to build their own churches. Rumor had it that he even secretly converted to Christianity. His hagiographic sermons were charged with political undertones similar to the use of *taratil* and *alhan*.[37]

As the anthropologists Deborah Durham and Frederick Klaits write, funerals are key occasions when issues of citizenship and civility can be debated and contested in public spaces.[38] In Coptic requiem services immigrant congregants mourn and sing, not only about the loss of life but also about the loss of their own sense of belonging in Egypt. In these funerary contexts congregants have not only wrestled with their ambivalent relationship to Egypt, but have also negotiated their own changing state allegiances to Canada. As the Coptic-Canadian community grew, and sectarian violence increased, these requiems began to take on the appearance of an alternative show of force, particularly as they became publicized through the advent of Coptic Orthodox satellite television in 2005 and the growing attendance of Canadian public officials.[39] Additionally, these services began literally to move outside of the church, first to larger halls to accommodate the growing number of church attendees from all over the city and then to sprawling demonstrations that traveled down the streets of downtown Toronto. Standing directly in front of Toronto's City Hall in Nathan Phillips Square or surrounding the Ontario Legislative Building, Copts relished the open disclosures allotted to them as emerging Canadian citizens. Considering what happened to demonstrators in front of the Maspero television building in Egypt, the freedom of peaceful assembly and expression became invested with whole new meanings here. And as they practiced their new civic liberties, among other things, Coptic-Canadians sang.

Singing Strategic Multiculturalism as Relational Practice

> And they'll know we are Christians by our love, by our love
> And they'll know we are Christians by our love

At the Nag Hammadi demonstration in front of the Ontario Legislative Building in late January 2010, in the frigid cold, after Coptic youth had just finished singing a popular evangelical hymn, "They'll Know We Are Christians," Conservative Parliament member for Mississauga-Erindale, Bob Dechert, took the podium to the cheers of the crowd. On behalf of the minister of immigration, Jason Kenny, and the prime minister, Stephen Harper, Dechert wanted to reassure the gathered Copts that the government of Canada "stands shoulder to shoulder in condemning these senseless acts of violence." He emphasized that these victims were innocent civilians gathering in celebration of Orthodox Christmas, which made the attack especially tragic. He reminded the audience that he was already in attendance at the Christmas liturgy at Saint Mary and Saint Athanasius of Mississauga on that fateful night, comforting the congregation alongside Father Angelos Saad, the community's head priest. Dechert also informed the crowd that, as an official liaison between the Coptic community and the government, he would travel to Ottawa and raise their concerns to members of the Canadian cabinet. By way of concluding his speech he praised Coptic-Canadians as models of successful integration into Canada, evoking multiculturalist threads that resonated with the themes of unity in the youth's initial hymn: "Prime minster Stephen Harper said pluralism is the principle that binds our diverse peoples together. My friends, you are proud Canadians, actively participating, learning, and working together and the example you set helps to form a stronger and more cohesive Canada and for this, we are most grateful to you."

Cheer became especially boisterous when Dechert ended his speech "May God bless you all." The crowd erupted and began to chant "God Bless Canada! God

Bless Canada!" As the rally's master of ceremonies continued these chants into the microphone, an Orthodox priest leaned close to his ear. The emcee paused and then began to chant "God Bless Egypt, God Bless Egypt!" Without missing a beat, the crowd took up his chants and soon followed them with an Arabic *tartila*, *"Bi Dimuʿ Ya Rabb Kalimtak,"* translated "With Tears, I Beseech You, O Lord."

> With tears, I have beseeched you, O Lord (2)
> Chorus
> O Jesus, O Jesus, I have made a covenant with you

In his work on Pentecostal Christian citizenship in Guatemala, the anthropologist Kevin O'Neill reminds us that prayer, fasting, and other rituals of piety are relational and relation-making activities.[40] Durham and Klaits add that funeral songs and laments ostensibly have the power to invite or divide, to demarcate lines of inclusion as well as exclusion. In this context Coptic-Canadian demonstrators sang Coptic *alhan*, Arabic and translated *taratil*, and even borrowed Protestant Christian hymns to maneuver strategically a narrative of Canadian multiculturalism. In doing so they looked to forge new state allegiances to Canada and to position themselves outside of the state's scope of tolerance. Historically, Canadian multiculturalism emerged to deal with an English-French rivalry that acknowledged two "founding races" of Canada while negating the aboriginal Indian population.[41] It became officially enacted as a state enterprise in 1971 at the height of French Canada's armed struggle for independence and a time when an influx of third-world immigrants was entering the country. Bannerji argues that Prime Minister Eliot Trudeau's policy of multiculturalism served as a device for diffusing both Francophone and American Indian national aspirations, while coping with a large number of non-European immigrant arrivals.[42] The sociologist Richard Day adds that the policy became "state sponsored attempts to define, to know and structure the action of a field of problematic Others (Savages, Québécois, Half-breeds, Immigrants) who have been distinguished from unproblematic Selves (French, British, British-Canadian, European) through a variety of means."[43]

By emphasizing their Christian identity and downplaying their Egyptian links,[44] many Coptic Canadians work to move closer to the Anglo-Canadian unproblematic Selves by using non-Christian communities as foils for what they are *not*: namely Muslim, problematic Others who needed to be tolerated. "They'll Know We Are Christians," a hymn that has recently become popular at Coptic youth meetings and Sunday schools, took on a different meaning in front of the Ontario Legislative Building. Originally an ecumenical banner for a 1960s hippie counterculture movement on the American West Coast, it clearly demarcated an Us-versus-Them stance during the Coptic demonstrations against sectarian-related violence in Egypt.[45] Furthermore, drawing on orientalist discourses of Egypt's last remaining Christians as sons of the pharaohs, Coptic-Canadian demonstrators also evoked familiar tropes of a persecuted Christian minority at the hands of Islamic terrorists that played on existing state biases against Arabs and Muslims.[46] In turn, members of Parliament themselves reinterpreted these same discourses to illicit visceral responses of loss and fear to maintain a reliable, if not growing, polity of voters.

Nearly two years later, on October 16, 2011, following the Maspero Massacre in Cairo, Coptic-Canadians organized another translocal funeral service. More of a political rally than a prayer meeting, the Conference of the Council of Coptic Churches began with requiem, the liturgical prayer for the departed. The church was packed as a large choir of deacons, in blue liturgical vestments, sang the Trisagion hymn in the mourning tune. Women donned black and men wore dark suits fit for funerals. Priests from all over Toronto looked tired and weary as they stood opposite the deacon choir. Among them stood the three clerical leaders of the largest Coptic communities in the area, each taking turns leading prayer: Father Marcos Marcos of Saint Mark's, Father Angelos Saad of Saint Mary and Saint Athanasius, and Father Rueiss Awad from Saint George and Saint Rueiss. Seated at long table arranged at the front of the church were local dignitaries and political officials who joined a handful of ministers from neighboring churches.

After prayers and introductions, a young woman stepped to the microphone and led the audience in a somber rendition of "O Canada." Not many people knew the words, but the anthem resonating in the church's hall was a gesture to shifting political formations. Despite how contested non-devotional musics are in the holy and liturgical spaces of a Coptic church, the Canadian anthem was openly welcomed here and began the long service, signifying a new arrangement of loyalties, especially with the host of local politicians sitting at the front end of the church hall. As it was performed in a solemn a cappella manner, it also became a fitting coda to the liturgical service; Copts were mourning not only the loss of Maspero's victims, but a larger loss as well—their own sense of place in Egypt. With the landslide victory for Islamist parties over the Parliament seats that preceding fall, Egypt as they remembered it seemed to be disappearing before their eyes, highlighting Canada further as an alternative home.[47] Jim Karygiannis, a Liberal member of Parliament in attendance, reaffirmed this loss by comparing the Maspero incident to the Armenian genocide under the Ottoman Empire, intentionally peppering his own speech with such terms *sectarian cleansing* and *massacre*. He further described a major exodus from Egypt and extended a protective, almost parental, arm of the Canadian nation-state.

Jim Karygiannis has been a familiar face at many of these demonstrations. Member of Parliament of the Scarborough-Agincourt district since 1987, he had been working closely with Saint Mark's Coptic Orthodox Church in his constituency. He did not become such an outspoken figure on the Copts until 2008, when he visited Egypt after the Abu Fana Monastery incident.[48] Born in Athens, Greece, and an immigrant to Canada as a young teenager, he is widely popular with the Coptic community. He frequently empathizes with their experiences as immigrants and always reminds audiences that his grandparents too were victims of sectarian violence when Turks invaded the city of Izmir in 1922, killing thousands of Armenian and Greek Christians. To the cheers of his Coptic supporters, he is known for frequently beginning his speeches "Hello, fellow Orthodox Christians" and referring to Father Marcos as "my father."[49]

Karygiannis is a portly, charismatic, and even theatrical figure, and when he took the microphone at the Coptic Canadian Center on October 16, his political agenda never hovered far from his fiery speech of consolation. Rather, he deftly criticized the opposing Conservative Party as being too passive to represent Coptic demands, both in the past and in the present. To the visible and growing agitation of Conservative member of Parliament Bob Dechert, he quoted his competing colleague's previous promise of "standing shoulder to shoulder" with the Copts and promised to do even more. By calling for an emergency debate at the United Nations, Karygiannis offered that it would be "*the whole world* standing shoulder to shoulder, with your priests in front of you and us beside you." Hearing this, the crowd jumped to their feet with excitement and gave the politician a hearty standing ovation. It was at this point that Dechert stood up and approached the podium in his party's defense. The scene bordered on the comical when Karygiannis refused Dechert his microphone, and Dechert attempted to address the huge crowd without one. Finally, Father Angelos Saad diplomatically handed the beleaguered politician another microphone with which Dechert assured the crowd that his party would certainly demand an emergency meeting and an independent investigation by the United Nations. Furthermore, the Canadian Parliament in Ottawa would also charge the Foreign Affairs Committee with undertaking their own investigations. The crowd was ecstatic, continuing their standing ovation, though at this point, it was unclear for whom.

While these kinds of political banter are not surprising, it was Karygiannis's astute insight to Coptic community politics that promoted his popularity among their ranks. Indeed, on October 17, just one day after this meeting, Karygiannis was successful in introducing a motion in the Canadian House of Commons, condemning the violence against Coptic Christians and asking the United Nations Human Rights Commission to conduct an open and transparent investigation into the Maspero massacres. The bill passed unanimously, and the next day, Karygiannis's administration team posted it on a YouTube archive as a testament of his success.[50] This was his first step to achieving his pledge of getting the whole world to "stand shoulder to shoulder" with the Copts in their plight, even if just as a global digital audience. It was the fact that he recognized the order of "your priests in front of you and us beside you" that gave him such leverage with the Orthodox clergy who served as mediators of diasporic as well as transnational politics. In other words Karygiannis offered to work within an already existing political system in which Coptic priests served as political liaisons between the Canadian government and their Coptic-Canadian constituencies, mirroring the informal entente that Pope Shenouda III had negotiated with Mubarak's regime in Egypt. In turn, Copts themselves cheered whoever pushed their cause forward, their loyalties strategically ambiguous, multivocal, and layered.

Some Conclusions

Himmani Bannerji writes: "The representational politics which gave claims to give us history or tradition 'as it was,' free of changes brought on by its own movements as history, free of a content changed by its contexts, needs to be contrasted to a liberatory or emancipatory use of culture as a basis for political identities and agencies."[51] Canada's state enterprise of multiculturalism has broadly helped the Coptic-Canadian community achieve their initial aims. By singing a strategic multiculturalism and navigating the discursive politics of *taratil* and *alhan,* Coptic-Canadians have made themselves both visible and audible in a Canadian landscape in a way that has become increasingly problematic in Egypt since the January 25 uprising, singing their identities as specifically Christian citizens. Yet despite these disclosures encouraged by the Canadian state supplying security during public Coptic demonstrations, organizing delegations to travel to the Canadian Parliament, and involving the direct action of some members of Parliament in the Canadian House of Commons, Coptic immigrant churches continue closely to reflect their mother church's politics.[52] In the same way that the institutional Coptic Orthodox Church of Egypt reinterprets *al-wihda al wataniya,* or national unity, to negotiate an entente with current Egypt's regimes, Coptic immigrant churches navigate Canada's multiculturalist discourse to position themselves closer to the state's scope of tolerance. Yet by emphasizing their Christian identities in hopes of more closely resembling an Anglo-Canadian ethnic unproblematic self, Coptic political agency is entangled in multiculturalism's orientalist and racialized biases. Additionally, Copts are embroiled in similar technologies of power and state containment that marginalized their civic power back home, deferring civic engagement to clerics and other hierarchs. As Coptic clergy increasingly emerge as the political mediators between Canadian politicians and their constituents, Coptic-Canadians risk losing what they initially bemoaned in Egypt: political clout as voters and as citizens. In the end, they sing. But that is it.

COPTIC MIGRANT CHURCHES
Transnationalism and the Negotiation of Different Roles

Ghada Botros

It is the evening of March 20, 2012. I am at the Toronto airport waiting for a plane to Cairo via a stop in Europe. Sitting in front of me at the terminal gate were seven men with long gray beards, dressed in black cloaks and wearing leather crosses on long necklaces. They were some of the Coptic priests in Toronto and its surrounding area. When our plane arrived at the European transit airport, the gate for our second plane had more than fifteen Coptic priests and monks, all heading to Cairo, who joined us from other countries. This was an unusual sight that had to do with a grand unusual event, the funeral of the Coptic Pope Shenouda, who had passed away two days earlier. His photo was on the front page of the *International Herald Tribune* sold at the airport on that day.

The Coptic Orthodox Church has gone transnational. This is a new reality for students of the Church who have long understood it as a localized religious institution within the boundaries of Egypt. Since the 1960s Coptic religious communities in North America, Europe, and Australia, usually described in Egypt as *mahgar*, or land of migration, began to form and establish Coptic churches. These local migrant churches are affiliated with the mother church in Egypt and have clergy members ordained by the Coptic pope. Despite a shy beginning in the mid-1960s, the number of Coptic churches, with the number of Coptic immigrants, has been growing. Coptic immigrant churches owe their expansion to the vision of Pope Shenouda III and his predecessor Pope Kyrillos VI. As the Coptic Orthodox Church extends its service beyond its traditional boundaries within Egypt, immigrant churches become potent sites for the negotiation of a Coptic identity outside Egypt and, therefore, witness a complex process of adaptation. Closely connected to the mother church in Egypt, immigrant local churches are an extension of its service outside the national borders of Egypt, and, hence, a transnational religious role emerges. This role involves a complex organizational structure as well as informally lived practices by migrants.

Immigrant churches play an important role in the lives of Copts that has been little addressed in research. This essay argues that the Coptic Orthodox Church seeks to provide pastoral care to the different needs of Coptic migrants that are at times competing and contradictory. To most new immigrants the local church is tasked with the role of a helper, providing a point of entrance into the new society. The Church is also required to play the role of consoler, helping to abate the emotional and psychological burdens of migration. The migrant church is in addition tasked with the transmission of the Coptic heritage and faith to second-generation Copts. Reaching out to this second generation of Copts, who have become culturally localized in the migrant society, is a grand task that requires enormous adaptation and negotiation. "A Church without youth is a Church without a future" is an often-repeated quotation of the late Pope Shenouda III. Youth remain at the center of most of the activities of migrant churches, the target group of its programs and expansion projects, and the main subject in the discourse of the clergy. Because of these different roles, the local migrant church is a potent site for competing and overlapping discourses.

This essay seeks to capture a moment in the adaptation process of migrant churches to accommodate the different roles mandated by the migration experience. It is a moment when the Coptic Orthodox Church moves beyond its traditional geography and opens its doors to the outside society and seeks to attract a second generation that has become culturally localized in new societies.

The research provided here builds on fieldwork conducted in Toronto and other North American cities during the period from 2001 to 2005.[1] More recent data were collected during short visits to Toronto in the summers of 2010, 2012, and 2013.

The Study of Immigrant Religious Gatherings

Researchers have recently began to recognize the role of religious gatherings in the lives of immigrants and their children. Several classic studies have provided the groundwork for this relatively nascent area of research. Prominently, Will Herbergs's emphasis on the role of religion in the lives of immigrants is seen as a key milestone in this area. He notes: "Of the immigrant who came to this country it was expected that, sooner or later, either in his own person or through his children, he would give up virtually everything he had brought with him from the 'old country.'... Within broad limits, however, his becoming American did not involve his abandoning the old religion; ... it was largely in and through his religion that he, or rather his children and grandchildren, found an identifiable place in American life."[2]

Another milestone in the field of the study of religious gatherings is the contribution by Raymond Brady Williams, who studied migrants from India and Pakistan. Williams not only emphasizes the salience of religion in the lives of immigrants, but he also refers to the reformulation process that religions undertake as they are lived by migrants and examines its social role: "Immigrants are religious—by all counts more religious than they were before they left home—... ; the emphasis on religious affiliation and identity is one of the strategies that allows the immigrant to maintain self-identity while simultaneously acquiring community acceptance. ... Apart from its spiritual dimension, religion is a major force in social participation; it develops and at the same time sacralizes one's self-identity, and thus the religious bond is one of the strongest social ties. Migration, however, forces reformulation of the religious identity."[3]

Timothy L. Smith goes beyond the assertion that migrants are religious by describing the migration experience as a "theologizing experience" owing to the emotional consequences of leaving the home country. He describes the situation of the immigrant: "Loneliness, the romanticizing of memories, the guilt for imagined desertion of parents and other relatives, and the search for community and identity in a world of strangers, ... separation from both personal and physical associations of one's childhood community."[4]

A growing body of literature seeks to capture moments in the transformative process that ethnoreligious gatherings in North America and Europe undertake.[5] The study of Coptic immigrant churches is an important addition to this literature on account of the unique historical trajectory of the Church from centuries of isolation following the historical religious schisms of the fifth century and the subsequent legacy of subjugation upon the Arab conquest of Egypt.

Coptic Migrants and Their Churches: Small Beginnings and a Growth in Leaps

The Copts in Egypt are best described, to borrow the term from Donald Horwitz, as an "unranked" group.[6] The Copts are represented among the poorest and richest classes in Egypt. Among migrant Copts in North America, the same description holds true. While there are established specialized physicians, engineers, and scientists who regularly attend Coptic migrant churches, there are also recent migrants with education credentials that do not translate in the North American labor market and people whose visas have expired. Additionally, while some have migrated as part of an elite cohort fleeing the socialist policies of the 1950s, others came for lack of other options because of limited economic resources.[7]

The early cohort of Coptic migrants started in the 1950s and 1960s. Immigrant Copts at the time were primarily from among the educated liberals who were fleeing the socialist policies of the regime of Gamal Abdel Nasser (1954–1970) in Egypt. Interviews with some of the migrants of this cohort attribute their decision to the police-state policies of the 1952 coup d'état. While these policies affected Egyptians from all religions, elite Copts had more reasons to worry.[8] Researchers focusing on this historic period relate these reasons to various issues. First, the Revolution Leadership Council had no Copt on it, despite the Copts' extended presence in the political arena at the time. Second, when Fayek Farid, a Copt and a previous member of the Parliament, was sentenced to five years for being member of a so-called communist group in 1959, this was seen as a sign of anti-Coptic trends among the leadership.[9] Because of their high education level and their fortunes, migrants from Egypt in the 1950s and 1960s found themselves a place either in Europe or North America. This migration movement, however, remained limited. The Egyptian state curbed the movement of Egyptians by imposing difficult measures for obtaining a passport or an exit visa.[10]

Beginning in the 1970s emigration from Egypt trickled down to the middle and lower-middle classes. The majority of these migrants had university education, a large percentage of which was in the health sector. The abolition of the policies curbing travel and the complex process to obtain exit visas coincided with changes in migration laws in the host countries, particularly in the United States and Canada. In the United States the Immigration Act of 1965 and the abolition of country of origin quotas opened the door for migrants from all over the world and particularly from countries that used to be called Third World countries during the Cold War. In Canada the 1967 immigration policies similarly opened the door to newcomers from all countries.

This more recent wave of emigrants from Egypt had different reasons for migration from those of the earlier cohorts. The emigration movement of the 1970s onward is related to economic reasons and to rising ethnoreligious tensions in the country. These two factors, however, are intertwined. Economic crises spark ethnic and sectarian strife. Michael Brown notes that inflation and unemployment stir ethnic conflict.[11] Similarly, John Hutchinson and Anthony Smith note that scarce resources exacerbate cultural differences.[12] In the 1970s in Egypt rapid changes of the open-door policies that followed the Nasserist socialist policies and the growing economic crisis had their toll on Christian-Muslim relations. Support from Anwar Sadat's administration (1970–1981) for Islamic extremist groups to counteract the leftist and socialist groups that supported his predecessor was seen by Copts as an alarming sign. During the thirty-year rule of Sadat's successor, Hosni Mubarak, and despite the cordial relationship between the Church leadership and the regime, the migration of Copts continued.

New developments in Egypt, specifically after the January 25 uprising and change of regime, provided impetus for a new wave of migration of Copts. Panic due to sectarian tensions and attacks on churches in a number of villages and urban neighborhoods, combined with a worsening economic situation and compromised state security, accelerated migration among Copts. While most of the sectarian tensions take place in relatively low-income urban neighborhoods and villages, it is mainly educated and middle class Copts who seek migration with a sense of urgency. This very recent wave of accelerated migration has been reported by NGOs in Egypt and has even attracted media attention.[13]

The establishment and growth of the number of Coptic churches in North America has followed the path of the Copts. It is safe to argue that the establishment of migrant churches is the outcome of an initiative by the mother church in Egypt that was backed and encouraged by migrant lay Copts. Interviews with the first priest in North America show that the suggestion to establish a first church came from the Church leadership. However, it was and continues to be the lay Copts who have supported the idea and provided the means to make new churches possible by financing the establishment of migrant churches and their maintenance. The Church in Egypt supports these migrant churches by ordaining priests and hosting regular papal and pastoral visits from Egypt. However, it is the immigrant communities that welcome these ordained priests, are consulted in their selection, and financially provide for them.

In 1964 Wagdi Elias arrived in Toronto carrying his new name as Father Marcos (Mark)[14] to be the first Coptic priest ordained "Priest for the Altar of God at the Coptic Church in North America," as announced in the service of his ordination.[15] The choice of the name of Marcos was not coincidental, as it shows the pride the Coptic Orthodox Church takes in its apostolic founding by Saint Mark and its long history in Christianity. This pride is also shown in the naming of migrant churches, with many named after Saint Mark. The first Coptic church in North America was registered in the province of Ontario in 1965. The choice of Wagdi Elias was not coincidental and would show the philosophy of the mother church in choosing priests to serve in migrant communities. Wagdi Elias was an instructor at the Coptic Seminary in Cairo and a deacon in the church with solid knowledge of the Church faith and tradition; he had also studied ethnomusicology focusing on Coptic music in the United States. This profile signifies what the Church saw as the required traits in the clergy to serve in immigrant societies: familiarity with the culture in the new society, a high level of education, and a strong background in the Church teaching.[16]

By 1970 four priests were permanently based in North America with continued visits from members of the clergy in Egypt. The second priest, Father Rofail Nakhla, was ordained in 1967 to be based in Montreal, a city of high concentration of Coptic migrants. The third church was established in Los Angeles in 1969 by a priest who was already very popular in Egypt, Father Bishoy Kamel. The fourth priest, Father Gabriel Abdelsayed, was ordained in New Jersey in 1970. Notably, Los Angeles had the first church building to be owned by a Coptic community, followed by another in New Jersey.[17]

Four churches in 1970 had grown to eighty Coptic Orthodox churches in the United States in 2012 and twenty-one churches in Canada in 2002. The sprawling of Coptic churches in North America was gradual and was more spontaneous than planned by the mother church in Egypt. When Pope Shenouda III made his first visit to North America in 1977, there were four churches in Canada and sixteen in the United States. During his visit he laid the cornerstones for churches in New York, New Jersey, Michigan, and California.[18] Each local immigrant church has a story of its establishment. In most cases the establishment of Coptic churches in the expansion phase was primarily a lay initiative. Usually, a group of Copts would want to have their own church because they were tired of the long commute to the nearest church or were eager to have more than the periodical services offered by a "flying priest" from another city. The role these centers of faith play in the lives of migrants cannot be underestimated. Migrant Copts build these churches so that these churches can address their different emotional and spiritual needs. The migrant church plays many roles in the lives of Copts.

Transnationalism and the Different Roles of a Migrant Church

It would be a mistake to assume that the role of the migrant church is limited to the spiritual service of performing liturgies and giving sermons at religious meetings.

Rather, it transcends this need to involve an intricate set of activities that are closely tied to the needs of migrants and their families. This complex role changes over time and is often subject to negotiation and adaption.

The migrant church plays three specific roles in the lives of migrants. As helper, the church provides a whole gamut of services, primarily determined by the size of the church and the capacity of laypeople and clergy to support migrants in the settlement process. As consoler, the migrant church provides migrants with a sense of a community within the new society and a piece from home, away from home. To quote Stephen R. Warner, the migrant church becomes "*gemeinschaft* within the *gesellschaft*, a remembrance of Zion in the midst of Babylon."[19] As a consoler, the immigrant church plays the important role of easing the emotional burdens of adjusting to a new society. The very locale of the immigrant church becomes a source of emotional support to the migrant; it is a place where she or he can speak the language of the homeland, tell the jokes of the old country, and talk to people who share a common background. Sermons, individual counseling, and family mediation are essential tools for this complex role of easing the emotional burdens of migration.

As competitor, the Coptic Orthodox Church takes pains to reach out to Copts from the second generation. "Competing" for the second generation is one major objective of Coptic immigrant churches. The term, used in one of the meetings for youth chaperons, has been recurring in the literature about the second generation in immigrant religious gatherings.[20] The goal of reaching out to the youth dominates the discourse of the Church leadership, members of the clergy and church volunteers. Toward this goal, different adaptation changes are endorsed by the church particularly in relation to the language of service.

Immigrant religious organizations are not transplanted imports severed from organizations in the homeland. Peggy Levitt's description of the Catholic Church as articulating a vision of a religious community across different national boundaries resembles the recent role of the Coptic Orthodox Church as a transnational religious institution with a global network "from one end of the universe to the other," as proclaimed in the Coptic patriarchate's English-language monthly magazine, *Al-Kiraza*.[21]

This transnational linkage of the Coptic Orthodox Church is expressed in different manners. Frequent papal visits by the late Pope Shenouda III have played a central role in maintaining the transnational linkages, along with a steady stream of visits by different bishops from Egypt. These visitors are warmly welcomed by migrant Copts. The mother church in Egypt also ordains most of the priests in churches outside Egypt, and the papal trips often include the consecration ceremonies for new churches established by immigrants. Moreover, books and lectures from Egypt are available in the bookshops of Coptic churches outside Egypt, many in translated versions. Coptic migrant churches follow the same liturgical prayers of the Coptic tradition. These churches also follow, as closely as possible, the architectural design, layout, and iconography of the churches in Egypt, particularly the older churches in Egypt that closely follow the Coptic tradition.

Despite the strong transnational linkages, it is important to stress a role that Coptic immigrant churches have long been discouraged from undertaking. This role relates to involvement in the politics surrounding the situation of Copts in Egypt. Incidents of sectarian strife in Egypt take central attention in discussions in the social gatherings of lay Copts. Some activist migrant Copts have sought to partake in action, primarily by whistle-blowing or by sending petitions to their governments. Historically there are many incidents in which a group of migrant Copts has placed paid advertisements in major newspapers in the United States condemning the acts of Islamic militant groups in Egypt against the Copts and accusing the state of not being firm enough.[22] However, the recommended course of action by the migrant church, following instructions from the mother church, is to "pray for our brothers and sisters in Egypt." Prayer is a form of transnational politics that is unique to Coptic migrant churches. The mother church considers the political situation of the Copts in Egypt highly sensitive, and the concern is that the meddling of immigrant Copts might have negative consequences. Activist groups among migrant Copts, however, resent this rather pacifist approach of the Church. An interesting incident was when Pope Shenouda III in 1982, while under house arrest by Sadat, sent delegates of bishops to Copts in the United States, urging them to meet the then newly elected president Hosni Mubarak "with prayers, not demonstrations."[23] The cleavage between the stance of the migrant church toward the politics in Egypt and the attitude of lay migrants has created instances of tension.[24]

The events of June 30, 2013, are of great significance to the discussion of the transnational politics of Coptic migrant churches. This day marked the anniversary of the first year of the first president after the January 25 uprising, Mohamed Morsi.[25] This was a big day in Egypt too, as many groups had decided to take to the street protest government failures. *Tamaroud*, or Rebel, was a movement championed by many youth groups in Egypt that collected signatures, reportedly thirty million signatures, to impeach the president. On this day in Toronto groups of migrant Egyptians, both Copts and Muslims, went to Queens Park to voice their protests. The migrant church played a delicate, yet significantly different, role in these events. Coincidently, June 30 was a Sunday. This made a migrant church a convenient meeting point for groups that had decided to demonstrate. Flags of Egypt were sold in front of churches. This was an unusual sight that can only be understood in view of the pressures from the new migrants, particularly those who arrived after the January 25, 2011, uprising and who maintained strong ownership of the situation in Egypt.

The June 30 events are a precedent and a break in the norm witnessed in the relationship between the Coptic Orthodox Church and the ruling regime in Egypt. The Coptic migrant churches have traditionally steered away from being "a center of political and cultural activism," to borrow the phrase from Raymond A. Mohl and Neil Betten in their discussion of immigrant churches early in the twentieth century that constituted minorities in their country of origin, such as the Greek Church under the Turks or the rabbis in czarist Russia.[26] The general approach of

Coptic migrant churches has been to focus on their spiritual and religious role with various added social services that are responsive to the needs of migrants and their families as they settle in the new society and as their children grow and become the center of attention at the church.

The Migrant Church as Helper

Providing support in the settlement of new migrants remains a major social task of the migrant church. Describing his service in the early years as the first Coptic priest in North America, Father Marcos, notes: "I was not just a priest. We used to do almost everything. . . . They [newcomers] used to come to our house. They'd stay until we find them housing, help them find a job, and even get them furniture. I'd help in the moving, my wife would go shopping with the wives for what furniture to buy."[27]

As Coptic churches in North America grow in number and size, the task of helping new migrants is primarily delegated to committees of lay volunteers. It is also rare now for a newcomer to lodge in the house of the priest. First, there is almost always a distant relative who will host the newcomer for days or even weeks. Second, most migrants are expected to have money to cover their rent. The newcomer now is helped with finding an apartment to rent. The church can act as guarantor to the landlord and provide references, if needed. A volunteer from the church can also accompany a newcomer to obtain a social insurance number (in Canada), open a bank account, or apply for health insurance.

Also, as churches grow, Coptic churches with large congregations build what is usually described as a center. It can be in the basement of the church or a separate elegant building attached to the church, depending on the size of the community and its resources. The center often includes a gymnasium for the youth, a large meeting room for meals after the liturgy on Sundays, and room for different services.

The help provided by migrant Coptic churches is not limited to planned services provided by priests or committees. The locale of the church provides a potent site for networking to find a job, a house, and even a marriage partner. Following a tradition started in the early years of the church in North America, almost all migrant churches open the church after the service for a meal to be shared by congregants; the meal is called *agape*, the biblical term for a feast of love. The meal might be free, as is the case in some churches, or it might be provided for a fee by a kitchen run by volunteers or even a professional cook. The funds raised support other services. After the liturgy, the meeting room is usually a busy place with Copts chatting about issues of interest. These face-to-face interactions provide excellent opportunities for networking; for example, congregants can ask the priest where they should send their children to school.

The social support of a migrant church can be traced by following the major life events of a migrant. It starts with help in finding a job in the new society and settling in. For the migrant family the church is where the children go not only for Sunday school but also for daycare, schooling, weekly meetings, counseling, gymnasium and recreational facilities, or help with studies. As the congregants age, the church might build retirement homes or cemeteries. Of course, the availability of these services differs from one localized Coptic church to the other, based on the church's size.

The Migrant Church as Consoler

There is a psychological and emotional burden associated with the migration experience. Being uprooted from family and friends in the homeland, on the one hand, and facing immediate needs, such as housing and employment, on the other hand, place enormous emotional burdens on an immigrant. Priests, most of them migrants themselves, are receptive to these needs. One priest in the United States echoes Smith's words, quoted earlier, on the feeling of displacement caused by the migration experience. He describes his congregants by noting that "the people here, when they come to the land of immigration, it is not easy for them. It is a very hard feeling that they are away from their families and friends. It affects the way they think, their psychology, so this gives the priest [a] hard time to [provide] relief [to] everybody and to comfort everybody and to deal with everybody, to gain them and to get them together and to avoid any problems and schisms in the church. It is not an easy task of course."[28] A bishop in North America echoes the same notion, noting that the migrants "have an identification with the church, driving long distances [to go to church]. Even if away, they support the church. The church is like a home, or a group therapy; . . . they get relief [there]."[29]

The task of relieving, comforting, and reaching out to congregants is enormous. It is a task that is even more complex than the tasks that come with the role of helper. It takes its toll on the priest's time and energy. It is the task of "sharing the pain," to borrow a phrase from Anitra Bingham-Kolenkow, who highlights the role that Coptic monks currently play in Egypt as Copts consult them about personal problems and prayer requests.[30]

Salman Akhtar notes that ethnic centers play a major role in the "emotional rejuvenation" of immigrants by bringing them closer to the homeland.[31] As much as the locale of the church is a component of the helping role, it is also a component of the consoling role. The locale of the church becomes a piece from home, away from home. It is the place where an immigrant can speak the language of her or his homeland, recount old jokes from back home, and even make jokes about things in the new society with co-ethnics. These casual conversations alleviate the sense of displacement that comes with migration. The theme of making the church "a piece from home" is very common. I was present as some church members were discussing having a festival in the church, and one congregant presented a project that would make the church look like "a piece from Egypt." The proposal was to have replicas of carts similar to those used by street vendors in lower income areas in Cairo and to have palm trees.

Looking similar to the church in Egypt is part of the objective of establishing new churches. A website describing the establishment of a Coptic church in one

North American city notes: "In no time the new church wasn't different in any way from any other Coptic church in Egypt, regarding the service." Raymond Brady Williams notes that immigration involves a crisis of epistemology that causes people to revive their tradition to establish a known world in their new societies. Creating a "piece from home" is an engagement with nostalgia.[32] In churches built by immigrant Copts, as opposed to churches purchased, the church architecture follows the Byzantine style used in Egypt. Purchased churches are decorated with Coptic icons.

Moreover, the celebration of festivities such as Christmas and Easter following the traditions at home, with a late Mass that ends with a shared meal, and the commemoration of Coptic saints are integral to the emotional role the migrant church plays. During Lent authentic Egyptian vegetarian meals are distributed or sold at a migrant church, including *foul* (beans), *bisara* (a thick soup of mashed beans and vegetables), *ta'amia* (fried mashed beans with vegetables), and *koshari* (rice, macaroni, and lentil). Several researchers have highlighted the centrality of food and shared meals in the reproduction of ethnicity and of relieving the psychological burdens of migration. Helen Rose Ebough and Janet Saltzman Chafetz note that communal eating is a regular and frequent feature of congregational life.[33] Similarly, Goldsmith describes how eating together fostered a sense of community in a black Pentecostal church in Georgia.[34]

Hymns and sermons as part of the service are central to the emotional role of the Coptic migrant church. Tapes of Christian songs produced in Egypt are sold in the bookshops of the church. During services deacons sing hymns in Arabic that are usually known to Copts from the first generation. Sermons addressing first-generation migrants are reflective of their emotional needs. Among the most common themes and Bible verses is "Cast all your cares upon him for he cares for you" (1 Peter 5:7). Stories, either biblical or from the lives of saints, are used to convey the same message. "Depending on God" is the major advice given.

In addition to that helping and consoling first-generation Copts, the activities of the Coptic migrant church focus particularly on serving the youth and the adolescents from the second and third generations. Because it is a young church in North America, and has the legacy of a minority status in Egypt, it is obvious why the Coptic Orthodox Church considers the youth the most important group. The youth are simply the future of the Church in immigrant societies. In a meeting of chaperons in one Coptic churches in Toronto, a bishop who primarily serves the youth invoked the same notion, noting that "it [would] be depressing if we lose our children. We need to compete. . . . We have a secret weapon, our secret weapon is that we have a good CEO [referring to Jesus Christ]; he guides us; . . . he gives us [an] example."[35]

As we have noted, "competing" for the youth is a recurrent theme in literature on immigrant religious gatherings. Karen Chai documents how different Korean organizations, both religious and nonreligious, compete for second-generation Koreans in the United States.[36] Shoshanah Feher discusses a similar case in which the Iranian-Jewish community in the United States focuses on youth as the most important demographic group and the target for most expansion projects.[37]

Competing for the youth also means competing for their time, particularly their leisure time. One youth servant, a university student, describes why meetings for high school youth are held on Friday nights, noting: "We want to trick them out of going somewhere else on Friday night by coming to church. We just have a social club, where after Sunday school they can go have some religious music, some games, some popcorn, stuff like that. We really want to get them from going outside, you know whatever, a late movie or a club or whatever it is maybe, to coming to church Friday night."[38]

Meetings, sports tournaments, and sometimes a gymnasium are offered to young people through the migrant church. These benefits are appreciated by many youth among second-generation Copts, who see the local church as an important element of group formation and the construction of an identity for second-generation Copts. One high school girl notes that "the reason why we like the church is that it brings us together and makes us a community. It is something that you belong to and you have your friends from church and you have your own way of doing things, like you have youth group and stuff. It is like it identifies you with the people. And . . . there [are not] a lot of Coptic people anyway, so it brings people together."[39]

The church becomes a safe haven where ethnicity and religion can be weaved together. Another second-generation male Copt notes that "the church is more than a service, that's the thing. We do go to church for services, but it doesn't stop there. There are other events that hold people together like after church, before church, things happening in the church, so there [are] fundraisers, dinners, events, or trips. The church tries to make everybody come to it. In a sense we are more than a church; through the church we can do other stuff, and that's how we get the connection, like we're having senior trips, with families, they take it a step further, but the church is the essence and they try to expand."[40] The objective of reaching out to young Copts from the second generation is manifest in many ways. Whenever there is a bishop visiting, the first meeting scheduled is the one for the youth. In fact the emphasis is to bring in bishops who are popular among the youth.

Two major changes seem to capture the Church's interest and its willingness to adapt to reach out to youth. First, there has been a strong movement to translate all services into English. Second, there has been a movement to ordain priests who are either brought up in immigrant societies or have spent some time as immigrants. These two major steps are described by a priest in the United States as steps toward moving from being "a church of immigrants to a church of citizens."

Moreover, the relatively new experience of establishing Coptic schools in the immigrant societies is another example of the Church's efforts to attract the second generation. This is a relatively new initiative that started in Australia and is being experimented with in North America. In the Greater Toronto Area there were two schools, each attached to a Coptic church, in 2004. There were schools in Montreal and Nashville. There were also plans by other churches to build schools.

The competition for youth is also manifest in the level of youth involvement in many of the church activities. This has been a notion emphasized in interviews with members of the clergy in churches with successful youth programs. One priest notes: "I always put it as a stipulation for anybody who wants to have a service in the church, [to] use the youth. . . . This way, they feel they are part of the church. It is important for them. I have a guy in church for the maintenance, the most wonderful thing he does is that, if he wants to change the bulbs, he gets a group of teenagers with him on a Saturday without telling anyone from the grownups."[41]

In this quotation "without telling anyone from the grownups" signifies a shift in the ownership of the locale of the migrant church, where the youth are given primacy as the group in charge of maintenance and eventually for the sustenance of the migrant church. Another priest refers to involving the youth in the governance of the local church by giving them membership on the board of deacons, which controls the major issues related to the church on the local level. He notes: "We need for the youth to feel that this is their church, they have a say in this church, so we have a huge number of [young] deacons, we have some youth representing the youth in the board of deacons in the church, and we have a lot of activities for the youth: spiritual, social, you know, like sports and athletic activities. We are trying to involve the youth in everything in the church and it is giving very promising results. The youth now are pretty involved and attending the church regularly, enjoying the service, knowing more about the Church."[42]

Reaching out to the youth also involves a celebration of the Coptic Church's history in order to invoke feelings of pride about being Copts. Pride in the history of the Coptic Orthodox Church is manifest in the discourse of the Copts in interviews and books and on websites. Among the highlights are the Coptic Church's contributions to early Christianity and the Church's role in the formulation of the first Christian creed (the Nicene Creed); the Catechetical School of Alexandria; and the role of the Coptic Church in the introduction of Christian monasticism. According to one bishop, the Church wants the youth to "appreciate the richness of the Orthodox church. In conventions [for youth] in the previous years, we tried to implant this spirit, for the youth to appreciate who they are; they come out of the conventions saying, wow, we are proud that we are orthodox."[43]

The objective of reaching out to the youth requires the Church to be in harmony with society in general. The different measures to reach out to the youth and play the role of "competitor" serve in many ways to "de-ethnicize" the church, to borrow the term from Mark Mullins.[44] This very notion is echoed by the Coptic priest's description of the process as moving from a "church of immigrants" to a "church of citizens."

Significantly, the active role of young people in the service can develop the role of helper for the migrant church to extend its outreach to society in general, rather than just to focus on helping newcomers within the migrant community. In one case, the church in Mississauga in Canada has been heavily involved in providing food-bank service to the entire local community, covering about 60 percent of the needs of the Peel region.[45]

Adaptation and the Accommodation of Difference

Because of the different roles of the migrant church and the different demographic and social characteristics of migrant Copts, adaptation and change are not without contention. In fact, the roles of the migrant church as a helper and consoler are not always compatible with its objective of competing for the second generation. To put it simply, what pleases the second generation and the youth may not necessarily please the first generation. On the contrary, the way these two groups envision the church setting, the language of prayers, and the role of the clergy are quite dissimilar. The nostalgia for the homeland that the first generation brings to the church stands in contrast with the second generation's need to have the service in the language they understand and to have their church assimilated into a society to which they have been acculturated.

The process of moving from a church of immigrants to a church of citizens starts with the language used in prayers. Yet it transcends the language issue to include many subtle issues concerning the local church and the type of services offered. The debate on the language, however, exemplifies this tension and the whole process of the adaptation and accommodation of difference in Coptic migrant churches.

Research on the use of language in services in migrant churches shows a structural linguistic shift in a three-generation process. Mullins notes that in an ethnic church the language of prayers evolves from a monolingual non-English stage to a bilingual stage, with the language of the country of origin used side by side with English in the prayers, and eventually to a monolingual stage in which English is the language of prayers.[46] This linguistic shift constitutes the language conundrum for Coptic migrant churches as they seek to cater to different cohorts of migrants at different generation cycles.

The continuation of successive waves of migrants and the very nature of the Coptic community with its diverse background render this language transition a highly contested process. One bishop in North America succinctly describes the situation as a struggle, noting: "We are struggling with the language; should we pray in Arabic or English? Even English, old English or new English? . . . If you pray in English, the older generation will be very upset, if you pray in Arabic you lose the new generation."[47]

This quotation summarizes the language dilemma in Coptic immigrant churches. First-generation migrants want the immigrant church to be a continuation of the church left at home, with its language, tunes, and services. Second-generation Copts, the group that is the center of the attention of the Church leadership, wants a church that speaks their language and sings and prays in tunes familiar to their Westernized ears. To the Church leadership this is the group that will constitute the future of the Church, and therefore their demands have to be reckoned with. The guiding policy of the mother church on the language issue is to translate everything into English. Indeed there has been a strong movement to translate all prayers to English in North America. One bishop notes that "the need for English has now superseded the need for Arabic . . . and that is a good natural progression. We are moving relatively quickly compared to other churches [other denominations] but I think that we are moving with a direction, that direction is very much based on the importance that we place on pastoral care."[48] However, the process of language shift in Coptic migrant churches is not linear. It remains contingent on several variables. While priests follow the guidelines of the Church leadership, the level of their English proficiency ultimately defines which language is used most often in services and prayers. The demographic composition of the local community is also central to the choice of language for services.

Moreover, the size of the congregation determines the number of priests serving it. According to the Coptic Orthodox Church canons, a priest cannot pray more than one liturgy in a day because he has to be fasting to perform the liturgy. If there is more than one priest, a full Mass can be offered in English and another in Arabic. On Sundays, if there is only one priest in the church the outcome is a liturgy that is a hybrid of English (to please the second generation) and Arabic (to please the first generation).

Also relevant as to how the composition of the congregation defines the language used in prayers is whether there are converts from the new society within the community. In this case the use of English is encouraged not only to reach the youth but also to include these new members. The relationship between serving converts and the use of English is reciprocal.

The language issue signifies a generational and cultural struggle over the ownership of the immigrant church. The following anecdote, repeatedly recounted by a priest who is a strong proponent of the sole use of English in prayers, captures this struggle. The incident took place in the 1980s, before his ordination as a priest. "Let me give you one occasion, which changed my whole thinking about this [language issue]. It was Good Friday. . . . I looked around; there were no youth or children in the church. I asked around; they said they are in the basement. I went downstairs, and I found a group of teenagers. I told them, 'Guys this is the most solemn day of the year and how come you are here in the basement?' One of them told me, 'How would you feel if I put you in a Chinese temple for six hours?' And I said, 'I would not like it.' And he said, 'That's the way we feel. This is your church. This is a church for grownups. It is not for us.'"[49]

The decision of the Church to shift the language of prayers to English has been in response to the resentment of the second-generation youth and their need for a church that speaks their language. This shift, however, forces all members of the migrant church, priests as well as first-generation members, to adapt. The situation of the older members is complex. While the role of a church as helper can continue in any language, it is the needed role of the consoler that is immediately compromised with the change of the language of prayers. For this reason a recent migrant describes her church, saying that it "seems to be the same [as in Egypt] yet does not feel the same."[50]

To accommodate the resentment of the first generation various notions are repeatedly invoked by priests who use English as the sole language of prayers. First, there is often the argument that "these are your children; . . . you don't want to lose your children so that you enjoy the Mass." In that sense the call for the use of the language of the homeland is framed as a selfish act on the part of the first-generation immigrant. In churches where the service has been completely shifted to English, a midweek Mass is often offered in Arabic for those who yearn for one in their native language.

The notion of struggle is not unique to Coptic immigrant churches. Paul David Numrich coined the term "parallel congregations" to describe the tension existing between different groups within the same congregation.[51] Reporting on thirteen churches, Ebough and Chafetz refer to tensions between different ethnic groups in multiethnic congregations, between different nationalities in churches of one ethnic group from different countries, between recent immigrants and established immigrants in churches with immigrants of one home country, and between people of different regions in the same country.[52]

Subtle Adaptations: Hierarchy Deference and Gender Roles

Priests have to deal not only with a shift in the language of prayers, but with other subtle changes from the mother church in Egypt as well. These changes are subtle in the sense that they reflect a gradual and smooth adaptation that can only be discerned by having a reference point of comparison.

One of these changes relates to the culture of deference toward members of the clergy. Priests in immigrant communities are called *Abouna,* the Arabic equivalent of "father," similar to the way they are addressed in Egypt. However, a general observation in immigrant churches is that priests are treated with less deference. A priest relates the compromise in the level of respect and deference to the effect of the American culture, noting that "the priest [in North America] is another person; they [the society] don't believe in hierarchy and the authority of hierarchy. . . . [They have] ideas of freedom and equality, . . . where you call people by their first name. The [Coptic] Church is not like this. We have fatherhood and respect. They are free of this. This creates a big problem. People are immersed in this culture, even if they believe in orthodoxy."[53]

In Egypt when a priest passes by a group of youth standing outside the church, they normally flock to him to salute him by kissing his hand or the cross he holds in his hands. In Canada the priest enters almost unnoticed. Some might nod, but in general the priest hurries to his office unless he stops to talk to someone specifically. In that situation kissing his hand or the cross in his hand would not necessarily take place. To a newly migrated priest this failure might be perceived as a sign of compromised respect in the community.

Another change relates to the increasing role of women in migrant churches. In Egypt boards of deacons, which are the governing bodies of each local church that approve projects and church-related activities, are usually comprised of older men. The situation in Canada and the United States is different. Women and youth have been members on many of the boards of deacons of immigrant churches. The involvement of the youth has, as we have noted, been a deliberate act. The increasing role of women is a change that has no relation with Church policy but instead reflects the impact of the local society.

In one church in Canada the head of the Sunday school services for boys and girls was a woman. Women were also involved in reviewing the church accounts and in a whole gamut of other services. In churches in Egypt men usually lead the singing. This was not always the case in the church where participatory observation took place in Canada. Particularly when there was singing in Coptic outside the liturgy, a woman who was proficient in the Coptic language led the singing many evenings. There is voluminous literature on the negotiation of the role of women in immigrant communities.[54] Writing about Hindu women in Southern California, Prema Kurien describes the increasing role of women in leading the singing and contributing to religious instructions.[55] Paradoxically, Sheba George documents the opposite in an Indian Orthodox church for families coming from Kerala, arguing that, because men in that community came as dependent immigrants with wives who were employed as nurses, they find in the church a venue to compensate for their diminishing social role and status.[56]

Also related to the negotiation of gender roles is the flexible seating arrangement in immigrant Coptic churches. In Egypt women sit on the right side of the church, while men sit on the left side. Gender segregation in seating is very strict there. In many immigrant churches families and couples tend to sit together. Because this is a change that has no direct guidelines, it is not commonplace in all migrant churches. In fact, it is rejected by some members of the clergy in some migrant communities as a violation of the church order.

The same argument is repeated with regard to women covering their heads in church. In Egypt covering the head in church is encouraged following biblical recommendations. In some immigrant churches there is no mention of the need for women to cover her head during prayers. In other churches covers are placed at the entrance of the church, constituting a reminder that women should cover their hair during prayers.

Finally, the depoliticization of the church from ethnoreligious conflicts in Egypt, discussed earlier, can also be considered a measure of adaptation by the migrant church in its move from a church of immigrants to a church of citizens. Against the strong feelings of many first-generation Copts, the migrant church steers away from politics in Egypt and adopts a spiritual stance of praying for those in the homeland.

Conclusion

Coptic immigrant churches are a new addition to the tapestry of religious communities in North America. Their story continues to unfold as a relatively young community in the land of migration, and, like all adaptation, theirs is a process in flux, with no definitive or determinist answer to how the process evolves.

The role of the immigrant church transcends the spiritual and conventional pastoral services to include an intricate set of roles—those of helper, consoler, and competitor—that are closely tied to the needs of migrants and their families. It is the task of reaching out to youth that has required the church to undertake a number of adaptations, most notable among them the shifting of the language of prayer from Arabic to the language of the new society. Adaptation, contestation, and accommodation of difference are interwoven processes that take place in the minutiae of the everyday. The process is fluid and is subject to reversal based on the power structure within a community and the intensity of the negotiation process between groups with different needs. The process is a milestone in the shift from being a church of immigrants to a church of citizens.

STRATEGIES OF ADAPTATION FOR SURVIVAL

The Introduction of Converts to the Coptic Orthodox Community in the Greater Toronto Area

Rachel Loewen

At a summer camp run by Coptic women at one of the Coptic churches in the Greater Toronto Area (GTA), a girl of about seven or eight years of age asked me if I was a visitor. I asked her if I did not look Coptic, to which she replied that I did not; I looked Canadian. To this little girl a Copt is Egyptian, and she is not the only one who shares this view of Coptic identity. Coptic is usually assumed by Copts to be synonymous with being Egyptian. However, with continued contact between the Egyptian Coptic Orthodox diaspora and the larger Canadian society, and the persistent introduction of non-Copts and non-Egyptians to the community through intercultural marriage and conversion, the ethnic makeup of the Coptic Orthodox community in the diaspora will become more diverse.[1]

Mark Mullins reasons that ethnic churches in Canada must adopt adaptive strategies in order to survive the changes in the needs of their congregants as new generations are born.[2] The initial purpose for the establishment of an ethnic church, such as the Coptic Orthodox Church in Canada, is to provide a sense of home for new immigrants in their new surroundings. Therefore, "the services and activities are naturally dominated by the language and clergy from the old country."[3] With the birth of the second generation, however, issues of language and cultural adaptation or assimilation occur.[4] Mullins claims that, by the third generation, intermarriage with nongroup members can lead to a loss in membership, as the younger generation can no longer relate to the Church, or the Church will move toward becoming a "multiethnic" organization.[5]

This essay concerns the adaptive strategies adopted by the Coptic Orthodox Church in the GTA, which include, among others: the conscious decision to try to separate the religious identity of the Coptic Church from an Egyptian or ethnic identity, emphasizing the Coptic Church's apostolic history in an attempt to prove that its beliefs, rituals, and practices are an authentic form of Christianity, and the introduction of a new Coptic church in the GTA, which was the first Coptic church in North America that focused on mission and conversion.[6] Also of interest are the beliefs, practices, and strategies of converts to the Coptic Orthodox Church in the GTA.

Background and Context

My fieldwork[7] and research interests were greatly influenced by the Coptic priest Father Peter who was the driving force behind both special meetings for university graduates and the creation of a new type of Coptic Orthodox Church.[8] My interest in the relationship between ethnic identity and religious identity was triggered by the increase in intercultural marriages within the Coptic community and the multicultural nature of the attendees at the meetings for the university graduates. Most participants at meetings that I attended at Coptic churches in the GTA were Egyptian; however, at the university graduates' meetings there was an unusually high number of non-Egyptians in attendance, which I soon learned was a direct result of Father Peter's "Ministry of Invitation." At the end of many meetings he would point to the empty chairs in the room and remind those in attendance of his outreach agenda. He said, "Keep bringing friends, no matter what their background." This was the first mission-centered program undertaken by a member of the Coptic clergy in the GTA.[9] Father Peter's actions resulted in a refinement of my research question. Therefore, during my twenty-one in-depth individual interviews, I asked my informants about the possibility of separating the Egyptian ethnic identity from the Coptic religious identity.

An Ethnic Church in Canada

The Coptic Orthodox Church in Canada is what Mark Mullins refers to as a "foreign-oriented minority church."[10] The leadership of the Coptic Orthodox Church in Canada is located in Egypt, which makes the Coptic diaspora inseparable from its homeland.[11] The Coptic Orthodox Church has its own pope and during my fieldwork Pope Shenouda III (1971–2012) was the 117th Coptic pope. The Copts believe that the Apostle Mark was their first patriarch and the founder of their Church. Egypt is divided into numerous dioceses or bishoprics over which a bishops are given control, including of the economic resources.[12] Until April 2013 the pope was considered to be the bishop in charge of the entire Coptic diaspora in Canada, however, Pope Tawadros II officially delegated Bishop Mina to be the bishop for the areas of Mississauga, Vancouver, and all of the surrounding cities, towns, and villages. Bishop Mina was enthroned on April 7, 2013, in Mississauga, Ontario, and the pope is expected to name a bishop to oversee the rest of Canada in the near future.

Mullins argues that an ethnic church in Canada must develop adaptation strategies to survive; otherwise, it will become obsolete within the third stage of its life cycle.[13] Ghada Botros describes the different roles that the Coptic Orthodox Church must fulfill in order to meet the needs of its followers in the North

American diaspora. In the beginning, during the first stage of its life cycle, the Church must act as a "comforter" by being a home away from home, or in other words, a little piece of Egypt in an unknown, and sometimes misunderstood, society.[14] This is a common role among immigrant churches in North America. In her study of the Greek community in Houston, Texas, Maria V. Gasi described how the community's Greek Orthodox church was expected to provide not only religious and spiritual guidance, but also "instruction in the language, history, and geography of Greece."[15] It was also believed that the use of the Greek language in the ritual and social life of the Greek community was paramount to the continuation of the Orthodox faith.[16] Since the early Coptic immigrants to the GTA held the same belief, in the 1960s, 1970s, and much of the 1980s all of the priests in the Canadian Coptic diaspora were sent from Egypt. Arabic and Coptic languages were the primary ones used during every ritual and at almost every event.

According to Mullins, issues of cultural assimilation between the first and second generations are what leads to the second stage of an ethnic church's life cycle.[17] At this point language becomes a problem. The second generation adopts English as their primary language, which requires the Church to locate bilingual leaders to provide English services, Sunday school materials, and religious texts.[18] Botros calls attention to the new role of "competitor" that the Coptic Orthodox Church must fulfill as it focuses on the needs of the second-generation youth in an effort to retain their interest in the beliefs and practices of the community.[19] In the 1980s the issue of language was at the forefront of many debates in Coptic churches in North America.[20] Fayek Ishak wrote that "insistence on using Arabic in our liturgies and church services is undeniably short-sighted. Others have given up the church altogether after irritation and distraction caused by the stubborn accommodation of the elderly generation of churchgoers."[21] Beth, a Canadian convert married to a Copt, recalls that in a Coptic church in the GTA during the 1980s "a lot of his [the priest's] youth were leaving. He had many, many youth leaving the Church because they had Canadian friends and they couldn't bring them in because there was no English. Minimal English! So he wanted to change it and he asked me to get involved. There was such a resistance and opposition to English." On account of the Coptic community's reaction to the issue of language, Beth added,

> I decided to leave after that; I thought I don't have English here. One of the women, one of the wives at the time of this meeting got up and said that if they want to have their Coptic Church and their language they have the right to. But she was a spectator. She would sit up in the balcony and watch. She was only there for an hour at the most and then she would pick up her children and go. I wanted to worship God! I wanted to be involved! I had been promised before marriage, by the priest who married us, that there would be English and that there had to be because they were living in Canada. We have to take care of ourselves. We have to meet our needs. Jesus says love others as we love ourselves. Before when I was in the Coptic Church wholly, I was not fed. I was very thwarted and very

frustrated. Trying to force myself to worship God in a different language by reading a book. On the other hand, for them, the older people, this is a way they need to worship God. Like they did in Egypt. They need both. They need the cultural Church, or that aspect for the immigrants, and they need the English-speaking Church that has the flavour, or what not, for the youth that are born here to be able to worship God.

The debate over bilingualism in most Coptic churches in the GTA has since been resolved. The Divine Liturgy is often performed twice, once in English and then in Arabic, or both languages are used interchangeably with the sermon first being given in one language after the gospel reading and a translated recitation of the original sermon heard after the Eucharist in the second language. Sunday school classes are held in English at every church, and there has been a significant increase in the amount of educational materials translated into English that discuss Coptic religious and cultural beliefs and rituals.

Beth's story is a good introduction to the issues that Mullins attributes to the third stage of an immigrant church's life cycle: the increasing number of intermarriages between members of the church or ethnic community and nonmembers due to the fact that the third generation of a community is more assimilated and adapted to the larger society than their parents and grandparents.[22] Mullins argues that if the mixed or intercultural couples are accepted in the church, the church will become de-ethnicized or multiethnic, and if the couples do not feel accepted, they will leave and go elsewhere.[23] In their comparative study of the function of ethnicity and religion in the life cycles of the Coptic and Dutch Calvinist Churches in Canada, Joanne van Dijk and Ghada Botros conclude that the Coptic Church is at a stage in its life cycle that they call "voluntary pluralism" in which the Coptic community's religious identity and ethnic identity are still distinct and separate from those of the larger Canadian community.[24] However, they speculate that the needs of future generations will diminish the strength of the ethnic identity of the community, while the religious identity will remain strong.[25] Gasi's study of the Greek community in Houston illustrates how an ethnoreligious immigrant community has focused on its religious identity overtime, rather than on its ethnic identity, and it provides a comparative model for the state of the Coptic Church in the GTA. At the time of her fieldwork Gasi found that most second- and third-generation Greek Americans wanted the Church to be a welcoming place for all baptized Orthodox believers, whereas new immigrants wanted the Church to remain "a means to ethnic survival and Greek language maintenance."[26] In the third stage of its life cycle the Coptic Church in the diaspora must fulfill both the roles of comforter and competitor, which can lead to conflict within the community.

A decision must be made by the Church about how to proceed. Sometimes it is a conscious choice while in other cases change just happens to accommodate new generations.[27] Intercultural marriage is becoming a very important issue within the community, because Copts who marry outside the Church excommunicate themselves and can no longer participate in Coptic sacraments.[28] Only baptisms performed in Oriental Orthodox churches are recognized by the Coptic Church.[29] Individuals baptized in Eastern Orthodox churches need to be confirmed through anointing with the holy chrism oil, while those baptized by any other Christian denomination must be rebaptized in the Orthodox faith and anointed with the holy chrism oil. Therefore, the question of rebaptism has become important in relation to intercultural marriage, because some couples choose to leave the Coptic Church since other Christian denominations accept Coptic and non-Coptic baptism. The choice of rebaptism is up to each individual couple and their decision on the importance of the Coptic Orthodox Church in their lives.

As a result the Church feels threatened by Copts marrying outsiders, as they could be lost to the Church.[30] Intercultural marriage tests the Coptic Orthodox Church's ability to separate its ethnic identity from its religious identity. It forces Coptic priests and parents to come face to face with the larger Canadian society and their own religious views and practices. Ashraf, a Copt in his mid-twenties, dated a girl who was not Coptic. When he told his father of confession about the relationship, the priest asked if he was ready to walk a long and difficult path. Ashraf believes that many priests dissuade Copts from marrying non-Copts. Mary, a Coptic university student in her early twenties stated, "You have to marry a nice Coptic boy. Yes, he has to be Coptic. It's sort of understood." Unfortunately, some priests hold biases against intercultural marriages and argue that non-Copts do not believe in the sacrament of marriage as a sacred and lasting union or that the introduction of non-Copts to the community will dilute the Coptic culture and traditions.[31]

One response to intercultural marriage and the potential introduction of other types of converts, by a Coptic priest, has been to form a new Coptic church in the GTA whose sole purpose is to missionize and administer to Copts and non-Copts alike. To establish his new church Father Peter had to leave the existing church that he served. Three weeks before the inaugural Divine Liturgy of the new mission church, Father Peter explained: "Why do mission? Why evangelize? Why disturb the peace when we've already decided that God loves everyone? How do people enter a predominantly ethnocentric community? For example, when a non-Egyptian walks into a Coptic church and gets 'the look,' which implies, 'You don't belong here.' The church has changed from a spiritual place to a place of community. There is a need for a missionary community. What is the difference between a missionary community and an ethnocentric community? They will only complement each other and never contradict."

There does seem to be a conscious, or perhaps semiconscious, restructuring of the Coptic churches in the GTA taking place. Specific churches are coping with the introduction of new immigrants to Canada, while others are catering to the needs of the youth, and a new church is focusing on converts.

Strategies for Adaptation used by the Coptic Church in the GTA

Paul Bramadat has argued that most people do not think about "the ways in which religious and ethnic identities influence, or even determine, one another."[32] In a similar vein Anne Mackenzie Pearson claims that Hindus did not have to contemplate the difficult task of separating their "culture" from their "religion" until the formation of the diaspora outside of India's borders.[33] Religious, ethnic, and cultural identities are always defined and then redefined in the Coptic community in the GTA. The Copts have had to study the relationship between their ethnic and religious identities because, as one Coptic informant explained to me, an Egyptian identity is slowly becoming synonymous with an Arab identity, which some consider to be Muslim in nature. However, as Father Marcos writes, "It is important to note that Coptic Christianity and Coptic culture are tightly interwoven to the extent that a person can hardly differentiate one from the other. . . . Therefore, when we speak, here below, about the Coptic Church we mean to include with its framework the Coptic culture."[34] For Father Marcos the Church has its own culture, which is different from Egyptian culture. This distinction was also made by Father Peter, who stated that it is important for the Church and its servants to emphasize to Coptic children that they are Christian, not Egyptian, because often a child will ask an adult why they do something and the response is "That's the way we do it in Egypt" or "That's the Egyptian way." The children, however, answer with the response that they are not Egyptian, but Canadian. Father Peter stressed that it is the Church's job to give the children a Christian faith. The family's task, in contrast, is to give the children a sense of their Egyptian heritage.

One strategy used by the Coptic Orthodox Church in the GTA, in an attempt to establish and maintain a relationship with intercultural couples and converts, is to emphasize that Coptic culture can and must be separated from the culture of Egypt. In other words one identity is religious in nature, Coptic or Orthodox, while the other is ethnic, Egyptian. Another approach used by the Coptic Church in the GTA, to create and sustain relationships with non-Egyptians, is undertaken by emphasizing the Church's apostolic roots in an effort to demonstrate that the beliefs, practices, and rituals of the Coptic Orthodox Church are authentically Christian. The construction of authenticity is a common practice among religious groups. For example, in a study of Yehi Ohr, a New Age / Jewish healing group, Celia Rothenberg observes numerous "authenticating strategies" used by members of the group to support the Jewish origin of its healing practices.[35] Such strategies include identifying themselves as Jewish, using Hebrew during rituals, and the presence of rabbis at meetings.[36] Most of the rabbis did not believe that Yehi Ohr was Jewish in origin; however, that fact did not seem important to the leader of the group or to his fellow participants.[37] The need for a sense of Jewish authenticity is strictly felt by the group's members. It seems to them that if the "authentic Jewish" religious identity was not attributed to the healing practices, healing would not occur.

Ellen Badone also notes the use of authenticating strategies associated with New Age rituals in Brittany. The family that she describes, The Floc'hs, believe that they live on a piece of land that is imbued with energy that past inhabitants recognized and harnessed.[38] Using *radiesthesie*, which is "both a method of diagnosing illness and a divinatory technique for discovering things hidden beneath the earth," the Floc'hs believe that there is a buried Christian chapel and underground tunnels and vaults from the Celtic era below their backyard.[39] The specifics of the Floc'hs' beliefs are not important here, but what is significant is their focus on the importance of the history of their property as proof of its authenticity as a place of healing. In Badone's example, as in my own fieldwork among the Canadian Copts, authenticity is constructed through reference to the past and to a historical legacy.

Rothenberg and Badone demonstrate that religious groups employ numerous authenticating strategies including, but not limited to, the use of the past and specific rituals that are considered religious in origin but can be altered to suit the needs of the participants. In an article Botros discusses how the Copts in diaspora in North America use their history to establish their identity and the authenticity of the Christianity of the Coptic Church.[40] Botros argues that the specific aspects of their historical narrative that they stress are their relationship with the pharaohs, their monastic past, and the Church's role in the early ecumenical councils during the fourth and fifth centuries.[41] During my fieldwork I came across references to the Copts as the "Children of the Pharaohs" only in literature written by Copts for other Copts.[42] However, I also observed frequent reminders about the Church's long history of monasticism and about the events at the Council of Chalcedon in 451 A.D.

The Coptic Church in the GTA also uses its apostolic roots as a means to prove its authenticity as a Christian church. First, Copts emphasize that their church was founded by Saint Mark. Therefore, their beliefs, practices, and rituals are directly descended from the teachings of an apostle. On more than one occasion I have been told that the rituals of the Coptic Orthodox Church have gone unaltered for two thousand years, which means that, compared to other denominations, it is a more authentic representation of the character of the early Christian churches.[43] When a Coptic layperson asks a priest for advice on how to deal with or react to different situations in her life, the priest almost always responds with the suggestion that the individual turn to the teachings and life experiences of the prophets, apostles, saints, and martyrs.

The reading of the *Agpeya* at the beginning of every meeting for university graduates is a good example of the Coptic community's (re)established or continued relationship with the apostolic church. The *Agpeya* is a prayer book that contains the seven canonical prayers, each read at a different hour of the day with corresponding readings from Psalms and the Gospels. The Coptic Orthodox Church traces the origin of the *Agpeya* to Saint Mark. During the different student group meetings that I attended, reading the *Agpeya* usually took twenty to thirty minutes, and it was always accompanied by the singing of hymns. At one church the hymns were always sung in English, whereas at another church, with a smaller number of people in attendance, all of them ethnically Egyptian, most hymns were sung in Arabic.

Articulating and defining the "authentic" nature of the Coptic Orthodox Church is one strategy used by the Coptic diaspora in the GTA in an attempt to missionize and convert non-Copts and non-Egyptians. A third strategy was officially inaugurated on December 15, 2007, with the establishment of Father Peter's new church. In November 2007 Father Peter met with Pope Shenouda and was granted the blessing of the Church hierarchy to found a new Coptic church in the GTA.[44] Father Peter emphasizes the possibilities and spiritual opportunities that the Coptic Orthodox Church can provide for non-Egyptians and views the future of the Coptic Church in the GTA as one that must include non-Egyptians. He is trying to establish a future church like the one predicted by van Dijk and Botros by creating a new Coptic church for Egyptians and non-Egyptians alike. The goal of the new church is to emphasize the religious identity of the Coptic Orthodox Church in an attempt to minimize the ethnic identity of the Church. Father Peter's goal is to introduce the larger Canadian society to Coptic Orthodox Christianity.

The Beliefs, Practices, and Strategies of Coptic Converts

Conversion is an ongoing, ever-evolving process that rarely includes a complete break from a convert's past life. At the beginning of the conversion process the convert must interpret and translate the new beliefs and practices through the prism of his or her old life. Therefore, individual agency and the history and structure of a group must be analyzed to determine a comprehensive understanding of why individuals convert and the changes that occur after conversion.[45]

There are three types of converts in the Coptic community in the GTA. The majority of the converts are Christian to begin with and have been introduced to the Coptic Orthodox Church through their potential spouses. However, some converts have come into contact with the beliefs and practices of the Coptic Church through friends or simply by accident. The third type of convert is Father Peter's dream for the future of the Coptic Church in the GTA, an individual who becomes familiar with the Orthodox beliefs of the Church through the proselytizing of its members.

Angela, a potential convert, is an example of the second category of converts:"I met a bunch of girls and became friends with them and they said that I should come to this Thursday meeting. So I went and I really, really liked it! When I first started going I loved reading the *Agpeya* and I felt a real reverence for God there. I would take notes and I was so eager and it could be that I was in a different place then, spiritually I was in a better place. It was just feeding me." Angela's introduction to the Coptic Church came by accident; however, one significant aspect of her statement is the mention of the *Agpeya*. It seems that the authenticating strategies of the Coptic Orthodox Church have worked in the case of Angela who feels "reverence for God" when she prays from a book of prayers that was established during the Apostolic Age. At the time of my fieldwork Angela had yet to decide if she would convert and be rebaptized in the Coptic Church; however, she was heavily involved in certain church activities.

Another convert, Marcus, also seems to have been drawn to the Coptic Orthodox Church because of its ongoing relationship with its past. He says,

> The amazing thing about the Church is that within the Orthodox churches you can find people with the same spiritual zeal as in the Bible. When-

ever people lost hope in the Bible, they always looked to the Prophets. We have Father Matery who is an exorcist. You can watch exorcisms on the Internet. Not everyone would want to see that. He also heals people. We have Father Fanous of whom it is said that he flies. He's a hermit. People see him in California when he is supposed to be in Egypt. For instance, the Protestants have no example of that, like the people in the Bible. When I was very young, I would read the Bible and I couldn't match it with the people in the Church. The people dress up in a jacket and tie. Show me a Moses, someone who is carrying on the tradition of the Bible. Show me a John the Baptist.

Marcus feels that the Coptic saints, martyrs, and miracles make the Coptic Orthodox Church more authentic than other Christian denominations because Copts are presented with a vision of the original Christian Church when the apostles were alive. Angela, like Marcus, has adopted certain aspects of the Coptic worldview. However, this adoption process takes time and during that time converts will try to reconcile their new worldview with the way that they live their lives and remember their past. For example, when Angela describes the veneration of saints by most Copts, she uses an example from her past experience with another Christian denomination. She says, "I'm starting to understand the reverence for their saints is just kind of like using them as examples. So if I rationalize it, it's sort of like following Billy Graham."

Not all of the converts are happy with the present Coptic worldview. Beth believes that the Coptic Church still focuses too much on its Egyptian heritage and ethnic identity. She argues,

I have heard so many sermons in the past about your Mother Church in Egypt, you are Egyptian, you are a part of Egypt, don't forget Egypt! They promote Egypt with so much pride. What is Egypt? I still have the same attitude about Canada. What is Canada? We're supposed to be Christians! Culture shouldn't play that heavy a part, but, unfortunately, it does for the Egyptian people, but I think that it's for protection as well. A cocoon! But they should not do that. When you live in a country like Canada you should be able to become Canadian and not be ashamed of it. There's a lot of history in Egypt and I respect that history.

However, she does praise the efforts of Father Peter: "I pray that God will choose others like Father Peter who has the courage and the strength to reach out and have the lack of prejudice to embrace other nationalities and cultures. I know that he's in a dangerous position because a lot of people are still ethnic in the hierarchy and give him a hard time."

A difference between the experience and opinions of Beth and those of Angela and Marcus is due, in part, to their differing motivations for conversion. Beth converted in order to marry her husband, while Angela and Marcus are not dating, engaged to, or planning to marry a Copt. Their conversions occurred because they adopted a new worldview and ethos based upon the Coptic model. Beth, in contrast, has respect for the Coptic Church, but still retains parts of the Protestant worldview she grew up with. Beth has also adopted a strategy to deal with what she feels is the ethnocentric nature of the Coptic Orthodox Church. She attends another non-Coptic church in the GTA that she feels is more multicultural. She explains that at this church, "You don't have the prejudices of an ethnic church." At the same time she is still involved with different committees at Father Peter's Coptic church.

Conclusion

The Coptic diaspora in the GTA is attempting to survive in the religiously and culturally diverse Canadian society through the implementation and execution of three strategies that include the separation of their religious identity from their Egyptian ethnic identity, the establishment of an "authentic" Christian identity based on their apostolic roots, and the founding of a new Coptic church in the GTA that recognizes and assumes that its survival depends on the inclusion of non-Egyptians as members of its community. Most non-Egyptians who choose to convert to Coptic Orthodoxy are already familiar with the beliefs and practices shared by most Christians. Their conversion is a means to an end, in the sense that it allows them to marry a Copt within the Coptic Orthodox Church. Therefore, many of the converts do not cut ties with their families or former religious communities. Instead, they choose aspects of the Coptic Orthodox Church to which they relate and participate in the activities of small groups within the larger Coptic community.

BELONGING TO THE CHURCH COMMUNITY
From Childhood Years Onward

Nora Stene

On November 4, 2012, in Saint Mark's Cathedral in Cairo an altar-lot was to reveal the name of the 118th patriarch of the Coptic Orthodox Church. A chalice contained the names of three nominees. Blindfolded, six-year-old Bishoy Girgis Masaad picked the piece of paper with the name of the one to lead the Church.

The pictures of Bishoy drew a lot of attention from international media, but, as might be expected, without any in-depth analysis of why a child was included in the practice of the altar-lot. In the field of Coptic studies the historical and political contexts of the election procedures have been studied, but, apart from mentioning that the child is believed to be "ignorant of sin,"[1] a wider framework for the understanding of children in the Coptic Orthodox Church has not been explored. Therefore, is it not timely that we give children our attention, especially when it comes to questions of identity?

This essay considers how perceptions of age are central to the Coptic tradition and asks what consequences these perceptions might have. Can the altar-lot be seen as an example of the Coptic notion of the child being celebrated? And to broaden the picture: what other roles with corresponding rights and duties are Coptic children given? Academic research exploring the question of religious identity will benefit from looking more closely at how Coptic children learn to embody their identity as Church members from childhood years onward. Important questions include how do Coptic children take part in the hallowed tradition of the Church? Linking identity to the term *belonging*, how is their belonging created and recreated? As the anthropologist Anthony Cohen has pointed out, "belonging implies very much more than being born [into a group]. It suggests that one is an integral part of that marvelously complicated fabric which constitutes the community; that one is the recipient of its proudly distinctive and consciously preserved culture—a repository of its traditions and values; a performer of its hallowed skills, an expert in its idioms and idiosyncrasies."[2] Studying children's belonging can be linked to what has become known as the new social studies of childhood. A short introduction to this field is in order.

An Emerging Paradigm for Childhood Studies

Since the 1980s researchers have challenged established ideas about children and childhood. Within the social sciences, publications by Chris Jenks, Allison James and Alan Prout, and Leena Alanen[3] all underline the narrow perspectives in previous research that both restricted theoretical discussions and limited the collection of new research material. Such research had seen children as "unfinished" human beings and addressed only "stages" by which they became mature adults. Researchers had taken a keen interest in socialization processes, but the social significance of childhood still lay in adult life, where the result of childhood socialization could be observed, often in the form of established identities. However, following the growing interest in gender and minority studies, more childhood researchers began to use the methods of interpretive sociology and social anthropology. A starting point was to see social life as continuously created and recreated by social actors.[4] Researchers have emphasized that children should also be seen as social actors, as active participants and competent interpreters of the world they live in. It has been stressed that children negotiate with their environments, "within the structural constraints of childhood in relation to more powerful, adult, social actors."[5]

When Samantha Punch points to "the structural constraints of childhood," she accentuates the second main premise for the new social studies of childhood, that is, childhood seen as a social and cultural construct. Within this framework what might appear to be "natural" (that is, what childhood "is") is rather seen as images (that is, images of childhood). To the childhood researcher these images are cultural constructions of social and biological relations, and they are understood in relation to their historical and cultural context.

In this essay the perspective of seeing children as social actors is combined with a discussion of constructions of childhood through an examination of how Coptic girls and boys take part in religious traditions.[6] Based on fieldwork material I have chosen to investigate children's participation in the sacramental life of the Coptic Orthodox Church. This participation is shaped by how childhood in general is viewed by Copts. It is important for researchers to see children as people important in their own right and also to look at the context they live in, that is, at childhood as culturally defined. Being a Copt is not postponed until the mature years. Children and adults share their belonging to the Church, and the roles of children and adults are interconnected. Moreover, what appear to be activities directed solely at the needs of children are closely connected to the needs of adults. In other words religious instruction is a place where generations meet and where the religious identities of both groups are strengthened.

Methodological Approach

My first fieldwork project took place in Cairo and the second took place in London.[7] Both projects lasted close to ten months. In both locations I focused on children from four to twelve years of age. I spent my time in Cairo among mostly low-income families in a densely populated part of town, while in London a substantial number of the migrant families I worked with were middle class. I found many similarities between the two groups when it came to how children took part in church life. It is these patterns of similarity that are highlighted here, and the focus is on continuity between Egypt and the diaspora.

In both fieldworks I used a local Coptic church as my starting point, using the method of participant observation. The arenas I had access to were the churches,[8] homes of families, and places where I accompanied families in their spare time. This included visiting several other Coptic churches in Egypt and Great Britain. This method of fieldwork makes the number of Church members I had contact with hard to estimate, but approximately two hundred children ages four to twelve came regularly to each of the local churches I had as my base.

My primary language of communication was Arabic in Cairo and English in London. I used an approach of informal small talk and unstructured interviews, where I usually left the initiative of raising topics to the informants, following up with questions whenever natural. The aim of this method is to be led by the informants and thereby learn about their worldview. For my London fieldwork I was also inspired by an interview guide in a previous study of children in religious groups.[9] I found some questions especially useful. For example, to start talking about Sunday schools I often asked "How do weekends differ from weekdays in your family?" To talk about religious practice I asked, "Are there special things Christian children should do?" Answers were not recorded, but I made notes as soon as possible. These notes encompass quotations from children. Some of them are included here, in English or translated from Arabic. Names of the children are changed in order to protect their identities, but gender and age are kept in line with general guidelines for childhood studies.

Studying Children in the Coptic Orthodox Church

Often overlooked by outsiders, one of the striking features of the Coptic Orthodox Church is the degree to which children are seen as natural participants in its sacramental life. Several studies of the sacraments as religious practice have already been carried out.[10] However, these studies are focused on adults. My questions are: In what ways do children participate? Is there a pattern of difference between boys and girls? And how do children themselves talk about their participation? In this text, I will give special attention to the role of children in the Eucharistic liturgy. The next section features empirical data and statements from the children as an introduction to the following discussion.

Children and the Seven Sacraments

According to the Church, Christian life starts with baptism. Nonbaptized children are outside the fellowship of the Church. Their families consider them vulnerable and in need of the sacraments. The first of these are baptism and anointment with holy oil (*mairoun*). From a theological point of view they are from that day onward Church members and Christians on their way to sanctification (*theosis*).[11] Children may not explain this in theological terms, but most will stress the importance of these initiation rituals. Peter, age eleven: Baptism "is very important. It washes the baby clean, and makes him strong. Everybody does it"; Botros, age eight: "He is made strong by the *mairoun,* you know, signed with a cross on every part of the body, 36 times!"; Angel, age seven: "We baptize children, then they can get an angel to protect them and can receive Holy Communion." If several children are brought to baptism on the same day, boys are always baptized before girls. Most children accept this as the way of the Church, but some girls objected. Katreen, age twelve: "Maybe *abuna* [the priest] should do it by age, the oldest first. Then the girls would be first!"[12]

From baptism onward all children receive, as Angel stated, the most holy substance of the Church, that is, the Eucharist. Even if all take part, again the pattern of male precedence is repeated. Both gender groups are of mixed ages. The Eucharist is seen as the most important spiritual nourishment needed to go through life. Murqus, age ten, expressed this in a dramatic way: "With the *minawla* [Eucharist] we are cleaned in our bodies. Without it we would be condemned to hell!"

Murqus had also learned that most Christians stray from the path of God. The sacrament of confession is therefore offered to restore the relationship between God and believer. Even small children may receive this sacrament, although usually they start at a later age. The sacrament consists of confessing to a priest, then receiving his blessing and absolution. Usually this takes place at the beginning of the liturgy. Rebecca, age twelve: "I feel 'forgivenish' at the end, like your sins *have* been forgiven, when *abuna* puts his cross on your head and says something, . . . I don't know what. You feel O.K. afterwards." Problems do arise, however. Marianne, age eight: "I go maybe every two months. I just started that. It's quite good; except the priest takes ages with the adults and when it's your turn he says 'sorry' and then I have to come back next week. . . . Maybe the adults have more problems, but I would like a [another] system."

On a regular basis and at least once a year, the whole congregation may also participate in the sacrament of the anointing of the sick. This sacrament is used as a prophylactic. Again the pattern of male before female is repeated, and there is participation of mixed age groups. Nayer, age seven: "I get anointed with holy oil by the priest in case I will get ill. So I am a bit strong in advance."

The sacrament of matrimony is meant to organize the congregations into stable families. The family is presented as a safe environment for children. In this "small church"[13] children come to know the ways of Coptic faith and practice. Children are generally enthusiastic about weddings, especially when this involves the handing out of sweets. Weddings confirm children's place within their community, as they come to watch and take part in the celebrations of the sacrament.

The seventh sacrament is that of the ordination to the priesthood. This sacrament makes sure that men (women are excluded) are chosen to lead the Church and make the necessary sacraments available to its members. However, in this work priests must have aides. These aides are called *shamamsa* (deacons), and they have particular roles and privileges. The deaconate has five formal degrees, and boys from the age of approximately five years of age may be chosen for the lowest degrees.[14] Whatever the degree, the status of the *shamamsa* can hardly be overestimated in a Church setting. For child-deacons being a *shamas* means intensified ritual participation. Philopos, age nine: "I wear a white *tunya*, stand up at the platform in front of the *haikal* (altar room) and sing; sometimes I get chosen to be with the priest inside the *haikal*." The setting to which Philopos refers is the Eucharistic liturgy.

Children and the Celebration of the Eucharistic Liturgy

Celebrating the Eucharistic liturgy starts before one enters the church, as fasting prepares one to approach the divine sphere. This means that the believers cannot eat or drink for a certain number of hours before receiving the Eucharist.[15] Even young children fast. The practice is supposed to be introduced gradually and varies greatly from family to family. The following quotations are from London and show differences in both children's understanding and family practice. Mira, age seven: "We don't eat Sunday morning. It's difficult. If I eat, I'm not allowed Communion." Rifat, age ten: "I have breakfast Sundays, but I'm not allowed to eat in church before Communion." Peter, age eleven: "I never fast, except Sundays." Mina, age six: "I fast every Sunday. I get a cup of milk [before going to church], but I am still starving!"

Coptic children are also taught the habit of food abstinence in the form of vegetarian or vegan diets in several periods throughout the liturgical year.[16] These periods are supposed to be accompanied by intensified religious practices. The Church has no rules concerning how children should abstain from certain kinds of food, generally leaving the question for parents or children themselves to decide.[17] What I observed when it came to changing diet was a spectrum of observance within each family. The children I knew all fasted to some degree, some less, some at times more than their parents. This is how Sophie living in London (age eight) described Lent: "Sometimes my Mum makes me fast if it is Lent, normally one week and Good Friday and some important days. Mina [younger brother] doesn't fast. When we fast we don't eat meat or margarine or cheese or anything from animals."

Conversation between adults and children could at times show how knowledge of fasting was a part of the children's vocabulary of what it means to be a Copt, as demonstrated in field notes from Cairo:

> Local priest: "What does fasting mean?" Group of children, ages six to nine:
> "We won't eat *fitary* [nonfasting food]."
> "We won't eat anything that had a spirit in it."
> "We won't have *samna* [butter], only oil."
> "We won't do wrong things, we must not steal, lie, beat someone or swear."
> Priest: "But are we not also supposed to do good things during the fast?"
> Children: "Yes, to pray!"; "To go to confession and have the *minawla*"; "To do our homework."
> Priest: "Right, Christian boys and girls will do their homework, right? Now, who will fast?"
> All children raise their hand.

Children sometimes use fasting practice to distinguish their own church from other churches. For example, in London seven-year-old Angel observed that "Those who go to an English [non-Coptic] Church can have breakfast [on Sundays]. And other times . . . no difference with food for them [that is, no periods with a different diet]. Even before Easter they just eat what they like, . . . I think."

Fasting children have through experience been taught about the ascetic tradition of their Church. The most Holy is offered to the believers, but in order to receive, it is necessary to "strive." Striving (*yit'ab*) means fasting and praying, but also taking part in a liturgy that lasts almost three hours during which adults, as well as children, stand upright most of the time. In this way they may show their commitment to the Church. However, according to my observations of children taking part in liturgies, it was clear that great leeway was given to children. Young children might eat in church, shortening their Eucharist fast. It was also common for children to wander in and out of the church during the long service. All adults were expected to show tolerance for babies crying and children walking about, making all-age participation clearly visible.

Inside the main church room there was a gender aspect to how children used the church; the male congregation members prayed to the left side, female members to the right. Apart from babies, children usually followed this division: the older they were, the less often they would cross gender lines. But whether boys or girls, in all churches I visited I observed that children were given positive attention by adults, heads were patted, cheeks touched, and questions asked. An adult not relating to a child nearby was the exception rather than the norm. The very young were met with lots of attention, often expressed as joyous admiration. We will return to this point below.

In the beginning of the liturgy some children lined up with others in order to confess. Again all-age participation was clearly visible. At the same time children did not always succeed in their endeavor. Some adults, often men of a certain social standing, would walk straight to the front of the queue. Children and others had to wait behind, sometimes never making it to the priest before he started his liturgical duties.

For children the liturgy was often a time to meet other children and to play. The churches usually had many rooms that made this possible. Only those who made too much noise were reprimanded. In my conversations with children about what attending the liturgy was like, this balance of limits and freedom was evident. From London, Mina, age six: "You can play during the Mass outside the main church, but it must be quiet. After Mass, you can be as noisy as you like!" Joanne, age eight: "You must behave well and not shout. But you are allowed to play." Irene, age eleven: "You are not allowed to scream and shout and throw wrappers; you must be quiet." Freedom of movement, however, did not apply to the child deacons. Their place was close to the altar, helping the priests. However, child deacons did not necessarily act as *shamamsa* every week. If they did not serve, they usually joined other children in the church.

Girls never had liturgical duties like the *shamamsa*, but some of them were in charge of ongoing socialization of the young by teaching them the ways of the church, including prayers and actions like *mataniyat* (prostrations). Girls also often kept the church room tidy; tidying candles and carrying glasses of water consumed after the Eucharist to the kitchen. For these activities girls were praised and called *banat al-baraka* (girls of blessing).

Toward the end of the liturgy the atmosphere in the church intensified. Children came inside and all present crammed into the side *haikals* where they would receive the Eucharist. The main *haikal* is the part of the church where the altar is situated. It is a section mainly reserved for the priest and the deacons. Women and girls beyond puberty are never allowed to enter.

Receiving the Eucharist with others of the same gender is the norm, but I observed that small boys often stayed with their mothers. Older boys, however, never walked over to receive with the women. The male members of the congregations entered the side *haikal* and then filed into the main *haikal* where they walked around the altar and received the consecrated bread and wine. When all male members had received, the priest moved to the side where female members pushed forward toward the Eucharist window. The pushing and shoving may be due to the architectural structure of the church room and the rule that no women are allowed into the main *haikal*. But another reason may also be at work. When I talked to women about this matter no one complained about the crowded room, but rather they pointed out that they all pushed to the front because they were eager to receive the holy substances. Pushing was a part of showing religious eagerness. Children, however, being small, could find the crowdedness challenging. This sentiment was especially expressed by girls, but it might also be a case for boys: Michael, age twelve: "My uncle says we should go for Communion early.... Then there's a long wait [inside the side-*haikal*]. Mum lets me go in later. Because it is really crowded and difficult to breathe. All those people on all sides. Like right here." (He moves his hands in front of his face.)

Michael found the crowd of men to be a problem. However, a handful of girls saw the "men's side" to be less of a trial than the "the women's side" and joined the boys when receiving Communion. Still, most of the girls kept up the traditions of gender separation. Sandra, age seven: "It's good to have a women's side and a men's side, 'cause ... I just think it is good"; Jessica, age eight: "I like it the way it is, to be with the others [other girls and women]."

After the Eucharist had been handed out, the priest walked down the aisle sprinkling blessed water on the congregation. Children ran after him, shouting loud when the water hit them. Returning to the altar the priest drew the curtain that hid the *haikal* from view. The formal liturgy was over.

Spending the Day in Church

Historians of religion analyze rituals in a wide context. A part of this is looking at both the fast and the feast.[18] This perspective is useful when it comes to a ritual like the Coptic Eucharistic liturgy. It has fasting as preparation and a long liturgical introduction to be followed by an intense climax: the moment of the Eucharist. The feast continues, however. After the liturgy the congregation gathers together.

Almost all line up for the handing out of "blessed bread" (that is, bread baked in the church and blessed by the priest but not chosen to become the body of Christ.) Meals are served and the kiosk opens for the sale of candy and magazines. While all of this is happening, children move about between friends and relatives. Still acting within boundaries of "good behavior," children may be observed dancing and jumping among eating and talking adults. On rare occasions I also saw younger children making use of a privilege most adults do not have; children may move around freely inside a church, including entering the main *haikal*. At times some who wanted to sit and talk quietly passed behind the curtain to sit on the floor of the *haikal*. I observed this kind of behavior by both girls and boys in Cairo and London.

The day spent in church continued with Sunday school classes for all the children. The children knew their teachers well and in London used family terms like *aunty* and *uncle* when they talked to or about them. In Cairo the children used terms taken from a school context such as *ustaz* (teacher) and *Miss*. The classes were sometimes noisy, but although teachers at times complained about this, none of the children did. On the contrary, the children appeared to enjoy the relaxed and friendly atmosphere. There were exceptions to this; some teachers were stricter than others and some children had objections to how things were organized. In spite of this I believe it is fair to say that to most children Sunday school was a "room of their own." The adults provided the frame; they were the leading agents, but the children were active participants. They were, among other things, one another's peers and fellow pupils. Except the youngest and oldest, who attended gender-mixed classes in Cairo, they were all in same-age, same-gender groups. The most active children used the classes as a place where they could show their abilities and where they could ask questions of religious nature. Some children were more quiet; others defied the teachers to some degree, but for all of the children Sunday school was, at least for the time being, a place where they were drawn into the community. It was an arena where all efforts were made to strengthen their belonging to the Church.

Sunday school classes were followed by meetings for adults, and all together the day spent in church lasted for many families from about nine in the morning until three or four in the afternoon. Many children spoke to me about these days and complained about the liturgy being long and that they got tired from fasting and standing up to pray. No one, however, complained about the amount of time spent in the church. This was rather referred to as "when we have Communion," "when I meet my friends," and "when we have fun." The days spent in church seemed to be days during which intensified religious life coincided with intensified social life.

Analyzing the Empirical Data

How might we analyze children's participation in the Coptic Church? We have seen how children gradually obtain ritual competence. By doing this children take part in the continuous recreation of their community. The children's participation makes them become active Church members in their own right. Both in their own eyes and in the eyes of adults they are seen to involve themselves with the faith of the Church, as expressed in general involvement and in ritual action. Using the terminology of the new social studies of childhood, they may be seen as both religious and social actors.

When children are actors in a church setting, they interact with adults. The examples given here have shown only a few of these interactions. They speak of a high degree of all-age participation and equality among Church members. At the same time it also happens that children are pushed aside when facing adults; adults take more space. The idea of being equal does therefore not always fall out in children's favor. Another part of the children's skills as Copts is, as shown by the data, knowledge of gender divisions and of the male precedence. Consequently, children adjust the idea of equality of all believers to ideas of gender distinctions.

As religious and social actors Coptic children relate to the idea of continuity, not change, within the Church. The Church wants continuity and children's ongoing participation is a necessary part of this. Verbally, children often defended the ways of the Church and underlined that they did not call for change. Still, when talking to me several children expressed that they wanted things to "change a little" or be "made so that it is easier for kids." Girls talked about gender divisions and called for "more fair systems." None of the girls expressed that she wanted radical changes, like becoming a *shamas* or priest herself. The girls' wishes were in the direction of having a different system for confessions and the possibility to receive the Eucharist under less-crowded circumstances. However, in London both girls and boys had called for language change during the liturgy, with some success. Already in the 1990s there was an increased use of English. In this field children seemed to be leading the way, followed by adults who agreed that a combination of Coptic, Arabic, and English worked well during the liturgies. This was however never referred to as a "change" but rather as a necessary adaptation.[19]

In presenting how children partake of the sacraments of the Coptic Orthodox Church my aim has been to make this part of the religious world of Coptic children visible, as it increases our understanding of the Coptic identity. It may also point out how belonging to the Church is continuously recreated as ritual participation takes place. However, it is necessary to look further and ask which ideas about the phase of childhood have the power to shape children's participation within the Church today. How can observations of Coptic children in a church setting be analyzed in the light of childhood understood as a social and cultural construction? These questions can be related to the teachings of the Church, as well as to the social practices and hierarchies between Church members.

Construction of Childhood

In the teachings of the Church the equality of all baptized is stressed. Baptized children are acknowledged as Church members on the same level as adults.[20] As we have noted, this means that the other sacraments of the Church are given to them.[21] The theology here stresses that, as long as the initiation of baptism has created the important bond to the Church, all ages are equal when facing the divine.

When it comes to liturgical life this idea of equality is expressed by the prominent Egyptian priest Tadros Malaty in the following way: "The church does not exclude children during the liturgy, and this is one of the resources of our church; . . . the child feels his positive membership and acknowledges his right in participating in church liturgies. The beautiful rite and heavenly hymns encourage children in worship without feeling bored, in spite of the lengthy services. . . . Children partake . . . especially of the liturgy of the Eucharist. . . . They are not isolated in a special place outside the nave; . . . this attaches the child to church worship, so that they may feel that the church appreciates their membership."[22] A consequence of placing children alongside adults is, in other words, that children are included, and also that usually no special arrangements are made for them during the liturgy. The liturgy of the Eucharist is important to all, and all are expected to take part according to ability.

The term *potential religiosity* has been used to describe the ways children act out their religious belonging.[23] The term suggests that children's religiosity may manifest itself only occasionally and under certain conditions. However, when it comes to discussing my empirical data on Coptic children, I do not find the term *potential religiosity* to be useful. In my material children's religious life could rather be characterized as one of being active alongside adults. I interpret this in the light of the Church's recognition of children as Church members equal to adults and from the understanding that there is nothing *potential* about the children's religiosity.

The idea of equality among believers is common to most Christian churches. However, sacramental practices differ: some denominations postpone baptism until the "age of conscious faith" (often early adulthood); the Roman-Catholic Church has First Communion at the "age of reason" (often age eight or nine); and several Churches celebrate confirmation in the teenage years. The Orthodox churches (both Oriental and Eastern), in contrast, do not postpone giving children these sacraments. Talking to adult Copts, I often heard criticism of other denominations because of what was perceived as their restrictive attitude toward children. Both in Cairo and London children's full participation in ritual life was taken as the natural way of organizing a church. Childhood should be a period for receiving grace through the sacraments. Among children, I met the same attitude. Few expressed this in theological terms, but all seemed to agree that they belonged and that age was no reason to bar someone from what was referred to as the blessings of the Church.

Child participation alongside adults may furthermore be analyzed in light of family patterns. Such patterns often stress that children should imitate the actions of older relatives. The Coptic children I knew often talked about church life as being with their family. To most children the family was the frame of their church experience. They belonged to the Church, because the whole family did. Several studies from the Middle East discuss the position of children within the family unit.[24] These studies all maintain that children are understood to belong to their parents. My fieldwork highlights the notion that Church tradition parallels the image of childhood as a period spent with the family. The family is upheld as the unit where the child naturally takes part. Researchers have also argued that being a minority, Copts put a special emphasis on tight family bonds.[25] This creates a cultural construction of childhood according to which children are merged with the family unit. In other words, although researchers such as Leena Alanen and Berry Mayall have warned against seeing children as family members only,[26] the context of the family unit should not be disregarded. On the contrary, in some instances the family setting may be crucial to understanding ongoing social and ritual practice.

However, further clarification needs to be made: within the family there is a clear hierarchy that places children below adults. Childhood is a phase in life in which one should know one's place and act accordingly. A social construction of childhood that stresses subordination is evident in the manner in which boys and girls are expected to show acceptance of the rules of the older generations; and at the moment of the Eucharist, children usually have to wait behind larger and more powerful adults who (in what was conceived to be a pious way) pushed their way forward. These forms of social practice make it possible to speak of a construction of childhood according to which the subordination of children is accepted as the norm. This norm runs alongside ideas of equality.

From a third angle, however, childhood according to a Coptic world view may also be seen as a stage that places children above adults. Their high status is reflected when they are allowed to receive the Eucharist without abstinence and in the tradition of using boys as *shamamsa*, or deacons. For certain tasks a very young *shammas* is even preferred. As we have seen, this preference is evident in the exceptional case of choosing a new patriarch of the Church. After a long process during which adults (lay and clergy) shorten a list of nominees, the final stage is left to divine intervention. The Church prays for guidance by the Holy Spirit, and a young child is chosen to be the one to act as the agent of the intervention.[27]

In short, Coptic children have certain privileges in a church setting. In addition they are usually allowed freedom to move around, often embraced with signs of affection, and met with admiration by adults. It must be asked, why are they admired? Here we need to pay attention to the way adult Copts usually consider children and childhood. During my fieldwork I asked adults what ideas they had about children. They often answered with references to children as "God's blessing upon a marriage," "those who do not sin," or "those who have simplicity of faith." The word most often used, however, especially about the youngest, was *malaika*, or angel. This term was elaborated in statements describing a child before puberty as innocent, pure, and closer to God than adults. It is important to note that the term carries connotations that are different from those it might have in a Western context. Among others, Jeanette Sky and Allison James[28] have discussed how idealization of childhood in the West is often linked to sentimentality. Angel-like children are presented as living in a world of fantasy, often apart from the world of adults. They are sweet, beautiful, admired, and in need of protection. As James writes, "children's bodies become confined in designated safe, but peripheral spaces:

schools, playgroups, playgrounds [and] paddling pools."[29] In a Coptic context children are also believed to be in need of protection, but the term *angel* does not refer to their sweetness. It refers to their ritual purity because of their perceived nearness to God. It also refers to the idea that prepubescent children are persons without sexual desires. Ritual purity is important to grasp in order to understand the privileges of children in the Church.

In her study of Coptic women the historian of religion Berit Thorbjørnsrud has shown how sexual desires and the "open" bodies of adults are seen as problematic within a Church context. To link the possible holiness of humankind with sex and the discharge of bodily fluids is seen as especially difficult.[30] These signs of adulthood limit partaking in the liturgies of the Church. Children, in contrast, are seen as outside of the defiling zone of sexual desire. With some exceptions, they are always welcome to receive the Eucharist.[31]

The local priests I interviewed all stressed that it is the teachings of the Church that give children certain privileges. Like other Orthodox churches, the Coptic Church teaches that original sin does not attach guilt to humans, even though the fall of Adam and Eve brought death into the world. Like Adam and Eve, human beings sin when they disobey God. When they are aware of right and wrong, children also sin, but only in what the priests called "minor ways." Children are neither believed by the Church to have overcome sin as the saints have nor to have been tainted by it like adults. In other words, childhood is seen as a state of virginity, near the divine world. In summary, Coptic constructions of childhood have many facets, all playing a part in Church life. These constructions may be thought of as three hierarchies.

Hierarchies of Childhood

A hierarchy that distinguishes between the baptized and the non–baptized: This hierarchy stresses the equality of all baptized and places children alongside adults. A family structure according to which all are supposed to take part in church activities together strengthens the idea of equality. Gender aspects, however, often give male members priority and privileges when it comes to actual church practice.

A social hierarchy related to age and position within the family: This hierarchy places children, both boys and girls, within the family unit below parents and adult caretakers. In local churches the same system is at work. The ideal is that all children should subordinate themselves and behave within the limits set by the older generation.

A hierarchy based on ideas about purity: This hierarchy positions human beings in varying degrees of closeness to the divine. The highest degree is assigned to sanctified saints, but children before puberty are ranked above all other adults, because they are considered to be "like angels"—pure, innocent, and asexual. The child's gender is of no importance in this regard.

These hierarchies related to childhood are abstractions. Therefore, how do the categories look like to an inside participant? The "new social studies of childhood" teaches us the importance of also talking with children when we study questions of group identity. It is therefore natural to ask: Do Coptic children see themselves as alongside adult Church members, below them, or above them?

Children on the topic of constructions of childhood

When I asked children how they saw themselves within a church setting I naturally received different answers. However, it was clear that to the children the idea of being a Church member alongside adults was a natural one. It was an idea they did not question. In Cairo the children I knew were not familiar with other churches, but in London several children pointed out differences between "their Church" and other denominations. They were skeptical to any child restriction when it came to the sacraments, and they emphasized the opportunity the liturgy gave them to play while in church. I have mentioned that girls at times complained that they could not do all the things boys could do, but they still insisted that they took part. Mary, age eleven: "We take part, just like the adults."

Nevertheless, children were well aware of the ideal of child obedience. Some seemed to have internalized this ideal and some rebelled. At times child obedience was linked to everything they saw as unfair in the church, be it adult preference or strict parenting. Children, both in Cairo and in London, were clearly aware of the social hierarchy that gave them a subordinate position. Rifat, age nine: "In church and at home, it is children second."

The topic of children's closeness to God was the area in which I found most divergence between adults and children. All the children with whom I had contact were familiar with the term *angel* used about young ones. Even so, no one used the expression to describe him- or herself, their peers, or older children. Answering my question about what it means that children are angels, James, age five, suggested that "they call us angels, and our [Sunday school] class 'angel-class'. Maybe at the Christmas play we will be angels?" Children did use the term to describe younger children, "those who wouldn't know if they did something wrong" (Mira, age nine) and "those who are like God's gift" (Sherif, age seven). In other words the adults' general classification of purity before puberty was not reflected in how the children talked about themselves. Children did not seem to draw the line at puberty. Still, the idea of a stage of purity was present among them, although always linked to a younger age group than the one in which they placed themselves. This might be because the children had internalized the ideals of humility; you do not talk about yourself as an angel. However, the fact that children did not use the term about their peers or older children could suggest that they make use of sets of classifications other than those used by adults. Whereas adults join all children before puberty together in one group, children construct childhood as a series of phases, with "younger children" clearly distinguished from themselves. About themselves they want to stress their own age as a sign of maturity, having left earlier phases behind. This way of classification was clearly of importance to children, overruling the potential high status they all could claim because of their before-puberty stage. In their eyes different ages mattered more.

Linking Children and Adults

As a Christian minority in Muslim surroundings, Copts do not engage in missionary activities. The active participation of the children has therefore become vital to the continuation of the Church. This may be the reason why both children's liturgical participation and organized Sunday schools (*madaris al-ahad*) have increasingly become part of church life. Local religious nurture has grown into large-scale religious education programs. Previous research about Coptic Christians has pointed out the immense importance of the Sunday School Movement.[32] Scholarship has not addressed how the Sunday school arena has given both adults and children important roles to play, thereby strengthening a common religious identity.

From the adults' point of view, the children are the raison d'être of the Sunday school. The teachers stressed that children need to be taught, and they need to spend time together in the atmosphere of the Church. Even if the youngest have a closeness to God that adults lack, as they grow in age it is important that they receive the right mix of instruction about expected moral behavior and correct religious practice, as well as about the teachings of the Church. This should not be done in a strict way, but in a way that will please the children and make them want to attend classes. Adults should be aware of children's needs, social as well as religious, and try to meet them.[33]

These perceived needs give children a position in the local churches. They are given the role of receiving religious instruction. Such a role is easily recognizable in other religious groups as well.[34] In studying the role of the pupils we need also to look at how adults create activities for pupils in relation to the adults' own needs. In looking at the interwoven roles of adults and children we see that children are not only pupils waiting for their lessons; they are also people adults want to teach and care for.

During my fieldwork I observed that the role of the Sunday school teacher was greatly valued within the local congregations. None of the teachers would brag about fulfilling the role, but rather they presented it as a service to God. Belonging to the inner circles of the church could often be shown through involvement in Sunday school. "Everybody" knew who was a Sunday school teacher, and this position was obtained only with the blessing of the priest. Many put themselves forward to serve as teachers, both men and women. To illustrate: in London in the 1990s about 130 children gathered for classes held in Arabic, and altogether 65 adults were involved as teachers, trainee teachers, bus drivers, and committee members.[35]

I interpret the level of activity among adults engaged in Sunday school work as a sign of reciprocal roles. When adults talked about the needs of children, this coincided with adults wanting tasks to fulfill and important roles to play within the congregation. In other words Sunday school meets the adults' need for children. A construction of childhood takes place according to which the casting of children as pupils is evident. Adults give children the role of needing to be served; children give adults roles as important people within the Church. To use both the local Arabic term and the terminology of this chapter: the construction of children as *makhdumin* (those being served) coincides with the construction of adults as *khuddam* (those who serve). Therefore, when we study the Coptic Orthodox Church and the question of belonging to this Church, we should include all age groups in our studies. When we look at the Sunday School Movement, we should not limit ourselves to focusing only on adults nor only on children. We should both be aware of how adults need to place children within the frame of their religious life and how children have a religious life of their own, which in part is nourished by the Sunday schools.

Conclusion

Belonging, as we have seen, may be considered as more than simply being born into a group. Coptic children have their identity as Copts created and recreated when they receive the sacraments, as well as when they take part in congregational life. For those who are active in the Church, being a Copt thereby becomes an integral part of life. A Coptic childhood is constructed relating to different hierarchies, according to which age, gender, and family patterns matter. Belonging is shaped by all these factors, linking children and adults together in Church membership.

With this background in mind it is important to note the paradigm of childhood studies has much to offer to Coptic studies. Its tools may help us understand the core of identity formation within the Church. However, this approach requires that researchers must be willing to listen to children, to enter into the arenas where their everyday life takes place, and to give importance to the early phases of life. In this way research may make clearer the cultural frames of Coptic childhood construction, as well as how children themselves may be seen as religious and social actors within the Church. Further in-depth studies of ongoing religious life should make this an important part of Coptic studies.

PART 3

TRADITION

THE REVIVAL OF THE COPTIC LANGUAGE AND THE FORMATION OF COPTIC ETHNORELIGIOUS IDENTITY IN MODERN EGYPT

Hiroko Miyokawa

For the Coptic Orthodox Christians, preserving the Coptic cultural heritage is an important initiative to strengthen their religious as well as cultural identity. This essay discusses one of the main tools to build Coptic identity: attempts to revive a spoken version of the Coptic language. Interest in the early roots of Coptic culture started as early as the nineteenth century during a time when Copts gradually gained full citizenship within the Egyptian nation-state. About the mid-1800s Egyptians had become interested in their pharaonic heritage, and when the Coptic Museum in Cairo opened in 1910, Copts could witness aspects of their earliest history for the first time. These processes call up questions as to how the Copts constructed their ethnoreligious identity during that period and what strategies they developed to be part of the nation-state. This essay focuses especially on the effort of Iqladiyus Labib (1868–1918), who initiated the first movement to revive Coptic as a spoken language.

The Coptic Language and Its Revival by Pope Kyrillos IV

The Coptic language, the final stage of the ancient Egyptian language, was the spoken language of the Egyptians at the time of the Arab conquest in the seventh century. As the Arabization and Islamization of the Egyptian population accelerated, Coptic gradually dissolved as the spoken language. It disappeared in the Delta about the eleventh century and in Upper Egypt between the fourteenth and seventeenth centuries. However, the language survived as the liturgical language of the Coptic Orthodox Church. As J. R. Zaborowsky has pointed out, the Coptic language became an indexical symbol of Coptic Christian identity after its disappearance as a daily spoken language.[1]

In the mid-nineteenth century Pope Kyrillos IV (r. 1854–1861, the 110th pope of Alexandria) initiated the reform of the Coptic language by mandating a uniform pronunciation, which had previously varied across regions. During this era knowledge of the Coptic language was reserved to a limited number of clergymen. The average priest was unable to read the Coptic alphabet. To remedy these deficiencies the pope strongly promoted the study of the Coptic language in the schools he established.[2] This reform, or revival, sparked interest in the Coptic language among both clergymen and lay intellectuals.

The Revival of the Coptic Language: Iqladiyus Labib

Under the influence of the Coptic revival launched by Pope Kyrillos IV, Iqladiyus Labib initiated the movement to revive Coptic as a spoken language in the modern era.[3] Labib was born in village called Mir in the Asyut Governorate, and he first encountered the language during his childhood when visiting the Muharraq monastery in Qusiya.[4] He later moved to Cairo and learned Coptic at the patriarchal school. He taught Coptic at the Coptic seminary, where he compiled a five-volume Coptic-Arabic dictionary. Upon recommendation of the pope, Khedive Abbas Helmy II bestowed on him the rank of bey in 1903 for his achievements in the research and education of the Coptic language.[5] Furthermore, he belonged to the first generation of Egyptian Egyptologists who learned hieroglyphs.

Labib was so fascinated with the Coptic language that he attempted to revive it as a daily spoken language and began teaching it to his family members and servants, encouraging them all to use it. To adjust the language to daily modern life, he inserted many neologisms, including the Coptic words for *automobile* and *telephone*, as well as replacing words of Greek origin in Coptic with those of Egyptian origin. His children had pharaonic names such as Pahor and Nefertari.[6] Labib explained his thoughts on the necessity and importance of the Coptic revival in a monthly magazine he published from 1900 to 1904 entitled *'Ayn Shams*.

'Ayn Shams

Figure 12 shows the cover of the first issue of *'Ayn Shams*. At the top the date is written in Arabic following the Coptic calendar. It reads "Egypt, Monday, the first of the month of Tūt, 1617," which was New Year's Day. It shows Horus in the center, and the title of the journal is written around him in four languages: English, Arabic, Coptic, and Egyptian in hieroglyphs. The title *'Ayn Shams* (Heliopolis) refers to the name of the district in Cairo where Labib lived, which is known for its ancient obelisk and the holy site of the tree of the Virgin Mary.[7] It also suggests that Labib's interest in Coptic was based on the fact that it connected ancient and modern Egypt.

In the first issue of *'Ayn Shams*, Labib explained that his goals for the journal were to let the readers know about the science and knowledge of the great ancient Egyptian civilization and to show its importance. He also noted that his other aims were "to study some of our ancient Egyptian customs that other civilized empires glory" and "to place a dedicated gate for the education of our Egyptian language."[8]

The Revival of the Coptic Language

Fig. 12. First page from thee journal *'Ayn Shams*, no.1 (Cairo, 1900 C.E., 1617 A.M., Tūt). Photograph by the author.

The journal was written mainly in Arabic with some parts in the so-called Bohairic dialect of the Coptic language, which originated in the Delta and by the eleventh century had become the main dialect of Coptic. It contained much information about ancient Egyptian civilization, along with pictures of murals and temples. It also contained a Q&A section to allow dialogue between its editor and the readers.

When answering readers' questions, Labib advocated the importance of the Coptic language and its position for Egyptians. For example, in *'Ayn Shams*, no. 3 (Hātūr 1618 A.M.), a reader asked "Is there any benefit to learning and teaching the Coptic language for foreigners and local Egyptians?" According to Labib, "it is a duty and necessity for both foreigners and local Egyptians to learn and teach Coptic."[9] In his view it was necessary for foreigners—especially archaeologists, theologians, and historians—to learn from the great wisdom of ancient Egyptian civilization. He gave several reasons for local Egyptians to study Coptic: Coptic is the language of the homeland and the ancestors; second, it is the language of religion for the Egyptian people, as well as the language of science, research, honor, and glory. Finally, Labib argued that learning Coptic would keep the Egyptians from being "demons" without a homeland or religion. He asserted that a people who did not have their own language did not have a homeland, and those without a homeland did not have religion.[10] After enumerating a total of seven reasons for learning Coptic, Labib continued: "There may be a criticism that the language we use is Arabic and that it is the language of our homeland."[11] Refuting this claim himself, he pointed out that Egyptian Arabic was strongly influenced by Coptic in its pronunciation and vocabulary[12] and asserted that "Arabic is not your true language."[13] Therefore, "the greater glory and the higher honor is in preserving your original language."[14] Considering "Coptic the first language for you before any other languages for several reasons," he concluded that "in order to be called an Egyptian, not nominally but actually, one has to learn this Egyptian language, its literature, its wisdom, and its traces. And on that basis, a person can properly be called Coptic or Egyptian, either Christian or Muslim, and vice versa."[15] Labib positioned the Coptic language as the ethnic language of the Egyptian people and as one of the important indices for Egyptian ethnicity, disregarding the Arab–Islamic elements of Egyptian national identity.

To the question from ʿAyn Shams, nos. 5–6 (Ṭūba-Amshīr 1619 A.M.), "Who are the true Egyptians?"[16] Labib answered that a true Egyptian is someone who speaks the language of his or her ancestors, the pharaohs; believes in the religion of the pharaohs; performs the customs of his or her ancestors; is devoted to learning the language, religion, and customs both past and present of his or her ancestors; and does not lose his or her own language, religion, customs, and patriotism, even after experiencing atrocities and persecution by foreign invaders such as the Persians, Greeks, Romans, and Arabs.[17]

Thus Labib defined the Egyptian people based on their cultural characteristics, such as language, religion, and customs. Although the religion of ancient Egypt was polytheistic, and therefore incompatible with Christianity, he regarded it to be the origin of the concepts and symbols of Christianity. He pointed out the similarity between the shape and meaning of the ankh, the key of life, and the Christian cross, even asserting that the latter derived from the former.[18] He also compared the Holy Trinity of ancient Egypt, which consisted of the deities Osiris, Isis, and Horus, to that of Christianity. He asserted that the Holy Spirit was sent for giving people comfort and protecting them from evil and sin. Labib argued that Isis played the same role in ancient Egyptian religion as the Holy Spirit in Christianity—giving comfort and protecting from the evil. Showing pictures of Isis holding her son Horus, he also pointed out the similarities between the pictures of Isis and the Virgin Mary holding the infant Jesus.[19] Thus, he connected the ancient Egyptian religion to Christianity.

As for the customs, he published a long article about the Coptic calendar and the Nayruz festival, or New Year's Day.[20] The Coptic calendar is used as the ecclesiastical calendar, and Nayruz is conventionally celebrated as the martyrs' festival that commemorates the martyrs persecuted in the Coptic Orthodox Church by the Roman emperor Diocletian. However, the festival was given a new meaning when it became clear through the findings of Egyptology that the Coptic calendar was almost identical to the ancient Egyptian calendar. The Nayruz festival was revived as a festival with ancient roots by a Coptic layman named Tadrus Shenuda al-Manqabadi in 1883. Labib participated in the Nayruz celebrations of 1899, even giving a speech in Coptic.[21]

Arabs were considered to be the foreign invaders of Egypt. Therefore, in Labib's view, ethnically authentic Egyptians were indigenous Egyptians who had lived in Egypt since before the Arab invasion and who had maintained characteristics of their original. In his view if such characteristics had been lost they needed to be revived.

It was not only the Arabs whom Labib considered to be foreign to Egyptians. Greek and Hebrew cultural influences were foreign as well. Labib asserted that "if you wish to go back to the right way and be inclined to something related to the revival of your language, you have to give your sons and daughters, and members of your families in general, Egyptian names with the original pronunciation and meaning."[22] He pointed out that names that were commonly used and widely considered to be Egyptian, such as Armaniyus, Iqludiyus, Sergiyus, Luqa, Marqus, Hanna, Kyrillos, Mikhail, Basili, Benyamin, and Girgis, and female names such as Helana, Sofia, and Maryam did not have their origin in "our language."[23] Rather, they were of Hebrew or Greek origin. Then he published a list of Egyptian names for both boys and girls, including names such as Ahmes, Shenouti, Bakhoum, Totmes, and Nefertari.

Even though Muslim Egyptians were not entirely excluded from his argument, Labib's interest was mainly focused on Copts and how to make them ethnically authentic Egyptians. He tried to show the connection between ancient Egyptian religion and Christianity. In addition, he did not try to revive the ancient Egyptian language itself, although he regarded ancient Egyptian civilization as the source of Egyptian cultural authenticity. Instead, he focused on reviving the Coptic language, which he called "the current Egyptian language." In fact, he tried to connect the Coptic culture, more specifically the Coptic language and Christianity itself, to ancient Egypt, thus positioning it as authentic Egyptian culture. As a result, the Copts' Christianity did not diminish their authenticity as Egyptians. Rather, Copts were positioned as heirs of the ancient Egyptian cultural heritage which had been transmitted to them in Christianized forms. This point becomes even clearer when we remember that Labib included Shenouti and Bakhoum on his list of Egyptian names; these are associated with Shenoute the Archimandrite and Pachomius the Great, Egyptian saints from the fourth century.

Conclusion

As we have seen, Iqladiyus Labib, the first reviver of Coptic as a spoken language, positioned the language as the ethnic language of the Egyptian people. Moreover, in his view Egyptian ethnicity is defined by cultural characteristics that originated in ancient Egypt, such as the Coptic language.

Even though Labib devoted considerable effort to reviving Coptic as a spoken language, he succeeded only on a very small scale. It is said that currently there are only three families, including Labib's, who speak Coptic as a result of the revival.[24] However, the significance of his efforts lies in the fact that the Coptic language was reevaluated and assigned a new meaning as the ethnic language of the Copts and Egyptian people.

Labib's vision of Coptic as the ethnic language of the Egyptian people evolved along with the development of Egyptian nationalism and the study of Egyptology in the late nineteenth century. He attempted to link Coptic culture with ancient Egyptian civilization and to reevaluate it as the national culture of Egypt. His main objective in reviving the Coptic language was neither to advocate national unity on the basis of a common pharaonic past shared by Muslims and Copts nor to revitalize Christian culture among the Coptic Christians. Rather, it was to raise the status of the Coptic language from the religious language of the Copts to the ethnic language of the Egyptian people, and thus elevate the status of the Copts themselves from a non-Muslim minority to ethnically authentic Egyptians. From Labib's point of view, Coptic Christianity played an important role in shaping Egyptian ethnic identity, because it had preserved ancient Egyptian culture among the Copts.

READING THE CHURCH'S STORY
The "'Amr-Benjamin Paradigm" and Its Echoes in *The History of the Patriarchs of Alexandria*

Mark Swanson

―――――――――――――◇――○――◇―――――――――――――

The Copto-Arabic ecclesiastical history usually known as *The History of the Patriarchs of Alexandria* (*HP* for short) is a text that has long been shaping Coptic Orthodox Christians' knowledge and perception of their community and its leaders.[1] Many Copts have read all or some of the text (in one of the various publications mentioned below), but many more have had contact with *HP* indirectly, through readings in the Copto-Arabic *Synaxarion*, stories shared at church events, published books of history, or pamphlets about individual patriarchs. *HP* is the origin, for example, of one of the very best known and widely celebrated stories in the Coptic community today: the account of the Muqaṭṭam miracle in the days of Patriarch Afrahām ibn Zurʿah (the 62nd patriarch, 975–978).[2] The story of how the patriarch, clergy, and laity (especially a faith-filled one-eyed tanner) averted disaster to their community by moving the Muqaṭṭam Mountain in accordance with Matthew 17:20 has been told, retold, and elaborated over the centuries. It has inspired the cult of Abuna Samaan the Cobbler (or Tanner),[3] and recently has given rise to the development of a major church complex and pilgrimage center in the Muqaṭṭam hills. Every Copt knows the story—and it has shaped the imagination of Coptic Orthodox Christians in important ways.[4] However, as far as we know, the earliest version of it (in which the tanner is still anonymous!) is that of *HP*.

If *HP* has a deep (but not always recognized) place in the imaginations of the faithful, for historians of the Coptic Orthodox Church it is simply indispensable. This may be seen from a quick perusal of Arabic-language treatments of Coptic history, including Bishop Īsūdhūrus's *al-Kharīdah al-nafīsah fī tārīkh al-kanīsah* (1923),[5] Manassā Yūḥannā's *Tārīkh al-kanīsah al-qibṭiyyah* (1924),[6] the pioneering studies of Kāmil Ṣāliḥ Nakhlah (1940s and 50s),[7] Iris Habib el Masri's *Qiṣṣat al-kanīsah al-qibṭiyyah* (begun in 1948),[8] and many other works. Western scholars have been using *HP* since Eusèbe Renaudot's extensive paraphrases in *Historia patriarcharum Alexandrinorum Jacobitarum*, published in Paris in 1713.[9] For some recent examples, a glance at the notes, index, or bibliography is sufficient to see the importance of *HP* to Aziz S. Atiya's *A History of Eastern Christianity* (1968),[10] the entries for the Coptic patriarchs in *The Coptic Encyclopedia* (1991),[11] Theodore Hall Partrick's *Traditional Egyptian Christianity* (1996),[12] Alberto Elli's *Storia della chiesa copta* (2003),[13] or my own *Coptic Papacy in Islamic Egypt* (2010).

Whether working in Arabic or in European languages, scholars have been aided by the accessibility of the text of *HP*, starting with the dueling European editions of Christian Friedrich Seybold and B. T A. Evetts (from 1904).[14] The Patrologia Orientalis (PO) edition of Evetts (1904–1915) was accompanied by an English translation, as was its continuation published in Cairo by the Société d'Archéologie Copte (SAC, 1943–1974).[15] This combined PO–SAC edition has contributed enormously to making *HP* known. While the English translation has been widely read by scholars and students in the West,[16] the Arabic text has been reproduced and reprinted in a variety of ways, so that inexpensive copies of the Arabic text are (intermittently) available in the bookshops of Cairo.[17]

Developments in the study of
The History of the Patriarchs of Alexandria

HP has often been used quite uncritically: many writers have been content to quote from, paraphrase, or summarize passages of interest, often allowing *HP* to form a framework which can occasionally be filled in from other sources (for example, Islamic ones for contemporary political developments). However, there is a growing sophistication in the utilization of this work for historical study. Three developments in particular come to mind.

First, the source history of *HP* has been decisively clarified. The researches of scholars such as Kāmil Ṣāliḥ Nakhlah, David Johnson, and Johannes den Heijer have demonstrated that *HP* is a compilation of sources, mostly by authors whose names have been preserved.[18] The sources through the year 1046 were written in Coptic. Beginning in 1088, a deacon of Alexandria, Mawhūb ibn Manṣūr ibn Mufarrij, directed a project to collect, translate, and edit these sources into a single history in Arabic. Mawhūb then became the first of a series of continuators who kept the history up to date with *Lives* of subsequent patriarchs, henceforth written directly in the Arabic language.[19]

The clarification of the source history of *HP* is a great gain for students of the work: in it we find the contributions of several authors of different periods, each of whom wrote about patriarchs with whom he was personally familiar. For example, one of these authors was George the Archdeacon, who wrote his Coptic-language history somewhere around the year 700. He was the spiritual son of Patriarch John III (the 40th, 680–689) and secretary to Patriarch Simon (the 42nd, 692–700). Thus for the patriarchs of the final decades of the seventh century, *HP* more or less preserves an account by a well-connected contemporary.

This phrase *more or less* points to some caveats that must be stated. George the Archdeacon wrote in Coptic—and no part of his Coptic original has been preserved. That Coptic original was translated into Arabic and edited as part of the process of fitting it into the new comprehensive *History of the Patriarchs*. To add to the confusion, *HP* underwent further development in the manuscript tradition, so that the accessible published texts of the work are those of what is usually called the "Vulgate recension," which occasionally differs in important respects from the older so-called Primitive recension, only part of which has ever been published—and that in an exceedingly rare volume.[20] It is easy (and here I speak from embarrassing experience) to fall into the trap of attributing to an author of one of *HP*'s Coptic sources literary features that, in fact, stem from later editors, whether Mawhūb or the shapers of the Vulgate recension.[21]

Again, the clarification of the *HP*'s source history allows us to identify a succession of history writers spanning long stretches of Coptic history; repeatedly we are given accounts by contemporaries or near contemporaries of the events described. In addition, the identification of *HP*'s sources allows (in a way reminiscent of a certain strain of New Testament redaction criticism) for the investigation of the theological-historical vision of each of these writers, their sense of how God and Satan are at work in the world, their vision of the Church and its leaders—all of which may help in the interpretation of particular passages.[22] Furthermore, we may investigate the ecclesial and social location of each writer: while George the Archdeacon was a monk who served as secretary to Patriarch Simon, Mawhūb was a lay notable of Alexandria, in the thick of both the ecclesiastical and the political life of that city. Both were committed sons of the Church, but their background, circles of associates, interests, and loyalties were quite different. Such matters may now be studied and taken into account when reading their histories.

Second, also of importance to the scholarly study of *HP* has been the careful investigation of convergences between this text and other witnesses—as opposed to older works in which *HP* is followed almost exclusively and often uncritically. An early example of this might be Kāmil Ṣāliḥ Nakhlah's 1947 study of a great twelfth-century patriarch, *Sīrat al-bābā Ghubriyāl Ibn Turayk*,[23] which wove together a variety of sources alongside *HP*, in particular the *History of the Patriarchs* attributed to the thirteenth-century bishop Yūsāb of Fuwwah. In this work *HP* can be seen as one of a number of independent sources together bearing a fairly coherent witness.[24] Recent historical work tends to treat *HP* as *a* source—an important, sometimes overestimated, and also sometimes overlooked source[25]— among *other* sources, including documentary papyri, Islamic literary works, and archaeological remains and inscriptions.[26] The discovery of coherence (or its lack) as these various sources are brought into conversation with one another contributes to a more nuanced assessment of *HP*—or, better, of each of *HP*'s component parts—as a witness to the events it describes.

A third development is an interest in "discursive history," where the focus is not so much on "what actually happened" but on how, in *HP*, the patriarchs are portrayed— and how these portrayals reflect and participate in the creation and reconstitution of Coptic Orthodox identity over the course of the centuries. One rationale for such a study is hinted at by the fact that *The History of the Patriarchs of Alexandria* is not, in fact, the title of the text. Its actual title is something like *Siyar al-bīʿah al-muqaddasah*, "Lives" or "Biographies of the Holy Church," with a "Life" for each patriarch. It does not take the reader long to realize that a *Sīrah*, or Life, is not a fixed genre in *HP*: in some lives we find a complex weave of historiography and hagiography; others are chroniclelike compositions that focus mostly on secular history; some consist merely in brief notices; and one, the Life of Matthew I (87th patriarch, 1378–1408), is an encomium of a saint shorn of its homiletic introduction and conclusion. The term *history* in the title *History of the Patriarchs* masks considerable complexity at the literary level. How *HP* functions at this level is surely a fit subject for study.

Stephen J. Davis adopted and provided a model of this "discursive historical" approach to texts for the study of the early Egyptian church, including *HP*, in his *Early Coptic Papacy*, the first volume in the American University in Cairo Press's Popes of Egypt series; I did my best to follow him in my own contribution to the series.[27] This approach brackets out certain questions of historicity (which was necessary in order to complete the series in three slim volumes!) and thus leaves many possible questions unanswered. However, by taking the text of *HP* as consisting in portrayals that not only reflect the community's self-understanding but also helped to shape that self-understanding, attention is drawn to literary and rhetorical aspects of the text that appeal to the imagination and possess community-shaping power; these include recurrent themes, intertextual references, and ongoing allusion and echo.

Looking Forward

Looking forward, we can anticipate progress in all three of the areas outlined above. First, our understanding of the history of the text itself, its sources and its redaction, will be greatly aided by a project that has now been announced: the preparation and publication of a critical edition of the "Primitive recension" of *HP*, directed by Johannes den Heijer and Perrine Pilette.[28] Second, studies that bring *HP* into conversation with the widest range of other sources will test and take the measure of *HP* as a historical source; one very instructive example is Maged S. A. Mikhail's *From Byzantine to Islamic Egypt*,[29] which fully exploits Christian and Islamic literary sources as well as documentary papyri and other evidence.

In this essay, I would like to make a small contribution in the third area, which pays special attention to some of the literary features of *HP*. The contemporary student of *HP* needs to be alert to the way in which its constituent texts engage other texts—including the other texts that came to be incorporated in *HP*. Most of the authors of *HP*'s various sources were well aware of the contributions of their predecessors; some of them had copied out the entire work before bringing it up to date with their own contributions. Furthermore, these authors shared many elements of a Coptic Christian culture, including wide familiarity with scripture, apocryphal legend, and the stories of the saints and martyrs. It is only to be expected, then, that certain themes, motifs, and allusions will recur throughout the *HP*, contributing to a certain unity of plot and vision. As readers we must pay attention to such literary connections and interweaving, to themes and variations. We are not dealing with a mere recital of discrete events that allows us to penetrate

Reading the Church's Story

in Rankean fashion to a reconstruction of what actually happened (*wie es eigentlich gewesen ist*), but with a complex fabric of event, representation, and ideology, tied together by repeated motifs, allusion, and echo.

The Coptic Patriarch and the Muslim Ruler

There are several themes and motifs that might be investigated here and that are critical to an understanding of the Coptic Orthodox worldview to which *HP* is not only a witness but also a contributor: martyrdom and sainthood (and the patriarch's participation in these), exile, and patriarch–lay relations are all important themes that run through the collected work. In the space available here, I would like to present a "theme with variations" to which we might give the title "The Coptic Patriarch and the Muslim Ruler." *The History of the Patriarchs of Alexandria* provides a very clear paradigmatic example for what this relationship should be, and then, repeatedly, presents variations on the theme.

The Paradigm

As for the paradigmatic example, it is a text that every educated Copt knows:[30] the story of the meeting between the Arab conqueror of Egypt, ʿAmr ibn al-ʿĀṣ, and Patriarch Benjamin I (the 38th patriarch, 623–662).[31] At the time of the Arab invasion of Egypt, Benjamin (Anbā Binyāmīn) was patriarch of the anti-Chalcedonian community that would eventually come to be known as Coptic Orthodox. He had already for several years been on the run from the agents of the Byzantine-appointed governor and patriarch, Cyrus, known to posterity as al-Muqawqas, who had been sent to Egypt with authority to impose imperially sanctioned Chalcedonian doctrine, using force if necessary. Nevertheless, as Byzantine authority in Egypt collapsed and ʿAmr established himself in Alexandria, new possibilities arose. According to *HP* it was the *dux* Sanutius (that is, Shenoute), "the Christian believer," who brought Benjamin's case to ʿAmr's attention—perhaps realizing that ʿAmr would need to establish lines of communication and authority with a Church leader who would command the widest possible acceptance and recognition from the Egyptian Christian population. ʿAmr sent a decree out to the provinces: "Let there be guidance, security, and peace from God, to the place where Benjamin, chief of the Christians, is found! Let him come and attend to the condition of his Church."[32]

Benjamin, who had spent thirteen years in exile (ten of them in flight from the Byzantines, and three since the advent of the Arabs—placing these events in about the year 644), returned in joy and was given a joyful reception by the people of Alexandria. Soon afterward, a meeting between patriarch and the Muslim emir took place. George the Archdeacon tells the story of their meeting as follows:

> [Sanutius the *dux*] went and informed the emir [ʿAmr] of his arrival, and [the emir] ordered that he be brought with honor and love.
> When [the emir] saw [Benjamin], he turned to his commanders and said to them: "In all the lands of which we have taken possession up to

now, I have not seen a man of God who resembles this man!" (For his appearance was very beautiful.) Then he turned to him and said, "Take control of all of your churches and all of your men! And if you pray for me, that I go to the West and the Pentapolis and take possession of them as I have of Egypt, and return to you quickly, then I shall do for you all that you demand of me."

Then the saintly confessor delivered a lengthy discourse [*lit.*, "said much speech"], and [the emir] and all who were present marveled at him; in his discourse there was exhortation and great benefit to whoever heard it. And [Benjamin] enunciated [hidden?] things to [the emir]. And then he departed from him in honor.

Everything that the Blessed One said, the emir 'Amr found it to be true. It came true for him, and there did not fall from him a word that did not come to pass.[33]

There are several interesting features of this story. To begin with, simply the appearance of the patriarch is enough to provoke admiring comment. The governor treats the patriarch with great respect, and listens in astonishment as he preaches a sermon! Most important, the governor grants the patriarch autonomy in affairs of the Church and promises his support in return for effective prayers. Their roles are defined, as also is the role of the *dux* Shenoute, the faithful lay notable: while he plays an important role in engineering the meeting between 'Amr and Benjamin, he backs out of the spotlight once the patriarch has arrived.

The text given above is translated from the Primitive recension of *HP*. If we compare the Vulgate recension, we find that this later recension underlines the most salient points of this episode with small additions:

Primitive Recension[34]	Vulgate Recension[35]
Let him come and attend to the condition of his Church	Let him come and attend to the condition of his Church **and the rule of his community.**
[the emir] ordered that he be brought with honor and love	[the emir] ordered that he be brought with honor, **esteem**, and love
When [the emir] saw [Benjamin],	When [the emir] saw [Benjamin], ... **he honored him** ...
(For his appearance was very beautiful.)	(For his appearance was very beautiful, **and his speech was excellent, marked by calm and dignity.**)

Take control of all your churches and all of your men!	Take control of all of your churches and all of your men, **and attend to their conditions!**[36]
"... then I shall do for you all that you demand of me."	"... then I shall do for you all that you demand of me." **And St. Benjamin prayed for him.**
And then he departed from him in honor.	And then he departed from him in in honor **and reverence**.

The additions of the Vulgate recension do not change anything of importance in this story,[37] but they do accentuate some of the story's most striking features: the patriarch's very presence and words evoke reverence; the Muslim ruler holds the patriarch in honor and listens to him with benefit; the patriarch is granted autonomy in the affairs of the Church; in return, the patriarch will pray for and otherwise bring blessing to the ruler.

While I have no doubt that some kind of encounter between ʿAmr and Benjamin did indeed take place after the Arab conquest of Egypt, it is important to note that George the Archdeacon wrote his account some sixty years after the event. He does not give us minutes of their meeting but rather an idealized depiction, a paradigm, a pattern to which appeal can be made. Here is what the relationship between the patriarch and the governor *ought* to look like. Subsequent rulers may be judged on the basis of whether they conform to this ideal pattern, or not.

The Triumph of the Paradigm

The same Archdeacon George who gave us the ʿAmr-Benjamin paradigm is also the source of the story of the initial encounters between Patriarch John III of Samannud (the 40th patriarch, 680–689 or thereabouts) and governor ʿAbd al-ʿAzīz ibn Marwān (685–705, the son and brother of Umayyad caliphs).[38] According to Archdeacon George, their relationship got off to a rocky start when ʿAbd al-ʿAzīz arrived in Alexandria and Patriarch John was not on hand to greet him. The patriarch's Chalcedonian enemies denounced John, saying that he had declined to greet the governor "on account of his haughtiness and wealth."[39] ʿAbd al-ʿAziz was enraged, summoned John, gave him a dressing-down, and delivered him to one of his officers in order to extract a fine of onne hundred thousand dinars, by any means necessary.

The next part of the story is full of familiar echoes for experienced readers of Christian literature. In the first place, we are told that John's imprisonment takes place during Holy Week; immediately a parallel is set up between the patriarch's ordeal and that of Jesus Christ. When the patriarch's jailer puts the demand of one hundred thousand dinars to the patriarch, he asserts his own evangelical poverty (since money is "the root of all evil," 1 Timothy 6:10), but then speaks a language well known from countless martyrdom accounts, saying: "Whatever you desire to do [to me], do it! My body is in your hands, but my soul and body together are in the hand of my Lord Jesus Christ."[40]

John's jailer was enraged at that and was preparing to torture the patriarch into submission when a message came from the governor's wife: "Beware lest you do any harm to the man of God who has been handed over to you! This night I have endured great trials on account of him."[41] The governor's wife? This would seem a bizarre plot twist, except that for scripturally literate readers it recalls the passion narrative of Saint Matthew, in which, even as the Roman procurator Pontius Pilate sat on the judgment seat pondering what to do with one Jesus called the Messiah, he received a message from his wife: "Have nothing to do with that innocent man, for today I have suffered a great deal because of a dream about him" (Matthew 27:19). And so, by allusion, Patriarch John takes on aspects of Christ in this story—while ʿAbd al-ʿAzīz is subtly identified with Pontius Pilate.[42]

George the Archdeacon goes on to relate how the intervention of the governor's wife was sufficient to save the patriarch from torture but not to gain his release; indeed, his would-be torturer continued to press the patriarch to agree to a fine, if not one hundred thousand dinars, then fifty thousand; or perhaps less. Once the sum was reduced to ten thousand, a delegation of Copts of the secretarial class stepped in to urge a settlement. From here on out, the story closely follows the ʿAmr-Benjamin paradigm. The Coptic secretaries arranged a meeting between the governor and the patriarch. The patriarch arrived, and "when [ʿAbd al-ʿAzīz] raised his eyes to him, he saw him as if he were an angel of God."[43] As was the case with Benjamin, the patriarch's very appearance is enough to inspire awe. The governor welcomes the patriarch, calls for a comfortable cushion, and invites him to sit. A conversation ensues:

> [The governor] said to him: "Don't you know that the sultan is not to be opposed?"
>
> The saint responded and said to him: "The command of the sultan is to be obeyed as it is necessary and when it does not provoke the wrath of God! Beyond this, God has bid us, as it is said to us [in scripture]: "Do not fear the one who kills your bodies, but has no authority over your souls" [Matthew 10:28].
>
> The emir said to him: "Your God loves faithfulness and truth."
>
> The patriarch said to him: "My God is wholly Truth, and in Him there is no falsehood [cf. 1 John 1:5], but He destroys everyone who pronounces falsehood."[44]

After this mixture of scripture quotation and sharp exhortation—a brief sermon, if you will—the governor and patriarch quickly come to agreement on the terms of the latter's release. Then, "[the governor] released him with honor [*lit.*, 'glory']. [At this,] the Orthodox experienced joy, gladness, and delight, while the enemies of the Church experienced distress and shame. And the blessed patriarch emerged from the emir's palace, and the people were surrounding him and going before him."[45]

Reading the Church's Story

What I have been calling the 'Amr-Benjamin paradigm is so closely followed here that one might almost forget that the patriarch and his Church have just been shaken down for ten thousand dinars! But never mind that, because Patriarch John emerges from the episode covered with honor, and the governor 'Abd al-'Azīz also emerges from it as a figure whom the narrator would have us evaluate positively—here and in the episodes that follow. This might be surprising, in the light of the biblical allusions that had loosely identified the Umayyad governor 'Abd al-'Azīz with the Roman procurator Pontius Pilate. But here, perhaps, there is another set of texts in the background. Egyptian Christians were well aware of the stories according to which Pontius Pilate repented of his role in the crucifixion of Christ, was baptized, and eventually suffered martyrdom for his Christian faith.[46] For the governor 'Abd al-'Azīz to be portrayed as a seventh-century Pontius Pilate did not necessarily put him beyond a change of heart toward his saintly prisoner.

Inversions in the Paradigm

My next example is set in the eleventh century, from a text originally written in Coptic by Michael of Damrū (Mīkhā'īl al-Damrāwī), Bishop of Tinnīs, in about the year 1051. His contribution to *HP* consists of ten patriarchal biographies, including that of Patriarch Zacharias (the 64th patriarch, 1004–1032).[47] The decisive reality of Zacharias's term as patriarch was the persecution of the Fatimid caliph al-Ḥākim bi-Amr Allāh (r. 996–1020). For a period of several years, culminating about the year 1012, the Christian community suffered from a series of discriminatory and hostile actions: Christian civil servants were dismissed or pressured into converting to Islam; churches were closed and destroyed; the celebration of the liturgy was limited to the monasteries or to secret house churches; and the patriarch himself was imprisoned for a time, after which he took refuge in the monasteries of Sketis (the Wādī l-Naṭrūn).[48]

Toward the end of the decade, however, the intensity of the persecution slackened; Bishop Michael reports that some civil servants asked for, and received, permission to return to Christian observance.[49] The time of trouble now winding down, but with the Coptic patriarch away in a desert monastery, the stage is set for an 'Amr-Benjamin "moment"—and Bishop Michael presents one. If the *dux* Sanutius had set up the meeting between 'Amr ibn al-'Āṣ and Patriarch Benjamin, or the Coptic secretaries the one between 'Abd al-'Azīz and Patriarch John, this time that role is played by the monk Poemen, who had become a confidant of the caliph at the Shahrān Monastery south of Cairo-Misr, where al-Ḥākim used to go for recreation (following a pattern of Fatimid caliphs seeking refreshment at their favorite monasteries). The patriarch is summoned, along with a delegation of bishops, presumably to the Dayr Shahrān. Then, according to Bishop Michael, events unfold as follows:

> When al-Ḥākim came to [Poemen] as was his custom, [Poemen] brought out to him the patriarch, who greeted him with the salutation of kings, invoked blessings upon him, and prayed for him.

> Al-Ḥākim said to Poemen the monk: "Who is this?" He said: "This is our father the patriarch. I have sent for and brought him here as you commanded." [Al-Ḥākim] gestured to him with his finger and greeted him.
>
> A group of bishops was with [the patriarch]. [Al-Ḥākim] said: "Who are these?" Poemen the monk said to him: "These are his deputies in the land, the bishops." Al-Ḥākim regarded [the patriarch] closely and marveled at him.[50]

As in the case of Benjamin or of John III, the mere appearance of the patriarch is enough to cause the ruler to marvel. All seems to be proceeding according to established pattern! However, we need to complete the sentence:

> Al-Ḥākim regarded [the patriarch] closely and marveled at him, because he was insignificant to the eye (if venerable in spirit). He was short-statured, sparsely bearded, and ugly of constitution. He saw the bishops who were with him, elders who were beautiful of countenance, splendid of figure, and perfect of stature. [Al-Ḥākim] said to them: "*This* man is the chief of all of you?" They said to him: "Yes, our master, may the Lord give growth to your kingdom!" Then [al-Ḥākim] marveled.[51]

A conversation ensues between al-Ḥākim and the bishops:

> Then [al-Ḥākim] marveled and said to them: "How far does his rule extend?" They said to him: "His rule is carried out in the lands of Egypt, Abyssinia, Nubia, the Western Pentapolis of Africa, and elsewhere." [Al-Ḥākim's] astonishment increased. He said: "How is it that all of these obey him without soldiers or wealth to expend among them?" They said to him: "By one cross, all these tribes obey him." He said to them: "And what is this cross?" They said to him: "The sign of that upon which Christ was crucified. So whatever he desires from them, he writes to them and puts it [the cross] between the lines of the writing, in the place of the king's mark. And he says to them, 'Do this or that, lest the cross be against you,' and they obey what he says and do what he commands them—and that without soldiers or warfare."[52]

Al-Ḥākim sums up his amazement and grants relief to the Church:

> [Al-Ḥākim] said: "Truly, in all the world there is no established religion like the religion of the Christians. Here are we: we spill blood and expend wealth and send out armies, and we are not obeyed! But this old man, insignificant in appearance, ugly of constitution—the people of all these lands obey him at a word, and nothing other."
>
> Then [al-Ḥākim] said to the patriarch and to the bishops: "Remain here until I carry out for you your requirements." He left them, and they were happy at what they had heard from him.[53]

In many ways this scene has proceeded true to what we have called the 'Amr-Benjamin paradigm—but with some curious twists. We remember that Patriarch Benjamin was described as beautiful in appearance; Patriarch Zacharias, in contrast, is "short-statured, sparsely bearded, and ugly of constitution"—a poor specimen of churchman in comparison to his stately bishops. Furthermore, after his initial greeting Patriarch Zacharias does not say another word in the entire scene. It is his bishops who pray for the caliph and who conduct an edifying conversation on the power of the cross.

In fact, this scene fits perfectly into the whole of Bishop Michael's portrayal of Zacharias in *The History of the Patriarchs*.[54] Zacharias began his patriarchate as an amiable weakling, chosen for the patriarchate precisely because he could be manipulated by a clique that operated the patriarchate as a for-profit enterprise. Bishop Michael wants to show, however, how God "raises the poor from the ground and the needy from the dunghill, and sets him upon the throne of glory" (Psalm 113:7–8, quoted at the beginning of the biography).[55] Zacharias came through the fires of persecution as a confessor of the faith; and so, despite his weakness and initial ineffectiveness as patriarch, he proved himself a saint of the Church. This judgment is underlined in the episode we have just recounted: the encounter between patriarch and ruler comes to a happy conclusion, in spite of the fact—or, is it ironically because *of* the fact?—that the patriarch does not meet anyone's expectations with respect to appearance, speech, or gravitas.

Conclusion

We can multiply examples of patriarch–ruler encounters in *The History of the Patriarchs of Alexandria* in which the 'Amr-Benjamin paradigm seems to hover in the background. We could, for example, look in detail at the patriarchal biographies written by the first "general editor" of *HP*, Mawhūb ibn Manṣūr ibn Mufarrij. His account of the first meeting between Patriarch Christodoulos (66th patriarch, 1046–1077) and the military governor Badr al-Jamālī (r. 1074–1094) runs along the lines of the story of Patriarch John and Governor 'Abd al-'Azīz: initial antagonism as the result of false witness gives way to earnest conversation and, finally, to the patriarch's departure in honor.[56] Later, Mawhūb relates the story of an encounter between the same Badr al-Jamālī and Patriarch Cyril II (67th patriarch, 1078–1092) along with his bishops meeting in synod—in which Badr "addressed to them a severe speech which God pronounced through him."[57] In other words, contrary to the expectation of the 'Amr-Benjamin paradigm, here it was the Muslim Badr who preached the sermon. But that serves to underscore Mawhūb's positive evaluation of the Armenian general Badr, who brought stability to Egypt after the "great tribulation" of 1066–1073, when the miseries of civil war contributed to and were exacerbated by famine and outbreaks of disease.[58]

There have been regular meetings between the Coptic patriarchs and Egypt's rulers, throughout the history of the Church. We have accounts of some of these meetings in Coptic sources, notably *The History of the Patriarchs of Alexandria*. The simple point of this essay is that these accounts need to be read not as if they were minutes, but rather with attention to their shaping as literary constructions in conversation with one another and with an entire library of biblical and hagiographical sources. Attending to this conversation may help us to perceive the manner and artistry with which the authors portray the patriarchs, their Church, and their place in the world—and, just so, how they have contributed to their community's imagination and self-understanding.

THE EVOLUTION OF LENT IN ALEXANDRIA AND THE ALLEGED REFORMS OF PATRIARCH DEMETRIUS

Maged S. A. Mikhail

The Coptic Orthodox Church and community recognize a long litany of saints, prominent among whom is Patriarch Demetrius "the Vinedresser" (189–232 C.E.), whose biography may be readily summarized by young and old alike. His humble origins, elevation to the episcopate despite his marital status, miraculous erudition, and the vivid proof of his chaste marriage are constantly extolled. I have analyzed the hagio-historical literature pertaining to the archbishop elsewhere;[1] here, my focus shifts to the Lenten traditions that credit him with a reform that joined Lent, which is presumed to have been observed in Alexandria immediately after the Feast of Epiphany (Theophany), to Holy Week.

Over the years both the Coptic and scholarly communities have become heavily invested in these traditions. Among the Copts, Demetrius's reform and *Epact* calculations, which ensured that Easter would never coincide with or precede the Jewish Passover, have been central to discussions of the liturgical calendar for nearly a millennium.[2] As for scholars, they have read the pertinent texts as historical relics reflecting Alexandrian ante-Nicean practice and have proceeded along two distinct, though overlapping, trajectories. Those studying the early baptismal rite in Alexandria, which was at one time associated with the Sixth Sunday of Lent, sought to reconstruct the lectionary readings and liturgical calendar of third-century Alexandria based on rather fragmentary (and in the case of the *Mar Sabas Clementine Fragment*, likely fraudulent) evidence. That line of investigation has proven fruitless and beyond rehabilitation.[3] Another bevy of scholars, who focus on the historical development of Lent proper, read the post-Epiphany Lent as historical and attempt to situate it with the aid of various patristic and medieval glosses,[4] including a recently identified reference in the writings of the Armenian Catholicos Isaac (d. ca. 1200 C.E.).[5] That line of investigation continues to gain wide acceptance and frequently appears as a given in academic discussions of other aspects of the liturgical cycle in Alexandria and the Early Church.[6]

This study challenges the interpretive paradigms of the Coptic and academic communities by arguing for what may initially seem as a radical thesis; namely, that Patriarch Demetrius's alleged reform and the evidence supporting the post-Epiphany Lent thesis are apologetic literary traditions engendered by the confessional rivalries that flourished under Islamic rule and that they have little, if anything, to do with third-century Alexandria. This study also contests the presumed purity of Coptic sources, proving that, at least where Demetrius's reform is concerned, Bohairic Coptic literature is informed by Arabic traditions rather than by Sahidic texts. Finally, it underscores the importance of Arabic texts for Coptic studies, and the vital importance of reading these sources within their historical contexts. The examination begins with a survey of the incontestable markers in the history of Lent in Egypt and then delves into two interdependent discussions; one focuses on the initial week of Lent according to the current eight-week cycle (the so-called Week of Heraclius), while another scrutinizes the evidence for a post-Epiphany fast in Alexandria and Patriarch Demetrius's reform of that practice.

Definitive Markers

Throughout the early Christian centuries, the duration, dietary restrictions, and ascetic austerity of Lent fluctuated greatly. In the second and third centuries only three- and six-day observances are documented (Paschal fasts, really), with three-, six-, seven-, and eight-week rogations emerging in the fourth and fifth centuries.[7] These provincial and jurisdictional variations persisted well into the Byzantine era and under Islamic rule.[8]

In Jerusalem and Gaza an eight-week Lent is attested in the late fourth century, though it remained but one of several competing observances in those regions until the sixth century, when it prevailed.[9] In Alexandria conclusive evidence for the duration of Lent prior to the fourth century is extremely scarce, and in the main only the observance of a six-day fast is documented from the mid-third century until the 330s.[10] (It is here that Demetrian traditions have been read in hope of illuminating ante-Nicean practice.) By contrast, fourth-century developments are well documented due to the festal letters of Patriarch Athanasius (326–373 C.E.) and his successors, permitting scholars to postulate with a fair degree of certainty that Egypt reluctantly adopted a six-week Lent that *included* Holy Week during the second quarter of the fourth century[11]—an observance that may be positively identified in Alexandria as late as 596 C.E..[12]

By the mid-seventh[13] or early eighth century,[14] the Copts appended two weeks to their Great Fast; one by separating their six-week Lent from Holy Week (likely due to the influence of an interpolated passage in the *Didascalia*),[15] and another by adopting the "Week of Preparation," better known in premodern literature as the "Fast of Heraclius." Together these two developments merged to forge the eight-week cycle observed by the Coptic Orthodox until today. Nonetheless, that transition was less than flawless; traces of the older observance remained behind, complicating attempts to rationalize the Egyptian eight-week cycle until today. The Gospel readings for the first two Sundays of that cycle (Matthew 6:1–18 and 6:19–33) address fasting in passing, but are not specifically Lenten. The first significant

Gospel in that regard, the Temptation of Christ (Matthew 4:1–11), which provides the context for the liturgical hymns and prayers chanted throughout that season, is read on the Third Sunday.[16] Counting forty days beginning with the Monday immediately following the "Sunday of Temptation" (no fast can begin on a Sunday), one meets with Easter—the Athanasian six-week cycle remains imbedded within the later observance.

As for the Melkites of Alexandria, they also appear to have separated Lent from Pascha by ca. 700 C.E., but the adoption of an extra (eighth) week took on several manifestations within that confession. It is interesting that in the early Middle Ages the Alexandrians altered their six-week observance to mimic that of their coreligionists. Both Copts and Melkites adopted an eight-week cycle, which for the Copts resembled that of their West Syrian colleagues (hence, the insistence on fasting that week as though it were Lent despite the irregularities that causes, see below), while the Melkites adopted an eight-week cycle that began with a preparatory "Week of Cheese," which mirrored the observance of the pro-Chalcedonains of Jerusalem, Antioch, and Constantinople. Under early Islamic rule, theological unity in the face of new political realities helped foster greater uniformity within confessional blocks.

The "Fast of Heraclius"

Currently, three unrelated explanations attempt to account for the first week of the Coptic eight-week cycle, though none is particularly convincing in light of historical evidence. One rationalization is that, while not part of Lent proper, it prepares one for that austere rogation.[17] Another interpretation maintains that Lent was always observed for eight weeks to accommodate the lack of abstinence on Saturdays and Sundays. Borrowed from Jerusalem, this justification is untenable in Egypt on historical and liturgical grounds. (Moreover, during the patristic era it appears that fasting was only relaxed on the Sundays of Lent in Egypt.)[18] The third explanation, which prevails in premodern Christian Arabic literature, associates the fast with the alleged actions of Emperor Heraclius in Jerusalem; it presents the initial week as something entirely different and not at all related to Lent or Pascha. These conflicting interpretations are largely the product of overlapping historical and liturgical traditions, which were initially distinct or had no relation to Egyptian practice.

Among the Copts, the separation of Lent from Pascha led to the labeling of the Friday before Palm Sunday as *jumʿat khitām al-ṣawm*, "The *Concluding* Friday of the Fast" (emphasis mine), which has a distinctive rite and is prayed in the Annual rather than Lenten tone. This explicit identification negates the notion that the eight weeks should be regarded as a unified whole in Egypt. By that Friday, the faithful would have fasted forty-seven days, if Saturdays and Sundays were included, or thirty-three days, if they were excluded. The reckoning and rite of The Concluding Friday are coherent only when the first week, that of Heraclius, is excluded altogether. Hence, The Concluding Friday provides evidence for an

Alexandrian seven-week cycle that was likely shared—ever so briefly—by Copts and Melkites in Egypt: a six-week Lent (forty days: including Saturdays and Sundays, as with the earlier Athanasian pattern), which concludes with *jum'at khitām al-ṣawm,* and was then followed by Passion Week.

While the eight-week cycle was observed since ca. 700 C.E., it seems that no one in Egypt attempted to rationalize the initial week's fast until the Melkite Patriarch Eutychius (d. 940 C.E.) forwarded an account whose stylistic moorings are decidedly borrowed from Arabic *futūḥ* (conquest) accounts.[19] Eutychius maintains that upon the reconquest of Jerusalem in 629 C.E., the Jewish community graciously welcomed Emperor Heraclius into the city and seized the opportunity to attain an assurance of safety (*amān*) from him.[20] Soon, however, Christians inundated the emperor with a long litany of the atrocities the Jews had inflicted upon them under Sasanid rule and demanded that he seek reprisal.[21] But Heraclius, fearing divine retribution, hesitated. At that juncture the clergy of Jerusalem purportedly swore to observe a week of fasting on his behalf so God would not condemn him for breaking his vow or for persecuting the Jews. Appeased, the emperor sanctioned the persecution; hence the inauguration of an extra week's fast and its designation (even among the Copts) as the Week of Heraclius (*jum'at Hiraql*).[22]

Historically, observance of the Week of Heraclius in Egypt was contested by the Melkites and the fast diverged along confessional lines, and even within the same sect. This is explicit when the Alexandrian (left column) and the later Antiochene recensions of Patriarch Eutychius's *Kitāb Naẓm al-jawhar* are compared.[23]

> And they instituted on his behalf the first week of the fast, in which the Melkites abandon the consumption of meat only and fast on behalf of the Emperor Heraclius as forgiveness for revoking the pact (*'ahd*) and killing the Jews. And they recorded this to all who (followed) the same confession (*al-awfāq*).

The people of Jerusalem and Egypt observe this fast, but not the Syrians and Byzantines (*rūm*), for they abandon the eating of meat during that week and only fast during Wednesday and Friday.	And the Copts (qibṭ) of Egypt observe this fast until today. As for the Syrians, Greeks, and Melkites, after the death of Heraclius they reverted to eating eggs, cheese, and fish during that week according to the canons of Saint Nicephorus, patriarch of Constantinople [d. 811], the martyr (and) the confessor, and the church remained upon this.

The earliest recension documents a lack of uniformity among the Melkites; those in Jerusalem and Egypt observed the fast while "Syrians and Byzantines," presumably the pro-Chalcedonians of Antioch and Constantinople, did not. The Antiochene recension, however, recasts the Melkites as a homogenous community

The Evolution of Lent in Alexandria

acting in concert, and forwards a distinct critique: briefly observed by some Melkites, the noncanonical fast was duly abandoned in favor of the White Week, though the heterodox Copts maintained its observance. This alignment of orthodox belief with correct practice is the common claim of both confessions. Here, the Melkites, positioning themselves as the orthodox, are faithful to both, while the Copts are said to err. Conversely, in the Coptic accounts discussed below, it is the Copts who maintain orthodox faith and worship, while the Melkites deviate.

If at all historical, Eutychius's account is certainly colored by his sectarian disposition and a touch of legend. Nonetheless, his explanation prevailed among Copts and Melkites, and set the stage for subsequent debates and polemics between the two confessions. Moreover, in Egypt the transition from the first, strict observance to the second, more lenient fast was not instantaneous or linear as the *Naẓm* seems to imply; for centuries that week functioned as a confessional signifier in the form of an anti-fast. Thus, as the Copts solemnly fasted,[24] the Melkites feasted, even on the Wednesday and Friday of that week.[25] The antithetical observances likely reinforced one another as fasting and feasting developed into tangible socioreligious markers. Significantly, both factions legitimized their divergent practices by referencing Patriarch Demetrius's alleged Lenten reform, which is the focus of the following section.

A Post-Epiphany Lent?

Of all the traditions pertaining to Demetrius of Alexandria, patristic and liturgical scholars have been especially interested in those describing his Lenten reform, which, they argue, retain a historical core.[26] Nonetheless, on the whole, scholars have misread the pertinent texts, and underestimated the historiography and complexity of the traditions at their disposal. Academic interest in this reform was largely sparked by a passage in Abū al-Barakāt's early-fourteenth-century *A Lamp in the Darkness* (*Miṣbāḥ al-ẓulma*).

> Our holy fathers, the pure Apostles . . . would [begin to] fast the Holy Forty days on the day after Epiphany, that is the twelfth of Ṭūbah [January 20]. And they would celebrate the glorious feast on the twenty-second of Amshīr [March 1]. They would [later] observe Passion Week after that by [many] days, and they concluded it with the Easter celebration. [Thus was the practice] until the days of the holy father Patriarch *anbā* Demetrius. . . . He was a peasant who could not read or write well, but God enlightened (*anara*) him through the spirit of grace so that he knew all the books of the church, delved deeply into their meaning, and commented upon many of them. He was inspired to set the *Epact* calculations, and to reform the observance of the holy fast according to the current practice and its connection to the Week of Passion and the celebration of the glorious feast [of the Resurrection] on the appointed month and time. He sent news of this to father Peter, Patriarch of Rome,

and to the Patriarch of Constantinople, and the Patriarch of Antioch. They agreed upon [Demetrius's reform] and it was thus maintained ever since.[27]

Several issues converge here that are best addressed separately: a Lenten reform, the *Epact* reckoning, and Demetrius's role vis-à-vis both developments. Here the analysis focuses on the Lenten reform and Patriarch Demetrius' alleged role.[28]

Text

In search of pre-Nicean evidence for Lent in Alexandria and the elusive origins of the forty-day observance in general (which suddenly emerges in the Fifth Canon of Nicea), several leading liturgists have advocated the case for Demetrius's reform. Minimally, they have interpreted the passage as a relic of an Alexandrian Lenten fast that was initially observed after the Feast of Epiphany and subsequently joined to Passion Week during the tenure of Demetrius or, as David Brakke has argued, Athanasius.[29] Proponents of this hypothesis have fortified it by identifying three ante-Nicean passages that allegedly document the practice: *Canons of Hippolytus* (§§ 12, 20); *Canonical Letter* of Peter of Alexandria (Canon 1); and Origen's *Commentary on Leviticus* (§ 10.2)—though none of these references may be interpreted in the context of the Feast of Epiphany. This is crucial. None of the alleged early references can substantiate the post-Epiphany Lent thesis on its own, but only when read through the lens of later texts, the earliest among which may date to ca. 900 C.E.

The lure of a post-Epiphany fast is compelling, since it would align early Christian practice with the Gospel narratives;[30] nonetheless, the evidence does not withstand scrutiny. The *Canons of Hippolytus* (which draw upon the *Apostolic Tradition*) reflect an Egyptian milieu,[31] but they only survive in Arabic recensions that reflect a lost Coptic antecedent of a presumed Greek original.[32] It is uncertain if the wording of that text has been faithfully retained over the various recensions, let alone while it circulated in a Coptic–Arabic milieu.[33] At best, the earliest stratum of the *Canons* dates to the second quarter of the fourth century, when Patriarch Athanasius had already introduced an Egyptian forty-day Lent based on the contemporary Roman model (where its actual duration was thirty six days until the sixth century).[34]

The argument based on the *Canons* runs as follows: since the text seems to discuss Lent and Holy week as two separate entities, which was not the case beginning in the 330s (Athanasius's six-week cycle included Pascha), then it must reflect a pre-Nicean pattern that was not yet overshadowed by Athanasius's Lenten reform. Nonetheless, this reading and interpretation are tentative. Neither of the references to forty days in Canons 12 or 20 mentions the Feast of Epiphany (lacking in the *Canons* altogether). Moreover, Canon 12 need not be interpreted in the context of Lent at all, and Canon 20, if anything, may be read as evidence for the acceptance of the Athanasian reform.[35] Even if we were to entertain the questionable reading of Holy Week and Lent as separate entities in the *Canons,* given that text's manuscript history, it would be more likely that this reflects post-seventh-century practice—when Holy Week and Lent were, indeed, separated—than a hypothetical third-century observance.

Origen's *Commentary on Leviticus* is said to provide another reference. Composed in Caesarea between 238 and 244 C.E., it reads: "Nor do we say, however, that we relax the restraints of Christian abstinence; for *we* have the forty days consecrated to fasting."[36] Nevertheless, assuming that the text was not augmented,[37] the subject of the pronoun is, at best, ambiguous. Origen delivered the sermons that constituted his *Commentary on Leviticus* seven years after he settled in Caesarea, and most likely he chose his words to resonate with his audience, not to reflect Alexandrian liturgical practice. Equally important, there is nothing in that passage to suggest that the forty days in question were observed after Epiphany.

A final alleged pre-Nicean reference comes from Archbishop Peter of Alexandria's 306 C.E. *Canonical Letter* on the lapsed (the Christians who sacrificed to idols during the Great Persecution); there he references "another forty days" (*allas tessarakonta*). Clearly, these forty days are predicated upon an antecedent, which earlier scholarship—I believe correctly—identified within the same passage as the three years of "grievous mourning" the lapsed had already endured.[38] Advocates for the post-Epiphany Lent, however, have interpreted this phrase in light of a passing reference to Christ's baptism in the letter. Read in context, *allas tessarakonta* likely references the final, intense phase of the penitential period during which the lapsed prepared to rejoin the Eucharistic community, rather than a forty-day Lent in Alexandria (post-Epiphany or pre-Paschal). As much may be gleaned from the canon itself: "And during these [forty] days through *hard spiritual exercise* and *keener vigilance* [the lapsed] will turn an alert mind to prayer and to profound study of what was said by the Lord to the one who tempted him *and sought to make the lord worship him:* 'Get behind me, Satan, for it is written, "You shall worship the Lord your God and him only shall you serve" (Matt. 4:10).'"[39]

The context here is not Lent, but the third temptation in particular. The lapsed made an offering to the pagan gods; they "worshiped" Satan (cf. Matthew 4:9). Consequently, they were instructed to focus their spiritual meditation and contrition on their fall and Jesus's triumph before the very same temptation (cf. Origen, *Exhortation to Martyrdom*, 32).[40] Ultimately, the primary context of this canon is the Great Persecution, not the liturgical cycle.

The absence of unequivocal patristic testimony for a post-Epiphany Lent challenges the historicity of that observation. Moreover, within Demetrius's hagio-historical corpus the tradition faces another formidable obstacle in its omission from Greek and Latin sources, the saint's Sahidic encomium, his biography in the Primitive (eleventh-century) and Vulgate (thirteenth-century) recensions of the *History of the Patriarchs,* and the *Chronicon orientale,* though it is well represented in Bohairic and later Coptic Arabic literature.[41]

Turning to Arabic traditions (and Bohairic texts), the nucleus of the account Abū al-Barakāt and the *Synaxarium* borrowed and embellished first appeared in *Naẓm al-jawhar,* by Eutychius (d. 940 C.E.), where the pertinent passage reads similarly in the Alexandrian and Antiochene recensions of that work: "At that time,

Demetrius, the Patriarch of Alexandria, wrote to Agapius, Bishop of Jerusalem, and to Maximus, Patriarch of Antioch, and Victor, Patriarch of Rome, concerning the calculations of the Passover of the Christians (*fiṣḥ al-naṣārā*) and their fast, and how to derive them from the feast of the Jews. And *they wrote many books and epistles* until they established the feast of the Christians (*naṣārā*) as to what they observe today."[42]

Here, wishing to resolve the regional irregularities associated with the observance of Lent and the celebration of Easter, Demetrius allegedly initiated several exchanges with his contemporaries, which culminated with a reform. Abū al-Barakāt and the *Synaxarium*'s accounts relied upon this tradition, but taking their cues from the then dominant hagiography, which lauded Demetrius's miraculous gift of erudition, they embellished his contribution. Thus, whereas Eutychius carefully presented a collaborative ecumenical reform, Coptic Arabic accounts (while introducing several careless mistakes in the process)[43] elevated Demetrius's role and depicted the other patriarchs as little more than passive agents who recognized the inherent genius of his reform and adopt it.[44]

Perplexing as they are, the texts and traditions forwarded here are better understood when Eutychius's sources and sociohistorical setting are scrutinized. One possibility is that the Melkite patriarch based his account on a misreading of a passage from a late-fourth-century Antiochene text, the *Apostolic Constitutions* (5.13): "Brothers and sisters, observe the festival days; and first of all the birthday which you are to celebrate on the twenty-fifth of the ninth month; after which let the Epiphany be to you the most honored, in which the Lord made to you a display of His own Godhead, and let it take place on the sixth of the tenth month; after which the fast of Lent is to be observed by you as containing a memorial of our Lord's mode of life and legislation."[45]

Here, the *Apostolic Constitutions* simply lists communal fasts and celebrations throughout the liturgical year.[46] Yet, whereas the feasts of Nativity and Epiphany are dated to month and day, Lent (a "floating" fast) is not; hence the abrupt shift from Epiphany to Lent, which Eutychius (or the source he relied upon) may have read as an apostolic injunction to observe Lent immediately after the Feast of Epiphany.[47] As demonstrated in the next section below, this would have been an attractive (mis)reading under Islamic rule.

With more certainty, it is clear that Patriarch Eutychius sought to resolve a discrepancy between what he perceived as universal apostolic practice and the later communal observance he knew prevailed. And he was not alone on that front. Pseudo-George of Arbela, a ninth- or tenth-century East Syrian author, also noted that discrepancy in his *Exposition of the Offices of the Church* (I.13).[48] There, he argues that Christians followed the example of Jesus by fasting for forty days after Epiphany until the Council of Nicea joined that fast to Holy Week. The contention that the fathers at Nicea set the length of Lent is ubiquitous in medieval literature, though, at best, they would have discussed only the date of the feast. But why did Eutychius and Pseudo-Geroge address the positioning of Lent within the liturgical cycle when that issue had been taken for granted previously? It is to that question that this study now turns.

Context

The textual analysis presented thus far is but one aspect of a complex tradition, the extant versions of which reflect the historical contours of the intra- and intercommunal polemics and apologetics rampant among Christians, Muslims, and Jews during the Middle Ages.[49] It was within that contentious atmosphere that the post-Epiphany Lent tradition emerged and is best interpreted. In essence the tradition functioned on two fronts. Within an intercommunal context it was an apology aimed at rebuffing a Lenten polemic leveled at Christians by Muslims (and perhaps Jews);[50] all the extant forms of the tradition function in that capacity. The Egyptian recensions of this topos, while retaining the basic jest of the tradition, honed its details to better resonate within the intracommunal feud surrounding the observance of the Week of Heraclius.

On the first front, that of intercommunal polemics, al-Makīn the Younger noted that "non-Christians" criticized the community for failing to observe Lent immediately after Epiphany in accordance with the biblical record (for example, Mark 1:9–13);[51] in essence Christians were accused of failing to follow their own scriptures. Although al-Makīn the Younger wrote in the fourteenth century, this specific Lenten polemic can be dated much earlier and appears to have been pervasive (the annual observance of the fast likely sustained it). This may be soundly deduced from the fact that, while the bulk of the evidence at hand is from the east, this specific Lenten polemic and the ensuing apology—the alleged post-Epiphany Lent and its reform—were documented by Ibn Ḥazm as far away as Cordoba in the early eleventh century C.E.[52] The narratives forwarded by Eutychius, Pseudo-George of Arbela, Catholicos Isaac, Abū al-Barakāt, and al-Makīn may be all read as variations of an apologetic topos addressing this specific Islamic polemic. Demonstrably, all explicit references to the post-Epiphany Lent were written under Islamic rule, and every one of them presents the biblical pattern as the original practice of the Church (an argument that erroneously assumes that Lent commenced in the first century). Moreover, all the above-named authors carefully maintain that the observance was modified through a *legitimate* means that would have resonated among Eastern Christians: Demetrius's reform and the subsequent endorsement of three other patriarchal sees and/or the Council of Nicea. On the whole the tradition sought to rebuff the Lenten polemic while assuring Christians of the veracity of their fast. Even Ibn Ḥazm noted that the Christians of his day attributed the reform to "five patriarchs," though the significance of the reference to the pentarchy was lost on him.[53]

The second, intracommunal context of this topos has been explored, in part, in the discussion above of the Fast of Heraclius. As demonstrated there, Copts and Melkites were very concerned with the correct observance—and rejection—of communal fasts.[54] Hence, while both factions accepted and propagated the basic outline of the apologetic narrative (that a post-Epiphany Lent was reformed through a canonically valid means), each faction tailored their respective accounts to bolster their confessional claims vis-à-vis the Week of Heraclius. Patriarch Eutychius had inaugurated that intraconfessional dynamic in his *Naẓm al-jawhar* by identifying Demetrius—a mutually recognized pre-Chalcedonian authority—as the nexus of orthopractice. This is the socioreligious context in which the accounts of Eutychius and Abū al-Barakāt must be read. Neither author was simply transmitting patristic traditions; rather they pursued an intracommunal apology enshrined within a seemingly mundane phrase: both maintained that the Demetrian reform was faithfully observed by his own community "until this very day" (*ilā yawminā hādha*).[55] Each author aimed to employ a mutually recognized authority to vindicate their community's normative practice.

In all, however, as effective as this apologetic topos may have been within intra- and intercommunal debates, none of the attestations can vouch for the historicity of the post-Epiphany Lent. Doubtless, other references to this pseudo-historical tradition are yet to be identified in the medieval literature of Eastern Christians living under Islamic rule.

Fourteenth-Century Coptic Historiography

While Copts and Melkites vehemently disagreed over specifics, both accepted Demetrius's role in forging the liturgical calendar and associated the emperor Heraclius with the initial week of Lent. In time the Melkites would contest that week's observance in the form of the anti-fast discussed above, but the Copts only challenged its designation and, if anything, reaffirmed its orthodoxy. In the fourteenth century Abū al-Barakāt and, more squarely, al-Makīn the Younger argued that that week's association with Heraclius was a mere misnomer since the Copts had fasted that week since antiquity, and it was sanctioned by Demetrius and the Council of Nicea (325 C.E.).[56] Hence the confessional dispute is framed as the faithful observance and blatant disregard of a canonical patristic tradition, rather than as divergent interpretations of a medieval rogation.

Al-Makīn forwarded the most complete version of this revisionist historiography, which was doubly informed by disputes with the Melkites and the criticism of "non-Christians." According to his recasting of traditions, the early Church had observed a forty-day fast immediately after Epiphany which was subsequently joined to Holy Week, but, rather than attributing the reform to Demetrius, he pushed it back to the apostolic era and, taking his cues from the Arabic *Didascalia*, attributed it to Saint Paul and Saint James.[57] Repeatedly, in his *Mukhtaṣar al-bayān* al-Makīn stresses the role of the apostles as a unique cohort—in a *Rāshidūn*-like manner—vested with the necessary authority to accomplish such a reform.[58] He then credited Demetrius with adding an extra week of fasting (to accommodate the lack of abstinence on Saturdays and Sundays),[59] which was later erroneously associated with the emperor Heraclius;[60] hence the eight-week cycle, which he affirms originated with Demetrius and was ratified at the Council of Nicea.[61] Al-Makīn argued that this observance was normative in the whole Church until the Council of Chalcedon sowed the seeds of schism and liturgical divergence.[62] His historiography addressed the Melkite's censure of the Copt's strict observance of the first week of Lent, and implicitly reversed the polemic. Herein also lies another manifestation of a theme already encountered above: the orthodox—the Copts in this case—observe correct doctrine and practice, while the heterodox err on both fronts. Al-Makīn is unequivocal: "Know that the Coptic Church maintains what the fathers the Apostles had arranged, and what their successor, the great father Demetrius, had arranged after them, and the great council that convened in the presence of the righteous King Constantine, that of the 318 [assembled at Nicea], and other accepted councils after them, before the schism [of Chalcedon]. And she has not deviated in her fasting of the Holy Forty days from what had been ordained in those [councils]."[63]

Strictly speaking, none of this is historical: the *Didascalia* does not date to the mid-first century, nor did it reference Lent or Egyptian practice in its original form; Nicea never addressed the length of Lent; and the eight-week cycle cannot be dated in Alexandria prior to the mid-seventh century—at the earliest. Yet none of that mattered in the fourteenth century. Al-Makīn succeeded in addressing the challenges posed by Melkites, Muslims, and Jews by arguing for the antiquity and orthodoxy of Coptic practice.

Wider Significance

The Demetrian corpus provides a salient example of the influence of Arabic Christian texts on modern Coptic sensibilities as well as on patristic, liturgical, and historical studies, which are often structured and analyzed as though they were isolated islands of knowledge. The analysis forwarded here has challenged the historicity of a post-Epiphany Lent in Egypt and Archbishop Demetrius's alleged reform of that observance. Demonstrably, these traditions are a product of a specific set of intra- and interconfessional polemics and a socioreligious environment that prevailed in the Middle Ages—not third-century Alexandria. Ultimately, the pattern delineated in the "Definitive Markers" section, above, provides the only historically verifiable scheme for the evolution of Lent in Egypt.

More subtle, this study undermines the assumption that Bohairic texts provide a faithful rendering of their Sahidic antecedents. Consistently, the Lenten traditions lauded in Bohairic doxologies and refrains find their roots in Arabic sources and are altogether absent in Sahidic literature.[64] This problematizes the common perception held by academics and the contemporary Coptic community alike that Coptic texts are somehow more "pure" or "authentic" than their Arabic counterparts.

Finally, as to Coptic studies, the discipline understandably emphasizes the importance of the Coptic language and literature, but with less justification it continues to minimize Greek influence and marginalizes Arabic sources. This study has demonstrated the intractable connections among Greek, Coptic, and Arabic texts and the need to better integrate liturgical, historical, and literary studies. In this light Arabic Coptic texts must be recognized as the third essential pillar of Coptic studies. The discipline and Coptic Christianity more broadly are best conceived as hybrids that defy the limitations imposed by a single language, a particular body of literature, or a distinct period of history.

THE PERFECT MONK
Ideals of Masculinity in the Monastery of Shenoute

Caroline T. Schroeder

The past two decades have witnessed a convergence of disciplines and methodologies in late antique Coptic studies. In North America in particular, archaeologists, documentary historians, literary scholars, historical theologians, art historians, papyrologists, and feminist scholars do not live in disciplinary silos. The linguistic divide between Greek and Coptic studies is eroding in academia, both are studied in Classics departments today. Nowhere has this flourishing of scholarship been more evident than in research on early asceticism and monasticism. This subfield is situated at an important moment in time, and the enterprise of studying early Coptic or Egyptian monasticism has radically transformed. A fuller understanding of the world of the early Coptic monk, male and female, becomes ever more available to us because we now understand our work as positioned at the intersections of traditional and new disciplines and methodologies.

This recent work on Coptic culture in antiquity bears significance for modernity and postmodernity in Egypt as well as in the Coptic diaspora. Over the past two decades the Coptic Orthodox Church has embarked upon a mission to solidify Coptic identity in Egypt. For example, the Church has reactivated ancient monasteries and cultivated a network of guest houses and festivals at these sites, encouraging contemporary Christians in Egypt to identify with the ancient places and their monks as part of their heritage. Thanks to organizations such as the Saint Shenouda the Archimandrite Coptic Society and the Saint Mark Foundation for Coptic History Studies, scholars, lay Coptic Christians, and clergy collaborate to make new discoveries about Coptic history that enrich our knowledge of this cultural heritage. Coptic studies is now more integrated into both academia and lay Coptic self-identity. This essay will begin by assessing the field of late antique Coptic studies, Egyptian monasticism in particular. Then it will examine a case study that exemplifies both the remarkable recent evolution of research in this area, the paths we still need to forge, and the work that still needs to be done.

The central question: How can the current trajectories illuminate the interior worlds of early monks as well as the very conscious and deliberate development of Coptic monasticism as a social enterprise by its leaders? The case study will focus on the writings of Shenoute of Atripe, who led a federation of three monastic communities (two male, one female) from the mid-380s until his death in 465 near the ancient town of Atripe (modern Sohag). Shenoute is also one of the Coptic Orthodox Church's most popular saints; thousands of pilgrims descend on the monastery each July to celebrate his feast day.[1] Shenoute's weighty corpus of writings consists of letters, sermons, treatises, and monastic rules. It provides an unparalleled non-hagiographical source for the study of early monasticism. This essay will hone in on the issue of ascetic perfection, a concept central to both individual monastic practice and to the overarching development of monasticism as a social movement. Moreover, it is an issue that can be addressed only through interdisciplinary investigation. Questions of whether a monk could even achieve ascetic perfection plagued the theological debates concerning Origenism and Pelagianism. Monks wrestled with the very practical concerns about which specific ascetic behaviors enabled one to strive toward perfection. Biblical interpretation proved critical for explaining and justifying ascetic theology and ascetic praxis. Monastic leaders crafted regulations and other systems of power to enforce their own authority and deal with political conflicts in their communities and the wider church. Additionally, the ascetics understanding and enactment of their own gender identities and sexualities lay at the heart of questions about what ascetic perfection might be and whether it could even be achieved (especially by women). This essay assesses the state of contemporary scholarship and then applies research methodologies and results from such work to select writings of Shenoute on masculinity and perfection. The perfect male monk acts according to both biblical and Hellenistic expectations of men in their roles as fathers and sons.

New Trends in Coptic Scholarship

A historiographic review of select innovative recent scholarship includes recent works that exemplify an interdisciplinary approach that has enabled new perspectives. Rebecca S. Krawiec's *Shenoute and the Women of the White Monastery*, published in 2002, examines the documents at Shenoute's monastery in order to produce simultaneously a social history of women in the community, an ideological and political analysis of power and authority, and a sense of how theology and biblical interpretation intersect with those other two issues.[2] Moreover, Krawiec uses documentary papyri by and about women (especially letters) to contextualize the correspondence between Shenoute and the women of the community. Next, Terry G. Wilfong in his book *Women of Jeme* provides an example of a documentary historian or papyrologist deploying gender analysis to produce a local history of a small community of women in Thebes, which gives us both a social history of these particular families and social networks and also illuminates broader trends in the history of gender, religion, and economy in the period.[3] *Women of Jeme* is a local history, but one that anyone studying gender in late antiquity or early Byzantium must read. Several scholars of material culture have in recent decades masterfully brought together art and archaeology with textual culture to help us understand the Coptic monk's use of physical space. Darlene L. Brooks Hedstrom's work on conceptualizations of the monk's cell integrates texts with insights from the monastic living quarters she excavates. Elizabeth S. Bolman's examinations of the artistic programs at Saint Anthony's and Saint Paul's monasteries by the Red Sea pairs literature about the saints with the art or rituals conducted in the churches in which those saints are venerated and images of them are viewed.[4]

Another scholar whose work connects multiple disciplines, methodologies, and theoretical perspectives is Stephen J. Davis. His book on the cult of Thecla presents a gendered analysis of literature and material culture.[5] His more recent book, *Coptic Christology in Practice*, stretches our understanding of Christology beyond historical theology in both innovative and illuminating ways.[6] He scrutinizes ritual, textiles, material culture, and the memory of a heritage to vivify what may be to some (especially our students) the dry topic of theology.

Finally, David Brakke's recent book, *Demons and the Making of the Monk*, deserves mention.[7] First, *Demons and the Making of the Monk* serves as the most potent example of a recent dramatic reorientation in the study of Egyptian asceticism. In the twentieth century's cosmology of the scholarship of early Christian asceticism and monasticism, the universe revolved around the *Life of Antony*; this vita was positioned as the text upon which ancient hagiography as a genre and asceticism as a social movement depended. Similarly, most studies of hagiography and asceticism somehow depend upon that text for their foundation. *Demons and the Making of the Monk* opens not with Anthony, nor even with the other "usual suspects" in the study of the desert monks, such as the *Apophthegmata Patrum*. Instead the book begins with an anecdote about the heretofore bastard child of monastic studies—Shenoute, whose imprint on Egypt is indelible, but whose presence in Western writings about Christian Egypt (whether ancient or modern) is only now being fully felt. Buried in footnote three of the first chapter lies the revelation that Shenoute has replaced the venerable Cassian in the "cast of characters" essential to the study of Egyptian monasticism; we no longer sit firmly in Gaul, Italy, Palestine, or even primarily Alexandria gazing back at Egypt through the eyes of Cassian, Jerome, and the Palestinian monks, but rather we stand in the "Egypt" of the ancient sense, Egypt beyond Alexandria. Shenoute is the first "desert father" mentioned, has his very own chapter aptly titled "The Prophet," and is treated in the thematic chapters of the book (the "War Stories") alongside world-renown monks such as Pachomius, Anthony, and Syncletica. The book is divided into two sections: first comes "The Monk in Combat," with chapters addressing individual figures (Anthony, Evagrius, Pachomius, Shenoute); then, in the second part, "War Stories," Brakke tackles thematic topics, such as Ethiopian demons and gender. Saturated with feminist, psychoanalytic, and postcolonial theory, the volume also displays a dazzling facility with ancient languages and history.

This work has been enabled by three broader trends in academia in the past few years: interdisciplinary work bridging traditional fields, such as philology, history, art history, classics/archaeology, and theology; an infusion of emerging disciplines (literary theory, feminist and gender studies, and so on) into traditional scholarship; and, finally, globalization. The ease with which we as scholars can travel internationally and share scholarship internationally has especially facilitated interdisciplinary work across literature and history, on the one hand (strong North American disciplines), and art history and philology on the other hand (strong European disciplines). This is not to say that Europeans do not excel in literature and history, and that North Americans do not excel in art history and philology, but Europe especially has long held expertise in the study and restoration of ancient artifacts and paintings, and in in-depth language study. Globalization has led to cross-pollination not only in terms of the content of our work but also in terms of our methodologies.

The rest of this essay explores how these aspects of scholarship in Coptic studies intersect and can point us to new questions in the field through a case study on masculinity and ascetic perfection in the writings of the archimandrite Shenoute of Atripe. Central to this examination are three themes, three places where Shenoute's ideas about masculinity intersect with his vision of ascetic perfection: paternity and fatherhood, genealogies, and emotions. Any study of Shenoute must be accompanied by several constraints, of course. Although he composed more than seventeen volumes of letters, monastic rules, sermons, and treatises (making him the most prolific author in the Sahidic dialect of the Coptic language), not all of his texts have been published. This essay primarily involves three specific texts: a sermon from the *Discourses* (his collection of texts for a broad monastic and nonmonastic audience) entitled *I Have Been Reading the Holy Gospels*, a text whose beginning has been lost and is now known as *Acephalous Work 1 (A1)*, and one of Shenoute's very first letters in volume one of the *Canons* (letters, rules, and texts primarily for the monasteries)—a letter he wrote before becoming leader of the monastery. Also considered are some monastic rules in *God Who Alone Is True*, from volume nine of the *Canons*.

Paternity and Fatherhood in Shenoute's Writings

Shenoute uses gendered discourse to persuade and shame the monks of the monastery. In his very first known letters he draws on the rhetoric of sexuality from the Christian Old Testament, specifically the language of harlotry (Greco-Coptic *porneia*) in the Prophetic books, in order to construct the monastery as a sexualized and feminine sinful figure (the harlot) in need of masculine discipline and control.[8] He also criticizes his very own monastic father for lacking the proper paternal stature. The father of the monastery at the time was the community's second leader, and we believe his name to have been Ebonh. Shenoute wrote two letters in the early 380s, before himself becoming the third leader of the community. He wrote them while in the midst of a dispute with Ebonh over his leadership, specifically his decision not to punish a certain group of monks whom Shenoute believed had sinned.[9] Shenoute thus begins his career chipping away at the reputation of his superior by questioning his ability to carry out his role as *father*. He accuses Ebonh of speaking to Shenoute "hatefully" during a dispute, not "lovingly" in the way a father speaks to a son.¹⁰ Here Shenoute compares the affective bond between father and son to the bond between monastic father and monk. He makes an emotional appeal by invoking a sense of intimacy between monk and superior. Even in dispute, the monastic father should treat his spiritual son with love (*agapē*). Implicitly, that love bond requires the father to respect and listen to his offspring. Moreover, Shenoute uses his accusation of Ebonh's betrayal of that bond to justify his own disrespect of his father figure; Shenoute admits that he spoke harshly in return.¹¹ Shenoute thus concedes that he has acted as a son in a dishonorable way, but he places the blame on the father, whom he accuses of mishandling his paternal role. The medium of exchange is the father-son relationship.

Once Shenoute advanced to lead the monastery, fatherhood continued to be an important way he conceptualized the roles of the community's leader and other high-status positions. Of course the words for a revered monk or monastic leader—*Abba* (Greek, from the Aramaic), *Apa* (Coptic), and *hllo* (Coptic)—literally mean father or old man, but the significance of fatherhood extends beyond the terminology. Men in positions of authority functioned as fathers. Established monks were judged by the expectations of a father or old man and exercise responsibilities in line with a head of household (or *pater familias*). In *God Who Alone Is True* Shenoute writes about men who "govern" the community and thus supervise food consumption among the monks. He describes these men as "truly fathers," and they possess the responsibility to determine how much food or fasting is beneficial for each person underneath them in the monastic hierarchy. They seem to have earned this authority by having demonstrated their own acute capacities for self-control and personal perfection.¹² Earlier in the text Shenoute describes successful monks as men who have "established themselves" and "subjugat[ed] their bodies" fully.¹³ This emphasis on self-control in a monastic leader would align with Greco-Roman expectations of the head of household, whose own self-control was a precursor for exerting control over his household.

Likewise, just as the right to beat children was held by the father of the family, the authority to beat monks was held solely by Shenoute and his deputy, or assistant old man. In a section of the monastery's rules about education and training, Shenoute identifies the old man (*hllo*) alone as the one with the power to carry out or alter Shenoute's commands to punish the monks physically. (Dwight Young translates this office as "abbot.") The one exception pertains to children. The children's immediate superiors seem to have the right to subject the children to beatings. The passage is a bit unclear, bearing the hallmark as it does of the typical Shenoutean style in which the relationship between clauses is not always obvious: "They know from God that there is a great injury and there is a great condemnation on everyone among us who will do anything for themselves on their own by their own authority without [approval by] the father [*hllo*, lit., old man] in our domain, whether man or woman, whether old or young, including he who will deal one in our domain or in your domain a blow with a rod or a slap, with the exception of boys and girls."¹⁴

It is possible to take this passage to mean that children were not allowed to be beaten at all. However, one other interpretation is quite the opposite, that the children's immediate superiors served as their "spiritual parents" and thus held the power to beat them in their hands; only Shenoute or his associate can beat (or order the beating of) a monk, unless that monk is a child. In this interpretation, the exception concerns not who can be beaten, but under what authority can a monk be beaten. No one can be beaten without Shenoute's or his associate's authorization, except for children (who can be beaten without their approval.) Another complication is that the terms for "boys and girls" are vague; since the other terms for rank in the monastery are age-related (old man, old woman), it is possible that "boys and girls" means not children but spiritual children—novices or junior monks. Thus the immediate supervisors of children and/or junior monks have permission to beat their novitiates, just as teachers and tutors (and mothers) in the wider Greco-Roman world had permission to beat their students or children. The tradition of corporal punishment in Egypt and the wider Mediterranean leads me to suspect that the second interpretation is the correct one. The monastery thus mirrors both the late-antique family and late-antique grammar school; the rights of *patria potestas* lie solely in the hands of Shenoute and his immediate second-in-command; as the monastery's *pater familias,* Shenoute outlines in writing the rights consigned to his deputy as well as the lower-level house leaders and supervisors, which include the rights to beat novices or children in the course of regular discipline and instruction (as one would see in a school). As Raffaela Cribiore has demonstrated, corporal punishment was standard in the lower-level schools of Greco-Roman Egypt; beatings lessened (though did not disappear) only as the male pupils advanced to an age at which they were expected to learn to be the dominant person of the household (one who meted out punishment rather than endured it).[15] At Shenoute's monastery, only Shenoute and his delegate, acting in the role of the head of household, could increase or lessen punishments originally established by the community's father/*pater,* Shenoute. As Krawiec has noted, there is a gendered dimension to this policy. In the past the women at Shenoute's monastery were responsible for their own discipline. The "mother" of the community determined who should be punished and how. During his tenure as leader of the federation, Shenoute usurps her authority, and thus a good portion of the women's community's self-determination.[16] This realignment of power is indeed gendered, and gendered in such a way that the authority of the monastic superior more closely resembles paternal authority in Greco-Roman families. Although there is much that we do not know about the early history of this monastery, especially about the relationship between the men's and women's communities prior to Shenoute's tenure, gender—Shenoute's own gender as well as the gender of the monks—certainly inflects Shenoute's interactions with them.

Monastic Genealogies

As the monastery's father, Shenoute envisions himself as establishing a monastic genealogy in which the monks of the community become his ascetic progeny and themselves proceed to spawn subsequent generations of monastic offspring.

Shenoute implicitly compares himself with the Old Testament patriarchs who begat generations of righteous believers. Through their adherence to or violation of monastic practices, the community will produce generation upon generation of either righteousness or wickedness. The monastic project of ascetic perfection, when followed properly, engenders a parallel, but more selective, genealogy, based not on biological reproduction but ascetic production. In exhorting the monks to repentance, righteousness, and obedience, he interweaves the ancient prophetic condemnation of "lawlessness" with his contemporary adjuration to monastic and ascetic discipline. The genealogy ends with "us," monks who "effect righteousness": "The offspring [*sperma*] of our fathers alone shall last forever and ever, and their remembrance to generation after generation, as it is written (cf. Eccl 44:13). But the offspring of the ungodly shall be cut off forever, according to the scriptures (Ps 36:28), and the Lord shall blot out every one who always perpetrates evil. The offspring of the ungodly are those of us who will ever perpetrate lawless deeds. The offspring of our fathers are those of us who will ever effect righteousness."[17] The responsibility to educate, even form, future generations also informs Shenoute's justification for corporal punishment. Despite a lack of scriptural evidence, Shenoute asserts that biblical patriarchs beat their children with rods. Accordingly, as monastic patriarch, Shenoute, too, holds that privilege—or as he would see it, obligation—in order to assure a righteous future for his own progeny. He explains this obligation in a letter to the women's community concerning the punishment of monks whose transgressions have been reported to him:

> They shall have to receive their instruction with blows, for they too are our brethren, just as our brothers who are in our domain here. And God being the father of all of us and our Lord Jesus, who said through his saints, "He who spares his rod, it is his sons and daughters whom he hates" (Prov 13:24), it is by these words that we instruct one another with scoldings and blows. . . . Truly, we are not unmindful that we have not found it written that the holy prophets and apostles chastised some with rods and not with their words alone. On the contrary, we believe that if they had had sons and daughters whom they begat after the flesh, or rather spiritual sons and daughters who had trusted them, we believe they would have beaten them and the others with rods whenever they were disobedient. We believe, moreover, that our fathers of old—Abraham, Isaac, Jacob, and all the others—chastised their sons and daughters whom they begat after the flesh. Now, if others of spiritual descent had obeyed them, they would not have persisted in beating them with rods whenever they transgressed the Lord's commandments or if they were ignorant so that they did not obey their instructions and everything that they were bid.[18]

Shenoute depicts a spiritual genealogy stretching from God the father of all to the biblical fathers down to the monastic fathers, in which corporal punishment is necessary to ensure the edification and obedience of the later generations.

Finally, elements of Stoic thought also infuse Shenoute's works and factor into his understanding of proper ascetic manhood. Shenoute is by no means a "pure" or true Stoic; his ideas about the human self bear the marks of many streams of thought, especially the book of Job in the Christian Old Testament. However, Stoicism, and especially Stoic views on emotions and the proper way men in particular should handle emotions and the objects and events that could possibly trigger emotions, contribute to Shenoute's understanding of how the ideal monk should act in the world. Brakke's *Demons and the Making of the Monk* must be credited for reintroducing the significance of Stoicism for ascetic theory. Brakke breaks down the Stoic influences on Evagrius of Pontus's demonology, and in the chapter on Anthony, he describes "the Stoic approach to virtue" as a "ready paradigm by which to understand the monk's conflict with demons."[19] Regarding Shenoute, however, he argues that the archimandrite's demonology is not influenced by Stoicism.[20] Nonetheless, Brakke's insights extend beyond demonology and beyond Antony to more widespread monastic understandings of the role of asceticism in addressing moral conflict and emotion. Even though Stoicism does not inform Shenoute's demonology, it does inform his understanding of the role of emotions in moral conflict.

Margaret Graver's recent book *Stoicism and Emotion* argues that Stoics understood the perfect person not to be someone who feels nothing, but to be someone who experiences appropriate feelings.[21] The Stoics thus distinguish between feelings (affective states of the human condition) and emotions. Emotions are defined as improper stirrings of the self in response to an event.[22] In Graver's words, "Every instance of emotion is in its very essence a judgment concerning some present or potential state of affairs."[23] One tries to suppress a feeling because it stems from an erroneous judgment, not because a person should not feel at all.[24] Stoics determine the propriety and rationality of an effective response in part by looking to the objects that inspire feelings. Graver explains, "By far the most distinctive feature of the Stoic position, however, is its insistence that psychological claims about how emotions are generated must be integrated with other, prescriptive or normative claims as to the kinds of objects that can legitimately be valued."[25] The judgment is based not in determining whether something or an event is good or evil, but in evaluating whether an already predetermined good or evil thing is present or about to be present, and a preestablished evaluation already in one's character about the appropriate feelings for such a situation. These prejudgments form the matrix or framework in the psyche that determines a person's affective response to something. So the perfect man does not feel distress at an impending negative event (such as a looming battle), because he knows before ever foreseeing this event that such is a time for action, not anger or fear.[26] The perfect man feels love and affection for a friend or a child; these feelings are *eupatheiai* (good feelings or "normative affect") not *pathē* (emotions).

Emotions, argue the Stoics, "imply false judgments."[27] The judgment is based not on the determination of something as good or evil, but on whether an already established good or evil thing is present or about to be present. There are several levels of judgments and assessments: whether something is good or evil (a classification a person has already made, before that thing appears on the scene), and a determination of the appropriate response for situations (a predetermined judgment, as well—one which occurs over time as a result of education and character formation).[28] Only a physical event can trigger emotions; the event or impending event triggers the psyche, which has been shaped, formed, and developed by these preestablished judgments about good and evil things, and appropriate contexts for affect; the person has a framework in the mind which is activated by the event or sense of an impending event. The psyche in turn physically responds by moving, shifting, or changing, which is why emotions often manifest physically as well. A person with a strong psyche does not respond inappropriately to those potential triggers; a weak psyche is susceptible. Judgments are in part a result of the character of a person, developed over time through education, upbringing life experience, and so on. A perfect man, with a strong psyche, can experience feelings, but they are *eupatheiai* such as a love-bond between friends or a parent and child, because they are good and appropriate responses to a good object (the friend or child). The wise sage or perfect man uses reason to prevent pre-emotions—initial movements of body (such as tears that well upon hearing of the death of a friend)—from leading to inappropriate *pathē*, such as extended or dramatic public grief.

In his sermon *I Have Been Reading the Holy Gospels*, Shenoute articulates two of the core elements of Stoic emotional theory: a belief that emotional triggers are physical, and that the perfect monk cultivates his soul in order to display only appropriate affect and to reject or fend off inappropriate emotions. Shenoute's emotional theory is more complex, though, and his emotional discourse also adapts from biblical discourse an emphasis on closeness and distance, or intimacy and estrangement, as well as the reciprocity of obligations between parties who share an emotional bond. The sermon is a treatise on the final judgment, a moment of final unification with or separation from the divine.

I have examined nine terms for emotions in *I Have Been Reading the Holy Gospels*: *orgē* (anger or wrath), *cōnt* (anger or wrath), *me* (love), *moste* (hate or abhor), *mkah nhēt* and *lupē* (grief, sorrow, sadness), *rashe* (joy), *kataphronei* (hate or despise), *hote/r-hote* (fear). In addition, the concepts of rest, peace, and movement or suffering, which are central to both Stoic and Platonic understandings of the self, figure prominently in the sermon (*mton, hise, tōt nhēt*). I have left out of this study shame, which of course is an important emotion in the construction of ancient identity and social relations. As a "caution against correct censure," shame also counts among the Stoic *eupatheia*.[29]

In the emotional matrix of the sermon, appropriate feelings consist of joy (*rashe*) and peace or harmony (*tōt nhēt*) or rest (*mton*), and only in a specific context: "It is good that the Gospel has already taught us about what will happen to us. It is even better when we distance ourselves from our sins, lest grief and wailing strike us in the place where it is more fitting for us to attain utter peace and joy."[30] Shenoute clearly means paradise or the afterlife in this passage, rather than any this-worldly context.³¹ He does, however, use emotions as clear indicators of people who had righteous or unrighteous souls in this life: grief (*mkah nhēt* and *lupē*) and distress plague those who are punished in the afterlife.³² Shenoute contrasts rest and peace—affective states of a stable soul—with the distress and suffering of the unrighteous.³³ Moreover, joy, when expressed in response to appropriate circumstances, counts among the Stoic *eupatheiai* or good affects.³⁴

Shenoute also privileges action over emotion in responding to potential emotional triggers. The devil, he says, "moves" against the monk or priest's soul with thoughts, thoughts designed to corrupt the purity of the ascetic.³⁵ The monk responds not with emotion but "actions," specifically the acts of combat. Ascetics "sharpen their swords against him through actions." Shenoute continues, emphasizing the physicality of the battle against the devil's "thoughts" and the strength of the righteous's weaponry: "Truly they will pierce him more than javelins and spears and sharp arrows." Finally, Shenoute appeals to a sense of emotional propriety: gladness inspired by purity that should prevail instead of grief: "Is that impure spirit any concern to those who do not wish to grieve [*lupei*] the Holy Spirit in His temple, but rather to gladden [*euphrane*] Him with the purity of their heart and their body?"³⁶

In this life monks should use their ascetic training to strive to fend off improper emotions physically. Only the proper spiritual education can prepare a monk to do so. In the text now known as *A1*, Shenoute describes lustful thoughts as material opponents that can leap up and attack people. Especially vulnerable are people who think they know how to resist such thoughts but in fact do not. "Thus also the thought or the spirit of fornication weakens people, but especially those who say, 'We have resisted it,' when they do not know how or with what to oppose it."³⁷

Shenoute is assuredly no "pure" Stoic—Zeno or Seneca would surely scoff. Emotions, including hatred and fear, appear on occasion as positive qualities. He exhorts his monks to fear God countless times. However, his understanding of even these affective states overlaps with Stoicism. Although fear, *phobos*, is a broad category of Stoic *pathē*, Shenoute's discourse of fear bears a closer resemblance to the Stoic concept of reverence (*hagneia*, "caution against misdeeds concerning the gods"³⁸). Shenoute praises fear *only* when understood as religious piety: multiple times he exhorts Christians to fear God. In this passage he juxtaposes fear and reverence against impiety: "Whose words have you kept? You have not feared [*r-hote*] God. You have not revered a prophet nor an apostle and even the saints and all the righteous. You have cast out their sayings behind you. You brought only these impieties before you, which become much sweeter to you than those who love your souls. You have reproached those living with you, who desire your salvation. You have angered those who look out for where you are going."³⁹ He also urges his followers not to reject without fear the teachings of Apa Athanasius: "If there is one who does not accept these remarks, let him not dare reject fearlessly [*hnoumntathote*] the words of the richest of men in Christ (Lk 12:21), the archbishop Apa Athanasius.⁴⁰

Thus, Shenoute's "fear of God" equates with Stoic religious reverence and is entirely normative. Like the Stoics, however, he finds another form of fear inappropriate: fear of pain and difficulty. "If someone says that these sayings are difficult and he says further that this sermon is like a medical treatment, let him listen to this. There is no special sort of scalpel, truly, that is available to the physician to use on the timid. Or does [the patient] not wish to bear the pain for a moment in order to find relief, but rather he is afraid [*hote*] to see [the physician's] tools and their sharpness?"[41]

Shenoute also calls on his readers to "abhor sin" and "hate evil."[42] His embrace of the negative feelings of hatred (*moste*), anger (*orgē*), and grief reflects the influence of biblical emotional discourse on his worldview. In *I Have Been Reading the Holy Gospels* and *A1* these emotions are circumscribed. The appropriate experience of anger and hate falls not to known current human experience, but is bounded off and experienced in a positive way by God. The prophets, who were in fact human, express public grief, but they remain an exceptional category of holy person who stands apart even from ascetics, and their grief is also limited, even socially acceptable, in classical terms.

Only God, in *I Have Been Reading the Holy Gospels*, is allowed to experience anger and wrath in response to human sin. The "wrath of anger" of God "descend[s] upon" and even "obliterates" the disobedient, lawless, and impious.[43] Shenoute's sermon praises and thanks God for showing mercy and the using discretion to "turn away" from "the wrath of your anger."[44] In this sermon Shenoute values wrath or anger as a legitimate feeling only when associated with divine judgment, and a just divine judgment, against sinners. The Stoics, of course, regarded anger as a *patheia* and defined *orgē* as the emotion expressed when a person perceives s/he has been treated unjustly. Shenoute uses *orgē* and *cōnt* in this way, but to designate *God's* reaction to injustice; as divine feelings, *orgē* and *cōnt* are not bad emotions.

Even with hatred, we can see the intersection of Hellenism with Shenoute's biblical worldview. Hatred, as endorsed by Shenoute, constitutes an action as much as an emotional state—a volitional, perhaps even rational response to a negative object. To hate, abhor, and despise sin is to turn away from it and leave it behind: "What is the difficult matter that has been taught to us by the Scriptures? What is the burden that is laid upon us? Have not burdens been lifted from us? For it is said, 'Hate evil and love good.' (Amos 5:15) And, 'Depart from evil, and do good.' (Ps 33:15 LXX)."[45]

Shenoute also condemns hatred as a negative emotion felt when a person improperly assesses a situation (or, in Stoic terms, renders a false judgment). Here the false judgment concerns spiritual education: "For if someone scolds me for the sake of the profit of my soul (cf. 1 Cor 10:10, Jud 11, 16), if I am wise, then I will love him. If I am foolish, I will hate him. Assuredly, just as it is written, 'The fool does not love the one who scolds him' (Prov 15:12), so also it says, 'Those who hate scoldings will die in scorn'" (Prov 15:10).[46] (144) Shenoute interweaves basic, classical concepts of education, wisdom, and emotion with biblical discourse to produce a spiritual instruction that is at home in a Hellenized Coptic monastery. Expressing love (the appropriate feeling) in response to chastisement exhibits wisdom. Expressing hatred exposes a false judgment, since, as Shenoute continues, the "fool" in this case does not recognize and understand the source and true nature of his emotional trigger: the scolding, while spoken by a human, actually originates from God.[47]

Grief and hatred appear in the text known as *A1*. Shenoute's understanding of grief is deeply biblical but also sits comfortably with the classical sensibility that public tears for a limited time may be expressed upon the loss of loved one. In *A1* the prophets weep over sinners in bondage to Satan just as they wept for the Israelites captured by the Babylonians.[48] In contrast, the humans who weep are the sinners themselves, who watch their friends ascend to heaven at the final judgment while they are condemned to hell.[49] As we have already seen, extensive grief has a negative association in *I Have Been Reading the Holy Gospels,* since it is expressed by the damned—people who clearly have not achieved a state of disciplined perfection. Shenoute's views on grief seem more influenced by biblical discourse, although they are not in conflict with Stoic emotional theory. Shenoute even takes pains to explain the injunction in John 12:25 to hate one's life in this world in order to achieve eternal life. His exegesis reveals the impropriety that may lie in "hating" a life that God has given you and an understanding that "hatred" qualifies as a *pathē*, a negative emotion. Hatred as a positive feeling, in Shenoute's interpretation, really means not to experience hatred but to experience love: "Surely then, the one who will forsake his life for his friend's sake (John 15:13), according to the word of the Lord, and will hate it (John 12:25) or lose it on account of him, he shall receive more blessings from him. Indeed, 'hate your life' [*mecte etekpsuchē*] is also struggling at the tasks that we specified and then did not hate [*ntanmectōou*]."[50] Thus the biblical command to hate one's own life transforms into imperatives to value a friend's life more than one's own and not to hate the daily tasks of life. Hatred becomes its opposite.

Finally, I wish to return the emotional language in Shenoute's account of his argument with his own monastic father in his first volume of canons. When Shenoute accuses Ebonh of treating him with hatred rather than love, he uses emotional rhetoric, drawing on monastic expectations and broader cultural expectations of the affective ties between fathers and sons—expectations influenced by, however diluted, Stoic values. Propriety dictates that a father love his son and act accordingly. As Shenoute sees it, both father and the son acted inappropriately by expressing hate and anger instead of *agapē*. Shenoute himself diagnoses the cause of his own emotional outburst as a Stoic might—he asserts that he reacted wrongly to an object/event (the hateful Ebonh). Again, although it is not possible to claim that Shenoute is a Stoic in the desert, his articulation of the relationship between emotion and ascetic self-discipline suggests that Stoic views of the self penetrated the Coptic monastic culture of Middle and Upper Egypt.

Conclusion

This examination of Shenoute on masculinity and ascetic perfection is possible only because of the trends in scholarship outlined earlier: interdisciplinary approaches, new methodologies and approaches, and globalization. It also owes much to recent work, specifically on Shenoute, especially by Stephen Emmel. Although Shenoute is our most important early Coptic author, his writings remained in scholarly disarray until recently. Only in 1993 did Stephen Emmel produce a codicological, or textual, reconstruction of the surviving manuscripts of Shenoute's writings—manuscripts dispersed, sometimes even page by page (folio by folio) across the globe in different collections. Later published as *Shenoute's Literary Corpus,* Emmel's reconstruction has enabled my work, along with the scholarship of several others. However, Emmel's codicological reconstruction is not sufficient for in-depth and contextualized analyses of Shenoute, since full critical editions and translations still do not exist. An international team of scholars led by Emmel has been working on a collaborative publication of Shenoute's works since the year 2000. They began with Shenoute's writings for monks, the *Canons,* and originally projected that those volumes would appear in print by 2010. The project has now expanded to the *Discourses.* Hopefully, these publications are on the horizon. While at work, the scholars on the team have been generous in sharing their materials with others, but understandably Shenoute research can only progress slowly in the meantime. Other scholars are deciding not to include Shenoute in studies of asceticism and monasticism or not to publish photographs, transcriptions, or translations of known unpublished manuscripts in anticipation of the editions. Our newest and most creative Ph.D. students in theology, history, asceticism, and linguistics in particular face a difficult choice: pursue a project that involves Shenoute (knowing that a team of experienced senior colleagues is preparing definitive editions) or choose a topic that excludes Shenoute (or even Coptic or late-antique Egypt altogether, given Shenoute's importance to both of those fields).

Likewise, a fuller understanding of the intersection of Hellenism, theology, biblical interpretation, and gender norms in Shenoute's writings must wait for the editions. Nonetheless, this excursus on masculinity and ascetic perfection has shed light on important issues in Coptic studies. In Shenoute's world, the concepts of monastic paternity and religious genealogies were instrumental in constructing a community identity and enforcing systems of authority. Emotional discourse, influenced by Hellenism and biblical discourse, was wielded in theological dialogue as well as in power struggles in early monasticism. Finally, the construction of an ascetic masculinity built from all of these elements (emotional expectations, paternity, genealogies, and legacies) accompanied the formation of conceptions of ascetic perfection in Egyptian monasticism.

THE PARADOX OF MONASTICISM
The Transformation of Ascetic Ideals from the Fourth to the Seventh Century

Karel C. Innemée

This essay discusses how the early ideals of the solitary life in the desert became overtaken by the realities and needs of the Church hierarchy. While most of the earliest materials about the men and women who moved deep into the desert to practice the Christian ideals have come to us via hagiographic writings, modern-day excavations provide material proof of how those seeking God in the desert had to give in to the everyday needs of the growing Church.

Although many legends tell about the origins of monasticism in Egypt, we have few historic accounts outside of those by travelers in search of these hermit monks and nuns who had removed themselves from the world in search of God. We do not always know for sure why individuals left behind wealth, family, and worldly pleasures, but we do know that their main goal was to achieve salvation of the soul. In coenobitic communities, those based on communal forms of monasticism, this was accompanied by obedience and submission to a superior and rules of the community. In contrast, the individual anchorite, or hermit, had the liberty of following his or her self-set goals of abstinence, thus reaching a state of "angelic life," half way between earth and heaven. The *Apophthegmata Patrum*, the Sayings of the Desert Fathers, show a great diversity in attitudes and degrees of austerity in this self-imposed asceticism.

Both the coenobitic and the anchoretic varieties of the monastic movement started as lay movements. Although there must have been appreciation and admiration for the early desert fathers, both at a popular level and in the ecclesiastical hierarchy, there is evidence for mistrust and rejection as well. Only when monastic communities and anchorites were officially placed under supervision of the Church was there a gradual integration and institutionalization of monasticism. Today the bond between monastic communities and the Church is confirmed and strengthened by the fact that most of the higher clergy are recruited from monastic circles.

This process of being integrated into the official Church profoundly influenced the monastic ideals of the fourth and fifth centuries. The strict imitation of Christ as it was practiced by many no longer seemed compatible with the rules of the Church once the monasteries came under ecclesiastical supervision. Monks had to adapt to a new situation both in their way of living and in their new physical space. For example, according to the tradition, one of the most influential models of early anchoretic monasticism, Macarius of the fourth century, spent his last years in seclusion close to the place where the Saint Macarius monastery currently resides (on the desert road between Cairo and Alexandria). The results of a recent survey around this monastery illustrate the changes in the material aspects of monastic life that resulted from the merger of Church and monasticism. Where at first hermits were living a modest lifestyle in self-made half-underground dwellings, a monastic settlement developed with several churches and industrial activities of various kinds.

The Monastic Ideal of Seclusion

In search of hermits living in absolute seclusion, the fourth-century saint Paphnoutios set out on a journey into the desert.[1] First he found a dead monk in his cell whom he buried. After a journey of seventeen days he found a man covered in his own hair and a girdle made of leaves. This man turned out to be Saint Onouphrios, now known as Abu Nofer. The saint told him that he had left his monastery at Ashmunayn sixty years before and had been in the desert ever since. Paphnoutius served him Communion and soon afterward the holy man died.[2] Coptic icons have traditionally depicted Saint Onouphrios as the naked hermit, and today he is considered a role-model of asceticism.[3]

We might ask ourselves which goals the two desert fathers that Paphnoutios encountered had set for themselves, and which one of the two had reached his goals. Of the first father we know nothing, only that he died nameless and in solitude. The second one became a saint and a model of abstinence and mortification. Both of them left society with the ideal of leaving the world behind, renouncing possessions and pleasure. Furthermore, the anchoretic ideals of the third and fourth centuries were to sever all ties to the world or "become dead to the world." The hermit fought a daily battle with his temptations, in order to reach a state of *apatheia*, the rejection and suppression of all passions, of which anger and pride are some of the worst.[4] Even the most renowned desert fathers would reject the slightest form of veneration of their person, in life as well as in death. In his vita, or biography, by Athanasius, it is said that Saint Anthony instructed his closest pupils to bury him in a secret place, to avoid a cult of his bodily remains.[5] Bearing this in mind, we might suppose that the first anonymous anchorite had reached some, if not all, of his goals. There must have been many in the third and fourth centuries who died like him, anonymously in absolute solitude. We could also wonder whether Onouphrios would have been pleased with his place in the synaxaria (the books about the lives of the saints and martyrs), the mural paintings, and icons, serving as an object of veneration to the faithful.

Here we have an illustration of what we might call the paradox of monasticism. The anchorite renounces and leaves the world, but the world tracks him down and brings him back, physically or as an icon, a saint and an object of veneration, through his hagiography, his icons, and his relics. His image and his biography become the property of the Church and a means to edify and teach the community. We might even say that his image in iconography and hagiography tells us more about the moral and theological ideals of the Church than about the historical person in question. In editing a vita, adding information where details are missing and polishing and enhancing the virtues, an idealized image is created that often borders on a stereotype. This hermit, however, does not consider him- or herself to be a saint. In numerous *apophthegmata,* or the words of the desert fathers, renowned desert fathers underscore their own sinfulness as a source of daily sorrow. For example, Saint Moses is quoted to have given advice to Saint Poimen: "If the monk does not think in his heart that he is a sinner, God will not hear him."[6] We can only guess how such fathers would react if they could have read their hagiographies, written long after their deaths.

Anchoretic monasticism began as a quest for solitude, poverty, and abstinence in order to achieve the salvation of the soul. Maybe most illustrative is the fact that the word *monk,* now generally interpreted as a term for one living in a community, has been derived from the term *monachos* (solitary). This quest for solitude and the difficulty in finding a lasting seclusion become clear in the traditions concerning Saint Macarius. After living as a village hermit and wishing to leave the world behind, he settled down in Sketis in the Western or Libyan Desert, sixty-five miles southwest of the Nile Delta. When his followers became too numerous, he retreated further into the desert to a place that must have been close to the present Monastery of Saint Macarius.[7] What happened around his first cell repeated itself here: followers settled around him and formed a community from which the Monastery of Saint Macarius later developed. The quest for solitude seemed to be in vain for hermits with reputations like his own.

One of the *apophthegmata* recounts: "Father Macarius said to the brethren concerning the destruction of Sketis: when you see a cell built close to the marsh, know that devastation of Sketis is near, when you see trees, know that it is at the doors, but when you see young children, take up your sheep-skins, and go away."[8] Indeed everyone who has ever visited a present-day monastery in Wadi Natrun on a Friday will have to admit that the destruction of Sketis according to Macarius has now been accomplished. Apart from modern means of transportation, smooth roads, and media, this high visibility can also be ascribed to the fact that all monasteries are now ensconced within the official Church structure. Their buildings, art, and inhabitants all serve at the pleasure of the Coptic pope and by extension of the Coptic community.

Incorporation of Monasticism by the Church

The institutions of the churches, not only the Coptic Orthodox Church, have gradually incorporated monasticism. It has gone so far that the Eastern Orthodox churches could no longer function without monasteries. This incorporation, however, has not been achieved without surmounting hurdles. The anchoretic ascetic movement was initially a completely extraecclesiastical one. It is not surprising that it must have been looked upon by many clerics with a certain skepticism in spite of, or perhaps because of, its growing popularity in the fourth century.

The organization of the Church from early on has been centered on the figure of a bishop who resided in a town, and thus Christianity has traditionally been an urban religion. It is no coincidence that the term *pagan* is derived from *paganus* (Latin, rural, of the countryside). The monastic movement not only escaped from the town and "the world" but, implicitly, also from the control of the bishop. For example, even Saint and Pope Athanasius of the fourth century, although he was an advocate of the monastic ideal (biographer of the first monk and hermit Saint Anthony), had his confrontations with monastic communities when he demanded that certain monks become bishops.[9]

Nowadays only monks are eligible for the office of bishop or patriarch. This is the result of a gradual process that started with the arduous task of convincing a monk to enter the clerical ranks. Athanasius was one of the first patriarchs who consciously recruited monks to become bishops.[10] Many anchorites, in spite of being advised or even forced to do so, resisted or refused even to be consecrated a priest. Anthony was never consecrated,[11] and Pachomius equally refused to become a priest when Bishop Serapion of Tentyra insisted.[12]

Being removed from the central Church authorities also carried the risk of diversion from the Church's teaching. Large groups of hermits were living far away from society, without clerical guidance or supervision but nevertheless attracting followers and believers in search of spiritual advice or healing. The risk that unorthodox teachings might take root in the desert was a real one. One example is the confrontation of Theophilus of Alexandria (384–412 C.E.) with various monastic communities concerning anthropomorphic ideas about God.[13] John Cassian reports how in his Paschal Letter of 399 Theophilus condemned such ideas. In three out of four churches in Sketis the letter was not even read as it was rejected by the monks.[14]

The detection of any deviant thoughts, acts, or teachings was one thing; a second problem was how to correct them or to enforce sanctions. Within the non-coenobitic communities there was apparently no uniform system of regulations and sanctions. On the contrary, some were even opposed to any kind of sanction on transgressions, bearing in mind the words from Matthew 7:1, "Judge not, that ye be not judged."

Imitatio Christi: Imitating Christ as a Ground for Conflict with the Church

A number of *apophthegmata* are dedicated to the idea that one sinner should not judge the sins of the other. Even some of the most senior desert fathers would stick to that mantra. This stands in sharp contrast to the coenobitic communities of Upper Egypt, where the rules of Pachomius (fourth century) and Shenoute (fifth century) were unequivocal in dealing with offenses.[15] Without taking these *apophthegmata* as rendering historical events, we can nevertheless consider them an illustration of the attitude certain hermits had toward their environment. They preferred to teach by example or leave matters in God's hand. For example, according to one anecdote, a monk in Sketis refused to believe that the Eucharist was the body and blood of Christ. Two fellow brethren tried to persuade him of the Orthodox view, but decided that it would be God himself that should convince him. After their prayers for him he had a vision during the liturgy in which the bread on the altar took the shape of a small child, and when the priest was about to break the bread, an angel appeared who slaughtered the child. The bread he received from the priest turned out to be a morsel of bloody flesh and only turned into bread after he confessed his faith in the divine presence in the Eucharist.[16]

Father Poimen, according to one of the *apophthegma*, rejected straightaway the condemnation of all sinners.[17] Abba Theodore advised not to judge the fornicator, since judging would be as much of a sin as fornication itself.[18] While this stance is a literal interpretation of Matthew 7:1, "Judge not, that ye be not judged," this attitude towards heterodoxy and sin was hardly acceptable in a regulated community, where the clergy had a responsibility to guide their flock on the path of correct beliefs. This atmosphere of rejecting judgment as a result of what we could call theocratic anarchy would therefore not last forever in monastic communities.[19]

By the end of the fourth century Church authorities tried more and more to get control of monastic and ascetic movements, not only in Egypt but also in the eastern Mediterranean and Mesopotamia in general. It seems that the potential of a large group of spiritually motivated people was recognized, but the clergy must have considered it a kind of wild plant that needed pruning and cultivation in order for the Church to harvest its fruits.

The *Imitatio Christi*, an important aspect in the anchoretic/ascetic ideal, meant not only abstaining from judgment but also taking on complete poverty as instructed by Jesus in Mathew 6:19–34. To some these verses were an inspiration to lead the life of a begging, itinerant monk. The heresies of a solitary hermit might be unacceptable to the Church, but as long as he remained isolated he posed less danger to the Church than itinerant monks who would frequently preach.

In 431 C.E. the Council of Ephesus condemned in fierce formulations the "most noxious heresy in memory," by which was meant Messalianism, a movement that must have started in the third quarter of the fourth century. It is difficult to give an exact definition of Messalianism, since the name was used by the "orthodox" as a term for a group of believers considered to be heterodox, but without a real organization or a well-defined corpus of teachings. Messalians (derived from the Syriac term for "those who pray") believed that the human soul could not be delivered from evil by the sacraments, not even baptism, but only through prayer. They practiced a life of poverty, celibacy, and fasting, while wandering as itinerant ascetics, taking their inspiration for this lifestyle from Matthew 6.[20]

In their outward appearance non-Messalian itinerants could easily be confused with Messalians, and this apparently discredited many of them. The ascetic movement of Lower Egypt was further compromised by the writings of the Pseudo-Macarius (the *Great Letter* and the *Spiritual Homilies*) that were considered to be of a Messalian character. At the end of the fourth century they were taken for genuine and must have confirmed the belief that the Lower Egyptian anchoretic/ascetic movement was not to be trusted. Although there is reason to believe that what was considered by many a heretical sect was in fact a much less-well-defined movement of begging wanderers with sometimes orthodox, sometimes heterodox convictions, they were opposed with great zeal.[21] Perhaps their greatest threat was the fact that they escaped social and ecclesiastical control, did not work but begged, and consequently did not fit in the system. In a period when Christianity became the official state religion and the position of the Church in the empire and the Trinitarian dogma were consolidated, it is not surprising that persons and movements that escaped control by worldly and clerical authorities were especially mistrusted and persecuted.

Control of monastic communities in general was achieved twenty years later at the Council of Chalcedon (451C.E.), when bishops were put in charge of monasteries and anchoretic communities and wandering and travelling were restricted.[22] The spirit of Mathew 7:1 was now gradually replaced by one of punishment for sin. Disciplinary measures as they would be applied in coenobitic monasteries or in lay society were apparently now also practiced in the monastic communities of Lower Egypt that were gradually developing into (semi-) coenobitic communities. In the *History of the Patriarchs of Alexandria* we even read of one case, at the end of the seventh century, in which a monk from Sketis (now called Wadi Habib) was beaten so severely on the orders of the bishop for having sexual contacts with a woman that he died of his injuries.[23]

Merger of Church and Monastic Life: The Case of the Monastery of Saint Macarius

In the centuries to follow there was a growing integration of the Church and monastic communities, both the coenobitic and semi-coenobitic ones. Until the thirteenth century it was apparently still possible for a man of virtue who had not been married more than once to become a bishop or patriarch,[24] but in practice we see that from thesixth century onward, more and more of the higher clergy were recruited from monasteries. The 29th and 30th patriarchs, John I (496–505) and John II (505–516), are mentioned as a monk (John I was probably from Saint Macarius monastery) and a hermit respectively.[25] The ties between the Patriarchate of Alexandria and the Monastery of Saint Macarius became especially close when the monastery became the patriarchal residence in the middle of the sixth century. Following measures by Justinian against the anti-Chalcedonian Copts in Alexandria, the position of the patriarch became more and more difficult. Churches were confiscated by the Melkites and, according to Eutychius[26] and the historian Maqrizi,[27] many citizens fled to Sketis when Patriarch Theodosius moved his residence to the Saint Macarius monastery.

Since then a considerable number of patriarchs have been monks from this monastery, by far the majority until the twelfth century. Here we see a more physical "return to the world." Whereas Paphnoutios only brought the vita and the veneration of Onouphrios back to the Church, now we see that the monk or hermit in some ways feels compelled to accept active office or to return to a world he thought he had left behind. His humbleness obliges him to refuse; his obedience to his superiors forces him to say yes. Although we have little or no information about the personal feelings or attitudes of individual monks who were elected to become bishops or patriarchs, it is not unlikely that they might have objected to this unexpected change in their career. The fact that the ritual for the consecration of a patriarch prescribes that the candidate be brought into the church in fetters represents this conflict, as does the criterion that the best candidate for the patriarchate is the one who does not aspire to it.[28]

There is little material evidence so far for the changing position of the Saint Macarius monastery as mentioned by Eutychius and Maqrizi. The latter wrote his account almost 850 years later, and it is difficult to say how much of their time the anti-Chalcedonian (Coptic) patriarchs really spent in the monastery. We have, however, certain reasons to believe that the monastery grew considerably in size and importance and that it brought about a considerable change in the lifestyle of its inhabitants. The anti-Chalcedonian patriarch Benjamin I (622–661 C.E.) lived in the period when Heraclius, after having reconquered Egypt from the Persians in 629 C.E., embarked on a violent campaign to subdue the anti-Chalcedonians in Egypt and appointed Cyrus as prefect and patriarch in Alexandria to carry out this task. Benjamin was forced to flee and hide in monasteries in the Fayoum and Upper Egypt. From December 18, 645 C.E. to January 646 C.E. (or 647), when following the Arab conquest the position of the Melkite Church had been reduced considerably, he was asked to consecrate the new church of the Saint Macarius monastery, a building of apparently impressive size and splendor. It must have been Benjamin himself who supported and fostered the redevelopment of monasteries, especially that of Saint Macarius, and his involvement is elaborately described in the *Book of the Consecration of the Sanctuary of Benjamin* and in the *History of the Patriarchs of Alexandria*. The appearance of Macarius to Benjamin in a vision and, later on, even the hand of God that performed the anointing of the sanctuary, are miracles that underline the importance of the church.[29] The special position of the monastery is also apparent from the fact that here for some time the head of Saint Mark the Apostle, the major relic of the Coptic Orthodox Church, was kept.[30]

The Survey around the Monastery of Saint Macarius

We can follow the development of and the changes in monastic life in Sketis on the basis of texts and archaeological evidence that seem to support some of these conclusions. Until the 1990s hardly any archaeological fieldwork had been done in this region, but since the excavations at the Monastery al-Baramus by Leiden University and the site of John the Little, first by the Scriptorium and continued by Yale University, more insight in the development of the monasteries here has been gained.[31] In the first stage of their development monastic settlements must have consisted of a group of hermitages, or *manshobiyyas*, spread over a wide area with a radius of about two miles. The center of such a settlement would consist of a church, sometimes in combination with a tower and, in the course of the centuries, we see a gradual contraction with a higher density of habitation in the direct vicinity of this center. In the ninth and tenth centuries defensive walls were constructed around these complexes, and only then we can speak of real monasteries in the architectural sense of the word. A similar process must have taken place in the area of the Saint Macarius monastery.

Beginning in the summer of 2009, with additional work in January 2010, and May 2012, a team from Leiden University undertook a survey in the direct vicinity of the Saint Macarius monastery, the area to the north, west, and south within the modern perimeter wall of the monastery. Hugh G. Evelyn White had published a small but accurate survey map of this area,[32] but the preliminary results of the Leiden survey show that even more remains than suspected are still present, giving us insight into the transformation of the area (see fig. 13).

The southernmost part of the area is mainly occupied by small hermitages of a type found elsewhere in Wadi Natrun: caves dug into the soft sediment or half-underground *manshobiyyas*, partly dug into the bedrock, half constructed in brick and limestone. This is a type of dwelling that can be dated to the fifth and sixth centuries and later. The present-day monastery probably developed around the new church that was consecrated by Benjamin I in the middle of the seventh century; the possible location of the earlier church has not been established yet. From the sixth to the tenth centuries the area around the present monastery must have undergone a metamorphosis from a small-scale settlement into a monastic suburbia where at least several hundred monks (and possibly lay personnel) lived. An exact dating of these buildings on the basis of preliminary survey results is not yet possible, but in the amount of pottery found at the surface of a number of structures, sixth to eleventh century artefacts are dominant. In some cases parallels can be drawn with dated structures elsewhere. An example of this is a large rectangular mud brick structure (approximately forty by twenty-five meters) with a complex floor plan (see figure 14). Most of the rooms seem to have been decorated with a dado-painting (a decorative pattern covering the wall up to a height of about 1.5 meters) in a style that corresponds to sixth- and seventh-century mural paintings from the Deir al-Baramus excavation. Apart from this building, there have been several buildings of comparable size surrounding the still existing monastery. Most of these are of a later date. From the late ninth century onward there is evidence of monastic complexes surrounded by a defensive wall, and the clearly visible remains of such buildings are extant north of the modern monastery. Several pottery kilns and metal workshops have also been located. The overall impression is that archaeological remains confirm the information from written sources: the area of the Saint Macarius monastery was a densely populated settlement until a decline in the thirteenth century. Maqrizi, writing about 1400, mentions only a few monks

Fig. 13. Survey map of the surroundings of the Monastery of Saint Macarius, including structures mapped by Hugh G. Evelyn White, indicated in gray. Drawing by Martin Hense. Used with permission.

Fig. 14. Structure 25, preliminary reconstruction. Drawing by Martin Hense. Used with permission.

living there[33], but for at least six centuries the place, where one of the founding fathers of the Egyptian anchoretic movement had hoped finally to find the ultimate seclusion, had become a bustling site that embodied the fusion of monasticism and ecclesiastical hierarchy.

Conclusion

Iconography and hagiography have much in common; they complement each other as picture and word in presenting the image of a saint. Neither of the two is (meant to be) realistic, and, rather than giving a true biographical image, they give an idealized representation that often repeats the paradigms and stereotypes of the ideal martyr, the ideal monk, and so on. As such, they were used as objects of veneration and educative instruments in the hands of the Church that could easily be edited or modified to fulfill this purpose.

In spite of changes in the real-life circumstances of the monks, the ideals of monasticism have left untouched certain elements in the hagiographic image of the fourth-century desert fathers. Saints such as Macarius, Pambo, and Poimen could hardly be ignored as founding fathers, but their teachings and behavior would no longer be accepted in sixth-century Sketis. Naked hermits such as Onouphrios and others showing extreme behavior would hardly fit in anymore. The almost anarchistic/theocratic ascetic movement of the fourth century with its diversity in ideals, many of which were only feasible in the isolation of the desert, and which had even been seen as a threat to the authority of the Church, had been successfully absorbed, transformed, and incorporated by the Church by the sixth century. It is remarkable to see that the place where Macarius sought seclusion in the final years of his life has become the embodiment of this transformation and a center of ecclesiastical authority.

RECONSIDERING THE EMERGING MONASTIC DESERTSCAPE

Darlene L. Brooks Hedstrom

Reading accounts of the Egyptian landscape in early monastic literature provides a taxonomy of place, which shapes how many scholars have interpreted where monastics lived. Early monastic literature presents an ideal of early ascetic living in a landscape often described as deserted. With agricultural fields present only on a narrow strip hugging the Nile valley, the desert is ubiquitous. The desert is very near; one can see large parts of the desert from a boat on the Nile. The extensive archaeological remains of monastic life prove that locations of new Christian communities were frequently on the boundaries of lay settlements. Monastic settlements were not hidden. The majority could be seen on limestone escarpments; in natural caves, quarries, and remodeled tombs visible from the Nile; on desert plains with newly purpose-built settlements; and even in revitalized abandoned buildings. All, regardless of place, were made suitable for monastic habitation. The spiritual vitality fostered in Egypt enhanced a monastic desert typos that was then transported, modified, amplified, and reproduced in other monastic communities across the Mediterranean.[1] The desert fathers, the first founders of Egyptian monasticism, would soon take on a popularity that had little to do with where they lived and more with how they lived.[2] And the desert, as described in monastic literature, became merely an architecturally free landscape for the battles with demons, apathy, temptation, and gossip.

Despite the elevation of ascetics as iconic figures of late antiquity, the archaeological study of the spaces in which Egyptian monastics lived is largely unexamined and, until now, largely bereft of well-defined methodological approaches that would help to contextualize the physical remains as part of larger issues related to late-antique and Coptic studies. The research agendas for the first generation of archaeologists who explored Egypt and the Near East in the nineteenth and early twentieth centuries were shaped in large part by a desire to fill national museums with treasures of ancient peoples.[3] Moreover, the earlier scholars who did document monastic sites in the course of nineteenth- and early twentieth-century surveys of pharaonic remains tended to reject the Egyptian desert as an appropriate location of habitation, thereby dismissing monastic spaces.[4] They were essentially unworthy of critical analysis. Scholars could not find a place for including the artifacts and the material culture of monastic history or late antiquity as an area of genuine interest.[5] Additionally, the scholarly ascription of authority to literary texts resulted in rigid paradigms for describing the evolution of monastic habitation. Foremost among these is the inherited binary model that identified monastics as adopting either eremitic (anchoretic) or coenobitic monasticism, as represented by the forerunners Anthony (ca. 251–356 C.E.) and Pachomius (292–346 C.E.). Without a critical rereading of the literary sources and consideration of the authorial motivations behind crafting a monastic history, early scholars recited and recorded a narrative of monastic history that provided a literary typology that was overlaid upon actual physical remains. Anything that did not physically fall within the categorization of a space to live alone, identified as Anthonian monasticism, or within a walled monastery, known more commonly as coenobitic or Pachomian monasticism, was something else.

A preferential regard for documenting monumental architecture led archaeologists to dismiss the value of the ubiquitous mud-brick structures of the late-antique and medieval periods.[6] The high regard for pharaonic architectural plans led to a rather singular view of the multiphased settlement evidence. The indications of a Coptic presence were frequently regarded as of little archaeological interest and of diminished value for financial patrons.[7] One only needs to view early photographs of the densely inhabited temples at Karnak and Luxor, in Upper Egypt, and further south at Philae, to consider how much material was stripped away in an effort to recreate a sanitized and restored pharaonic landscape for scholars and tourists.[8] This essay examines how the application and appropriation of archaeological theory contextualizes the reading of monastic remains. Before examining those theories, a brief overview of the historiography of how monks lived in Egypt is necessary in order to articulate the challenges faced in viewing the artifactual evidence and putting forward a revised portrait of the monastic desertscape.

Old Theories of Fanatics, Structuralism, and Processual Theory in Archaeology

Vivid fourth-century ascetic portraits of John of Lycopolis entombed on a cliff for decades in Middle Egypt or Macarius the Alexandrian living alone in the remote desert like a hyena make for good stories.[9] Few readers forget the account of the young monk Zacharius, who embraces self-harm by submerging his beautiful body in a pit of natron (a deposit of natural sodium carbonate) in order to put an end to the wagging tongues of fellow monks in his community.[10] His use of the natural environment to scar his body can be read as act of mutilation or profound spiritual devotion.[11] These accounts, and the others like them found in the *Apophthegmata Patrum* and the accounts of visitors such as John Cassian (ca. 360–435 C.E.) and Palladius (ca. 363–420 C.E.), were and are evocative of an extreme asceticism and Christianity that would mystify modern readers. Nineteenth-century scholars adopted Edward Gibbon's view that monks were extremists and asserted that such behavior revealed the signs of a fanatical, insane, or uneducated populace.[12] The stories are repeated in scholarly discussions as examples of iconic asceticism. They capture the imagination as figures who exhibit a life of hardship and commitment—so holy were these early desert inhabitants that they were willing to subject their bodies to the harshness of the natural environment. Their bodies could be monitored and controlled by dwelling in a physical residence, whose walls would restrain the weak flesh.[13] Separation, as least in part, was necessary in order to create the physical space for the new training grounds. The elevated Egyptian mountain cliffs and associated deserts were excellent spaces for designing a landscape dedicated to spiritual living. The newly emerging monastic desert of late antiquity was a space that communicated religious ideals to the outside world while simultaneously interweaving religious geography with ideals of monastic spiritual progress.[14]

The religious rhetoric of monastic accounts regarding space and place essentially limits our ability to see early monastic building practices in a clear light. The authorial intent of writers seeking to attach spiritual value to acts of habitation, incubation, and engagement with the world overshadows what actual monks experienced in the spaces they built. Fortunately, extensive physical evidence remains of monastic habitation, along with documentary evidence that challenges and calls into question the ascetic ideals espoused in devotional literature. The challenge in considering how the Egyptian monastic landscape was understood in antiquity is not shaped solely by access to material or textual evidence. Rather, it is the interpreter of those artifacts, buildings, and documents who also provides an obstacle to our ability to know and understand the past. The success of these studies demonstrates that all such fields can benefit from the appropriation of theories from related fields. Egyptian monastic archaeology is about to enter a new stage in which theorized research designs will greatly enhance how we approach the study of monastic history and allow us to consider carefully how monastic space became monastic. We, much like our nineteenth-century colleagues who first gathered evidence of monastic history, present a past shaped by modern attitudes toward monasticism, religion, and land usage.

For the nineteenth-century historian Leopold von Ranke, the task of the historian was to understand the past as it actually was. This descriptive approach was upheld in the field of archaeology and history until the middle of the twentieth century. In the 1960s and 1970s the American archaeologist Lewis Binford and the British historian David Clarke developed two different, but related, theoretical models for applying quantitative methods to archaeological research and understanding the past.[15] Their theories would inspire a generation of archaeologists who embraced what would be later known as New Archaeology or Processual Archaeology. This means that one can read the archaeology within a structure of predictable patterns that would involve environmental or site-formation processes and predictable societal actions. Binford, writing in two articles, presented a scientific approach to excavation methodologies by incorporating statistical and matrix analyses; by applying models of cultural formation to explain site formation; and by integrating anthropological theories with archaeological interpretations.[16] Clarke, working independently of Binford, created a four-tiered systems theory for explaining culture, change over time, and phasing. He argued that a close analysis of systems could allow the archaeologist to predict and explain particular features and components in the material record. One could use systems theory to quantify past societies in knowable ways. Writing in *Analytical Archaeology*, Clarke argued for a structuralist approach by which the archaeologist could "expect to both find regularities in his data and to be able so to rearrange his data as to produce yet other regularities."[17] In his construction Clarke identified four states that could be arranged to explain society effectively. The models of economy, social pattern, material culture, and religious pattern moved the archaeological outside of the realm of taxonomy to more theorized and scientific analysis.

One could argue that Egyptian monastic archaeology still remains firmly within an outdated structuralist interpretive worldview. While few of the earlier archaeologists working in Egypt consciously considered site-formation theory when identifying monastic settlements, their descriptions reflect underlying assumptions. The foundational belief is that all settlements must be divided into one of two categories. C. C. Walters's general introduction in *Monastic Archaeology in Egypt* typifies the basic view of the binary reading of monastic space:

> Any consideration of the monastic communities in Egypt must always differentiate between the two types normally termed Anthonian and Pakhomian after their founders. This differentiation is concerned primarily with the degree and manner of organization within the respective communities, with whether the emphasis was on the individual or the community. Their origins were quite different, on the one hand spontaneous and on the other the result of a deliberate act at a given moment in time. The character of the Pakhomian institutions remained fundamentally unchanged. Inevitably their differences found expression in the overall form of the communities and to some extent in the design of some of their buildings.[18]

Scholars repeat and reinforce this bimodal classification, or typology, in many introductions to monastic settlement patterns. Two distinct and charismatic figures, Anthony and Pachomius, would become catalysts for regional variations in monastic living. Anthony's final habitation by the coast of the Red Sea was a modified cave and a few followers resided nearby. Today it rests within a crag in one of the sharply rising vertical cliffs. Anthony's cliff dwelling then becomes the inspiration for hermetical living. The community continues to this day nestling at the base of the wadi cliffs as a visible marker of Anthony's residence.[19]

In contrast, Pachomius espoused a more deliberate, man-made reclamation of abandoned spaces and areas on the outskirts of towns, especially in Middle and Upper Egypt.[20] Inspired in part by his prior experience in the military, his call for communal living makes him the namesake for the cenobitic movement. His many purpose-built communities did not survive past the sixth century, although he did inspire others, such as Shenoute of Atripe (348–465 C.E.) and his great White Monastery Federation in Sohag in southern Egypt.[21] Although this is not to say that monastic settlements with houses, churches, refectories, gatehouses, gardens, and the like did not have continuity to the modern period; quite the contrary is true. Many monastic communities today owe their form to the vision of Pachomius who encouraged the creation of self-sufficient settlements.

What then is the problem with the typology of monastic settlements if in fact we may trace some form of continuity back to the earliest visionaries? The settlement evidence from Egypt is much more diverse than what these two forms represent. Owing to variations in form, size, materials used, and location, archaeologists have opted for further cumbersome language such as semi-hermetic or semi-cenobitic classifications. At times these terms are replaced with nomenclature that is not necessarily drawn from the Egyptian milieu. So terms such as *hermitages*, *lavras*, and *oratories* are used to describe spaces that were frequently described in Coptic sources by more generic terms, such as *place* (Greek/Coptic, *topos*), *mountain* (Coptic, *toou*), or *dwelling place* (*ma nshōpe*).[22]

New Theoretical Modes: Post-Processualism, Cognitive Archaeology, Spatial and Landscape Theory

The field of monastic archaeology is now positioned to move forward with the benefits of thirty years of archaeological theory that critiqued and modified the New Archaeology or Processual Archaeology of Binford and Clarke. New Archaeology is now regarded by some theorists as too empirical and drawing upon an overly positivist view of the data. Certainly the field of archaeology is not unique in its adoption and modifications of new theoretical models. With the impact of postmodernism in several disciplines, a new generation of archaeologists offered counter-narratives for how to question and integrate the data. The post-processualists, as they have become known, have stepped away from the structuralism of earlier work and raised a series of questions that challenged our ability to know the past. For example, Ian Hodder acknowledges that the "past is meaningfully constituted," suggesting that individuals, rather than systems, create material culture.[23] To ignore the individual, agency, behaviors, and beliefs is to dehumanize the past and the artifacts that testify to a complex world.

Post-processualists sought to overturn the heavy structuralism of the processualists who believed that changes to the environment were predictable and knowable. With post-processualism, as with this discussion, the aim is to explore both how we as the interpreters of the past shape our own readings of the evidence and to also recognize the importance of personal agency in the way in which the past came to be. As Hayden White has argued, there is a difference in how we read and explain history:

> Here arises a division between the historian who wishes primarily to "reconstruct" or "explain" the past and one who is interested either in "interpreting" it or using its detritus as an occasion for his own speculations on the present (and future).... Historians have always had to draw upon

theories from other fields in the humanities and social sciences, when they have not credited current common sense or traditional wisdom, for their analytical strategies.... Historians have always used some version of a theory of language to assist them in their work of "translating" meaning across the historical continuum in order to "make sense" of their documents.[24]

The translation of monastic archaeology and its associated artifacts is in need of translating and not just reconstructing. As White has claimed, it is just as important to consider how scholars have written about monastic spatial configuration as it is to describe the actual elements of the settlements themselves.

Outsider Spaces and New Theoretical Frameworks

Readings of artifacts, buildings, and archaeological monographs should be interwoven in the construction of a reading of monastic archaeology. Archaeologists and historians read and distill the evidence as individuals. Therefore, to consider how we may approach monastic landscape requires us first to consider what underlying themes are being brought to bear in our interpretations of the past. I propose that theoretical models from cultural geography, historical ecology, and the phenomenology of landscape studies should be used to write a more nuanced history of monastic settlements and the placement of monks within the broader history of late-antique and medieval Egypt. As a Byzantine archaeologist who specializes in monastic archaeology in Egypt, I believe that not only Coptic studies but also, more broadly, Byzantine and medieval studies of the Mediterranean world are well poised to be reexamined through the application of theoretical archaeology. In this discussion I examine the relationships between landscape and religious geography and how we may come to reevaluate the emplacement of monastic settlement within the Egyptian landscape. Ultimately, I want to question how monastic space became monastic and if the markers of monastic habits can be observed within the archaeological record.

Architectural historians point to the importance of the urban environment as the central defining feature of civilization. With the built form, historians are able to discern the processes that make a civilization function. Cultural geographers speak of society as divided along lines of insiders and outsiders such that cultures identify those who belong to society and those who live outside the accepted norm. Monastics self-identify as being outsiders and seek to reside within a world that is designed according to particular religious and sacred objectives. Monastic literature is filled with accounts of the difficult process of separation from one's biological family and the impulse to embrace fully the sacred family of the monastic community.[25] For example, when Isaac of Alexandria first adopted the monastic life in Sketis, in modern Wadi Natrun, his family was said to set out on a hunt for him. All the while the other monks helped deceive his family by not revealing his true location.[26] This late-seventh-century Coptic account was designed to affirm monastic collusion to protect monks from distractions, even from their own families. Although the story alludes to the displeasure with familial encounters, the numerous incidents in which visitors and family members intruded upon the monastic community suggests that monks were not fully segregated from their past worlds. The monastic desertscape, therefore, was not hidden, but was knowable and findable.[27] Hagiographical authors explained to their audiences how individuals could escape difficult encounters and create distance, both emotional and physical, from these previous affiliations. As Peter Brown has eloquently expressed this tension, "the settlements ... combined geographical proximity to the settled land with a sense of measureless imaginative distance."[28]

The otherness of the monastic-built environments helped foster the imaginative distance of which Brown speaks. The monastic settlements at Kellia, Wadi Natrun, Saqqara, Bawit, Dayr al-Bala'izah, Sohag, Thebes, and Esna, just to name the best-known examples, contain features which create specifically religious spaces.[29] The fact that the settlements span from the fifth to the thirteenth century and have regional diversity speaks to the fact that monasticism in Egypt was not entirely uniform. The importance of the Church, often elevated in the text, is only one feature of the monastic settlement. Little attention is given in the texts to the spaces in which monastic living is actually undertaken. The cells with elaborately painted programs and kitchen facilities extensive enough to feed several inhabitants and visitors typify the components of several of these settlements.[30] Areas for storage of food, pens for animals, and wells with accompanying cisterns and inspection tanks all contribute to the site plan for these communities. However, there are still substantial differences between the sites to indicate that monastic authority did not dictate a universal design. In monastic literature there is a clear objective to recognize the sacredness of monastic space. The geography of monasticism was crafted by ancient authors intent to illustrate that monastic settlements were the realms of angels.[31] These writers also reinforced the importance of religious travel to these spaces. For example, in a letter to Rufinus, Jerome (ca. 347–420 C.E.) writes that he heard that his friend had journeyed to the "hidden places of Egypt" where he had visited monks who were members of "heaven's family on earth."[32] This otherworldliness helps explain the locative value of monastic settlements.

The theoretical construction of the outsider mentality in scholarship and in the monastic literature assists us in reflecting on the ways in which we have come to know about monastics and the landscapes in which they reside. By considering the theoretical view of outsider societies and how they inhabit the land, we are able to repopulate the monastic landscape, knowing the degree to which our modern conceptions of insider/outsider societies impinge upon the history of monastic settlement. The anthropologist Lewis Binford described the quest to understand how the land has been inhabited as a desire to understand the "life space" of the human community. Binford's life space explains why specific areas are arranged with artifactual assemblages to facilitate daily living.[33] Within the ancient city or village the ability to interpret settlement patterns is easier to digest than it is for settlements on the perceived boundaries of society. Desertscapes, by their very nature, are regarded as boundaries. It is at the edge of the Nile's cultivation that the escarpment vividly rises up in contrast to the lush fields below. The near desert is the transition between the profane world—the city, the marketplace—and the spiritual realm, where demons were frequently thought to reside.

David Sibley notes that the construction of marginal communities is characterized by a language of deliberate misrepresentation. Gypsies and nomads, for example, are often presented in history as living outside of the norms of the civilized. They come to represent minority cultures and are tied closely to where and how they live. The fact that both groups move, rather than settle, creates the impression of instability and a rejection of the sedentary urban environment and society.[34] The exclusivity of the outsider group makes it difficult for the perceived insider group to understand the settlement choices of the other. The outsider identity is an elected exclusivity as it is self-crafted and refined over generations, but it may have its roots in a response to external pressures to conform or settle. In the case of the Egyptian monastic movement, private individuals with disposable wealth frequently provided money or physical housing for monks seeking to establish themselves in new residences, away from their familial homes. Thus the history of monasticism is blurred by the support of nonmonastics in assisting holy men and women to establish themselves in new late-antique landscapes.[35]

Two features of the "landscape of exclusion" are important to note in considering monastic settlement as an exclusive landscape. First, communities select "places which are avoided by members of the dominant society because they appear threatening—a fear of the 'other' becomes a fear of place."[36] The desert was throughout antiquity known as a dangerous landscape where spiritual actors could impart harm upon individuals. Monastic literature is filled with the image of the untrained monk being attacked by demons or by temptations while in the desert.[37] The Egyptian desert, in particular, was not the realm for the faint of heart. Those who were not spiritually strong were not encouraged to venture into this space alone. Therefore when monastics did seek residence in this fearful place, they became individuals to be feared as they reflected the fierce desertscape.[38] Further "the labeling of places as threatening confirms the otherness of the minorities with whom the places are associated, and relegation to marginal spaces serves to amplify deviance."[39] The threatening nature of the Egyptian desert works on many levels of representation.

While the desert is valued in religious literature as a testing ground for spiritual development, it is also recognized as a physically and emotionally demanding space. Therefore those who are able to navigate these challenges successfully are in turn regarded as being different, perhaps even deviant. Whereas gypsies might be scorned for their difference, monastics were described with qualities that made their deviance acceptable. They became angels and the soldiers of Christ; they were otherworld beings.[40] Furthermore, by remaining within these fearful landscapes, the inhabitants were then understood in mythological and stereotypical ways. Narratives emerged within the insider communities to explain why individuals would willingly elect to move into such different places.[41]

A second feature of the "landscape of exclusion" is how the built environment creates boundaries around the society and thereby provides particular spatial divisions. The community's ability to configure the land spatially is then directly linked to its power to exert control. Power and spatial divisions confer the "power to exclude."[42] The location of monastic communities predominately within a neglected or abandoned landscape of the cliffs, edges of cultivation, wadis, abandoned quarries, and tombs, makes it possible for monks to elect their own boundaries. Their residences are separated from the insider community by the pure nature that they elect to inhabit a world not considered worth living in. The power of the monastic built form is tied firmly to the belief that sacred places are imbued with religious power. The writing of religious topography in monastic literature provided narrations of why some regions were more exclusive than others. The built monastic settlement was a visible sign of those who were different from others. Beyond this settlement further into the "inner desert," were the residences of the monks who were able to live on very little and were said to find companionship only with God. How did marginalized and excluded dwellings relate to the larger, social community? Were these in fact temporary shelters or residences? Do we have the vocabulary to talk about temporary marginal dwellings and how they might relate to spiritual living?

As self-appointed outsiders, monastics placed themselves in historically neglected landscapes. In examining the need to bring the somatization of archaeology together with landscape theory, Vuk Trifkovc identifies a central methodological deficiency in how we study the past: "There is no concept of these reconstructed persons being situated in any spatial or environmental locale, let alone the exploration of the mutually defining relationships between spaces, agents and their bodies."[43] Without an effort to treat the body within the landscape that was inhabited we have "finely crafted individuals floating in an empty black void of history."[44] Trifkovc argues for a reterritorialization in which the body, personhood, and landscape are intertwined. This goal is achieved if we consider two central concepts of "taskscapes" and "embodied agents."[45] Tim Ingold's concept of the taskscape links individuals to a spatial context and thereby grounds people within the landscape through their actions.[46] The need to consider how individuals acted within a space and created specific areas for monastic living is essential for considering the materiality of religious life. For Ingold there is essential value in objects, architecture, and materials. Yet he cautions us to understand the past not only through theoretical models; we must, he argues, "take materials seriously," by which he means that scholars should return to the artifacts and buildings as real elements and not just as reflections of social and communal beliefs.[47] The landscape is not just a theoretical construct for Ingold, but a real canvas upon which the built environment is painted.

The Archaeology of Religion and the New Monastic Desert Canvas

What then are the relationships between the landscape, the environment, and monastic settlements? In what ways are monastic sites particularly monastic and not more broadly Christian settlements? While answers to these questions may seem obvious, the larger question is more epistemological. What would indicate monastic habitation clearly and not the residence of an Egyptian Christian? Do we have enough comparable material to assess the differences between a Christian village and a monastic settlement? Or how does one ascertain whether a space was inhabited by an ascetic and not a Christian guard on a desert post?[48]

Our approach toward Egyptian monasticism does not yet reflect a heavily theorized understanding of what the study of the archaeology of religion may entail. The theoretical consideration is to examine what links may be established between the religious dimensions observed in the material record with cognitive dimensions of the individuals behind such physical markings. Anthropologists are now considering the ways in which religion and the individual interact in ways that are evident with material culture.[49] Harvey Whitehouse, for example, has provided a heuristic model to differentiate between "doctrinal and imagistic modes of religiosity."[50] He argues that much of what scholars identify as religion is a myopic or monolithic definition for a belief system that is not framed by individuals and agency. Archaeologists who work primarily with religious spaces are finding the work of anthropologists Timothy Insoll and Harvey Whitehouse to be especially helpful in reframing how archaeologists interpret archaeological material and behavior. Insoll states that archaeologists are naïve when it comes to religion and our ability to understand it archaeologically. We are, as he claims, unwilling and untrained in the archaeology of religion. We use terms such as *ritual* and *religion* merely to describe things that are "odd" or not well understood.[51] Further, Insoll laments the current practice of linking the past to the present in an effort to understand the physicality of religion and the very materials that make up monastic life.

Cognitive processual archaeologists, such as Colin Renfrew, argue that we *should* use our present understanding of human actions to investigate the past.[52] The position of cognitive processualists is that there are systems, or processes, which are repeatable and observable in the archaeological record. If we recognize marks of repetitive actions, such as the inscribing of walls with intercessory prayers, then we can explain the ritualized behavior by looking for parallels in the modern world. This methodology is called cognitive because its proponents assert that we may know or experience the ancient or medieval world once we find linkages between the past and present. For example, it is common to observe graffiti at contemporary Coptic sites.[53] By employing anthropological and cognitive readings of such performative acts, Renfrew would assert that we can extend our knowledge of current behaviors, motivations, and desires from observed experiences at religious sites and then apply them to the past. How well cognitive processual interpretations might translate to architectural designs and spatial configuration is more difficult to defend, as we shall see shortly. Insoll, as a critic of Renfrew and other cognitive processualists, challenges archaeologists who work with specifically religious material to be more aware of how they imbue their own religious understanding onto the past. I would agree that his challenge is well timed for Coptic archaeology and the study of the materiality of monasticism, as the interpretation of monastic space has been viewed through the lens of Western monasticism and a critical view of early monasticism as overly stringent, ascetic, and isolationist.

It is the task of the archaeologist to ask questions as to how we know what we know. This phenomenological approach is particularly important as archaeology now embraces more philosophical approaches in how material remains are read and presented for examination. The walls, middens, plaster layers, and dipinti are scrutinized to the same degree as the textual evidence, whose value has long superseded that of the archaeological evidence. We may then regard the material evidences as byproducts of acts of religion.[54] As an example we have ample evidence of the spaces that were heavily marked with crosses, dipinti, and graffiti with the intent to focus the attention of the monks in prayer. The site of Esna, located in southern Egypt, is one such example where we have physical indicators of religious markings inscribed by the entrances to rooms within a monastic context.[55] The presence of a central niche flanked by secondary niches; numerous intercessory prayers; and the inscription of crosses by the entrance to the space led many to conclude that the space was sacred and thus unique in comparison to the other rooms in the residences. These spaces are generally referred to as oratories (Greek, *Euktērion*) by modern scholars. There is no evidence, textual or other, that the inhabitants considered these spaces as bearing a single function, nor did they use this Greek term. Instead they called the space, and by extension the whole building, a "dwelling place" (Coptic *ma nshōpe*). Thus, I believe that employing a term, such as *oratory*, restricts our ability to consider the variegated functions and broader purposes for the spaces in which such markings appear. The "dwelling place" becomes a space for public or private prayer, for working handcrafts, and for eating the daily meal. Without a convincing textual guide, it is perhaps more fruitful to consider the spaces in more objective terms.

For example, the layout of specific monastic residences or the wider monastic settlement bears signs of divisions between public space with the inclusion of doors and gates. Large walls did not enclose all monastic settlements in Egypt. Some walls were not thick enough even to be defensive, in fact.[56] They may have served as natural boundaries, defining the monastic space or community. Or they could have been built to deal with the environmental threats, such as wind and sand, or aggressive animals that could not climb or jump over the walls. Finally, the ability to document and examine wear marks on stoops, niches, and other features may help us look more closely at the individual rooms of a settlement to observe religious activities that are not necessarily making an appearance in the texts. Do modifications within the architecture reflect changes in personal taste, piety, or communal needs? Could we discern answers to these questions by reading the material remains closely? As scholars specializing in the archaeology of religion, it is natural to look for motivations with the religious practice, but in practical terms, not all physical changes can or should be embedded in religious needs. What other factors, therefore, could be impacting the design and alterations in the physical remains?

In *The Social Logic of Space* Bill Hillier and Julienne Hanson lament how frequently the environment, as a canvas for living, has no serious impact upon the building of structures or their placement within a larger interpretative framework. Hillier and Hanson point to a problematic paradigm by which scholars regard a building as "an object whose spatial form is a form of social ordering.... The physical environment has no social content and society has no spatial content."[57] A dismissive view of the environment, in this case the Egyptian desertscape, cliffs, and associated cultivated lands, fosters a one-dimensional view of the landscape. With these considerations we can begin to put the overly spiritualized landscape to one side while we take a comprehensive view of the placement of the settlements, the environmental reasons for living in specific locations, and the modifications of the natural environment for living.

Of course much of this conversation about the value of the desertscape and the construction of the monastic built form is overshadowed by the fact that we are limited by the uneven nature of the evidence, both artifactual and textual. The fact that we have far more substantial architectural evidence for large communities, such as those at Saqqara, Kellia, Bawit, Naqlun, Wadi Natrun, and Sohag, than what the textual records in fact describe means that archaeologists must be encouraged to apply theoretical models to interpret the material remains. Similarly, the publication of papyri and ostraca, forming the bulk of documentary evidence for monasticism, continues to challenge the myth we have of monastic life. As Leslie S. B. MacCoull explains: "Although entrants were supposed to renounce both their property and their blood family upon joining a monastery, all our documentation shows that this norm was a long way from being observed."[58] The dating for these sites, some of which were excavated in more antiquated periods, also creates methodological challenges as to how we classify the sites for comparison. To simply describe and catalogue artifacts and structures does little to help us grapple with the possible meaning behind what has been preserved.

Conclusion

Several suggestions emerge for positioning the field of monastic archaeology to be enhanced by appropriating new methodologies. First, we can establish a clearer phenomenological framework in which we articulate specifically what elements of a site led to the interpretation that it was once occupied by monastic individuals. While this might appear to be obvious, very little discussion is given to whether those same elements might be indications of a Christian community. For example, what would be sufficient evidence at a settlement to indicate that it was not a monastic residence but instead the residence of a lay Christian? Consider the reused quarries at Dayr al-Dik in Middle Egypt. The modified spaces are frequently identified as part of a monastic community, and yet there is very little in the way of substantive markers of monastic life that is found there aside from some inscriptions, painted crosses, and a space that functioned as a church.[59] Should this site be considered a monastic settlement, or a Christian community that took advantage of new locations for building, or a combination? If we present more evidence to explain what exactly constitutes the elements of a monastic settlement and if such features cannot be found in any other type of settlement, then we are creating clearer parameters to assessment of monastic site identification.

Second, greater efforts are needed to conduct comparative analysis with other Byzantine monastic settlements in the Near East, such as in Palestine and other regions of the Levant as part of the larger monastic movement in the Eastern Mediterranean.[60] There are only a few studies that consider early monastic parallels between Egypt and elsewhere, but more can be done now to look at monastic settlements after the Arab conquest as new building activities in late antiquity were undertaken by a variety of individuals and not just monastic builders.[61] Greater attention to changes in building activities during the late-antique and early medieval periods will provide an important historical framework for understanding monastic construction as part of a larger effort by private builders to expand investments at a time when building codes and regulations were more lax throughout the Byzantine and early Islamic empire.[62]

Third, when reading Egyptian monastic landscapes we need to reassess where monasteries were located in proximity to each other and their relationship to non-monastic settlements. My own interests lie primarily in considering this issue of the emplacement of the settlements and how late-antique spatial discourse may cloud the reality of where monastics actually resided and their economic interactions with the local communities. One of the assumptions that has plagued our understanding of the Egyptian monastic life is that they were living in isolation in areas that were difficult to reach and had elected to live in the remote desert. However, both archaeological and papyrological evidence significantly challenge this reconstruction. An enormous gain in revising the earlier model of ascetic isolationism with evidence from monastic archives in which we learn of the complex social and economic relationships between individual monks, their community, and individuals living in the nearby villages.[63] Recent archaeological work in Wadi Natrun, in the Fayuum, at Bawit, Edfu, and Thebes overturns this older model of exclusivity.[64] At these sites we can observe monastic settlements with structurally complex buildings, elaborately painted halls and rooms, and documentary evidence that each community was far from isolated from the nonmonastic world.

An adoption of theoretical models for classifying sites and reading archaeological material will foster a more textured portrait of Egyptian monasticism. An appreciation for the historiography of monastic archaeology is essential as the field comes to terms with the insights and limitations of early scholarship. In light of these limitations archaeologists working within monastic studies are now willing to revisit sites and reconsider artifacts, landscape, and space as independent sources for historical analysis. I firmly believe that we can learn from the successful methodological applications of theoretical work in Buddhist and Western Christian monastic archaeology, where more robust analysis is providing new frameworks for interpreting how monastics create a separate but accessible community.[65] The success of these studies demonstrates that all such fields can benefit from the appropriation of theories from related fields. Egyptian monastic archaeology is about to enter a new stage in which practice theory and theorized research designs will greatly enhance how we approach the study of monastic history and allow us to consider carefully how monastic space became monastic.

NOTES

Introduction

1. Although the Coptic Orthodox Church is the indigenous church of Egypt and remains the majority denomination (from 5 to 10 percent of Egyptians are Christian), by the end of the nineteenth century a Protestant Coptic Church (about 200,000 members) and a Catholic Coptic Church (about 160,000 members) were established in Egypt as well. There are also several other denominations present in Egypt: Greek Orthodox, Armenian Orthodox, and Episcopal. These, however, do not self-describe as Coptic. The essays in this volume deal with topics related to the Coptic Orthodox community only.

2. See the six-part analysis of Morsi's presidency in Al-Ahram online by Hani Shukrallah, http://english.ahram.org.eg/NewsContent/4/0/80716/Opinion/0/A-peoples-history-of-the-Egyptian-revolution-.aspx (accessed June 7, 2014).

3. April 7, 2013. Among others, see Aleem Maqbool, "Cairo Clashes at St. Mark's Coptic Cathedral after Funerals," *BBC World News,* April 7, 2013, http://www.bbc.co.uk/news/world-middle-east-22058570 (accessed April 28, 2015).

4. July 3, 2013.

5. Among others, see http://www.al-monitor.com/pulse/originals/2013/08/egypt-muslim-brotherhood-massacre-sisi.html (accessed 4-29-2015).

6. For one of the many news reports, see "Egypt: Mass Attacks on Churches," *Human Rights Watch,* August 21, 2013, http://www.hrw.org/news/2013/08/21/egypt-mass-attacks-churches (accessed April 28, 2015).

7. That era is mostly remembered for the year 1321 C.E., when sixty churches were destroyed in major anti-Christian rioting. Mark Swanson, *The Coptic Papacy in Islamic Egypt 641–1517,* The Popes of Egypt 2 (Cairo & New York: American University in Cairo Press, 2010), 102.

8. Among others, see Nelly van Doorn–Harder, "Copts Fully Egyptian but for a Tattoo," in *Nationalism and Minority Identities in Islamic Societies,* ed. Maya Schatzmiller (Montreal & Kingston: McGill–Queen's University Press, 2005), 22–57.

9. Throughout this book *church* refers to a local church, while *Church* refers to the Coptic Orthodox Church as a hierarchical structure.

10. Often we see the title of pope as well as that of patriarch being used for the prime leader of the Orthodox Copts. His official title is dual: Pope of Alexandria and Patriarch of All Africa on the Holy See of Saint Mark the Apostle.

11. Pope Tawadros II was elected on November 4, 2012, and officially installed as pope on November 18.

12. Among the many examples, see Pope Tawadros's interview with Egyptian TV, published by CopticWorld.org just after the widespread attacks on the churches: "Pope

Tawadros II Speaks on Events in Egypt," http://suscopts.org/press/2013/aug/17/pope-tawadros-ii-speaks-on-events-in-egypt/ (accessed April 28, 2015).

13. "Visit of an American Congressional Delegation," *Coptic Pope*, September 5, 2013.

14. For Coptic youth protest, see the chapter by Sebastian Elsässer in this volume. Furthermore, see Joseph Fahim, "Egypt's Copts May Soon Regret Supporting Sisi," *Al-Monitor*, July 4, 2014, http://www.al-monitor.com/pulse/originals/2014/07/egypt-coptic-christians-sisi-secular-islamist.html (accessed April 29, 2015).

15. Rogers Brubaker and Frederick Cooper, "Beyond 'Identity,'" *Theory and Society* 29 (2000): 1–47. In thinking about the concept of identity, I thank Levi Klempner (Vrije Universiteit, Amsterdam, 2016) for generously sharing with me the draft of his dissertation in progress on Coptic identity in diaspora, "Blessed Is Egypt My People: Recontextualizing Coptic Identity Outside of Egypt."

16. Mariz Tadros, *Copts at the Crossroads: The Challenges of Building Inclusive Democracy in Egypt* (Cairo & New York: American University in Cairo Press, 2013), 38.

17. Tadros, *Copts at the Crossroads*, 41.

18. Pierre Du Bourguet, S.J., points out in the entry "Copt" in *The Coptic Encyclopedia*, ed. Aziz S. Atiya (New York & Toronto: Macmillan, 1991), vol. 2, 599, that the Greek word *Aigyptos*, technically speaking, referred to the ancient city of Memphis in the north of Egypt where the principal sanctuary dedicated to the god Ptah was situated.

19. There is much debate about the actual numbers of Copts, and we have few publications with hard facts. The two main studies remain E. J. Chitham, *The Coptic Community in Egypt: Spatial and Social Change* (Durham, N.C.: Center for Middle Eastern and Islamic Studies, 1986), and Youssef Courbage and Philippe Fargues, *Chrétiens et juifs dans l'Islam arabe et turc* (Paris: Fayard, 1992).

20. Emile Maher, "Coptic Language, Spoken," *The Coptic Encyclopedia*, vol. 2, 604–7. Also see Mariam F. Ayad, "The Death of Coptic? A Reprisal," in *Coptic Culture: Past, Present and Future*, ed. Mariam F. Ayad (Stevenage, U.K.: Coptic Orthodox Church Center, 2012), 11–42.

21. Jurgen Habermas, *The Inclusion of the Other: Studies in Political Theory* (Cambridge, U.K.: Polity Press, 2005).

22. Among the many news features, see Sarah Carr's blog "Why is Maspero different?," October 10, 2013, http://www.madamasr.com/content/why-maspero-different-0, and "Maspero: A Massacre of Christians in Egypt," CBS, 60 Minutes Overtime, December 15, 2013, http://www.cbsnews.com/news/maspero-a-massacre-of-christians-in-egypt/ (both sites accessed December 20, 2013).

23. For an overview of sectarian incidents from 2008 to 2011, see Tadros, *Copts at the Crossroads*, chapter 2.

24. Paul R. Brass, ed., *Ethnic Groups and the State* (Totowa, N.J.: Barnes and Noble, 1985), 29–30.

25. For example, see Paul Sedra, "Class Cleavages and Ethnic Conflict: Coptic Christian Communities in Modern Egyptian Politics," *Islam and Christian-Muslim Relations* 10, no. 2 (1999): 219–35.

26. Andreas Wimmer, *Ethnic Boundary Making. Institutions, Power, Networks* (New York: Oxford University Press, 2013), 63.

27. Elizabeth Iskander, *Sectarian Conflict in Egypt: Coptic Media, Identity and Representation* (London & New York: Routledge, 2012), 11–17.

28. Fredrik Barth, "Pathan Identity and Its Maintenance," in *Ethnic Groups and Boundaries: The Social Organization of Culture Difference*, ed. F. Barth (Boston: Little, Brown, 1969), 117–34.

29. Simon Harrison, "The Politics of Resemblance: Ethnicity, Trademarks, Headhunting," *Journal of the Royal Anthropological Institute* vol. 8, no. 2 (2002): 211–32.

30. Magdi Guirguis and Nelly van Doorn-Harder, *The Emergence of the Modern Coptic Papacy*, The Popes of Egypt 3 (Cairo & New York: American University in Cairo Press, 2011), 140–42, 179–82.

31. The Saint Shenouda Society publishes the journal *Coptica* (2002–). Since 2009 the CSCS has published the *Journal of the Canadian Society for Coptic Studies*. The CSCS also runs the Coptic Museum in Toronto, the only one of its kind outside Egypt; see the website, St. Mark's Coptic Museum, http://www.copticmuseum-canada.org/ (accessed April 29, 2015).

32. *Le Monde Copte*, http://www.lemondecopte.com/ (accessed April 29, 2015); *Coptologia Journal*, Coptologia Publications, http://www.coptologia.com/presta/category.php?id_category=5 (accessed April 29, 2015); *Journal of the Canadian Society for Coptic Studies*, http://www.lockwoodpressjournals.com/loi/cscs (accessed April 29, 2015).

33. Among others, Shapinaz-Amal Naguib, "The Era of Martyrs: Texts and Contexts of Religious Memory," in Nelly van Doorn-Harder and Kari Vogt, eds., *Between Desert and City: The Coptic Orthodox Church Today* (Oslo: Novus, 1997), 127.

34. Iskander, *Sectarian Conflict*, 14.

35. The Coptic popes have used this title since the time of Pope Dyonisios (247–264 B.C.E.), which was fifty years before the same title was assigned to the bishop of Rome; Stephen J. Davis, *The Early Coptic Papacy, The Egyptian Church and Its Leadership in Late Antiquity*, The Popes of Egypt 1 (Cairo & New York: American University in Cairo Press, 2005), 27. However, in a list of Coptic Orthodox popes found on the Internet, it is stated that it was Dyonisios's predecessor, Heracles, who held the title first; "List of Coptic Orthodox Popes," *Wikipedia*, http://en.wikipedia.org/wiki/List_of_Coptic_Orthodox_Popes_of_Alexandria (accessed April 29, 2015).

36. Ayad, "Death of Coptic?" 19.

37. Among others, see Hany N. Takla, "The Coptic Bible," chapter 9, and Youhanna Nessim Youssef, "Coptic Literature," chapter 10 in *Coptic Civilization: Two Thousand Years of Christianity in Egypt*, ed. Gawdat Gabra (Cairo & New York: American University in Cairo Press, 2014), 105–30.

38. Samuel Moawad, "Coptic Historiography," in Gabra, *Coptic Civilization*, 1, 5.

39. Mark Swanson provides the bibliographic details for the classical story. For a modern-day rendition, see the website of the church complex on the Muqattam Mountain: "Miracle of Moving of the Mokattam Mountain," Monastery of St. Samaan the Tanner, http://www.samaanchurch.com/en/miracle_en.php (accessed April 29, 2015).

40. Febe Armanios, *Coptic Christianity in Ottoman Egypt* (New York: Oxford University Press, 2011), 16.

41. Maryann M. Shenoda, "Lamenting Islam, Imagining Persecution: Copto-Arabic Opposition to Islamization and Arabization in Fatimid Egypt (969–1171 C.E.)" (Ph.D. diss., Harvard University, 2010). Another work on this period is Marlis J. Saleh, "Government Relations with the Coptic Community in Egypt during the Fatimid Period (358–567 A.H. / 969–1171 C.E.)" (Ph.D. diss., University of Chicago, 1995).

42. Tamer el-Leithy, "Coptic Culture and Conversion in Medieval Cairo, 1293–1524 A.D." (Ph.D. diss., Princeton University, 2005).

43. Armanios, *Coptic Christianity in Ottoman Egypt*, 117–45.

44. Febe Armanios, "The Ottoman Period (1517–1798)," in *The Coptic Christian Heritage. History, Faith, and Culture*, ed. Lois M. Farag (Abingdon, U.K. & New York: Routledge, 2014), 65–67.

45. Guirguis and van Doorn–Harder, *Emergence of the Modern Coptic Papacy,* 80–82. Paul Sedra has studied the colonial and missionary influence on the Coptic Church. See, for example, his *From Mission to Modernity: Evangelicals, Reformers and Education in Nineteenth Century Egypt* (London & New York: Tauris Academic Studies, 2011). Also see Sedra, "Class Cleavages and Ethnic Conflict: Coptic Christian Communities in Modern Egyptian Politics," *Islam and Christian-Muslim Relations* 10, no. 2 (1999): 219–35, and "Ecclesiastical Warfare: Patriarch, Presbyterian, and Peasant in Nineteenth-Century Asyut," available at http://128.36.236.77/workpaper/pdfs/MESV5-10.pdf (accessed 3-30-2010); Sedra, "John Lieder and His Mission in Egypt: The Evangelical Ethos at Work among the Nineteenth-Century Copts," *Journal of Religious History* 28 (October 2004): 219–39.

46. Guirguis and van Doorn–Harder, *Emergence of the Modern Coptic Papacy,* 75.

47. Ibid., 106.

48. The Holy Synod of the Coptic Orthodox Church officially canonized Habib Guirguis and Pope Kyrillos VI as saints on June 20, 2013; Michael Collins Dunn, "Coptic Church's Synod Recognizes Two Modern Saints," *Middle East Institute: Editor's Blog,* June 20, 2013, http://mideasti.blogspot.com/2013/06/coptic-churchs-synod-recognizes-two.html (accessed April 29, 2015).

49. Especially at the beginning of the twentieth century, in the wake of the rediscovery of ancient Egyptian pharaonic treasures, Copts started to identify with this part of Egypt's history. See Donald Malcolm Reid, *Whose Pharaohs? Archaeology, Museums, and Egyptian National Identity from Napoleon to World War I* (Cairo: American University in Cairo Press, 2002).

50. Iskander, *Sectarian Conflict,* 16. Refer to note 3 in Brooks Hedstrom's essay.

51. See, for example, the articles and illustrations in Elizabeth S. Bolman and Patrick Godeau, eds., *Monastic Visions: Wall Paintings in the Monastery of St. Antony at the Red Sea* (New Haven: Yale University Press, 2002).

52. Now, more than two decades later, the entries that can be added to *The Coptic Encyclopedia* have multiplied to such great extent that it is being revised electronically in order to allow for new entries to be added continuously. The current editor is Gawdat Gabra, who supervises the Claremont Coptic Encyclopedia project: "Claremont Coptic Encyclopedia," http://ccdl.libraries.claremont.edu/cdm/landingpage/collection/cce (accessed April 29, 2015).

53. Ragheb Moftah, Margit Toth, and Martha Roy, *The Coptic Orthodox Liturgy of St. Basil; With Complete Musical Transcription* (Cairo: American University in Cairo Press, 1998).

54. See the first chapter of Carolyn M. Ramzy, "The Politics of (Dis) Engagement: Coptic Christian Revival and the Performative Politics of Song" (Ph.D. diss., University of Toronto, 2014).

55. Monica René, "Contemporary Coptic Art," in Gabra, *Coptic Civilization,* 252.

56. Guirguis and van Doorn–Harder, *Emergence of the Modern Coptic Papacy,* 127–88.

57. See the David Ensemble website, http://www.davidensemble.com/english/ensemble.htm (accessed August 23, 2016).

58. Among others, see my essay entitled "Coptic Visual Culture. Gendered Re-creations of Traditional Themes," in Ayad, *Coptic Culture,* 201–14.

59. For some of the many titles Pope Shenouda produced, see "His Holiness Pope Shenouda III," Orthodox Bookstore website, http://www.orthodoxbookstore.org/hisholinesspopeshenoudaiii.aspx (accessed April 29, 2015), and "His Holiness Pope Shenouda III," Coptic Orthodox Church Network, http://www.copticchurch.net/topics/pope/ (accessed August 23, 2016).

60. Arab West Report, March 22, 2012, http://www.arabwestreport.info/year-2012/week-12/43-ecumenical-relations-coptic-orthodox-church-mentioned-decisions-holy-synod (accessed April 29, 2015).

61. See D. Bell, *An Introduction to Cybercultures* (London: Routledge, 2001).

62. For example, see Ayad, *Coptic Culture*, and Gabra, *Coptic Civilization*.

63. In the year 1990 the most prominent study on the Copts in the twentieth century was written by Edward Wakin, a journalist reporting from Egypt during the time of the well-known Coptic Pope Cyril VI, whose reign from 1959 to 1971 coincided with part of the Nasser regime; Wakin, *A Lonely Minority: The Modern Story of Egypt's Copts* (New York: William Morrow, 1963). About the same time the German Coptologist Otto Meinardus lived in Cairo. His observations were later published as *Patriarchen unter Nasser und Sadat* (Hamburg: Deutsches Orient-Institut, 1998).

64. Some of Father Matta el-Miskin's work has been published in English. His best-known book is written under the name Matthew the Poor, *The Communion of Love* (New York: St. Vladimir's Press, 2004).

65. Also see Iskander, *Sectarian Conflict in Egypt*.

66. Among others, see "New Video Shows Egyptian Police Allowing Deadly Attack on Coptic Cathedral," *Fox News*, April 28, 2013, http://www.foxnews.com/world/2013/04/28/new-video-shows-egyptian-police-allowing-attack-on-coptic-cathedral/ (accessed April 29, 2015).

67. Guirguis and van Doorn–Harder, *Emergence of the Modern Coptic Papacy*, 134, 135.

68. Ibid., 141–42.

69. Nora Stene, "'Engler i platåsko': Religiøs sosialisering av koptisk-ortodokse barn i London" ("Angels in Platform Shoes": Religious Socialization of Coptic Orthodox Children in London) (Ph.D. diss., University of Oslo, 2005); "The Challenge of the Diaspora as Reflected in a Coptic Sunday School," *Journal of Eastern Christian Studies* 54, nos. 1–2 (2002): 77–90; "Into the Land of Immigration," in van Doorn–Harder and Vogt, *Between Desert and City*, 254–64.

70. The pope's role is so influential that the American University in Cairo Press commissioned a miniseries of three volumes about the history of the popes of Egypt. The first volume discusses the period until the Arab invasion (641) when popes created theology, were mired in theological disputes, or had to guide the community through times of persecution. The second volume concerns the medieval period when the Copts went from a majority to a minority community. The third volume covers the Ottoman Empire and the modern period. Stephen J. Davis, *The Early Coptic Papacy: The Egyptian Church and Its Leadership in Late Antiquity*, The Popes of Egypt 1 (Cairo & New York: American University in Cairo Press, 2004); Mark Swanson, *The Coptic Papacy in Islamic Egypt 641–1517*, The Popes of Egypt 2 (Cairo & New York: American University in Cairo Press, 2010); and Guirguis and van Doorn–Harder, *Emergence of the Modern Coptic Papacy*.

71. For quick orientation to this text, see Johannes den Heijer, "History of the Patriarchs of Alexandria," *The Coptic Encyclopedia*, vol. 4, 1238–42.

72. Also see Mikhail's work that focuses on the early Islamic period, when Coptic, Greek, and Arabic were used and processes of conversion and assimilation moved Egypt's culture from Christian to Islamic: "Egypt from Late Antiquity to Early Islam: Copts, Melkites, and Muslims Shaping a New Society" (Ph.D. diss., University of California, Los Angeles, 2004), and *From Byzantine to Islamic Egypt: Religion, Identity and Politics after the Arab Conquest*. (London: Tauris, 2014).

73. Even Bohairic Coptic literature, he maintains, reflects Arabic traditions rather than Sahidic or Greek antecedents.

74. The Institute of Coptic Studies conference took place in Cairo, December 5–7, 2014.

The Copts in the January Revolution of 2011

1. On the many facets of Egyptian sectarianism, see Laure Guirguis, *Les coptes d'Égypte: Violences communautaires et transformations politiques* (Paris: Karthala, 2012); Sebastian Elsässer, *The Coptic Question in the Mubarak Era* (New York: Oxford University Press, 2014); Elizabeth Iskander, *Sectarian Conflict in Egypt* (London: Routledge, 2012).

2. Rafīq Ḥabīb, *al-Jamāʿa al-qibṭiyya bayna l-indimāj wa-l-inʿizāl* (Cairo: Dār al-Shurūq al-Dawliyya, 2005); Nelly van-Doorn Harder, "Copts: Fully Egyptian but for a Tattoo?," in *Nationalism and Minority Identities in Islamic Societies*, ed. Maya Shatzmiller (Montreal & Kingston: McGill-Queens University Press, 2005), 22–57; Anne-Sophie Vivier, "Quand Le Caire se révèle copte: Traits et enjeux des pratiques de sociabilité des coptes orthodoxes dans Le Caire contemporain," *Revue des Mondes Musulmans et de la Méditerranée* (September 2005):107–10, 205–27.

3. See Sāmiḥ Fawzī, "Kayfiyyat tanāwul wasāʾil al-iʿlām wa-manāhij at-taʿlīm al-miṣriyya li-l-dīn al-masīḥī," in *al-Adyān wa-ḥurriyyat at-taʿbīr*, ed. Rajab S. Taha (Cairo: CIHRS, 2007), 217–62; and Samia Mehrez, "The New Kid on the Block: Bahibb Issima and the Emergence of the Coptic Community in the Egyptian Public Sphere," in Mehrez, *Egypt's Culture Wars: Politics and Practice* (London: Routledge, 2008), 188–207.

4. See Shawky F. Karas, *The Copts since the Arab Invasion: Strangers in their Land* (Jersey City: American Coptic Association, 1985); Mityās Naṣr, *al-Qibṭ: Kifāḥ min ajl al-baqāʾ* (Cairo: al-Katība al-ṭibiyya, 2007); Martyn Thomas and Adly A. Youssef, eds., *Copts in Egypt: A Christian Minority under Siege*, Papers presented at the First International Coptic Symposium, Zurich, September 23–25, 2004 (Zurich: G2W-Verlag, 2006).

5. See Maurits Berger, "Public Policy and Islamic Law: The Modern Dhimmi in Contemporary Egyptian Family Law," *Islamic Law and Society* 8, no. 1 (2001): 88–136; and Nathalie Bernard-Maugiron, "Les amendements à la loi du statut personnel des coptes orthodoxes: Vers la fin du projet du code unifié de la famille en Égypt?," in *Chroniques Égyptiennes 2008*, ed. Iman Farag (Cairo: Cedej, 2008), 124–49.

6. Sebastian Elsässer, "La 'question copte' entre crispations confessionelles et ouvertures civiques," in Farag, *Chroniques Égyptiennes 2008*, 101–21; Laure Guirguis, ed., *Conversions religieuses et mutations politiques en Egypte* (Paris: Non Lieu, 2008); Mariz Tadros, "Behind Egypt's Deep Red Lines," *Middle East Report Online*, 13 October 2010, http://merip.org/mero/mero101310 (accessed May 4, 2015).

7. Sebastian Elsässer, "Press Liberalization, the New Media, and the '"Coptic Question': Muslim-Coptic Relations in Egypt in a Changing Media Landscape," *Middle Eastern Studies* 46, no. 1 (2010): 131–50.

8. Mariz Tadros, *Copts at the Crossroads: The Challenges of Building Inclusive Democracy in Egypt* (Cairo & New York: American University in Cairo Press, 2013).

9. In *al-Kiraza* (April 1, 2011), the official mouthpiece of the Coptic Orthodox Church, Pope Shenouda mentioned only fourteen Coptic "martyrs" of the revolution, and other media reports do not suggest a higher number.

10. The political discourse of some Protestant spokesmen (for example, Ikram Lamei and Andrea Zaki) was different. They did not take a partisan stance for or against Mubarak, but they insisted that the right to demonstrate should be guaranteed and that the regime should fulfill its promises of political reforms (*Watani*, February 6, 2011). This shows that the churches could avoid being drawn into the political struggle but at

Notes to Pages 25–27

the same time stand firmly on the side of freedom and human rights, an option that the Coptic Orthodox Church did not take.

11. See the articles published on copts-united.com from January 25 to January 28, 2011. On January 26, Pope Shenouda, on the occasion of his weekly meeting in the cathedral, called on the people to "stay calm" and "overcome the current state of disconcertment and confusion" (*al-Misri al-Yawm,* January 28, 2011). Coptic activists Rami Kamil (interviewed by author on April 1, 2011) and Hany Elgezery (interviewed by author on September 6, 2011) stressed that the general sentiment in the Coptic community was initially not in favor of participating in the demonstrations.

12. Yasmine Fathi,"Egypt's Copts: A Cry of Pain," *Ahram Online,* October 14, 2011, http://english.ahram.org.eg/NewsContent/1/64/24107/Egypt/Politics-/Egypts-Copts-A-cry-of-pain.aspx (accessed May 4, 2015).

13. One exception needs to be noted: On January 29, there was an arson attack on a church in the border village Rafah in North Sinai (*Watani,* February 13, 2011). On February 17 construction work at a church in Hathata, governorate of al-Minya, triggered an attack by stone-throwing youth, which was stopped by the police (*Watani,* February 27, 2011).

14. On February 6 Copts organized an ecumenical Christian service (*khidma*) as part of a solemn ceremony in commemoration of some of the victims of police violence during the protests, two of whom were Christians. On February 9 thousands of Christians and Muslims held a traditional forty-day vigil for the victims of the terror attack on the al-Qiddisayn church in Alexandria on January 1. The ceremony featured two church choirs, one from the Protestant Qasr al-Dubbara congregation in downtown Cairo, the other from a Coptic-Orthodox church in 'Izbat an-Nakhl in northeastern Cairo, home of the activist priest Mityas Nasr (Minqarius).

15. This was confirmed to me by Khalid 'Abd al-Hamid, a veteran activist in leftist movements such as the Revolutionary Socialists (*al-ishtirākiyyūn al-thawriyyūn*) and the Youth for Freedom and Justice (*shabāb min ajl al-ḥurriyya wa-l-'adāla*) and one of the leading members of the Alliance of the Revolutionary Youth (*ittiḥād shabāb al-thawra*), interviewed on October 2, 2011.

16. *Watani,* March 6, 2011.

17. The citations are from a declaration of the patriarch concerning the second Coptic Maspero sit-in, which was read by Bishop Yu'annis on state television. Although they came in specific circumstances, I think that they are broadly representative of the Church leadership's attitude in this period. See *al-Misri al-Yawm,* March 15, 2011, and the clip "martin19041." "al-Anbā Yu'annis yulqī bayān al-Bābā li-faḍḍ i'tiṣām Māsbīrū," http://www.youtube.com/watch?v=T6p_vZS0k38 (accessed May 5, 2015).

18. Amr Izzat, "Muqāranāt al-adyān fannān sha'biyyān," *al-Shurūq,* October 7, 2010.

19. Mary Abdelmassih, "Muslims Protest at Church in Cairo," *Copts United.* May 1, 2011, http://www.coptsunited.com/Details.php?I=423&A=3539 (accessed May 4, 2015). For the background, see Tadros, "Behind Egypt's Deep Red Lines."

20. In late March and early April, Salafis were responsible for a series of arson attacks on Sufi shrines in the Delta. The media also reported incidents of Salafis meting out vigilante justice against people they accused of prostitution and other sinful behavior. The social media circulated rumors about threats of acid attacks against unveiled women, causing numerous Upper Egyptian women to stay at home on March 29. Moreover, Salafis played a major role in the protests against the appointment of Christian 'Imad Mikha'il as governor of Qena. The protests, which lasted more than one week and even temporarily interrupted traffic on the vital Cairo-Luxor-Aswan train line, effectively prevented Mikha'il from assuming office. In August 2011 he was replaced by a Muslim.

21. Interviews with Mityas Nasr on June 29, 2009, and on October 3, 2011, and with Hani Elgezery on September 6, 2011.

22. Although the public sphere was becoming more and more liberated in the 2000s, and opposition movements such as Kifaya were stretching the boundaries of dissent, confronting the regime remained risky. Philopater Gamil, an activist priest like Mityas Nasr and a major contributor to the magazine with articles commenting on the politics of the day, experienced this reality. In late 2005 a church court, most probably under pressure from the regime, defrocked him for two years and banned him from any publishing activities. However, he was pardoned and returned to his post in June 2007.

23. My information on this movement derives from personal interviews with Hani Elgezery, Mityas Nasr, and Rami Kamil, as well as from the press and the facebook page of the Copts for Egypt.

24. *Al-Misri al-Yawm,* September 12, 2011.

25. Mona el-Ghobahsy, "The Praxis of the Egyptian Revolution," Middle East Report 258, Spring 2011, http://www.merip.org/mer/mer258/praxis-egyptian-revolution (accessed September 2, 2016). For a description and analysis of the typical repertoire of oppositional and revolutionary action see El-Ghobashy 2011.

26. The funeral service was broadcast live by the Church-held television channel Aghapy TV. From this broadcast there is a clip on YouTube that shows the reaction of the audience to the president's message (from 4:30): "iʿtirāḍ ʿalā shukr al-Anbā Yuʾānis (sic!) lil-raʾīs wa-ṭalab bi-ʿazl al-muḥāfiẓ"), http://www.youtube.com/watch?v=-Ut7U06wHxU. The other events were reported in the show *al-ʿAshira Masaʾan* (Dream TV) on January 1, 2011; see the following clip: "Munā al-Shādhilī iʿtidā al-aqbāṭ ʿalā al-wuzarāʾ fī al-janāza", http://www.youtube.com/watch?v=TlpcNKnzmVo (accessed May 4, 2015).

27. For example, they demanded the reopening of churches closed for obscure "security reasons" and the liberation of Mataʾus Wahba, a Coptic Orthodox priest who in 2008 had been sentenced to five years in prison for forgery of documents because he had officiated at a marriage between a male Copt and a female convert from Islam.

28. *Watani,* May 22, 2011.

29. About this event, see Jason Casper, "11. Burning the Dome: AWR Investigates Sectarian Violence in Edfu," *Arab-West-Report,* October 2, 2011, http://www.arabwestreport.info/year-2011/week-40/11-burning-dome-awr-investigates-sectarian-violence-edfu (accessed May 4, 2015).

30. Hassan Elsaghier. "amatallah muslima" http://www.youtube.com/watch?v=5FiRoUaFfns (accessed May 4, 2015). "faḍīḥat muḥāfiẓ Aswān al-Liwāʾ Muṣṭafā al-Sayyid maʿa Sūzan Ḥirafī" and "Filūbatīr yasubb muḥāfiẓ Aswān ʿalā al-hawāʾ wa al-muḥāfiẓ yarudd ʿalayhi"l http://www.youtube.com/watch?v=YicyoGyMarM (accessed May 4, 2015).

31. *Daily News Egypt,* October 9, 2013.

32. The violence at Maspero foreshadowed the November 19–22 protests against the military council in Tahrir Square and at Muhammad Mahmud Street, in which security forces killed more than thirty-three people.

33. On Mina Daniel and his legend, see Yasmine Fathi,"Egypt's Mina Daniel: The Untold Story of a Revolutionary," *Ahram Online,* October 9, 2012, http://english.ahram.org.eg/NewsContent/1/64/55044/Egypt/Politics-/Egypts-Mina-Danial-The-untold-story-of-a-revolutio.aspx (accessed May 4, 2015).

34. *Al-Ahram,* May 11, 2011.

35. This was the opinion of Rami Kamil (interview on September 4, 2011) and Hani Hanna (September 11, 2011). In the subcommission, which met weekly from May to September 2011, the Maspero Youth was represented by Rami Kamil and Bishoi Tamri.

36. Countless video clips give an impression of Hassan's role in the mediation process, which was widely covered by the media. See, for example, ḥalqat al-Shaykh Muḥammad Ḥassān ḥawla qaryat Ṣūl wa-kanīsat Aṭfīḥ 'islāmunā 'izzunā'"), http://www.youtube.com/watch?v=m1uUOXmVdsA (accessed May 4, 2015). The Coptic weekly *Watani* commented critically on March 13 and 20.

37. According to press reports, the Free Egyptians were the first and only newly shaped liberal party to reach the mark of one hundred thousand supporters (*al-Misri al-Yawm*, August 26, 2011). Thanks to the support Sawiris and other like-minded businessmen, it was also one of the best-funded parties on the scene.

38. Georges Fahmi, "The Coptic Church and Politics in Egypt," Carnegie Middle East Center, December 18, 2014, http://carnegie-mec.org/2014/12/18/coptic-church-and-politics-in-egypt/hxlt (accessed May 4, 2015).

39. Mariz Tadros, "Copts under Morsi: Defiance in the Face of Denial," *Middle East Report* 267 (Summer 2013), http://www.merip.org/mer/mer267/copts-under-mursi (accessed May 4, 2015).

40. *al-Misri al-Yawm*, April 11 and September 25, 2011.

The Undesirables of Egypt

Some parts of this essay appear in my articles "Scapepigging: H1N1 Influenza in Egypt," in *Epidemics: Science, Governance, and Social Justice*, ed. Sarah Dry and Melissa Leach (Abingdon, U.K.: Earthscan, 2010), 213–38, elements of which also feature in Mariz Tadros, *Copts at the Crossroads: The Challenge of Building an Inclusive Democracy in Egypt* (Cairo & New York: American University in Cairo Press, 2013), 174–82.

1. S. Viney, "Despite New Regime, Cairo's Garbage Collectors Face Same Hardships," *Egypt Independent*, http://www.egyptindependent.com/news/despite-new-regime-cairo-s-garbage-collectors-face-same-hardships (published February 19, 2013; accessed May 14, 2013).

2. D. Rashed, *Al Ahram Weekly*, "Dumping the Zabaleen," http://weekly.ahram.org.eg/2002/594/eg7.htm (published July 11–17, 2002; accessed September 9, 2009).

3. Ibid.

4. Commonly referred to as swine flu, the H1N1 influenza virus is a novel strain of influenza that first emerged in Mexico and the United States. The virus contains a mixture of genes from humans, birds, and pigs. Despite this mixture of genetic material, it appeared to spread only between humans and no cases of animal-to-human transmission were reported. Swine flu proved to be a catchy but misleading nickname for the new virus. From its initial appearance in March 2009 the virus spread globally. While it appeared to cause a relatively mild form of influenza, it infected large numbers of people and, by October 2009, had killed nearly five thousand people worldwide. In June 2009 the WHO declared a global pandemic of H1N1 as a result of sustained human-to-human transmission in multiple countries.

5. H. Markell, *Ethical and Legal Considerations in Mitigating Pandemic Disease: Workshop Summary* (2007), p. 51. Published on line, Openbook access, https://www.nap.edu/read/11917/chapter/3 (accessed September 12, 2016), 51. D. McNeill, "Finding a Scapegoat when Epidemics strike," *New York Times*, September 1, 2009.

6. McNeill, "Finding a Scapegoat."

7. "Cairo under the Pigsties' Siege," *Al Masry Al Youm*, April 27, 2009, 1.

8. Al-Azhar is one of the oldest and largest places for Islamic teaching in the Muslim world.

9. A literal translation of the word *Coptic* is "Egyptian"; however, it is commonly used to refer to Christians of Egypt.

10. "The Coptic [Women] MPs Give the Muslim Brotherhood a Lesson in Civility," *Al Moussawer*, June 5, 2009.

11. "The People's Assembly [Parliament] Decides to Cull Pigs Immediately," *Al Ahrar*, April 2, 2009, front page.

12. "O ye Ummah," *Al Distour*, May 2, 2009, 6.

13. "The People's Assembly [Parliament] Obliges the Government to Kill the Pigs In Situ," *Ikhwan online*, 28 April 2009, http://www.ikhwanonline.com/Article.asp?ArtID=48291&SecID=250 (accessed August 19, 2009). It is exactly this measure that the minister of health would publicly announce pursuing in response to the pandemic.

14. I. Issa, "A Very Piggish Affair," *Al Distour*, May 7, 2009, front page.

15. Ibid.

16. In the past half century the Coptic Orthodox Church has also sought to assume the political representation of Copts as well, although not always successfully.

17. "The Pig *fitna* and the Wisdom of the Pope," *Al Moussawer*, May 6, 2009, 8.

18. For example, "Warning against Transforming the Influenza into Sectarianism," *Al Gomhorriyya*, May 3, 2009; also see "Enlightened Copts and Sectarian Lies," *Al Watani al Youm*, May 12, 2009. There are many similar stories in the press.

19. An analysis of the actual implementation of the policies related to this narrative is offered later in this essay.

20. See, for example, Shahdan Arram's excellent documentation of the government responses to avian flu: "Integrating Disaster Risk Reduction into Development Planning in Egypt. Case Study: The Impact of Avian Influenza Crisis on Traditional Poultry Keepers' Livelihoods in Fayoum" (M.A. thesis, American University in Cairo, June 2009).

21. See, for example, "Pigs in Government Refrigerators," *Al Ahrar*, May 1, 2009, 3, which specifically named some of the communities in which pigs were bred, such as the village of al Bayadeya in Minya, with strong urging that the pigs be immediately removed.

22. "Killing and Not Relocating [Pigs]," *Al Ahram al Araby*, May 2, 2009, 4.

23. "Kill the One Whose Religion You Know," *Al Akhbar*, May 3, 2009, 17.

24. "Mass graves for Egypt's pigs, Al Masry Al Youm, uploaded May 15th, 2009, http://www.youtube.com/watch?v=jwMIlw7rCSc (accessed October 10, 2009).

25. Dena Rashed "Capital Collection," *Al-Ahram Weekly*, February 28–March 6, 2002, features page, http://weekly.ahram.org.eg/2002/575/sc3.htm (accessed October 9, 2009).

26. Tadros, *Copts at the Crossroads*.

Examining the Role of Media in Coptic Studies

1. See Magdi Guirgis and Nelly van Doorn–Harder, *The Emergence of the Modern Coptic Papacy*, The Popes of Egypt 3 (Cairo & New York: American University in Cairo Press, 2011), and S. S. Hasan, *Christians versus Muslims in Modern Egypt* (Oxford: Oxford University Press, 2003).

2. Dina el-Khawaga, "The Laity at the Heart of the Coptic Clerical Reform," in *Between Desert and City: The Coptic Orthodox Church Today*, ed. Nelly van Doorn–Harder and Kari Vogt (Oslo: Novus, 1997), 145.

3. Less than one-third of the students are female. Despite the high numbers of enrollment each year, only two to three hundred have successfully completed the four-year program since its opening in 1988.The director of the clerical college in Shubra al-Kheima informed me that each of the colleges graduate roughly the same number of students from their programs each year. He explained that the academic rigor of the exams and the time required to finish are challenges to graduation. In the class of

Notes to Pages 54–67

forty students, which I attended, almost all the students juggled their studies with a job during the daytime.

4. Interview with author, January 2, 2013.
5. See the CYC website, http://cycnow.com/site (accessed May 5, 2015).
6. Interview with Author, January 10, 2013.
7. See Hent de Vries, "In Media Res: Global Religion, Public Spheres, and the Task of Contemporary Comparative Religious Studies," in *Religion and Media*, ed. Hent de Vries and Samuel Weber (Stanford: Stanford University Press, 2001): 3–42.
8. William Mazzarella, "Culture, Globalization, Mediation," *Annual Review of Anthropology* 33 (October 2004): 345–67.
9. Matthew the Poor, *Orthodox Prayer Life: The Interior Way* (Crestwood, N.Y.: St. Vladimir's Seminary Press, 2003), 190.
10. Elizabeth Iskander, *Sectarian Conflict in Egypt: Coptic Media, Identity and Representation* (London & New York: Routledge, 2012), 137–43.
11. Mariz Tadros, "Egypt's Bloody Sunday," in *Middle East Research and Information Report*, October 13, 2011. Http://www.merip.org (accessed April 10, 2017).

Father Samaan and the Charismatic Trend within the Coptic Church

I would like to thank for their help and readings of this text: Daniel Duque, Febe Armanios, Jamie Furniss, Konstantin Kastriassianakis, Carolyn M. Ramzy, Giedre Sabaseviciute, Clément Steuer and Nelly van Doorn-Harder.

1. John Waters, *Moving Mountains* (London: Triangle 1999), 44. I quote the story as it is narrated in Waters's book because I was not able to take notes when I witnessed this situation.
2. Stories about Father Samaan's youth have been collected in the English-language book *Moving Mountains* by the Anglican missionary John Waters, cited above.
3. Magdi Guirguis and Nelly Van Doorn-Harder, *The Emergence of the Modern Coptic Papacy*, The Popes of Egypt 3 (Cairo & New York: American University in Cairo Press, 2011).
4. See on Evangelicals and conversion, Sébastien Fath, ed., *Le protestantisme évangélique: Un christianisme de conversion* (Turnhout, Belgium: Brepols, 2004).
5. On the emergence of a charismatic movement among the Copts, see Febe Armanios and Andrew Amstutz, "Emerging Christian Media in Egypt: Clerical Authority and the Visualization of Women in Coptic Video Films," *International Journal of Middle East Studies* 45, no. 3, (2013): 513-33.
6. Jean-Baptiste Decherf, "Sociologie de l'extraordinaire : Une histoire du concept de charisme," *Revue d'Histoire des Sciences Humaines* 23, no. 2 (2010): 203-29.
7. Olivier Roy, *La sainte ignorance: Le temps de la religion sans culture* (Paris: Seuil, 2008).
8. Sylvie Pédron Colombani, " Entre 'local' et 'global': Les conversions au pentecôtisme au Guatemala, " in Fath, *Le protestantisme évangélique*, 98–114.
9. Brigitte Voile, *Les coptes d'Egypte sous Nasser: Sainteté miracle, apparitions* (Paris: CNRS, 2004), 44.
10. Elizabeth E. Oram, "Constructing Modern Copts: The Production of Coptic Christian Identity in Contemporary Egypt" (Ph.D. diss., Princeton University, 2004), 142.
11. Benedict Anderson, *Imagined Communities: Reflections on the Origins and Spread of Nationalism* (London & New York: Verso, 1991). Reality is, following Luc Boltanski, what is stabilized by the semantic power of institutions. It is opposed to the world, which includes all that happens, the flux of life. Reality covers just a small part of what happens in the world, and therefore can be contested by elements taken from this

unlimited flow. This protest against reality is obvious during revolutionary periods. See Luc Boltanski, *De la critique: Précis de sociologie de l'*émancipation (Paris: Gallimard, 2009).

12. See Anthony Shenoda, "Cultivating Mystery: Miracles and a Coptic Miracle imaginary" (Ph.D. diss., Harvard University, 2010).

13. The Sunday schools were launched in 1918 by Habib Guirguis based on the Protestant model to provide a basic religious education to Coptic children. The movement was therefore instrumental in proposing common benchmarks to the Copts. The Sunday School Movement was particularly active during the 1950s. Its leaders became figures of the revival of the Church, and some of them chose to become monks and continue the renewal in the monasteries. See Wolfram Reiss, *Erneuerung in der Koptisch-Orthodoxen Kirche: Die Geschichte der koptisch-orthodoxen Sonntagsschulbewegung und die Aufnahme ihrer Reformansätze in den Erneuerungsbewegungen der Koptisch-Orthodoxen Kirche der Gegenwart.* (Hamburg: Lit, 1998).

14. Dina el-Khawaga, "Le renouveau copte : La communauté comme acteur politique" (Ph.D. diss., IEP Paris 1993), 275.

15. Matta el-Miskin, *Al Masīhī fīl Mujtamaʿ* [The Christian in Society] (Monastery of Saint Macarius, 1968), quoted in Luc Barbulesco, *La participation politique de la communauté copte d'Egypte (1881–1981): Attitudes collectives et orientations idéologiques* (IEP Paris, 1990), 241.

16. Voile, *Les coptes d'Egypte sous Nasser*, 41.

17. This process is often referred to as the clericalization of the Coptic Church. See el-Khawaga, "Le renouveau copte."

18. For the example of reform of the Coptic pilgrimages, see Catherine Mayeur-Jaouen, "The Coptic Mouleds: Evolution of the Traditional Pilgrimages," in *Between Desert and City: The Coptic Orthodox Church Today*, ed. Nelly van Doorn–Harder and Kari Vogt (Oslo: Novus, 1997), 212–29.

19. Quoted in Voile, *Les coptes d'Egypte sous Nasser*, 250.

20. Al Haya was launched in 2003.

21. See Margaret Poloma, "The Millenarianism of the Pentecostal Movement," in *Christian Millenarianis: From the Early Church to Waco*, ed. Stephen Hunt (London: Hurst, 2001), 166–86. For dreams and visions in the Egyptian context, see Amira Mittermaier, *Dreams That Matter: Egyptian Landscapes of the Imagination* (Berkley & Los Angeles: University of California Press, 2011).

22. Sébastien Fath, "Les charismatiques troisième vague c'est quoi?" *Sébastien Fath's blog*, http://blogdesebastienfath.hautetfort.com/archive/2007/05/03/les-charismatiques-troisieme-vague-c-est-quoi2.html (accessed March 25, 2013). In premillenarianism the instauration of God's kingdom comes directly from Jesus's intervention; Stephen Hunt, "The Rise, Fall and Return of Post-Millenarianism," in Hunt, *Christian Millenarianism*, 50–61.

23. "The label Protestant remains a damning epithet to this day in Orthodox circles"; S. S Hasan, *Christian versus Muslims in Modern Egypt* (Oxford: Oxford University Press, 2003), 76.

24. It is not unusual to be ordained at a very young age as a deacon in the Coptic Orthodox Church, but to be a deacon at six is rare, and the aim here is probably to insist on his early vocation.

25. Waters, *Moving Mountains*, 41.

26. Ibid., 42.

27. Father Zakareya Boutros was the future Samaan's father of confession; he was living in Damanhur and was participating in such rural tours under Father Boulos's

Notes to Pages 70–72

supervision. Stuart Robinson, *Defying Death: Zakaria Botross: Apostle to Islam* (Davenport, Iowa: City Harvest Publications, 2008), 14.

28. El-Khawaga, "Le renouveau copte," 392–94; Reiss, *Erneuerung*, 227, 229.

29. Testimony from a member of the association from Minya in a video called *sawfa tarrâ a'zam* [you will see greater], online since September 11, 2011, http://www.youtube.com/watch?v=35rHUDv_sXE (accessed March 25, 2013).\

30. Personal interview with Dr. Samuel Labib Maher, son in law of Father Samaan, personal interview April 2, 2009. The Society for the Salvation of the Souls (SSS) is not a church and claims no particular denomination. The fact is that it is a *gam'iyya* (association) and, for example, has no legal status to perform marriages. (Based on Egyptian personal status laws, this right is reserved for state-recognized churches only.) SSS was founded in Assiout in 1927 and has spread all over Egypt. Today it has forty-five branches. One of its activities is translating religious books from all Christian denominations. It also organizes prayer meetings. See the SSS website, http://khalaselnefoos.org/about-us/about-khalas-el-nefoos (accessed August 26, 2016).

31. Waters, *Moving Mountains*, 48.

32. Robinson, *Defying Death*, 57.

33. There are several studies on the Zabbalin. See, for example, Gaétan du Roy, "Le miracle de la montagne et les chiffonniers du Moqattam," in *Figures contemporaines de la transmission*, ed. Nathalie Burnay and Annabelle Klein (Namur, Belgium: Presses Universitaires de Namur, 2009), 201-16 ; Gaétan du Roy and Jamie Furniss, "Sœur Emmanuelle et les chiffonniers : Partage de vie et développement: 1971–1982," in Mission et engagement politique après 1945 : Afrique, Amérique Latine, Europe, ed. Caroline Sappia and Olivier Servais (Paris: Karthala, 2010), 87-101; Jamie Furniss, "Metaphors of Waste: Several Ways of Seeing 'Development' and Cairo's Garbage Collectors" (Ph.D diss., Oxford University, 2012).

34. *Zarayeb* is the plural of *zariba*, which means enclosure. The Zabbalin neighborhood is often referred to as *al zarayeb* because of the pigs that are raised there.

35. Biography (anonymous), *The Biography of Saint Samaan the Shoemaker*, translated from Arabic (Cairo: Saint Samaan Church, 1998).

36. Ibid., 79–80.

37. This verse is now engraved high up on the cliff at the entrance of the monastery, and the page of the Bible, now framed, hangs on the priest's office wall. Ibid., 81.

38. For example, see this video from the program *"Insan 'Adi"* , part 1, ("Normal Person") SAT 7 2009, https://www.youtube.com/watch?v=G4axPuaUSXE (accessed September 5, 2016). In a move, I think, to protect himself, he always praised the pope in spite of his strained relationship with him. He speaks about his relation with Pope Shenouda in "Insan 'Adi", part 2, Sat 7 2009: https://www.youtube.com/watch?v=68Bib Bzbans (accessed September 5, 2016).

39. He said, for example, in an interview: "Our goal was the service of the souls; my work was to go to the houses and take them to the church" (*"Insan 'Adi"*): https://www.youtube.com/watch?v=68BibBzbans (accessed September 5, 2016).

40. The director of the film about Father Samaan's life explained to me that the Zabbalin came from Upper Egypt because they killed people in their village; "they were all criminals."

41. For example, in a recent movie in which the vocation of the priest in the area is reenacted by actors, an imposing and corpulent Sa'idi with a big mustache appears regularly, and we rapidly understand that he symbolizes Evil because he plays no role in the film and he looks very frightening and aggressive. He just appears on the screen

and does not interact with other characters. In the closing titles the actor is called "Personification of Evil." The film is entitled *Risala Samaweya* (Heavenly Message), directed by Ibrahim Abdel-Sayed, Agape Media Center, 2007.

42. Personal interview with Ragui Assaad, who was then working with Environmental Quality International (EQI), an organization affiliated with the World Bank, May 18, 2012.

43. Information found in an EQI report. Https://www.devex.com (accessed April 10, 2017).

44. Suleyman was thrown in jail after the revolution of January 25, 2011.

45. Information confirmed by Dr. Samuel, personal interview, April 2, 2009.

46. Personal interview with Mrs. Souad (in Egypt, married women, Muslim or Christian, keep their own name), March 17, 2009.

47. I analyze the story of this legend in my doctoral thesis : *Le prêtre des chiffonniers ou la construction d'une autorité religieuse au Caire, entre charisme, tradition et clientélisme* (1974-2014) (PhD. diss., Université catholique de Louvain, 2014), p. 202-290. The major studies of this story are Johannes Den Heijer, "Les patriarches coptes d'origine syrienne," in Studies on the Christian Arabic Heritage, ed. Rifaat Ebied and Herman Teule (Leuven: Peeters, 2004), p. 45-63 ; Youhanna Nessim Youssef, "The Miracle of Ibn Zar'ah in Coptic Tradition, Texts and Icons," Coptica 8 (2009), p. 81-96; Maryann Shenoda, "Displacing Dhimmī, Maintaining Hope: Unthinkable Coptic Representations of Fatimid Egypt," International Journal of Middle East Studies 39 (2007), p. 587-606. The vita subsisted mainly in the *History of the Patriarchs* and in the *Synaxarion*, embedded in the life story of the patriarch Abraham. The saint himself was of little importance; the key was the miracle in itself, as revealed by the fact that the name of the saint was not even mentioned in the first tales.

48. Father Samaan likes to stress this point.

49. This book, which was published anonymously, was written by Zakareya Boutros, as I learned from different sources. It shows the importance of Father Zakareya in pushing forward Samaan's "spiritual mission." The book was published in 1987 in Arabic and then republished in 1992 and translated in English in 1998.

50. One can buy a CD with archive films showing the construction of the monastery. Everything was filmed in Muqattam. A person close to the priest told me that he often cries out *"Da tarikh"* ("This is history").

51. Cornelis Hulsman, "Intolerant Climate in Egypt and Media Manipulations Result in Row around Bishop Bishuy," *Arab West Report*, week 43, October 2010.

52. In March 2012 Makari Younan was interviewed about the exorcisms in a talk show called *Ma'kum* (With You) on Arabic channel CBC, http://www.youtube.com/watch?v=Wk3hTyUmnrk (accessed, September 5, 2016).

53. Others are even more "Protestant." Mahir Fayezz himself describes many songs heard in Muqattam as "too Protestant for him." He describes himself as Orthodox and prefers to follow the Egyptian Coptic tradition. Personal interview with Mahir Fayezz, 2010, personal interview, April 9, 2010.

54. This channel was launched in 1996 by a British missionary, Terence Ascott. For its history, see the channel's website: http://www.sat7.org/en/sat7/history (accessed September 6 2016). His interview about Sat 7 on the Evangelical talk show *100 Huntley Street* can be found on YouTube: http://www.youtube.com/watch?v=UtjL3TOCSAQ&feature=relmfu (online, April 26, 2012 ; accessed September 6, 2016). This channel broadcasts in English, Arabic, Turkish, and Persian.

55. People criticizing the priest use the terms *Protestant* or *ingili* (evangelical) as opposed to traditional, *taqlidi*. Zakareya Boutros had already been attacked by Pope Shenouda, who wrote a book based on a series of articles in *al-Kirazah*. For more details

Notes to Pages 74–78

see Robinson, *Defying Death*, 59. The pope's book is entitled *Bid'a al Khalas fi Lahza* [The Heresy of Salvation in a Moment] (Cairo: Anba Ruways, 6th edition, 2009 [1988]).

56. This initiative was launched by South African Protestants in order to gather together the Christians in Africa. See the website The Global Day of Prayer, http://www.globaldayofprayer.com (accessed September 6, 2016).

57. As mentioned in *Ruz al Yusuf* for November 6, 2006, "Coptic authorities" didn't allow the meeting to take place in al Muqattam, see *Arab West Report* website, http://www.arabwestreport.info/year-2006/week-24/38-international-day-prayer-qasr-al-doub257ra-evangelical-church-after-coptic (accessed May 21, 2013).

58. Qasr al-Dubbara had organized "intercession prayer" for Egypt for eight years before the revolution. Anna Dowell, "The Church in the Square: Negotiations of Religion and Revolution at an Evangelical Church in Cairo" (M.A. thesis, American University in Cairo, 2012), 31.

59. See Nelly van Doorn–Harder *Contemporary Coptic Nuns* (Columbia: University of South Carolina Press, 1995), 189–90.

60. As of 2012, videos of exorcisms have been added to the monastery's website, http://www.samaanchurch.com/en/video_library.php (accessed September 6, 2016).

61. A good example is given by Anthony Shenoda when he asked a group of people gathered around a monk who himself has wonder-working qualities why miracles are important for the Copts. They answered that it is because of the pressure against them. And then Shenoda asked why some Muslims care about miracles as well: "The unison response in the room was that Muslims go to Christians for miracles. One man blurted out in his deep, gruff, know-it-all voice '*Sayyida Zaynab mish bita'mil hāga* [does nothing]." Shenoda, "Cultivating Mystery," 39–40.

62. Barbara Drieskens, *Living with Djinns: Understanding and Dealing with the Invisible in Cairo* (London, San Francisco & Beirut: Saqi, 2006).

63. For a similar interpretation of the exorcism, see Laure Guirguis, "Coptes d'Egypte: Un 'nationalisme utopique?'" *Cahiers de l'Institut Religioscope* 6 (July 2011): 22–25, http://www.religion.info/pdf/2011_07_Guirguis.pdf (accessed July 17, 2014).

64. Robinson, *Defying Death*, 48.

65. We can see her testimony in a film made by the monastery and directed by Ramy Samir in 2008, "Ad-deir al-jadid," http://www.youtube.com/watch?v=9fVlw_OIvzo&list=PL2908FoE2B5391AD3&index=3&featur e=plpp_video (accessed August 31, 2016).

66. On the question of conversions in Egypt, see Laure Guirguis, ed., *Conversions religieuses et mutations politiques en Egypte* (Paris: Non Lieu, 2007).

67. Voile, *Les coptes d'Egypte sous Nasser*, 250.

68. Catherine Mayeur-Jaouen, " Saints coptes et musulmans dans l'Egypte du XXe siècle," Revue de l'Histoire des Religions, vol. 2015, no. 1, (1998), p. 139–186; Voile, *Les coptes d'Egypte sous Nasser.*

69. André Mary, " Syncrétisme, " *Dictionnaire des faits religieux*, ed. Régine Azria and Danièle Hervieu-Léger (Paris: Quadrige/PUF, 2010), 1197–1202.

70. Voile, *Les coptes d'Egypte sous Nasser*, 245–57.

71. "Over and over again, worshippers at KDEC [Qasr al-Dubbara Church] told me with great feeling that while the events of January may seem to have come out of nowhere, they were in fact a direct, divine intervention in response to the faithful prayer movement that had been growing in KDEC over the last eight years." See Anna Dowell, "The Church in the Square: Negotiations of Religion and Revolution at an Evangelical Church in Cairo" (M.A. thesis, American University in Cairo, 2012), 34. See also Andrawus's talk show *Kâchif al Asrâr*, on January 21, 2012, on which he speaks about

the Egyptian revolution. Two young Christian women are interviewed by him, and they also affirm that the revolution was brought about by prayer.

72. Dowell, "The Church in the Square," 36.
73. *Ruz al Yusef*, May 24, 2009, 19.
74. This shift among American Evangelicals was called optimistic millenarianism by Sébastien Fath, "Les ONG évangéliques américaines ou les ruses de la Providence," in *Les ONG confessionnelles: Religions et action internationale*, ed. Bruno Duriez, François Mabille, and Kathy Rousselet (Paris: Harmattan, 2007), p. 249–262.
75. Which does not mean that he has no political practice. See Gaétan du Roy, "La campagne de Misriyin al Ahrar chez les chiffonniers de Manchiyit Nasir," *Égypte/Monde Arabe*, no. 10 (2013), Open access online journal, link to this feature: https://ema.revues.org/3176 (accessed September 6, 2016).
76. Visions are common in Egypt among Copts as well as Muslims. See, for example, Valerie J. Hoffman, "The Role of Visions in Contemporary Egyptian Religious Life," *Religion* 27, no. 1 (1997), p. 45–64.
77. He told his dream during the November 11, 2011 (11/11/11), prayer meeting.
78. SAT7Arabic, *Al-Qiss Sameh Mauris, Allah Kallimni min 40 sanna* [Pastor Sameh Maurice, God talked to me 40 years ago], December 30, 2011, http://www.youtube.com/watch?v=SecrZfC5MWQ, SAT 7 (accessed on December 30, 2011).
79. Personal interview with Mahir Fayez, May 24, 2011.
80. See du Roy, "La campagne de Mosriyin al Ahrar."

Transmitting Coptic Musical Heritage

1. See Carolyn M. Ramzy, "Taratil: Songs of Praise and the Musical Discourse of Nostalgia among Coptic Immigrants in Toronto, Canada" (M.A. thesis, Florida State University, 2006); Séverine Gabry-Thienpont, "Tarânîm et madîh: Chants liturgiques coptes ou chansons populaires égyptiennes?" *Cahiers Rémois de Musicologie* 7 (2013): 87–99.
2. For an overview of the process and issues of creating a Coptic music heritage, see Séverine Gabry-Thienpont, "Processus et enjeux de la patrimonialisation de la musique copte." *Égypte/Monde Arabe* 5–6 (2009): 133–58, https://ema.revues.org/2883 (accessed December 31, 2010).
3. Aziz S. Atiya, ed., *The Coptic Encyclopedia*, vol. 6 (New York: Macmillan, 1991), 1715–44.
4. Ragheb Moftah, Margit Toth, and Martha Roy, *The Coptic Orthodox Liturgy of St. Basil; With Complete Musical Transcription* (Cairo: American University in Cairo Press, 1998).
5. Other titles by Ragheb Moftah are "Coptic Music," *Bulletin de l'Institut des Études Coptes* (1958): 42–53; "The Study of the Recording of the Coptic Airs: The History of the Mu'allim Mikâ'il," *Al Kirazah*, January 10, 14, and 17, 1975; "Coptic Music, from Mothers Chanting to Mikhâ'il El-Batanony Hymns," *Akhbar El-Adab Literature News Magazine*, January 7, 1995.
6. Nikolaos Boukas and Ioannis Papathanasiou, "Early Diastematic Notation in Greek Christian Hymnographic Texts of Coptic Origin: A Reconsideration of the Source Material," *Palaeobyzantine Notations III: Acta of the Congress Held at Hernen Castle, The Netherlands, in March 2001*, edited by Gerda Wolfram, Eastern Christian Studies 4 (2004): 1–26.
7. Ragheb Moftah, "Music," *The Coptic Encyclopedia* 6, 1731–32.
8. Charles H. Cosgrove, *An Ancient Christian Hymn with Musical Notation: Papyrus Oxyrhynchus 1786: Text and Commentary* (Tübingen: Mohr Siebeck, 2011).
9. For more informations on the topic of manuscripts in Greek found in Egypt, see, among others, Céline Grassien, "Préliminaires à l'édition du corpus papyrologique des hymnes chrétiennes liturgiques de langue grecque" (Ph.D. diss., Paris IV University,

2011). Currently, Céline Grassien and the musicologist Alan Gampel are studying the musical notations in the earliest manuscripts found in Egypt.

10. Carolyn M. Ramzy, "Music: Performing Coptic Expressive Culture," in *The Coptic Christian Heritage: History, Faith, and Culture*, ed. Lois M. Farag (Abingdon, U.K. & New York: Routledge, 2014), 166.

11. Athanasius Kircher, *Lingua aegyptiaca restituta*. (Romae: H. Scheus, 1643), 515–16.

12. Guillaume André Villoteau, *De l'état actuel de l'art musical en Égypte, ou Relation historique et descriptive des recherches et observations faites sur la musique en ce pays, Description de l'Égypte* V (Paris: Imprimerie Charles Louis Fleury Panckoucke, 1826), 607–846.

13. Jules Blin, *Chants liturgiques des Coptes* (Cairo: National Printing House, 1888); Louis Badet, *Chants liturgiques des Coptes, notés et mis en ordre par le Père Louis Badet de la Cie de Jésus* (Cairo: Collège de la Sainte Famille, Petit Séminaire Copte, 1899).

14. For more details about the influence of Villoteau's, Blin's, Badet's, and Moftah's work, see Gabry-Thienpont, "Processus," 151–55, and Ramzy "Music," 166–72.

15. One example of that can be consulted in Ilona Borsai, "Le tropaire byzantin 'O Monogenès' dans la pratique du chant copte," *Studia Musicologica Academiae Scientiarum Hungaricae* 14 (1972): 329–54.

16. For example, connections such as those she mentioned in her article "Mélodies traditionnelles des Égyptiens," *Studia Musicologica Academiae Scientarium Hungaricae* 10 (1968) : 69-90.

17. From a sociological point of view it is important to begin any study of the music performed by these two groups by defining their musical material. First, it is essential to understand the context in which the practices, the magico-religious rites, and the diverse forms of worship take place. Second, it is fundamental to assess the influence of the works of scholars of Middle Eastern studies and musicologists on how the Copts—especially the clergy and the cantors—perceive their own music today.

18. Maurice Martin, "Les coptes catholiques, 1880–1920," *Proche-Orient Chrétien* 40 (1990): 37.

19. Wolfram Reiss, *Erneuerung in der Koptisch-Orthodoxen Kirche* (Hamburg: Lit, 1998), 54; Brigitte Voile, *Les coptes d'Égypte sous Nasser* (Paris: CNRS, 2004), 50–52.

20. Carolyn M. Ramzy, "Exploring Coptic Music Narratives: Collaborative Ethnography and the Study of Coptic *Taratîl*," paper presented at international conference The Future of Coptic Studies: Theories, Methodologies, and Subjects, Wake Forest University, Winston Salem, N.C., September 17–19, 2010.

21. M. P. Roncaglia, "Didymus the Blind," *The Coptic Encyclopedia*, vol. 3, 900.

22. Otto F. A. Meinardus, *Monks and Monasteries of the Egyptian Deserts* (Cairo: American University in Cairo Press, 1992), 156–57.

23. At the same time Magdalena Kuhn noticed similar types of notation in others parts of Egypt. See Magdalena Kuhn, *Koptische liturgische Melodien: die Relation zwischen Text und Musik in der koptischen Psalmodia* (Louvain: Peeters, 2011).

24. These are not ornaments but so-called melismas, which are composed in links with a regular rhythm, often measured, sung with long syllables ("yé," "waw," and so on) and considered as important as the syllabic parts.

Singing Strategic Multiculturalism

1. It should be noted that these six coffins only represented the Coptic casualties of Nag Hammadi. Rarely did demonstrators, Canadian members of Parliament, or priests mention the Muslim officer who also died in the drive-by shooting; nor did they mention other non-Christian casualties in sectarian conflicts.

2. As the anthropologist Angie Heo points out, the term *sectarian* is an opaque one, glossing all acts of Muslim-Christian violence as one category without regard for textual detail, personal and local dynamics, as well as strategies of larger political narratives. Soon after the January 25 revolution of 2011, rumors circulated that it was the ex-minister of interior Habib Adly who had orchestrated the Coptic church bombing as a divisive ploy to detract from larger Christian-Muslim protests, brought together by the brutal beatings and murder of one young man, Khalid Said, at the hands of the Alexandria police; see Angie Heo, "The Virgin Made Visible: Intercessory Images of the Church Territory in Egypt," *Comparative Studies in Society and History* 54, no. 2 (2012): 361–91.

3. Anthony Shenoda provides an excellent timeline of the major event that followed the Two Saints' Church bombing and the spike of sectarian violence that followed the January 25 uprising; Anthony Shenoda, "Reflections on the (In)Visibility of Copts in Egypt," *Jadaliyya.com*, May 18, 2011, http://www.jadaliyya.com/pages/index/1624/ (accessed May 13, 2013).

4. Other cities with significant Coptic-Christian communities were also active. These included Los Angeles, Houston, and Washington, D.C., in the United States, as well as other cities around the world including, Sydney, London, Stockholm, Dublin, and Paris, among others.

5. I am quoting Conservative member of Parliament of the Mississauga-Erindale district, Bob Dechert, as he addressed the Coptic crowds in front of the Ontario Legislative Building on January 30, 2010. On this day he also promised to organize a delegation of Coptic Orthodox priests from Montreal and Toronto to travel to Ottawa and raise their concerns to members of the Canadian cabinet. This included the minister of immigration, Jason Kenny, and the minster of foreign affairs, Laurence Cannon. Although this did not take place, Prime Minster Stephen Harper and Jason Kenny hosted a roundtable of Coptic clergy in Mississauga's Coptic Canadian Center the following year on January 13, 2011.

6. Webb Keane, *Signs of Recognition: Powers and Hazards of Representation in an Indonesian Society* (Berkeley: University of California Press, 1997). Angie Heo writes of the hazards that heightened Coptic Church visibility may bring to clerics during episodes of Marian apparitions; Heo, "The Virgin Made Visible," 374.

7. Humani Bannerji, *The Dark Side of the Nation: Essays on Multiculturalism, Nationalism and Gender* (Toronto: Canadian Scholars Press, 2000), 78.

8. The Coptic community uses the terms *taratil* and *taranim* interchangeably to describe nonliturgical devotional songs that complement the official Coptic liturgical hymnody known as *alhan*. The thirteenth-century linguist Muhammad Ibn Mukarram Ibn Manzur (1232–1311) mentions *ra-ta-la* and *ra-na-ma* as the verb "to sing" or "to chant" religious texts in his lexicon *Lisan al-ʿArab*. He specifically mentions *ra-ta-la* as a genre resulting from the addition of melodies to Christian prayers by those of mixed Arab ancestry. While Copts do not claim to have mixed Arab ancestry, by the thirteenth century their colloquial language began to change from Coptic to Arabic after the Arab conquest in the seventh century. For the sake of brevity and clarity, I will continue to refer to *taratil* and *taranim* solely as *taratil* (sing. *tartila*).

9. See Séverine Gabry-Thienpoint, "Anthropologie des Musiques Coptes en Égypte Contemporaine" (Ph.d.diss., Université Nanterre-Paris X, 2013); Hans Hickmann, "Koptische Musik," in *Ausstellungskatalog Koptische Kunst: Christentum am Nil* (Essen: 1963), 116–21; Ragheb Moftah, Martha Roy, and Margit Toth, *The Coptic Orthodox Liturgy of St. Basil; With Complete Musical Transcription* (Cairo: American University in Cairo

Notes to Pages 96–97

Press, 1998); Martha Roy, "The Coptic Orthodox Church and Its Music," in *The Garland Encyclopedia of World Music: The Middle East*, ed. Virginia Danielson, Scott Marcus, and Dwight Reynolds (New York: Routledge, 2002), 219–24.

10. Carolyn M. Ramzy, "*Taratil*: Songs of Praise and the Musical Discourse of Nostalgia among Coptic Immigrants in Toronto, Canada" (M.A. Thesis, Florida State University, 2007).

11. Saint Mark's status as the first church in North America is contested. While Father Marcos served as early as 1964, Scarborough's Saint Mark's only officially registered as a church in 1978, after New Jersey's St. Mark's Coptic Church was established in 1970. Fore more on Coptic diaspora history, please see Father Marcos Marcos's book Riḥlat al-Kanīsa al-Qibṭiyya al-Urthūdhukhsiyya ila Amrīkā al-Shamāliyya Arbaʿīn ʿman (The Journey of the Coptic Orthodox Church to North America: 1964–2004) 410 (Alexandria: St. Mina's Monastery Publishing House, 2004). In 2014, Father Marcos Marcos published an updated edition in English. See Father Marcos Marcos, *The History of the Coptic Orthodox Church in North America; The First 50 Years* (1965-2014) (Toronto, Canada: St. Mark's Coptic Orthodox Church, 2014).

12. Here I am indebted to Helene Moussa, volunteer curator at Saint Mark's Coptic Museum, for our rich conversations about all things Coptic-Canadian, her experiences at Saint Mark's museum, and her invaluable feedback in the course of writing this essay.

13. It is important to point out that, besides the ease with which it is possible to attain building permits and the desire to accommodate their growing communities, building new Coptic churches in Toronto is riddled with community politics between clergy and their supporters. Moussa points out that, since no bishop was initially assigned to the Ontario and Northeast region, many of the older priests hold considerable social and political sway with their congregants, and their own churches have come to operate as smaller dioceses. Today Bishop Mina is the first bishop of a newly created diocese of Mississauga, Vancouver, and Western Canada. Curiously, this diocese does not include Toronto, home of the one of the largest communities of Coptic Christians in North America.

14. Anthony Shenoda, "Confessing the Faith Coptic Christian Witnessing to Christ in an Islamic Public Sphere," paper presented at the annual meeting for the American Anthropological Association, Montreal, Canada, November 15–20, 2011.

15. The Coptic Church Network (http://www.copticchurch.net); Coptic Orthodox Patriarchate Archdiocese of North America (http://nacopts.org); *Wikipedia*, List of Coptic Orthodox Churches in Canada (http://en.wikipedia.org). While Wikipedia is not necessarily a reliable source, its ability to allow users to contribute and to add the churches in their cities makes it a noteworthy resource in this regard. (All sites listed accessed January 25, 2015.)

16. Statistics Canada, *2011 National Household Survey: Data Tables* 2011 Census, Catalogue Number 99–10-X2011028, in *Statistics Canada*, http://www12.statcan.gc.ca/nhs-enm/2011/dp-pd/dt-td/Rp-eng. cfm?TABID=2&LANG=E&APATH=3&DETAIL=0&DIM=0&FL=A&FREE=0&GC=0&GID=1118296&GK=0&GRP=0&PID=105396&PRID=0&PTYPE=105277&S=0&SHOWALL=0&SUB=0&Temporal=2013&THEME=95&VID=0&VNAMEE=&VNAMEF=&D1=0&D2=0&D3=0&D4=0&D5=0&D6=0 (accessed January 25, 2015); Fouad Assaad, "Egyptians" in *The Encyclopedia of Canada's Peoples*, ed. Paul Robert Magocsi (Toronto: University of Toronto Press, 1999), 459.

17. For a more detailed analysis of Coptic immigration patterns, refer to Ghada Botros's study "Competing for the Future: Adaptation and the Accommodation of

Difference in Coptic Immigrant Churches" (Ph.D., diss., University of Toronto, 2005): 42–57.

18. When President Abdel Fattah Sisi succeeded in the controversial removal of his predecessor, Muslim Brotherhood president Mohamed Morsi, in July 2013, there was a severe backlash against Christians in the country. On August 14 a total of forty-two churches were either burned or damaged, along with dozens of other Christian-owned businesses or homes. Human Rights Watch also reported that at least three people, Copts and one Muslim, were killed. It was the largest sectarian-related attack in modern Egyptian history, and there continues a trepid sense of security as insurgencies continue to blot Sisi's leadership. See "Egypt: Mass Attacks on Churches," http://www.hrw.org/news/2013/08/21/egypt-mass-attacks-churches, and "Sources: At least 26 killed in North Sinai Attack," http://www.cnn.com/2015/01/29/africa/egypt-north-sinai-attack/ (both accessed February 3, 2015).

19. Some CDs were less expensive, going for as little as $1.50 for copies of burned Arabic *taratil*. English copyrighted materials were more expensive, however, with one CD entitled "Best of the West" going for $10.00.

20. Thomas Turino, *Music as Social Life: The Politics of Participation* (Chicago: University of Chicago Press, 2008), 1.

21. For more on Islamic religious revival, refer to Gregory Starrett's *Putting Islam to Work: Education, Politics and Religious Transformation in Egypt* (Los Angeles: University of California Press, 2006), and Saba Mahmood's *Politics of Piety: The Islamic Revival and the Feminist Subject* (Princeton: Princeton University Press, 2005). In my dissertation (University of Toronto, 2014) "Politics of (Dis)Engagement: Coptic Christian Religious Revival and the Performative Politics of Song," I discuss, the trajectories of a Coptic religious revival as it emerged in Orthodox Sunday schools.

22. This is a habit that is not just limited to Coptic Christian youth. Young Muslims can also purchase samples of their favorite *inshad*, or Islamic devotional songs, as mobile ring tones. Besides using dress and other physical markers, such as facial hair or lack thereof, people can decipher one another's religious identity via a simple cellphone ringtone.

23. Michel Foucault, *History of Sexuality*, volume 1: *An Introduction* (New York: Random House, 1978), 11.

24. One example is S. H. Leeder's *Modern Sons of the Pharaohs* (London: Stoughton, 1918). For a more detailed discussion regarding the discursive politics of early Coptic liturgical music studies, refer to my article "Notating Coptic Music: A Brief Historical Survey," in *Coptic Orthodox Chant and Liturgical Hymnody: The Ragheb Moftah Collection at the Library of Congress* (Washington D.C.: Performing Arts Encyclopedia, 2008), http://www.loc.gov/performingarts/ (accessed May 13, 2013).

25. Saba Mahmood, *Politics of Piety*.

26. Father Marcos Marcos's name before ordination was Wagdy Elias Abdel Masih. It is also interesting to note that one of the first Egyptian grocery stories to open in Scarborough, in the plaza adjacent to St. Mark's Church was named San Marcos Place. It is also interesting to one of the first Egyptian grocery stores to open in Scarborough, just in next plaza to St. Mark's church, wasalso named San Marcos Place. In the United States the first Coptic Orthodox Church also took the name Saint Mark's when it was officially registered in Jersey City, New Jersey, in 1970. The vice president of the Coptic Association of America, Sami Boulos, describes the church's early history in this community publication: *The History of the Early Coptic Community in the U.S.A., 1955–1970* (n.p.: self-published, 2006).

Notes to Pages 100–103

27. American and European missionaries heavily proselytized Egyptians in the eighteenth and nineteenth centuries, leaving many lasting impressions on the Coptic Orthodox Church, one of them being an evangelical rhetoric in its services. This is particularly evident on the website of Saint Mark's Coptic Church of Scarborough, http://www.stmark.toronto.on.coptorthodox.ca (accessed April 10, 2017). For more on missionary activities and influence in Egypt, refer to Heather Sharkey's study *American Evangelicals in Egypt: Missionary Encounters in an Age of Empire* (Princeton: Princeton University Press, 2008), and Paul Sedra's work *From Mission to Modernity: Evangelicals, Reformers, and Education in Nineteenth-Century Egypt* (London & New York: Tauris, 2011).

28. Father Marcos Marcos, *Riḥlat al-Kanīsa al-Qibṭiyya*, 234 (accessed February 3, 2015).

29. "Egyptian Christians Want Own State, Journalist Says," *Toronto Daily Star*, November 11, 1969.

30. Father Marcos Marcos, "Religion in Egypt," *Toronto Daily Star*, undated. The piece is also referenced in Marcos, *The Journey of the Coptic Orthodox Church in North America*, (November 11, 1969) 259.

31. Nadia Ramsis Farah discusses the Khanka church burning incident in detail in *Religious Strife in Egypt: Crisis and Ideological Conflict in the Seventies* (New York: Gordon and Breach 1986), 112–13.

32. Father Marcos Marcos, *Riḥlat al-Kanīsa al-Qibṭiyya*, 238.

33. Mariz Tadros asserts it was the incident of the al-Khanka church burning that exacerbated the tensions between President Sadat and Pope Shenouda and contributed to the dissolve of their informal entente. See Tadros, "Vicissitudes in the Entente between Church and the State." *International Journal of Middle East Studies* 41, no. 2 (2009): 274–75.

34. Father Marcos Marcos, *Riḥlat al-Kanīsa al-Qibṭiyya*, 245–47.

35. There was also one Muslim victim who died in this incident; for more, refer to Nadia Abou-El Magd's article "The Meaning of Al-Kosheh," *Al Ahram Weekly Online*, no. 467 (February 3–9, 2000), http://weekly.ahram.org.eg/Archive/2000/467/eg7.htm (access August 29, 2016).

36. Father Marcos Marcos, *Riḥlat al-Kanīsa al-Qibṭiyya*, 264.

37. Febe Armanios provides an insightful chapter entitled "Weapons of the Faithful: Defining Orthodoxy through Sermons" in her *Coptic Christianity in Ottoman Egypt* (New York: Oxford University Press, 2011): 117–46.

38. Deborah Durham and Frederick Klaits, "Funerals and Public Space of Sentiment in Botswana," *Journal of Southern African Studies* 28 (December 2002): 773–91.

39. It is important to note that many of the area's largest churches, particularly Saint Mary and Saint Athanasius of the Coptic Canadian Center, now broadcast all of their services live via the Internet on http://www.cccnet.ca. There are also countless videos uploaded to sites such as YouTube and facebook by community members, including many demonstration videos that were integral to this research.

40. Kevin Lewis O'Neill, *City of God: Christian Citizenship in Postwar Guatemala* (Los Angeles: University of California Press, 2010), 4.

41. Richard Day, *Multiculturalism and the History of Canadian Diversity* (Toronto: University of Toronto Press, 2000).

42. Bannerji, *The Dark Side of the Nation*, 9.

43. Day, *Multiculturalism and the History of Canadian Diversity*, 5.

44. In many of these Coptic-Canadian demonstrations, crosses, banners with biblical verses, and pictures of the saints far outnumbered flags of any sort. In the Nag Hammadi demonstration in January 2010, I spotted one Egyptian flag.

45. This hymn was actually composed by a Catholic priest, Peter Sholtes, in 1966 and released as the solo "They'll Know We Are Christians" in 1968. For more on music of the Jesus People's movement, see John Haines, "The Emergence of Jesus Rock: On Taming the 'African Beat.'" *Black Music Research Journal* 31 (Fall 2011): 229–60.

46. The historian Paul Sedra has also written extensively about the use of exclusively political sectarian discourse and the strategic use of the persecution narrative. See Paul Sedra, "Class Cleavages and Ethnic Conflict: Coptic-Christian Communities in Modern Egyptian Politics," *Islam and Christian-Muslim Relations* 10, no. 2 (1999): 219–35.

47. According to the BBC news article "Egypt Islamist Parties Win Elections to Parliament," January 21, 2012, the Muslim Brotherhood's party, the Freedom and Justice Party, won more than 47 percent of the seats, while the Salafi Nour Party won more than 24 percent. BBC news, http://www.bbc.com/news/world-middle-east-16665748 (accessed 29 August 2016).

48. The attack on Abu Fana Monastery took place on May 31, 2008. Local Muslims in the area claim that there was initially a land dispute between monks and their neighbors that offset the violence. Others point to the kidnapping and unsuccessful conversion attempts of the monks to Islam and their subsequent beatings as purely sectarian incidents. Nonetheless, the domestic and international reaction to the incident illustrates the heated religious tensions in the area and throughout the rest of Egypt. For more on this, see "Abu Fana in Focus," by Reema Leila in *Al-Ahram Weekly Online*, no. 907 (July 24–30 2008), http://weekly.ahram.org.eg/2008/907/eg2.htm (accessed May 13, 2013).

49. Jim Karygiannis's speech on October 23, 2011, in front of the Ontario Legislative Building, http://www.youtube.com/watch?v=atFvUDXFyg8. Archives of his video speeches are available on his website http://www.karygiannismp.com (both accessed May 13, 2013).

50. Jim Karygiannis, "Karygiannis Thanks MP's for Unanimous Consent on Egyptian Coptic Motion," Karygiannismp.com, http://karygiannismp.com/spip/article.php3?id_article=1684 (accessed October 17, 2011).

51. Bannjerji, *The Dark Side of the Nation*, 2.

52. It is important here to point out that many of these conversations are neither homogeneous nor monolithic. Rather, many congregants are contesting their Church's dealings with Canadian politicians and even such overt political disclosures, contending that prayer in private is enough and that one should "leave the politics of out of it." Other interlocutors were critical of MPs roles as suspicious and divisive, "playing a game" to win Coptic votes for their constituencies, while others scrutinized their clergy's discriminatory rhetoric describing their Muslims friends and neighbors back home as Muslim "terrorists" and "enemies."

Coptic Migrant Churches

This essay builds on my unpublished dissertation submitted to the Department of Sociology at the University of Toronto: Ghada Barsoum Botros, "Competing for the Future: Adaptation and the Accommodation of Difference in Coptic Immigrant Churches" (Ph.D. diss., University of Toronto, 2005).

1. Ghada Barsoum Botros, "Competing for the Future: Adaptation and the Accommodation of Difference in Coptic Immigrant Churches" (Ph.D. diss., University of Toronto, 2005).

2. Will Herbergs. *Protestant, Catholic, Jew: An Essay in American Religious Sociology*, 2nd ed. (Garden City N.Y.: Doubleday, 1960), 27–28.

3. Raymond Brady Williams, *Religions of Immigrants from India and Pakistan: New Threads in the American Tapestry* (Cambridge: Cambridge University Press, 1988).

4. Timothy L. Smith, "Religion and Ethnicity in America," *American Historical Review* 83 (December 1978): 1174–75.

5. See Stephen R. Warner and Judith G. Wittner, eds., *Gatherings in Diaspora: Religious Communities and the New Immigration* (Philadelphia: Temple University Press, 1998), and Helen Rose Ebaugh and Janet Saltzman Chafetz, eds., *Religion and the New Immigrants: Continuities and Adaptations in Immigrant Congregations* (New York: Altamira Press, 2000).

6. Donald Horowitz, *Ethnic Groups in Conflict* (Los Angeles: University of California Press, 1985). Max Weber makes a similar distinction between a "caste structure," referring to hierarchically ordered groups, and "ethnic coexistence," referring to parallel groups, in *From Max Weber: Essays in Sociology*, ed. H. H. Gerth and C. Wright Mills (New York: Free Press, 1958).

7. Coptic migrant churches also serve Copts from Sudan. Interviews show that they followed a different trajectory as most of them came to Canada and the United States in the early 1990s as asylum seekers and refugees after the al-Bashir's coup d'état. Copts from Sudan are originally from Egypt. However, they continue to maintain a distinct identity as Sudanese within Egyptian immigrant churches.

8. Center for Political and Strategic Studies (CPSS), "The State of Religion in Egypt," *Al-Ahram Report* (Cairo, 1995), 218.

9. Ibid.

10. Leila Ahmed. *A Border Passage: From Cairo to America; A Woman's Journey* (New York: Farrar, Straus and Giroux, 1999).

11. Michael Brown, "Causes and Implications of Ethnic Conflict," in *The Ethnicity Reader, Nationalism, Multiculturalism and Migration*, ed. Guibernau Montserrat and John Rex (Cambridge, U.K.: Polity Press, 2000), 90–134.

12. John Hutchinson and Anthony Smith, eds., *Ethnicity* (Oxford: Oxford University Press, 1996), 3.

13. "NGO Report 93000 Copts Left Egypt since March," *Egypt Independent*, September 25, 2011, http://www.egyptindepen¬dent.com/news/ngo-report-93000-copts-left-egypt-march (accessed September 9, 2012).

14. Coptic priests carry a different Christian name upon their ordination to symbolize their starting of a new life.

15. Personal interview with Father Marcos Marcos, Toronto, March 12, 2002.

16. While the choice of the first priest and of his name were not coincidental, the choice of Toronto for the establishment of the first Coptic church in North America was mandated by visa regulations, with the Canadian government granting the new priest residence status at the time when the United States granted him entry visa.

17. Personal interview with Father Marcos Marcos, Toronto, April 16, 2002.

18. Gabriel Abdelsayed, "The Coptic-Americans: A Current African Contribution," in *The New Jersey Ethnic Experience*, ed. Barbara Cunningham (Union City, N.J.: W. H. Wise, 1977), 120–30.

19. Stephen R. Warner, "Work in Progress. Towards a New Paradigm for the Sociological Study of Religion in the United States," *American Journal of Sociology* 98 (March 1993): 1063.

20. See, for example, Karen Chai, "Competing for the Second Generation: English-Language Ministry at a Korean Protestant Church," in Warner and Wittner, *Gatherings in Diaspora*, 266–95, and Fenggang Yang, *Chinese Christians in America: Conversion*,

Assimilation, and Adhesive Identities. (University Park: Pennsylvania State University Press, 1999).

21. Peggy Levitt, *The Transnational Villagers* (Los Angeles: University of California Press, 2001).

22. Richard Jones, "Egyptian Copts in Detroit: Ethnic Community and Long-Distance Nationalism," in *Arab Detroit: From Margin to Mainstream*, ed. Nabeel Abraham and Andrew Shryock (Detroit: Wayne State University Press, 2000), 231–31.

23. Ibid., 227

24. Paul Sedra, "Class Cleavages and Ethnic Conflict: Coptic Christian Communities in Modern Egyptian Politics," *Islam and Christian-Muslim Relations* 10, no. 2 (1999): 219–35.

25. Rapid changes took place after this day, with the president leaving power on July 3, 2013.

26. Raymond A. Mohl and Neil Betton, "The Immigrant Church in Gary, Indiana: Religious Adjustment and Cultural Defense," *Ethnicity* 8, no. 1 (1981): 1–17.

27. Personal interview with Father Marcos Marcos, Toronto, April 14, 2002.

28. Personal interview, Atlanta, May 2, 2002.

29. Personal interview, Atlanta, May 2, 2002.

30. Anitra Bingham-Kolenkow, "The Copts in the United States of America," in *Between Desert and City: The Coptic Orthodox Church Today*, ed. Nelly van Doorn–Harder and Kari Vogt (Oslo: Novus, 1997), 265–72.

31. Salman Akhtar, *Immigration and Identity, Turmoil, Treatment and Transformation* (Lanham, Md.: Rowman & Littlefield, 1999).

32. Williams, *Religions of Immigrants from India and Pakistan*, 31.

33. Ebaugh and Chafetz, *Religion and the New Immigrants*, 397.

34. Quoted in Ebaugh and Chafetz, *Religion and the New Immigrants*, 396.

35. Personal interview, Toronto, March 3, 2002.

36. Chai, "Competing for the Second Generation."

37. Shoshanah Feher, "From Rivers of Babylon to the Valleys of Los Angeles: The Exodus and Adaptation of Iranian Jews," in Warner and Wittner, *Gatherings in Diaspora*, 38–71.

38. Personal interview, Toronto, April 14, 2002.

39. Personal interview, Toronto, October 2002.

40. Personal interview, Toronto, March 2002.

41. Personal interview, Kitchener, Ont., April 14, 2002.

42. Personal interview, Atlanta, May 2, 2002.

43. Quoted in Joanne Van Dijk and Ghada Barsoum Botros, "The Importance of Ethnicity and Religion in the Life Cycle of Immigrant Churches: A Comparison of Coptic and Calvinist Churches," *Canadian Ethnic Studies* 41, nos.1–2 (2009): 191–214.

44. Mark Mullins, "The Organizational Dilemmas of Ethnic Churches: A Case Study of Japanese Buddhism in Canada," *Sociological Analysis* 49 (Fall 1988): 217–33.

45. Personal interview with Father Angelous, Mississauga, Ont., July 18, 2013.

46. Mark Mullins, "The Life-Cycle of Ethnic Churches in Sociological Perspective," *Japanese Journal of Religious Studies* 14, no. 4 (1987): 320–34.

47. Personal interviews, Atlanta, May 17, 2002.

48. Personal interviews, Mississauga, Ont., March 3, 2002.

49. Personal interviews, Kitchener, Ont., April 14, 2002.

50. Personal interviews, Toronto, October 16, 2001.

51. Ebaugh and Chafetz, *Religion and the New Immigrants*, 20.

52. Ibid.
53. Personal interview, Cairo, August 2003; translation by the author.
54. Warner, "Work in Progress," 1044–93.
55. Prema Kurien, "Becoming American by Becoming Hindu: Indian Americans Take Their Place at the Multicultural Table," in Warner and Wittner, *Gatherings in Diaspora*, 37–70.
56. Sheba George, "Caroling with the Keralites: The Negotiation of Gendered Space in an Indian Immigrant Church," in Warner and Wittner, *Gatherings in Diaspora*, 265–94.

Strategies of Adaptation for Survival

1. I am borrowing the term *intercultural marriage* from Father Pishoy Salama. He uses the term to refer to a marriage wherein an individual of Coptic Egyptian heritage marries a "Canadian of any other racial, ethnic, or cultural background." Pishoy Salama, "Of All Nations: Exploring Intercultural Marriages in the Coptic Orthodox Church of the GTA" (D.Min. diss., University of St. Michael's College and University of Toronto, 2012), 55.
2. Mark Mullins, "The Life-Cycle of Ethnic Churches in Sociological Perspective," *Japanese Journal of Religious Studies*, 14, no. 4 (1987): 322–23.
3. Ibid., 323.
4. Ibid., 325.
5. Ibid., 327.
6. This first mission church in the GTA has since been joined by a second mission church in Toronto and three others in eastern Canada. Four mission churches have been established in the United States.
7. I began my fieldwork in June 2007 by attending a meeting for university graduates at one of the larger Coptic churches in the GTA. I completed my fieldwork in December 2007 after the inaugural Divine Liturgy of the first Coptic Orthodox mission church in North America. Originally, I had planned to study the relationship between the Coptic Orthodox Church and second-generation Canadian Copts, and I pursued this line of study through participant observation at four Coptic churches and a university campus located in different parts of the GTA. The churches' congregations ranged in size from two hundred families to two thousand families. At these four churches I participated in different types of meetings, including those held for high school students, university students, university graduates, the elderly, and potential converts, and I attended conferences for the youth and a retreat for university graduates and volunteered at a summer camp organized by women at one of the Coptic churches in the GTA. After meetings I was often invited to gatherings at different coffee shops and hookah bars, where I initiated informal interviews with individuals of the community.
8. Pseudonyms are used throughout this essay to protect the identities of my participants. The names of public figures are exempt from the rules.
9. Mission work is not necessarily frowned upon in the Coptic community; nevertheless, it is not widely promoted. One priest also mentioned that young Copts in the GTA are highly focused on their education and careers and are, therefore, unwilling to donate time to mission work.
10. Mark Mullins, "The Organizational Dilemmas of Ethnic Churches: A Case Study of Japanese Buddhism in Canada," *Sociological Analysis* 49, no. 3 (1988): 217.
11. The Coptic Orthodox Church was registered with the province of Ontario in 1965, which required the Church to establish a set of bylaws. The first bylaw highlights the importance placed on the relationship between the Coptic diaspora and the patriarch-

ate in Egypt. The bylaw is that the newly established church is "inseparable from the Coptic Orthodox Church in Egypt" headed by the Coptic Pope (Ghada Barsoum Botros, "Competing for the Future: Adaptation and the Accommodation of Difference in Coptic Orthodox Immigrant Churches" (Ph.D. diss., University of Toronto, 2005), 74.

12. The pope is the head of a council, which is called the Holy Synod. The Holy Synod consists of "all metropolitans, bishops, abbots, chorepiscopi, and patriarchal deputies"; Nelly van Doorn-Harder, *Contemporary Coptic Nuns* (Columbia: University of South Carolina Press, 1995), 34.

13. Mullins, "The Life-Cycle of Ethnic Churches," 323, and Mullins, "The Organizational Dilemmas of Ethnnic Churches," 218.

14. Botros, "Competing for the Future," 13.

15. Maria V. Gasi, "St. Nicholas Greek Orthodox Church: Maturing through the Generations," in *Religion and the New Immigrants: Continuities and Adaptations in Immigrant Congregations*, ed. Helen Rose Ebaugh, and Janet Saltzman Chafetz (New York: Altamira Press, 2000), 154.

16. Gasi, "St. Nicholas Greek Orthodox Church," 154.

17. Mullins, "The Life-Cycle of Ethnic Churches," 325.

18. Ibid.

19. Botros, "Competing for the Future," 13.

20. See Nora Stene, "In the Lands of Immigration," in *Between Desert and City: The Coptic Orthodox Church Today*, ed. Nelly van Doorn-Harder and Kari Vogt (Oslo: Novus, 1997), 259-60.

21. Fayek Ishak, "Immigrant Copts Striking Roots in the Lands of the Diaspora," *Coptologia* 10 (1989): 29-36.

22. Mullins, "The Life-Cycle of Ethnic Churches," 326.

23. Ibid., 327, and Mullins, "The Organizational Dilemmas of Ethnic Churches," 227.

24. Joanne van Dijk and Ghada Barsoum Botros, "The Importance of Ethnicity and Religion in the Life Cycle of Immigrant Churches: A Comparison of Coptic and Calvinist Churches," *Canadian Ethnic Studies* 41, no. 1 (2009): 195, 210.

25. Ibid., 211.

26. Gasi, "St. Nicholas Greek Orthodox Church," 161-62.

27. Mullins, "The Life-Cycle of Ethnic Churches," 327.

28. Salama, "Of All Nations," 8.

29. The Oriental Orthodox family includes the Egyptian, Ethiopian, Indian, Syrian, Armenian, and Eritrean churches.

30. Anitra Bingham-Kolenkow, "The Copts in the United States of America," in van Doorn-Harder and Vogt, *Between Desert and City,* 267. Also see Anba Marcos, "Coptic Culture in Italy: Centro Culturale Copto Ortodosso," *Coptologia* 10 (1989): 81.

31. Salama, "Of All Nations," 105.

32. Paul Bramadat, "Beyond Christian Canada: Religion and Ethnicity in a Multicultural Society," in *Religion and Ethnicity in Canada*, ed. Paul Bramadat and David Seljak. (Toronto: Pearson Longman, 2005), 1-29.

33. Anne Mackenzie Pearson, "Being Hindu in Canada: Personal Narratives from First and Second Generation Immigrant Hindu Women," *Religious Studies and Theology* 23, no. 1 (2004): 82.

34. Father Marcos Marcos, "The Copts of Canada: A Shining Star in a Galaxy of Diversified Celestial Bodies," *Coptologia* 1 (1981): 65.

35. Celia Rothenberg, "Hebrew Healing: Jewish Authenticity and Religious Healing in Canada," *Journal of Contemporary Religion* 21 no. 2 (2006): 163.

36. Ibid., 174–75.
37. Ibid., 172–73.
38. Ellen Badone, "Ethnography, Fiction, and the Meanings of the Past in Brittany," *American Ethnologist* 18, no. 3 (1991): 521.
39. Ibid., 518.
40. Ghada Barsoum Botros, "Religious Identity as a Historical Narrative: Coptic Orthodox Immigrant Churches and the Representation of History," *Journal of Historical Sociology* 19, no. 2 (2006): 180.
41. Ibid., 183–88.
42. Aziz S. Atiya, "The Copts and Christian Civilization," *Coptologia* 1 (1981): 10–46.
43. The belief that nothing has been altered within the rituals of the Coptic Orthodox Church for more than two thousand years is naïve, since the introduction of a sermon during the Mass is relatively new and only began in the past century.
44. The purpose of this church, however, is different from that of the other Coptic churches in the GTA and, at the time, the rest of North America. Missionary activity is new to the Coptic Orthodox Church in general, even though the Church has focused attention on doing mission work on the continent of Africa. Some of the African countries in which the Coptic Church has established mission churches are Kenya, Zambia, Congo, Tanzania, Nigeria, and the Ivory Coast.
45. R. S. Kipp, "Conversion by Affiliation: The History of the Karo Batak Protestant Church," *American Ethnologist* 22 no. 3 (1995): 872.

Belonging to the Church Community

1. Otto Meinardus, *Christian Egypt: Faith and Life* (Cairo: American University in Cairo Press, 1970), 108.
2. Anthony Cohen, *Belonging, Identity and Social Organization* (Manchester: Manchester University Press, 1982), 21.
3. Chris Jenks, *Childhood* (London: Routledge, 2005); Allison James and Alan Prout, *Constructing and Reconstructing Childhood: Contemporary Issues in the Sociological Study of Childhood* (London: Falmer Press, 1997); Leena Alanen, "Rethinking Childhood," *Acta Sociologica* 31 no. 1 (1988): 53–68.
4. Anthony Giddens, *New Rules of a Sociological Method: A Positive Critique of Interpretive Sociologies* (Cambridge, U.K.: Polity Press, 1993).
5. Samantha Punch, "Negotiating Autonomy: Childhood in Rural Bolivia," in *Conceptualizing Child-Adult Relations*, ed. Leena Alanen and Berry Mayall (London: Routledge/Falmer, 2001), 23.
6. Gender questions link with recent studies of gender issues in the Church, although these studies are related to adult women. See Febe Armanios, "The 'Virtuous Women': Images of Gender in Modern Coptic Society," *Middle Eastern Studies* no. 38 (2002): 110–30; Mariz Tadros, "The Non-Muslim 'Other': Gender and Contestation of Hierarchy of Rights," *Hawwa, Journal of Women of the Middle East and the Islamic World* no. 7 (2009): 111–43; and Nelly van Doorn-Harder, "Coptic Women Reshaping the Visual Culture," in *O Ye Gentlemen: Arabic Studies on Science and Literary Culture*, ed. Arnoud Vrolijk and Jan Hogendijk (Leiden: Brill, 2007) 511–26.
7. Nora Stene, "Fordi barn er som engler . . . En religionshistorisk studie av barn i den koptisk-ortodokse kirke i Egypt" (M.A. thesis, University of Oslo, 1991); "Becoming a Copt," in *Between Desert and City: The Coptic Orthodox Church Today*, ed. Nelly van Doorn-Harder and Kari Vogt (Oslo: Novus, 1997), 190–211; Nora Stene, "Into the Lands of Immigration," in van Doorn-Harder and Vogt, *Between Desert and City*, 254–64; and

Nora Stene, *Engler i platåsko. Religiøs sosialisering av koptisk-ortodokse barn i London* (Oslo: Unipub, 2005).

8. In this text *church* refers to a local church, while *Church* refers to the Coptic Church as a hierarchical structure.

9. See Kim Knott, *The Changing Character of the Religions of the Ethnic Minorities of Asian Origin in Britain*, final report of the Leverhulme Project, research paper no. 11 (Leeds: University of Leeds, Department of Theology and Religious Studies, 1992).

10. See for example O. H. E Burmester, *The Egyptian or Coptic Church: A Detailed Description of Her Liturgical Services and the Rites and Ceremonies Observed in the Administration of Her Sacraments* (Cairo: Societé d'Archéologie Copte, 1967), and Gerard Viaud, *La liturgie des coptes d'Égypt* (Paris: Librairie d'Amerique et d'Orient, 1978).

11. Johan Watson, *Among the Copts* (Brighton: Sussex Academic Press, 2002), 123.

12. A child is usually baptized when his or her mother can be present in the church. After the birth of a son the mother should not enter the church for forty days; after the birth of a daughter, eighty days. These Church rules refer to purity laws in Leviticus.

13. Bishop Moussa, *Youth & Family Life* (Cairo: Bishopric of Youth, St. Mark's Translation Group, n.d.), 35.

14. Adult deacons are ordained and have the highest degrees. Several Church leaders have pointed out that children are not really ordained. Also see O. H. E. Burmester, *Ordination Rites of the Coptic Church.* (Cairo: Publication de la Société d'Archéologie Copte, 1985), 124. However, in the minds of most laypeople this is but an academic question, as all deacons are considered to be chosen for a service that connects them to the priesthood.

15. For details, see Stene, *Engler i platåsko*, 141–149.

16. Berit Thorbjørnsrud, *Controlling the Body to Liberate the Soul: Towards an Analysis of the Coptic Orthodox Concept of the Body* (Oslo: Unipub, 1999), 216–224.

17. See Patriarch Shenouda, *The Spirituality of Fasting* (Cairo: Dar El Tebaa El Kawmiyya, 1990).

18. See Catherine Bell, *Ritual: Perspectives and Dimensions* (Oxford: Oxford University Press, 1997).

19. See Nora Stene, "Multiple Choices? Language Usage and Transmission of Religious Tradition in the Coptic Orthodox Community in London," *British Journal of Religious Education* 20, no. 2 (1998): 90–101.

20. See Morcos Daoud, *Church Sacraments: The Coptic Orthodox Church* (Cairo: Dar el Alam el Arabi, 1975).

21. The sacrament of matrimony is the exception. On the sacrament of ordination, see note 14 above.

22. Tadros Malaty, *Introduction to the Coptic Orthdox Church* (Alexandria: St. George's Coptic Orthodox Church, Sporting, 1993), 207–88. Malaty uses *church* without capital C, although he is referring to the institution.

23. Sissel Østberg, "Pakistani Children in Oslo: Islamic Nurture in a Secular Context" (Ph.D. diss., University of Warwick, 1998).

24. See Hoda Rashad, and Kathryn Yount, *Family Life in the Middle East* (London: Routledge, 2008); Andrea Rugh, *Within the Circle: Parents and Children in an Arab Village* (New York: Columbia University Press, 1997); and Unni Wikan, *Tomorrow, God Willing: Self-made Destinies in Cairo* (Chicago: University of Chicago Press, 1996).

25. Thorbjørnsrud, *Controlling the Body to Liberate the Soul*, 157; Andrea Rugh, *Family in Contemporary Egypt* (Cairo: American University in Cairo Press, 1985), 206.

26. Alanen and Mayall, *Conceptualizing Child-Adult Relations.*

Notes to Pages 144–152

27. On other exceptional situations involving the actions of child deacons, such as the ritual of Abu Tarbu against rabies, see Stene, "Becoming a Copt," 206; Burmester, *The Egyptian or Coptic Church*, 152; Gerard Viaud, *Magie et coutume populaires chez les coptes d'Égypte* (Sisteron: Éditions Présence, 1978), 48, 89.

28. Jeanette Sky, *From Demons to Angels: Fairies and Religious Creativity in Victorian Children's Literature* (Oslo: Unipub 2003); Allison James, *Childhood Identities: Self and Social Relationships in the Experience of the Child* (Edinburgh: Edinburgh University Press, 1993).

29. James, *Childhood Identities*, 107.

30. Thorbjørnsrud, *Controlling the Body to Liberate the Soul*.

31. Exceptions are if a child is bleeding from an open wound or suffering from a disease that causes sanctified substances to leave the body in an unwanted way.

32. See Wolfram Reiss, *Erneuerung in der Koptisch-Orthodoxen Kirche der Gegenwart* (Hamburg: Lit, 1998); Dina el-Khawaga, "Le renouveau copte: La communauté comme acteur politique" (Ph.D. diss., Institut d'Étude Politique de Paris, 1993); Dina el-Khawaga, "The Laity at the Heart of the Coptic Clerical Reform," in van Doorn–Harder and Vogt, *Between Desert and City*, 142–66.

33. Nora Stene, "The Challenge of the Diaspora as Reflected in a Coptic Sunday School," *Journal of Eastern Christian Studies* 54, nos. 1–2 (2002): 77–90.

34. About Sikh children, see Eleanor Nesbitt, "The Religious Lives of Sikh Children: A Coventry Based Study" (Ph.D. diss., University of Leeds, 2000). For Hindu children, see Robert Jackson and Eleanor Nesbitt, *Hindu Children in Britain* (Stoke-on-Trent: Trentham, 1993); for Muslim children, see Sissel Østberg, "Pakistani Children in Oslo."

35. See Stene, *Engler I platåsko*, 340.

The Revival of the Coptic Language and the Formation of Coptic Ethnoreligious Identity in Modern Egypt

1. J. R. Zaborowski, "From Coptic to Arabic in Medieval Egypt," *Medieval Encounters* 14, no. 1 (2008): 15–40.

2. Aḥmus Labīb Bāhūr, *Al-Duktūr Bāhūr Labīb ʿĀlim al-Āthār: Qiṣṣat Kifāḥ wa Najāḥ* (Mariyūṭ: Maṭbaʿat Dayr al-Shahīd al-ʿAẓīm Mār Mīnā al-ʿAjāʾibī, 2009): 34; and Nabīl Ṣabrī Isḥāq, *Al-Lughat al-Miṣriyya al-Qibṭiyya: Nashʾat-hā, wa Asbāb Ufūl-hā, Juhūd ʾIḥyāʾ-hā min al-Qarn al-Tāsiʿ ʿAshara, al-Nuṭq al-Kīrilusī wa al-Khilāf ʿalayhi* (Alexandria: Maṭbaʿa al-Diltā, 2012): 80.

3. We sometimes hear about "native Coptic speakers" who have preserved the language since ancient times. However, Isḥāq (*Al-Lughat al-Miṣriyya al-Qibṭiyya*, 84–85) points out that neither the letter of Pope Kyrillos IV nor the book written by the Coptic historian Yaʿqūb Nakhla make mention of native Coptic speakers in Upper Egypt in the mid-nineteenth century. In addition all existing Coptic speakers are from families who attempted to revive Coptic as a spoken language. Therefore, I presume that Coptic as a spoken language once disappeared and experienced a revitalization in the latter half of the nineteenth century.

4. Bāhūr, *Al-Duktūr*, 7.

5. Ibid., 22. *Bey* is a title that was conferred on Egyptian notables who had rendered significant services to the country. Bey is a rank below pasha.

6. Ibid., 12–13. Pahor Labib, his eldest son, later became an Egyptologist and served as director of the Coptic Museum from 1951 to 1965.

7. The obelisk was erected by Senusret I, the second pharaoh of the twelfth dynasty. Saint Mary's tree is a sycamore tree located in nearby district of al-Matariyya. It is believed that the Holy Family rested in its shade.

8. *'Ayn Shams* Tūt 1617 A.M. (September 1900 C.E.) 1: 4.
9. *'Ayn Shams* Hātūr 1618 A.M. (November 1901 C.E.) 3: 42.
10. Ibid., 3: 43.
11. Ibid.
12. Labib published a book titled *Collection de mots arabes vulgaires et littéraires d'origine égyptienne* in September 1902. See Bāhūr, *Al-Duktūr*, 15.
13. *'Ayn Shams* Hātūr 1618 AM (November 1901 C.E.) 3: 43.
14. Ibid.
15. Ibid., 3: 44.
16. *'Ayn Shams* Ṭūba-Amshīr 1619 A.M. (January–February 1903 C.E.) 5–6: 122.
17. Ibid., 5–6: 122–23.
18. *'Ayn Shams* Bāba 1617 A.M. (October 1900 C.E.) 2: 18–19.
19. *'Ayn Shams* Abīb 1617 A.M. (July 1901 C.E.) 11: 162–70.
20. *'Ayn Shams* Tūt 1618 A.M. (September 1901 C.E.) 1: 4–13.
21. *Miṣr* September 8, 1899: 3.
22. *'Ayn Shams* Abīb, Misrā, and Nasī 1619 A.M. (July-August 1903 C.E.) 11–12: 221.
23. Ibid.
24. Isḥāq, *Al-Lughat al-Miṣriyya al-Qibṭiyya*, 157.

Reading the Church's Story

1. For a quick orientation to this text, see Johannes den Heijer, "History of the Patriarchs of Alexandria," in *The Coptic Encyclopedia*, ed. Aziz S. Atiya (New York & Toronto: Macmillan, 1991), vol. 4, 1238–42. For a recent summary of the state of *HP* research, see Johannes den Heijer, "*The Martrydom of Bīfam Ibn Baqūra al-Ṣawwāf* by Mawhūb ibn Manṣūr ibn Mufarrij and Its Fatimid Background," *Medieval Encounters* 21, nos. 4–5 (2015): 452–84.

2. For an introduction to this text and its elaborations, see Johannes den Heijer, "Apologetic Elements in Coptic-Arabic Historiography: The Life of Afrahām ibn Zurʿah, 62nd Patriarch of Alexandria," in *Christian Arabic Apologetics during the Abbasid Period (750–1258)*, ed. Samir Khalil Samir and Jørgen S. Nielsen (Leiden & New York: Brill, 1994), 192–202; Mark Swanson, *The Coptic Papacy in Islamic Egypt (641–1517)*, The Popes of Egypt 2 (Cairo & New York: American University in Cairo Press, 2010), 48–52.

3. The saint's profession is discussed in an anonymous publication, *Sīrat al-qiddīs Simʿān al-kharrāz "al-dabbāgh,"* 2nd printing (Cairo: Church of St. Simʿān the Tanner in Muqaṭṭam, 1993), 28–30.

4. See Maryann M. Shenoda, "Displacing Dhimmī, Maintaining Hope: Unthinkable Coptic Representations of Fatimid Egypt," *International Journal of Middle East Studies* 39, no. 4 (2007): 587–606. Shenoda concentrates on the version of the story found in the *Synaxarion*.

5. Al-Rāhib al-Baramūsī [Bishop Īsūdhūrus], *al-Kharīdah al-nafīsah fī tārīkh al-kanīsah* (Cairo: Maktabat al-Maḥabbah, 1964 [1923]).

6. Manassā Yūḥannā, *Tārīkh al-kanīsah al-qibṭiyyah* (Cairo: Maktabat al-Maḥabbah, 1982 [1924]).

7. Kāmil Ṣāliḥ Nakhla, *Kitāb tārīkh wa-jadāwil baṭārikat al-Iskandariyyah al-qibṭ* (Cairo, 1943); *Silsilat Tārīkh al-bābāwāt baṭārikat al-kursī al-Iskandārī*, 5 fascicles, 2nd ed. (Cairo: Dayr al-Suryān, 2000 [1951–1954]). And see note 23 below.

8. Iris Habib al-Masri, *Qiṣṣat al-kanīsah al-qibṭiyyah, wa-hiya Tārīkh al-kanīsah al-urthūdhuksiyyah al-miṣriyyah allatī assasahā Mār Marqus al-bashīr*, 7 vols. My own

set is mixed: vols. 1–4 (Alexandria: Maṭbaʿat al-Karnak, 1969–1975), vols. 5–7 (Cairo: Maktabat al-Maḥabbah, 1984–1988)—but all of these are reprints.

9. Eusèbe Renaudot, *Historia patriarcharum Alexandrinorum Jacobitarum a D. Marco usque ad finem saec. XIII* (Paris, 1713).

10. Aziz S. Atiya, *A History of Eastern Christianity* (London: Methuen, 1968), part 1, "Alexandrian Christianity: The Copts and Their Church," 11–166.

11. *The Coptic Encyclopedia*, ed. Aziz S. Atiya, 8 vols. (New York & Toronto: Macmillan, 1991).

12. Theodore Hall Patrick, *Traditional Egyptian Christianity: A History of the Coptic Orthodox Church* (Greensboro, N.C.: Fisher Park Press, 1996).

13. Alberto Elli, *Storia della chiesa copta*, 3 vols., Studia Orientalia Christiana Monographiae 12–14 (Cairo: Franciscan Centre of Christian Oriental Studies / Jerusalem: Franciscan Printing Press, 2003).

14. Christian Friedrich Seybold, *Severus ben el Moqaffaʿ: Historia Patriarcharum Alexandrinorum*, 2 vols., Corpus Scriptorum Christianorum Orientalium 52 and 59 = ar. 8–9 (Beirut & Paris, 1904–1910); B. T. A. Evetts, *History of the Patriarchs of the Coptic Church of Alexandria*, 4 vols, Patrologia Orientalis, vol. 1, fasc. 2 and 4; vol. 5, fasc. 1; and vol. 10, fasc. 5 (Paris: Firmin-Didot, 1904–1915).

15. Yassā ʿAbd al-Masīḥ, O. H. E. Burmester, Aziz S. Atiya, and Antoine Khater, *History of the Patriarchs of the Egyptian Church, Known as the History of the Holy Church, by Sawīrus ibn al-Muḳaffaʿ, bishop of al-Ašmūnīn*, vol. 2, parts 1–3; vol. 3, parts 1–3; and vol. 4, parts 1–2 (Cairo: Société d'Archéologie Copte, 1943–1974).

16. Evetts's English translation is available online, on the website "Early Church Fathers—Additional Texts," ed. Roger Pearse: http://www.tertullian.org/fathers/severus_hermopolis_hist_alex_patr_00_intro.htm (accessed August 15, 2012).

17. Ṣamūʾīl al-Suryānī, later Bishop Samuel of Shibīn al-Qanāṭir, published a cut-and-pasted then mimeographed "edition" of the Arabic text of *HP* (from the Patrologia Orientalis–Société d'Archéologie Copte [PO–SAC] editions) sometime in the 1980s. Later he reissued the same text, but now transcribed by computer: *Tārīkh al-baṭārikah li-l-anbā Sāwīrūs ibn al-Muqaffaʿ usquf al-Ashmūnīn*, 3 vols., Silsilat iṣdārāt niyāfat al-anbā Ṣamūʾīl usquf Shibīn al-Qanāṭir wa-tawābiʿihā (Cairo, 1999). A few years later an impressively bound set of six volumes appeared in one of Cairo's leading bookshops: ʿAbd al-ʿAzīz Jamāl al-Dīn, *Tārīkh Miṣr min bidāyāt al-qarn al-awwal al-mīlādī ḥattā nihāyat al-qarn al-ʿishrīn min khilāl makhṭūṭāt Tārīkh al-baṭārikah li-Sāwīrus ibn al-Muqaffaʿ*, 4 parts in 6 vols. (Cairo: Maktabat Madbūlī, 2006). More recently, the PO–SAC text (through John VII, the 74th patriarch) has been reprinted as the first volume in a three-volume set: *Silsilat Tārīkh al-ābāʾ al-baṭārikah al-mansūb li-Sāwīrus ibn al-Muqaffaʿ usquf al-Ashmūnayn, ʿan al-Bāṭrūlūjiyā Ūranītālīs*, Tārīkh al-baṭārikah 1, 2nd printing (Maktabat Dayr al-Suryān: 2011).

18. See Johannes den Heijer, *Mawhūb ibn Manṣūr ibn Mufarriğ et l'historiographie copto-arabe: Étude sur la composition de l'Histoire des Patriarches d'Alexandrie*, Corpus Scriptorum Christianorum Orientalium 13 = subsidia 83 (Louvain: Peeters, 1989), with extensive bibliography.

19. Ibid. Den Heijer convincingly shows that the great tenth-century Coptic author Sāwīrus ibn al-Muqaffaʾ played no role in this process; however, such was his fame as a Coptic Orthodox author in Arabic that many Copto-Arabic works by unknown or obscure authors, including *The History of the Patriarchs of Alexandria*, came to be attributed to him.

20. Edition of the Primitive recension (that is, the older form, before the revisions of the Vulgate recension) of *Lives* 1–46: Christian Friedrich Seybold, ed., *Severus ibn al-Muqaffaʾ: Alexandrinische Patriarchengeschichte von. S. Marcus bis Michael I (61–767), nach der ältesten 1266 geschriebenen Hamburger Handschrift*, Veröffentlichungen aus der Hamburger Stadtbibliothek 3 (Hamburg: Lucas Gräfe, 1912). The recent research of Perrine Pilette indicates that it is an oversimplification to speak of *the* Vulgate recension as if it were a fixed entity: Perrine Pilette, "L'*Histoire des Patriarches d'Alexandrie*: Une nouvelle évaluation de la configuration du texte en recensions," *Le Muséon* 126, nos. 3–4 (2013): 419–50.

21. I fell into this trap in Mark Swanson, "Sainthood Achieved: Coptic Patriarch Zacharias according to *The History of the Patriarchs*," in *Writing "True Stories": Historians and Hagiographers in the Late-Antique and Medieval Near East*, ed. Arietta Papaconstantinou et al., CELAMA 9 (Turnhout, Belgium: Brepols, 2010), 219–30; see my corrections in Swanson, *Coptic Papacy*, 56 and note 111.

22. An attempt at this is made in Swanson, *Coptic Papacy*, where the chapter divisions reflect the source history of *HP*.

23. Kāmil Ṣāliḥ Nakhlah, *Sīrat al-bābā Ghubriyāl Ibn Turayk, al-baṭriyark al-sabʿīn* (Cairo: Maktabat al-Maḥabbah al-Qibṭiyyah, 1947).

24. For a study that benefits from Nakhlah's use of sources, see Mark Swanson, "The Coptic Patriarch and the Apostate Scribe: An Incident from the Career of Pope Gabriel II ibn Turayk (the 70th, 1131–1145)," *Parole de l'Orient* 37 (2012): 479–92.

25. One might point here to the studies of Johannes den Heijer which test and demonstrate the importance of *HP* for the study of Fatimid Egypt, especially in the time of Badr al-Jamālī; for example, Johannes den Heijer, "Considerations sur les communautés chrétiennes en Égypte fatimide: l'État et l'Église sous le vizirat de Badr al-Jamālī (1074–1094)," in *L'Égypte fatimide, son art et son histoire*, ed. Marianne Barrucand (Paris: Presses de l'Université Paris-Sorbonne, 1999), 569–78; den Heijer, "La rébellion de l'émir Al-Awḥad (477/1084): Étude comparative des sources historiques," in *Alexandrie medieval 3*, ed. Jean-Yves Empereur et Christian Décobert, Études Alexandrines 16 – 2008 (Cairo: Institut Français d'Archéologie Orientale, 2008), 171–81.

26. For an example that examines *HP* in the context of papyrological evidence, see Frank R. Trombley, "Sawirus ibn al-Muqaffaʿ and the Christians of Umayyad Egypt: War and Society in Documentary Context," in *Papyrology and the History of Early Islamic Egypt*, ed. Petra M. Sijpesteijn and Lennart Sundelin (Leiden & Boston: Brill, 2004), 199–226. For other examples of the use of *HP* in conjunction with many different kinds of evidence, see above, note 25, and below, note 29.

27. Stephen J. Davis, *The Early Coptic Papacy: The Egyptian Church and Its Leadership in Late Antiquity*, The Popes of Egypt 1 (Cairo & New York: American University in Cairo Press, 2004); Swanson, *Coptic Papacy*. My approach was also influenced by Maurice P. Martin's sensitivity to matters of continuity and plot in "Une lecture de *l'Histoire des Patriarches d'Alexandrie*," *Proche-Orient Chrétien* 35 nos. 1–2 (1985): 15–36.

28. Perrine Pilette, "International Coptic-Arabic Historiography Project (ICAHP)," paper given at the Ninth International Congress of Christian Arabic Studies, Valetta, Malta, July 19–21, 2012. For an update, see den Heijer, "*The Martyrdom of Bīfam*," 463.

29. Maged S. A. Mikhail, *From Byzantine to Islamic Egypt: Religion, Identity and Politics after the Arab Conquest* (London & New York: Tauris, 2014), which revises and expands upon his UCLA dissertation of 2004.

30. An investigation into the contemporary use of the story under consideration here is beyond the scope of this paper. Perhaps it is enough to say that the story of the en-

counter between Patriarch Benjamin and ʿAmr ibn al-ʿĀṣ has regularly been rehearsed in books or lectures on *al-waḥdah al-waṭaniyyah* (national unity), the ideology of Muslim-Christian harmony in the one Egyptian state. Examples from my shelves include William Sulaymān Qilādah, *al-Masīḥiyyah wa-l-Islām ʿalā arḍ Miṣr* [Christianity and Islam upon the Land of Egypt], Kitāb al-Ḥurriyyah 9 (Cairo: Dār al-Ḥurriyyah, 1986), 20–21 (a study by a Copt), and ʿAbd al-Tawwāb Yūsuf, *al-Hilāl wa-l-ṣalīb* [The Crescent and the Cross] (Cairo: Maktabat Rūz al-Yūsuf, 1980), 19–20 (a book intended for children).

31. The Primitive recension of the following story is found in Seybold, *Alexandrinische Patriarchengeschichte*, 100–101. For the accessible Vulgate recension of this story, with an English translation, see B. T. A. Evetts, *History of the Patriarchs of the Coptic Church of Alexandria*, vol. 2, *Peter I to Benjamin I (661)* (Paris: Firmin-Didot, 1904), 495–97. I have commented on this story previously: Swanson, *Coptic Papacy*, 7.

32. Seybold, *Alexandrinische Patriarchengeschichte*, 101/1–2.

33. Seybold, *Alexandrinische Patriarchengeschichte*, 101/6–13.

34. Ibid., 101.

35. Evetts, *History of the Patriarchs of the Coptic Church of Alexandria*, vol. 2, 495–97.

36. In a Christian-Muslim dialogue meeting in Cairo in the 1980s, I heard a Coptic priest relate the same story with yet another elaboration at this point: "Build all the churches you like!"

37. I emphasize, *this* story. Johannes den Heijer has shown how the tone of the entire passage on the Arab conquest of Egypt in *HP* changes, from more favorable to the Arabs to less, as one moves from the Primitive to the Vulgate recension. Given this fact, it is perhaps especially significant that the Vulgate recension here emphasizes the mutual respect between ʿAmr and Benjamin. See Johannes den Heijer, "La conquête arabe vue par les historiens coptes," in *Valeur et distance: Identités et sociétés en Égypte*, ed. Christian Décobert (Paris: Maisonneuve & Larose, Maison Méditerranéenne des Sciences de l'Homme, 2000), 227–45, here 229–31 (with a French translation of the passage considered here on 231).

38. The Primitive recension of the following story is found in Seybold, *Alexandrinische Patriarchengeschichte*, 116–18. For the accessible Vulgate recension of this story, with an English translation, see B. T. A. Evetts, ed., *History of the Patriarchs of the Coptic Church of Alexandria*, vol. 3, *Agathon to Michael I (766)* (Paris: Firmin-Didot, 1910), 13–18.

39. Seybold, *Alexandrinische Patriarchengeschichte*, 116/23.

40. Ibid., 117/14–15.

41. Ibid., 117/18–19.

42. The same motif of the governor's wife is found in the story of the tenth-century martyr Jirjis (Muzāḥim) and is briefly reported in the *Synaxarion* entry for Jirjis on 19 Baʾūnah: René Basset, *Le synaxaire arabe jacobite (redaction copte)*, V: *Les mois de Baouneh, Abib, Mesoré et jours complémentaires*, Patrologia Orientalis 17 (Paris, 1923), 578–80, here 579/3.

43. Seybold, *Alexandrinische Patriarchengeschichte*, 118/12.

44. Ibid., 118/13–17.

45. Ibid., 118/19–21.

46. See Philippe Luisier, "De Pilate chez les Coptes," *Orientalia Christiana Periodica* 62, no. 2 (1996): 411–25.

47. On Bishop Michael's contribution to *HP*, see Swanson, *Coptic Papacy*, chapter 4, "Saints and Sinners," 43–57. On his portrait of Patriarch Zacharias, see ibid., 52–56, and Swanson, "Sainthood Achieved."

48. For *HP*'s witness to this period, see Aziz S. Atiya, Yassā 'Abd al-Masīḥ, and O. H. E. Burmester, eds., *History of the Patriarchs of the Egyptian Church, Known as the History of the Holy Church, by Sawīrus ibn al-Muḳaffaʿ, bishop of al-Ašmūnīn*, vol. 2, part 2, *Khaël III – Shenouti II (AD 880–1066)* (Cairo: Société d'Archéologie Copte, 1948), 121–38 (Arabic text); 183–211 (English translation).

49. Atiya et al., *History of the Patriarchs of the Egyptian Church*, 2.2, 135 (Arabic text); 205 (English translation).

50. Ibid., 135/19–20 and 136/1–3 (Arabic text); Mark Swanson's English translation. It should be noted that this Arabic text represents the Vulgate recension; the Primitive recension of this part of *HP* has not yet been published.

51. Ibid., 136/3–5.
52. Ibid., 136/5–11.
53. Ibid., 136/11–15.
54. See Swanson, *Coptic Papacy*, 52–56, or Swanson, "Sainthood Achieved."
55. Atiya et al., *History of the Patriarchs of the Egyptian Church*, 2.2, 117/1–2.
56. Aziz S. Atiya, Yassa 'Abd al-Masih, and O. H. E. Burmester, eds., *History of the Patriarchs of the Egyptian Church, Known as the History of the Holy Church, by Sawirus ibn al-Mukaffaʿ, bishop of al-Ašmūnīn*, vol. 2, part 3, *Christodoulos – Michael (AD 1046–1102)* (Cairo: Société d'Archéologie Copte, 1959), 204–5 (Arabic text); 316–17 (English translation).

57. Ibid., 215 (Arabic text); 337 (English translation).
58. See den Heijer, *Mawhūb*; or, very briefly, Swanson, *Coptic Papacy*, 61–66.

The Evolution of Lent in Alexandria and the Alleged Reforms of Patriarch Demetrius

I am thankful to Professor Nelly van Doorn–Harder for her invitation to join The Future of Coptic Studies conference in 2010 and for her editorial guidance. I am also grateful to the faculty and staff at Wake Forest University, whose kindness and intellectual curiosity contributed to the success of a memorable conference.

1. Maged S.A. Mikhail, *The Legacy of Demetrius of Alexandria: The Form and Function of Hagiography in Late Antique and Islamic Egypt*, Routledge Studies in the Early Christian World (New York: Routledge Press, 2017), esp. ch. 8.

2. For example, Bishop Basilios, "Fastings," in *The Coptic Encyclopedia*, 8 vols., ed. Aziz S. Atiya (New York & Toronto: Macmillan, 1991), vol. 4, 1093–97. On the *Epact*, see Abu al-Barakāt Ibn Kabar, *Muṣbāḥ al-ẓulmā*, ed. Ṣamū'īl al-Suryānī, 2 vols. (Cairo: n.p., 1998), chapter 23; S. K. Samir, "Book of Epact," *The Coptic Encyclopedia*, vol. 2, 409–11; Mikhail, "Legacy of Demetrius."

3. See P. F. Bradshaw and M. E. Johnson, *The Origins of Feasts, Fasts and Seasons in Early Christianity* (Collegeville, Minn.: Liturgical Press, 2011), 102–5; N. V. Russo, "A Note on the Use of Secret Mark in the Search for the Origins of Lent," *Studia Liturgica* 37, no. 2 (2007): 181–97; Russo, "The Origins of Lent" (Ph.D. diss., University of Notre Dame, 2009), sec. 3.10. All these reconstructions were hypothetical.

4. Bradshaw and Johnson, *Origins of Feasts, Fasts and Seasons*, chapters 10–12; M. E. Johnson, *Rites of Christian Initiation*, 2nd rev. ed. (Collegeville, Minn.: Liturgical Press, 2007), chapters 2 and 5; P. F. Bradshaw, "Baptismal Practice in the Alexandrian Tradition: Eastern or Western," in *Living Water, Sealing Spirit: Readings on Christian Initiation*, ed. M. E. Johnson (Collegeville, Minn.: Liturgical Press, 1995), chapter 5; T. J. Talley, *The Origins of the Liturgical Year*, 2nd ed. (Collegeville, Minn.: Liturgical Press, 1991), 189–202, 214–22; J. P. Abdelsayed and M. Samaan, "A History of the Great Lent," *Coptic Church Review* 31, no. 1 (2010): 18–32. See the following note and note 29 below.

5. Catholicos Isaac maintains that the Church observed a post-Epiphany fast for 120 years after the Resurrection: Russo, "Origins of Lent," 398; cf. F. C. Conybeare, *The Key of Truth: A Manual of the Paulician Church of Armenia* (Oxford: Clarendon Press, 1898), lxxviii; Bradshaw and Johnson, *Origins of Feasts, Fasts and Seasons*, 105–8; Russo, "A Note on the Use of Secret Mark."

6. This has led to the layering of several tentative arguments; for example, Talley, "Origins of Lent at Alexandria," 199. This observance is assumed as fact in *The Canons of Hippolytus*, ed. P. F. Bradshaw, trans. C. Bebawi (Nottingham: Grove Books, 1987), 6, and notes to canons 12 and 20.

7. Pierre Maraval, ed./trans., *Socrate de Constantinople: Histoire Ecclésiastique*, Sources Chrétiennes 477, 493, 505, 506 (Paris: Éditions du Cerf, 2004-2007); A.C. Zenos, trans., "The Ecclesiastical History of Socrates Scholasticus," *Nicene and Post-Nicene Fathers* 2.2: 1–178; Sozomène, *Histoire ecclésiastique*, André-Jean Festugière, trans., annotation by Guy Sabbah, Sources Chrétiennes 306, 418 (Paris: Éditions du Cerf, 1983; repr., 1996); Chester D. Hartranft, trans., "The Ecclesiastical History of Sozomen," in *Nicene and Post-Nicene Fathers* 2.2: 239-427; J. B. Comings, *Aspects of the Liturgical Year in Cappadocia (325–430)* (New York & Berlin: Peter Lang, 2005), chapter 2; Talley, *Origins of the Liturgical Year*, part 3, surveys the bewildering accounts and the diversity of competing observances.

8. Anonymous, "A Chronicle Composed AD 640," in *The Seventh Century in West-Syrian Chronicles*, ed. and trans. A. Palmer (Liverpool: Liverpool University Press, 1993), 15; cf. E. Jeffreys, M. Jeffreys, and R. Scott, trans., *The Chronicle of John Malalas* (Melbourne: Melbourne Australian Association for Byzantine Studies, 1986), § 18.96 (M.G. Morony, *Iraq after the Muslim Conquest* (Princeton: Princeton University Press, 1984), 374.

9. Egérie, *Journal de voyage*, ed. and trans. P. Maraval, Sources Chrétiennes 296 (Paris: Cerf, 1997), chapter 27; G. E. Gingras, trans. *Egeria: Diary of a Pilgrimage* (New York: Newman Press, 1970), chapter 27 and note 321; E. P. Wheeler, trans. *Dorotheos of Gaza: Discourses and Sayings* (Kalamazoo: Cistercian Publications, 1977), chapter 15 (pg. 215). Also note 7, above.

10. See Dionysius of Alexandria (d. 264), *Letter to Bishop Basileides*; C. L. Feltoe, *The Letters and Other Remains of Dionysius of Alexandria* (New York: Macmillan, 1904); Feltoe, *St. Dionysius of Alexandria, Letters and Treatises* (New York: Macmillan, 1918). This was also the oldest observance in Syria, see R. H. Connolly, *Didascalia Apostolorum* (Oxford: Clarendon Press, 1929), § 21, 183 and note to line 15.

11. Athanasius, *Festal Letters*, 2.8 (dated 330 C.E.); 3.6 (331 C.E.); 6.13 (334 C.E.); cf. his Letter to Serapion; Socrates, *Ecclesiastical History*, 5.22; and Theophilus of Alexandria, *Festal Letter for 401* in Jerome, *Letter*, 96.20.4; I. Hilberg, ed., *Sancti Eusebii Hieronymi Epistulae*, Corpus scriptorum ecclesiasticorum Latinorum 54–56 (Vienna: Verlag der Osterreichischen Akademie der Wissenschaften, 1996); A. Camplani, "Sull' origine della Quaresima in Egitto," in *Acts of the Fifth International Congress of Coptic Studies*, ed. D. W. Johnson, 2 vols. (Rome: C.I.M, 1993), 2:105–21; David Brakke, "Jewish Flesh and Christian Spirit in Athanasius of Alexandria," *Journal of Early Christian Studies* 9, no. 4 (2001): 453–81, esp. 457–64; H. Buchinger, "On the Early History of the Quadragesima: A New Look at an Old Problem and Some Proposed Solutions," in *Liturgies in East and West: Ecumenical Relevance of Early Liturgical Development*, ed. Hans-Jurgen Feulner (Berlin: Lit Verlag, 2013), 99–117. Lent was designated as the "Forty Days" in Greek, Coptic, and Arabic sources regardless of the actual duration of the fast.

12. A. Camplani, "Coptic Fragments from a Festal Letter of the Late Sixth Century (John Rylands Library, Coptic Suppl. nos. 47–48): Damian or Eulogius?" in *Coptic*

Studies on the Threshold of a New Millennium: Proceedings of the Seventh International Congress of Coptic Studies, ed. M. Immerzeel and J. van der Vliet (Louvain: Peeters, 2004), vol. 1, 317–27.

13. Camplani, "Coptic Fragments;" Camplani, "La Quaresima egiziana nel VII secolo: note di cronologia su Mon.Epiph. 77, Manchester Ryland Suppl. 47–48, P. Grenf. II 112, P.Berol.10677, P.Köln 215 e un'omelia copta," *Augustinianum* 32.2 (1992): 423–32; Camplani places the shift during the tenure of Benjamin or Agathon.

14. *P.Mon.Epiph* 77 (Camplani, "La Qaresima egiziana") may be dated later. The earliest reference is in Patriarch Benjamin's *Thirty Fifth Festal Letter*, which is solely attested by two date clauses cited in John of Damascus's (d. ca. 749 C.E.) *De sacris ieiuniis* (PG 95:63–78, §505). Confident in John's attribution, scholars have followed A. Rahlfs lead by correcting the clause so that the Easter celebration it dates would fall during Benjamin's tenure (A. Rahlfs, *Die alttestamentlichen Lektionen der griechischen Kirche* (Berlin: Weidmann, 1915), 28–136; at page 86, note 3). Nonetheless, if we assume that the date clause is correct, but that the attribution is in error (or that John copied the clause identifying the beginning of Holy Week—which is common in festal letters—rather than that identifying Easter itself), then the date clause would identify a festal letter written some time during the first quarter of the eighth century—not the mid-seventh. The earliest unambiguous evidence for an Egyptian eight-week Lent is Patriarch Alexander II's festal letter dated to 713, 719, or 724 C.E.; see C. Schmidt and W. Schubart, *Altchristliche Texte* (Berlin: Weidmannsche Buchhandlung, 1910), chapter 5; Leslie S. B. MacCoull, "The Paschal Letter of Alexander II, Patriarch of Alexandria: A Greek Defense of Coptic Theology under Arab Rule," *Dumbarton Oaks Papers* 44 (1990), 27–40; reprinted in MacCoull, *Coptic Perspectives on Late Antiquity* (Brookfield: Variorum, 1993), 19.

15. The *Apostolic Constitutions* (§5.13; see note 45) may have also been influential, but Arabic Coptic authors appear slowly to be quoting the *Didascalia* in this context. The stipulation to conclude Lent *prior* to Holy Week is an altogether later addition, lacking in the earliest manuscripts of the *Didascalia* (see Connolly, §§18, 31). Nonetheless, Abū al-Barakāt, al-Makīn, and Ibn Sabbāʿ read the interpolated passages and interpreted that practice as normative within the early Church; see W. S. Qiladā, *Taʿlīm ar-rusul, al-dasqūliyah* (Cairo: n.p., 1979), § 29.4; § 29.4; Ṣalīb Suryāl, *Dirāsāt fī al-qawānīn al-kanasiyyah: Taʿlīm al-ābāʾ al-rusul al-maʿrūfah bi al-disqūliyah* (al-Jīzah, Egypt: Maktabat al-tarbiyyah al-kanasiyyah, 1992), § 18. These editions represent two recensions in which the order of chapters is different. For Ibn Sabbāc, see Yuḥannā ibn Abī Zakariyya ibn Sabbāʿ, *al-Jawharah al-nafīsah fī ʿulūm al-kanīsah/Pretiosa Margarita de scientiis ecclesiasticis*, ed. Vincentio P. Mistriḥ (Cairo: Éditions du Centre Franciscain d'Études Orientales Chrétiennes, 1966), § 32. The twelfth-century *Nomocanon* (§19) of Gabriyal Ibn Turayk simply cites the Arabic *Didascalia's* provision that the fast must conclude prior to the Week of Pascha; A. A. Mina, ed., *Le Nomocanon du patriarche copte Gabriel II ibn Turayk*, 2 vols. (Beirut: CEDRAC, 1993).

16. "Jesus Christ fasted for us forty days and forty nights" permeates all Coptic Lenten prayers. Cf. Talley, *Origins of the Liturgical Year*, 211. "The enumeration is: Pre-Lent (Matt 6:1–18); 1st Sunday (Matt. 6:19–33); 2nd Sunday (Matt. 4:1–11); 3rd Sunday (Lk. 15:11–32); 4th Sunday (Jn 4:1–42); 5th Sunday (Jn 5:1–18); 6th Sunday (Jn 9:1–41); Palm Sunday; Easter Sunday."

17. Coptic Arabic literature maintains that that week should be fasted with the same austerity as the rest of Lent; it is hard to argue for "preparation" here, as with the Melkite "Week of Cheese." Moreover, even ascetics did not measure asceticism based

on the length of abstinence or austerity of practice alone, but rather in relation to the individual's ability; for example, L. Papadopulos and G. Lizardos, trans., *Saint Paisios the Great by Saint John the Dwarf of Egypt* (Jordanville, N.Y.: Holy Trinity Monastery, 1998), 25–26.

18. Shenoute of Atripe, *Acephalous Work A14*, § 15. Hitherto, the only full translation is in Arabic: S. Moawad, *al-Anbā Shinūdah ra'īs al-mutawaḥḥidīn* (Heliopolis: Maktabat Banurāmā, 2009), 379–93.

19. Eutychius, *Naẓm al-jawhar*, 2.5–7 [=*Eutychii Patriarchae Alexandrini annales (Tārīkh)*, Corpus Scriptorum Christianorum Orientalium 50, 51, ed. L. Cheikho, B. C. de Vaux, and H. Zayat (Beirut: E Typographeo Catholico, 1905–1909; Louvain, 1954); al-Maqrīzī, *al-Mawāʿiẓ wal-iʿtibār fī dhikr al-khiṭaṭ wal-athār*, ed. A. F. Sayyid, 4 vols. (London: al-Furqān Foundation, 2002–2004), 4:995–96. Eutychius was the first to introduce this account of Heraclius.

20. Such stipulations are commonplace in *futūḥ* texts; A. Noth, *The Early Arabic Historical Tradition: A Source-Critical Study*, 2nd rev. ed., ed. L. I. Conrad (Princeton: Darwin Press, 1994), 151–52, 167–68.

21. Eutychius, *Naẓm al-jawhar*, 2.5–6; F. C. Conybeare, "Antiochus Strategos: The Capture of Jerusalem by the Persians in 614 AD," *English Historical Review* 25.99 (1910): 502–17.

22. Eutychius, *Naẓm al-jawhar*, 2.6; cf. al-Bīrūnī, *al-Āthār al-bāqiya ʿan al-qurūn al-khāliya*, *Chronologie orientalischer Völker von Albērūnī*, ed. C. E. Sachau (Leipzig: Deutsche Morgenl. Gesellschaft, 1878; repr. 1923); Sachau, trans., *The Chronology of Ancient Nations* (London: W. H. Allen, 1879; repr. Frankfurt, 1969), chapters 16 and 17. This may have been the recasting of the White Week into a strict fast for some, but the evidence is slim. Based on this account, several late Muslim historians tersely chronicled this persecution: see M. Gil, *A History of Palestine, 634–1099* (Cambridge: Cambridge University Press, 1992), 10, note 11; M. Avi-Yonah, *The Jews of Palestine: A Political History from the Bar Kokhba War to the Arab Conquest* (Oxford: Blackwell, 1976), 271.

23. Cf. M. Breydy, ed. *Das Annalenwerk des Eutychios von Alexandrien*, Corpus Scriptorum Christianorum Orientalium 471, 472 (Louvain: Peeters, 1985), 129; with L. Cheikho, Corpus Scriptorum Christianorum Orientalium 50 (=*Annals* vol. 2), pages 6–7; see also M. Breydy, *Études sur Saʿid ibn Batriq et ses sources* (Louvain, 1983), 96–98; S. H. Griffith, "Apologetics and Historiography in the Annals of Eutychius of Alexandria: Christian Self-Definition in the World of Islam," in *Studies on the Christian Arabic Heritage*, ed. R. Y. Ebied and H. G. B. Teule (Louvain: Peeters, 2004).

24. Al-Safī ibn al-ʿAssāl referenced the Week of Heraclius as the "Introduction to the Great Fast" (*muqaddimat al-ṣawm al-kabīr*); see his *al-Majmūʿ al-ṣafawī*, ed. J. F. ʿAwad, 2 vols. (Cairo, n.d.), vol. 1, 171.

25. Ibn al-ʿAmīd al-Makīn [the Younger], *al-Mawsūʿa al-lāhūtiyya* [that is, *Mukhtaṣar al-bayān*], ed. A Monk from the Monastery of al-Muḥarraq, 4 vols. (Egypt: Dayr al-Muḥarraq, 1999–2001), vol. 4, 64. This edition erroneously attributes the authorship of the text to the thirteenth-century author Ibn al-ʿAmīd; it is rather the product of the fourteenth-century author al-Makīn Jirjis ibn al-ʿAmīd [the Younger] (see Geschichte der christlichen arabischen Literatur 2:453 [§ 139.3]). The work's accurate title is *Mukhtaṣar al-bayān*. Mark Swanson had noted this error of attribution at the UCLA–St. Shenouda Conference for Coptic Studies some years ago.

26. See notes 3–5 and 29.

27. See Abū al-Barakāt, *Miṣbāḥ*, chapter 18, page 140; cf. *Synaxarium*, 10 Hātūr and 14 Baramhāt; Talley, *Origins of the Liturgical Year*, 197–98. For the Coptic Arabic *Sy-*

naxarium, see R. Basset, ed. and trans., *Le Synaxaire arabe-jacobite (rédaction copte),* Patrologia Orientalis 3, 13, 56, 78, 84, 100 (Paris: Firmin-Didot, 1905–1928); also see note 43, below.

28. On the other aspects, see Mikhail "Legacy of Demetrius."

29. R.-G. Coquin, "Les origins de l'Épiphanie en Égypte," *Lex Orandi* 40 (1967): 140–70; idem, "Une Reforme liturgique du concile de Nicee (325)?" *Comptes Rendus, Académie des Inscriptions et Belles-lettres* (Paris: Diffusion de Boccard Paris Masson, 1967), 178–92; Bradshaw and Johnson, *Origins,* chs. 10–12; Talley, *Origins of the Liturgical Year,* 189–202, 214–22; Talley, "Origin of Lent at Alexandria," in *Between Memory and Hope: Readings on the Liturgical Year,* ed. M. E. Johnson (Collegeville, Minn.: Liturgical Press, 2000); Brakke, "Jewish Flesh and Christian Spirit," esp. 459–61; P. F. Bradshaw, *The Search for the Origins of Christian Worship,* 2nd ed. (Oxford: Oxford University Press, 2002), 179–82; M. E. Johnson, "Preparation for Pascha? Lent in Christian Antiquity," in *Passover and Easter: The Symbolic Structuring of Sacred Seasons,* ed. P. F. Bradshaw and L. A. Hoffman, (Notre Dame: University of Notre Dame Press, 1999); reprinted in Johnson, *Memory and Hope*; P. Regan, "The Three Days and the Forty Days," in Johnson, *Memory and Hope.*

30. Matthew 3:13–4:11; Mark 1:9–13; Luke 3:21–22, 4:1–13.

31. G. Dix and H. Chadwick, eds., *The Treatise on the Apostolic Tradition of Saint Hippolytus of Rome, Bishop and Martyr,* 2nd ed. (London: SPCK, 1992); T. Vivian, *St. Peter of Alexandria: Bishop and Martyr* (Philadelphia: Fortress Press, 1988), chapter 3 and appendix 1; P. A. de Lagarde, *Reliquiae Iuris Ecclesiastici Antiquissimae* (Leipzig: B. G. Teubnerus, 1856), 63–73 (Patrologia Graeca 18:467–508); G. W. Barkley, trans., *Origen: Homilies on Leviticus 1–16, Fathers of the Church* 83 (Washington D.C.: Catholic University of America, 1990). Also see Talley, *Origins of the Liturgical Year,* 193.

32. R.-G. Coquin, *Les Canons d'Hippolyte,* Patrologia Orientalis 31.2 (Paris, 1966); Bradshaw and Bebawi, *Canons of Hippolytus.*

33. See R.-G. Coquin, "Canons of Saint Basil," *The Coptic Encyclopedia,* vol. 2, 459; Maged S. A. Mikhail, "The Fast of the Apostles in the Early Church and in Later Syrian and Coptic Practice." *Oriens Christianus* 98.2 (2015), 1–20, repeatedly demonstrates that Arabic translations of the *Didascalia* were harmonized with contemporary practice.

34. See the 330 C.E. *Festal Letter* of Athanasius of Alexandria, in A. Camplani, *Atanasio di Alessandria, Lettere festali* (Milan, 2003); Brakke, "Jewish Flesh and Christian Spirit;" L. Th. Lefort, "Les lettres festales de saint Athanase," *Bulletin de la Classe des Lettres et des Sciences Morales et Politiques et de la Classe des Beaux-Arts* ser. 5, 39 (1953) 643–56. Bradshaw surveys the various dating schemes for the *Canons* in his introduction to the English translation of that text.

35. It would better to interpret Canon 12 along the same lines as the passage in the *Canonical Letter* of Peter of Alexandria, discussed below, than as proof for an Alexandria post-Epiphany Lent. On a distinction between the fast and Holy Week even within the six-week cycle, see H. Buchinger, "On the Early History of the Quadragesima," 106, note 41.

36. Origen, *Commentary on Leviticus,* 10.2; my emphasis.

37. The extant recension is based on Rufinus's Latin translation, which he identified as the text with which he took the greatest liberties in translating.

38. A. Roberts and J. Donaldson, eds., *Ante-Nicene Christian Library,* vol. 14, *The Writings of Methodius, Alexander of Lycopolis, Peter of Alexandria* (Edinburgh: T. & T. Clark, 1869), 292–4; note the commentary by Th. Balsamon and J. Zonaras.

39. Vivian, *Peter of Alexandria,* 185, my emphasis.

40. P. Koetschau, ed., *Origenes Werke I, Die griechischen christlichen Schriftsteller* der ersten Jahrhunderte 2 (Leipzig: J. C. Hinrichs, 1899); R. A. Greer, trans., *Origen: Exhortation to Martyrdom, Prayer, and Selected Works* (New York: Paulist Press, 1979).

41. See Eusebius, *Ecclesiastical History*, trans. R. J. Deferrari, 2 vols. (Washington, D.C.: Catholic University of America Press, 1953, 1955; repr. 1969); *Encomium on Demetrius of Alexandria*, in *Coptic Martyrdoms in the Dialect of Upper Egypt*, ed. and trans. E. A. Wallis Budge (London: British Museum, 1914), Coptic, 137–56, translation, 390–408; the Primitive recension of the *History of the Patriarchs*, ed. Christian Friedrich Seybold, *Severus ibn al-Muqaffaʿ, Alexandrinische Patriarchengeschichte von S. Marcus bis Michael I (61–767)* (Hamburg: L. Gräfe, 1912); and the Vulgate recension, ed. and trans. Evetts, *History of the Patriarchs of the Coptic Church of Alexandria*, Patrologia Orientalis I.2 (Paris: Firmin-Didot, 1906; repr. 1947); L. Cheikho, ed., *Petrus Ibn Rahib: Chronicon Orientale*, Corpus Scriptorum Christianorum Orientalium 45, 46 (Beirut: E Typographeo Catholico, 1903; reprint Louvain: Peeters, 1955). See M.S.A. Mikhail, Legacy of Demetrius, Texts 2, 3, and 5.

42. Breydy, *Annalenwerk*, pages 59–60, §172, my emphasis; Eutychius, Nazm al-jawhar, in Cheikho, ed., Corpus Scriptorum Christianorum Orientalium 50, 104.20–105.6. Eutychius and Abū al-Barakāt believed that the post-Epiphany fast was normative within the early church not just Alexandria.

43. "Constantinople" did not yet exist, and Rome never had a pontiff named Peter other than the apostle—this likely resulted from reading "Peter," b-ṭ-r-s, for "Victor" b-q-ṭ-r-s (cf. *Patrologia Orientalis* III.3.13).

44. See the *Synaxarium*'s entry for Hātūr 10; Mikhail, "Legacy of Demetrius."

45. M. Metzger, *Les Constitutions Apostoliques*, 3 vols., Sources Chrétiennes 320, 329, 336 (Paris: Cerf, 1986), vol. 2, 246; English trans., by J. Donaldson, in *Ante-Nicene Fathers*, vol. 7, 391–500.

46. *Apostolic Constitutions*, 5.17, forwards additional instructions on the observance of Lent.

47. A later reference in the ninth-century Celtic metrical *Martyrology of Oengus* the Culdee likely stems from a similar, literal reading of the *Apostolic Constitutions* or the Gospels rather than from an older Egyptian precedent. Other aspects of Celtic practice were likewise transmitted through ecclesiastical literature rather than a living conduit: W. Stokes, ed. and trans., *Félire Óengusso Céli Dé: The Martyrology of Oengus the Culdee* (London: Harrison and Sons, 1905), verses for January 6 and 7 (page 34); text and current bibliography are on www.ucc.ie/celt/ (accessed May 4, 2015). Nonetheless, ninth-century Celtic evidence cannot prove the existence of a post-Epiphany fast in Egypt more than five hundred years earlier (cf. Talley, *Origins of the Liturgical Year*, 193, 201).

48. R. H. Connolly, ed.and trans., *Gīwargīs, Metropolitan of Arbela and Mosul, d. 987?: Anonymi auctoris Expositio officiorum ecclesiae*, Corpus Scriptorum Christianorum Orientalium 64, 71–72, 76; Scriptores Syri 25, 28–29, 32 (Louvain: Peeters, 1953–1954), I 13; S. Brock, *A Brief Outline of Syriac Literature*, Mōrān ʿEthʾō 9 (Kottayam: St. Ephrem Ecumenical Research Institute, 1997), 68, 138.

49. Maged S. A. Mikhail, *From Byzantine to Islamic Egypt: Religion, Identity and Politics after the Arab Conquest* (London & New York: Tauris, 2014), chapter 11.

50. This presents another aspect of the scriptural polemics, but rather than arguing that the text of an interlocutor was adulterated, the argument is that it was not followed.

51. Makīn, *Mukhtaṣar al-bayān*, vol. 4, 229.

52. ʿAlī ibn Aḥmad ibn Ḥazm, *al-Fiṣal fī al-milal wa al-ahwāʾ wa al-niḥal*, 5 vols. (Cairo: al-Maṭbaʿah al-adabīyah, 1899–1903), vol. 2, 72; T. Pulcini, *Exegesis as Polemical*

Discourse: Ibn Hazm on Jewish and Christian Scriptures (Atlanta: Scholars Press, 1998), 135–36, 159.

53. Ibn Ḥazm, *al-Fiṣal fī al-milal*, 2:72.

54. The three-day Fast of Nineveh (the "Fast of Jonah") functioned in an analogous manner to the Fast of Heraclius—Copts fasted, Melkites feasted; see Mikhail, *From Byzantine to Islamic Egypt*, chapter 11. That fast originated in the sixth century among the East Syrians ("Nestorians"); M. G. Morony, "History and Identity in the Syrian Churches," in *Redefining Christian Identity*, ed. J. J. van Ginkel et al. (Louvain: Peeters, 2005), 10, note 67.

55. This is implicit in the earlier Alexandrian recension of the *Nazm* (Breydy, *Annalenwerk*, 129) and is explicit in the Antiochene version (Cheikho, Corpus Scriptorum Christianorum Orientalium 50, 6–7); cf. *Synaxarium*, s.v. Ṭūbah 12, *Patrologia Orientalis* I.3.3, page 334.3; s.v. Hātūr 10, *Patrologia Orientalis* 3.13.3, page 75.12. Interestingly enough, a paraphrase (*ilā mā hum ʿalayhi al-yawm*: "what they observe today") appears in Ibn Ḥazm, *al-Fiṣal fī al-milal*, 2:72.

56. Makīn, *Mukhtaṣar al-bayān*, vol. 4, 238–239, cf. 241, 245–46; Abū al-Barakāt, *Muṣbāḥ*, vol. 2, 141.

57. Makīn, *Mukhtaṣar al-bayān*, vol. 4, 231–32, 236.

58. Ibid., 230, 244–46. The emphasis may have been to clarify the issue to Muslims. Earlier, Ibn Ḥazm (*al-Fiṣal fī al-milal*, 2:72) was not convinced of the validity of the reform.

59. Ibid., 238.

60. Ibid., 240.

61. Ibid., 238, 245.

62. Ibid., 236.

63. Ibid., 239, cf. 245–46.

64. This is demonstrated at length in Mikhail, "Legacy of Demetrius."

The Perfect Monk

1. Caroline T. Schroeder, *Monastic Bodies: Discipline and Salvation in Shenoute of Atripe*, Divinations (Philadelphia: University of Pennsylvania Press, 2007), chapter 3.

2. Rebecca S. Krawiec, *Shenoute and the Women of the White Monastery* (New York: Oxford University Press, 2002).

3. Terry G. Wilfong, *Women of Jeme: Lives in a Coptic Town in Late Antique Egypt* (Ann Arbor: University of Michigan Press, 2002).

4. Darlene L. Brooks Hedstrom, "The Geography of the Monastic Cell in Early Egyptian Monastic Literature," *Church History* 78, no. 4 (2009): 756–91; Elizabeth S. Bolman and Patrick Godeau, eds., *Monastic Visions: Wall Paintings in the Monastery of St. Antony at the Red Sea* (New Haven: Yale University Press, 2002); see also Bolman's contributions to William Lyster, *The Cave Church of Paul the Hermit: At the Monastery of St. Paul in Egypt* (New Haven: Yale University Press, 2008).

5. Stephen J. Davis, *The Cult of Saint Thecla: A Tradition of Women's Piety in Late Antiquity*, Oxford Early Christian Studies (Oxford: Oxford University Press, 2001).

6. Stephen J. Davis, *Coptic Christology in Practice: Incarnation and Divine Participation in Late Antique and Medieval Egypt*, Oxford Early Christian Studies (Oxford: Oxford University Press, 2008).

7. David Brakke, *Demons and the Making of the Monk: Spiritual Combat in Early Christianity* (Cambridge: Harvard University Press, 2006).

8. Caroline T. Schroeder, "Prophecy and *Porneia* in Shenoute's Letters: The Rhetoric of Sexuality in a Late Antique Egyptian Monastery," *Journal of Near Eastern Studies* 65 no.2 (2006): 81–97.

9. See Schroeder, *Monastic Bodies*, 24–53; Stephen Emmel, "Shenoute the Monk: The Early Monastic Career of Shenoute the Archimandrite," in *Il monachesimo tra eredità e aperture: Atti del simposio "Testi e temi nella tradizione del monachesimo cristiano" per il 50e anniversario dell'istituto monastico di Sant'Anselmo, Roma, 28 maggio-1e giugno 2002*, by Maciej Bielawski and Daniël Hombergen (Rome: Pontificio Ateneo S. Anselmo, 2004), 151–74.

10. Shenoute, Canon 1, YW 80, unpublished (FR-BN 1302 f. 2V): *epeidē akjnoui de hnoumine nshaje entaoueisht an te efshaje mn pefshēre hnouagapē alla taourōme te efshaje mn pethitouōf hnoumoste ekjō mmos nai je mē nsooun hnouōrj je nim pentafrnobe.*

11. Shenoute, *Canon 1*, YW 81 unpublished (FR-BN 1302 f. 3R): *hnounshot efnasht nthe namnte.* See also the treatment of this passage in Schroeder, *Monastic Bodies*.

12. [*hene*]*iote na*[*me*], in Shenoute, *Canons Vol. 9*, in Dwight Young, *Coptic Manuscripts from the White Monastery: Works of Shenute* (Vienna: Österreichische Nationalbibliothek and Brüder Hollinek, 1993) 62; English translation, 65.

13. Shenoute, *Canons Vol. 9*, in Young, *Coptic Manuscripts*, 55, and Johannes Leipoldt, *Sinuthii Archimandritae Vita et Opera Omnia*, 3 vols. (numbered 1, 3, 4), Corpus Scriptorum Christianorum Orientalium 41, 42, 73, SC 1, 2, 5 (Paris: 1906–1913), vol. 4, 156; English translation in Young, *Coptic Manuscripts*, 59.

14. Shenoute, *Why Oh Lord*, *Canons Vol. 4*, in Young, *Coptic Manuscripts*, 93–94; English translation (revised from Young), 108.

15. Raffaella Cribiore, *Gymnastics of the Mind: Greek Education in Hellenistic and Roman Egypt* (Princeton: Princeton University Press, 2001), 69–71.

16. On the role of the leader of the women's community, see now Rebecca S. Krawiec, "The Role of the Female Elder in Shenoute's White Monastery," in *Christianity and Monasticism in Upper Egypt: Akhmim and Sohag*, ed. Gawdat Gabra and Hany N. Takla (Cairo & New York: American University in Cairo Press, 2007), 59–71; See also Susanna Elm on the early history of the men's and women's communities: *"Virgins of God": The Making of Asceticism in Late Antiquity*, Oxford Early Christian Studies (Oxford & New York: Oxford University Press, 1994), 300.

17. Shenoute, *Why Oh Lord*, *Canons Vol. 4*, in Young, *Coptic Manuscripts*, 87–88; English translation, 90–91.

18. Shenoute, *Why Oh Lord*, *Canons Vol. 4*, in Young, *Coptic Manuscripts*, 95–96, 101; English translation, 109, 111.

19. Brakke, *Demons and the Making of the Monk*, 39.

20. Ibid., 119.

21. Margaret R. Graver, *Stoicism and Emotion* (Chicago: University of Chicago Press, 2007).

22. On the physicality of the changes to the human person involved in an emotion—the movement inside the soul (*psychē*)—see Graver, *Stoicism and Emotion*, chapter 1.

23. Ibid., 4.

24. Ibid., 5.

25. Ibid., 37.

26. Ibid., 36–40, 42–43 (the example of Agamemnon), 55.

27. Ibid., 5.

28. Ibid., 36–40.

29. Ibid., 56.

30. Shenoute, *I Have Been Reading the Holy Gospels, Discourses Vol. 8*, in Leipoldt, *Sinuthii*, vol. 3, 222; English translation in Mark Moussa, "*I Have Been Reading the Holy Gospels* by Shenoute of Atripe (Discourses 8, Work 1): Coptic Text, Translation, and Commentary" (Ph.D. diss. , Catholic University of America, 2010), 122–23.

31. He refers to a "paradise of joy" immediately preceding this passage (*pparadisos ntetruphē*)

32. Shenoute, *I Have Been Reading the Holy Gospels, Discourses 8*, in Leipoldt, *Sinuthii*, vol. 3, 221–22; English translation in Moussa, "*I Have Been Reading the Holy Gospels*," 122–23.

33. Shenoute, *I Have Been Reading the Holy Gospels*, in Leipoldt, *Sinuthii*, vol. 3, 221–22; English translation, Moussa, "*I Have Been Reading the Holy Gospels*," 122–23.

34. See Graver, *Stoicism and Emotion*, 52–53. She writes of *chara*/joy, using Seneca as an example.

35. Shenoute, *I Have Been Reading the Holy Gospels, Discourses 8*, in Moussa, "*I Have Been Reading the Holy Gospels*," 58; English translation, 152.

36. Ibid., 58–59; English translation, 152.

37. Young, *Coptic Manuscripts*, 150; English translation, 157.

38. Graver, *Stoicism and Emotion*, 58.

39. Shenoute, *I Have Been Reading the Holy Gospels, Discourses 8*, in Moussa, "*I Have Been Reading the Holy Gospels*," 38; English translation, 140.

40. Ibid., 43; English translation, 142. On fear, anger, and hatred, also see Ibid., 38, 58, 64–65; English translation, 140, 152, 156.

41. Ibid., 46; English translation, 143.

42. Shenoute, *I Have Been Reading the Holy Gospels, Discourses 8*, in Leipoldt, *Sinuthii*, vol. 3, 222, and Moussa, "*I Have Been Reading the Holy Gospels*," 30; English translation, 123, 129.

43. Shenoute, *I Have Been Reading the Holy Gospels, Discourses 8*, in Moussa, "*I Have Been Reading the Holy Gospels*," 34–35; English translation, 138.

44. Ibid., 51; English translation, 147.

45. Ibid., 30; English translation, 129.

46. Ibid., 47; English translation, 144

47. "How will the holy Word explain this to us except through the mouth and tongue of man? . . . For at all times 'it is the Lord who gives a teaching tongue' (Isa 50.4). . . . Yet it is the Lord . . . who will give the instructing tongue to the upright teacher," Ibid., 47–48; English translation, 144–45.

48. Young, *Coptic Manuscripts*, 151–52; English translation, 157–58.

49. Shenoute, *I Have Been Reading the Holy Gospels, Discourses 8*, in Young, *Coptic Manuscripts*, 125–26; English translation in Moussa, "*I Have Been Reading the Holy Gospels*," 120; see also Moussa, "*I Have Been Reading the Holy Gospels*," 49, 73; English translation, 145, 161, where hell is a place characterized by weeping and gnashing of teeth (a biblical, prophetic discourse).

50. Young, *Coptic Manuscripts*, 156; English translation, 160.

The Paradox of Monasticism

1. For a short vita, see De Lacy O'Leary, *The Saints of Egypt in the Coptic Calendar* (Amsterdam: Philo Press, 1974, reprint. Original publisher: the Society for Promoting Christian Knowledge, London, 1937): 219–20.

2. Emile Amélineau, "Voyage d'un moine égyptien," *Recueil de Travaux Relatifs à la Philologie* no.6 (1885):166–94; J. Chaleur, "Saint Onuphre, sa vie d'après le synaxaire

copte et le manuscrit oriental no. 7027 du British Museum," *Les Cahiers Coptes* 5 (Cairo: Institut Copte, 1954): 3–15.

3. G. Kaster, "Onuphrius," in *Lexikon der christlichen Ikonographie*, ed. E. Kirschbaum, vol. 8 (Rome: Herder, 1990), 84–88.

4. Richard Finn, *Asceticism in the Graeco-Roman World* (Cambridge: Cambridge University Press, 2009), 58–99.

5. Robert T. Meyer, *St. Athanasius: The Life of St. Antony* (New York: Newman Press, 1950), 94–95.

6. Benedicta Ward, *The Sayings of the Desert Fathers: The Alphabetical Collection* (New York: Macmillan, 1975), 141.

7. Toda Satoshi, *Vie de St. Macaire l'Égyptien: Édition et traduction des textes copte et syriaque* (Piscataway, N.J.: Gorgias, 2012), 450.

8. Ward, *Sayings of the Desert Fathers*, 128.

9. David Brakke, *Athanasius and Asceticism* (Baltimore & London: John Hopkins University Press 1995), 80–141. Brakke deals extensively with the relationships between Athanasius and the monastic communities.

10. Brakke, *Athanasius and Asceticism*, 82.

11. Satoshi, "Vie de St. Macaire l'Egyptien," 426.

12. Brakke, *Athanasius and Asceticism*, 113.

13. Stephen J. Davis, *The Early Coptic Papacy: The Egyptian Church and Its Leadership in Late Antiquity*, The Popes of Egypt 1 (Cairo & New York: American University in Cairo Press, 2004), 66–67.

14. John Cassian, *Conferences* 10.2., trans. C. Luibheid (New York: Paulist Press, 1985), 125–26.

15. Philip Rousseau, *Pachomius: The Making of a Community in Fourth-Century Egypt* (Berkeley: University of California Press, 1999), 87–104.

16. Ward, *Sayings of the Desert Fathers*, 53.

17. Ibid., 183, saying number 113.

18. Ibid., 80, saying number 3.

19. Thomas Merton in his introduction to a translation of the *Apophthegmata Patrum* describes the early monastics as "truly in certain sense 'anarchists,' and it will do no harm to think of them as such." Thomas Merton, *Wisdom of the Desert* (Abbey of Gethsemani, Kentucky, 1960), 5.

20. Columba Stewart, *Working the Heart of the Earth: The Messalian Controversy in History, Texts and Language to AD 431* (Oxford: Clarendon Press, 1991).

21. Daniel Caner, *Wandering, Begging Monks: Spiritual Authority and the Promotion of Monasticism in Late Antiquity* (Berkeley, Los Angeles & London: University of California Press, 2002), 83–87.

22. Caner, *Wandering, Begging Monks*, 206

23. B. T. A. Evetts, "History of the Patriarchs of the Coptic Church of Alexandria III," *Patrologia Orientalis* V (Paris: Firmin-Didot, 1910), 33.

24. Karel C. Innemée, *Ecclesiastical Dress in the Medieval Near East* (Leiden: Brill 1992), 22.

25. Evetts, "History of the Patriarchs," 448–49.

26. M. Breydy, *Das Annalenwerk des Eutychios von Alexandrien*, Corpus Scriptorum Christianorum Orientalium 472 (Louvain: Peeters 1985), 87.

27. F. Wüstenfeld, *Maqrizi's Geschichte der Copten* (Hildesheim: Olms 1979; reprint Göttingen: Dieterich, 1845), 44.

28. O. H. E Burmester, *The Rite of Consecration of the Patriarch of Alexandria (Text according to Ms. 253 lit, Coptic Museum)* (Cairo: Société d'Archélogie Copte, 1960), 9, 10, 55.

29. Davis, *The Early Coptic Papacy*, 126. René-Georges Coquin, *Livre de la consécration du sanctuaire de Benjamin*, Bibliothèque d'Études coptes 13 (Cairo : IFAO 1975); Evetts, "History of the Patriarchs," 502–18.

30. Gawdat Gabra, *Coptic Monasteries* (Cairo: American University in Cairo Press, 2002), 58.

31. Karel C. Innemée "Excavations at Deir al-Baramus 2002–2005," *Bulletin de la Société d'Archéologie Copte* 44 (2005): 55–68; Stephen J. Davis, Darlene Brooks Hedstrom, Tomasz Herbich, Gillian Pyke, and Dawn McCormack, "Yale Monastic Archaeological Project John the Little, Season 1 (June 7–27, 2006)," *Mishkah* 3 (2008): 47–52; Stephen J. Davis, Darlene Brooks Hedstrom, Tomasz Herbich, Gillian Pyke, and Dawn McCormack, "Yale Monastic Archaeological Project John the Little, Season 2 (May 14–June 16, 2007)," *Mishkah* 3 (2008): 59–64.

32. Hugh G. Evelyn White, *The Monasteries of the Wâdi 'n Natrûn*, vol. 3 (New York: Metropolitan Museum of Art, 1933), 50–52, plate 2.

33. Wüstenfeld, *Maqrizi's Geschichte*, 110.

Reconsidering the Emerging Monastic Desertscape

I would like to thank Nelly van Doorn–Harder for the invitation to participate in the 2010 conference "The Future of Coptic Studies: Theories, Methods, Topics" at Wake Forest University. An earlier version of this essay was presented in 2009 to the Roman Archaeology Conference. I thank Christian Raffensperger, Tammy Proctor, Nancy McHugh, and Molly Wood for commenting on earlier drafts. I am grateful for their suggestions and time.

1. James E. Goehring, "The Dark Side of Landscape: Ideology and Power in the Christian Myth of the Desert," *Journal of Medieval and Early Modern Studies* 33, no. 3 (2003): 437–51.

2. James E. Goehring, "The Encroaching Desert: Literary Production and Ascetic Space in Early Christian Egypt," *Journal of Early Christian Studies* 1, no. 3 (1993): 281–96; Darlene L. Brooks Hedstrom, "The Geography of the Monastic Cell in Early Egyptian Monastic Literature," *Church History* 78, no. 4 (2009): 756–91.

3. Donald Malcolm Reid, *Whose Pharaohs? Archaeology, Museums, and Egyptian National Identity from Napoleon to World War I* (Cairo: American University in Cairo Press, 2002).

4. Darlene L. Brooks Hedstrom, "Treading on Antiquity: Anglo-American Missionaries and the Religious Landscape of Nineteenth Century Coptic Egypt," *Material Religion* 8, no. 2 (2012): 127–52.

5. Derek Bryce, "Repackaging Orientalism: Discourses on Egypt and Turkey in British Outbound Tourism," *Tourist Studies* 7, no. 2 (2007): 165–91; Lynn Meskell, "The Practice and Politics of Archaeology in Egypt," *Annals of the New York Academy of Sciences* 925, no.1 (2000): 146–69; Scott Trafton, *Egypt Land: Race and Nineteenth-Century American Egyptomania* (Durham: Duke University Press, 2004); Elliott Colla, *Conflicted Antiquities: Egyptology, Egyptomania, Egyptian Modernity* (Durham: Duke University Press, 2007).

6. The fact that nineteenth- and twentieth-century excavations were dominated by architects and architectural historians means that the emphasis for excavation included large-scale clearing of sites, which was the common practice for the time. The point here is that the preference for exposing as much of a settlement as possible and for documenting its fullest extent means that stone architecture was considered a higher priority in excavation than structures made of mud brick. The majority of late-antique settlements in Egypt were made of mud bricks and were frequently considered poor

habitation and debris. The actual remains cluttered the view and appreciation of the more valued pharaonic monuments, which were frequently the focus of the excavations.

7. Mary Horbury, "The British and the Copts," in *Perspectives on Ancient Egypt since Napoleon Bonaparte: Imperialism, Colonialism and Modern Appropriations*, ed. David Jeffreys (London: UCL Press, 2003), 153–70; D. Medina Lasansky and Brian McLaren, *Architecture and Tourism: Perception, Performance and Place* (Oxford: Berg, 2004).

8. Renewed interest in monastic archeology at Thebes is producing satisfactory results at a variety of sites. Additionally, reassessments of previously recovered material illustrate the need to reconsider the monastic evidence with a fresh perspective. See Catherine Thirard, "Le monastère d'Épiphane à Thèbes: Nouvelle interprétation chronologique," *Études Coptes 9* (2006) 367–74; Von Ina Eichner and Ulrike Fauerbach, "Die spätantike / koptische Klosteranlage Deir el-Bachit in Dra' Abu el-Naga (Oberägypten). Zweiter Vorbericht," *Mitteilungen des Deutschen Archaologischen Instituts, Cairo* 61 (2005): 139–52; G. Burkard, M. Mackensen, and D. Polz, "Die spätantike / koptische Klosteranlage Deir el-Bachit in Dra' Abu el-Naga (Oberägypten). Erster Vorbericht," *Mitteilungen des Deutschen Archaologischen Instituts, Cairo* 59 (2003): 41–65. See also C. F. Calament, "Correspondence inédite entre moines dans la montagne thébaine," *Études Coptes 9* (2006): 81–101; Tamás Bács, "The So-called 'Monastery of Cyriacus' at Thebes," *Egyptian Archaeology* 17 (Autumn 2000): 34–36; Elisabeth O'Connell, "Transforming Monumental Landscapes in Late Antique Egypt: Monastic Dwellings in Legal Documents from Western Thebes," *Journal of Early Christian Studies* 15, no. 2 (Summer 2007): 239–73. For a comprehensive consideration of archaeological and textual evidence for Philae and Aswan, see Jitse H. F. Dijkstra, *Philae and the End of Ancient Egyptian Religion: A Regional Study of Religious Transformation (298–642 C.E.)* (Louvain: Peeters, 2008).

9. Norman Russell, trans., *Historia monachorum in Aegypto 1: The Lives of the Desert Fathers*. London: Mobray, 1980), 83.

10. Benedicta Ward, trans., *The Sayings of the Desert Fathers: The Alphabetical Collection* (Kalamazoo: Cistercian Publications, 1975): 116–18.

11. For a reading of the ascetic gaze, see Caroline T. Schroeder, "Queer Eye for the Ascetic Guy?: Homoeroticism, Children, and the Making of Monks in Late Antique Egypt," *Journal of the American Academy of Religion* 77, no. 2 (2009): 333–47; Derek Krueger, "Between Monks: Tales of Monastic Companionship in Early Byzantium," *Journal of the History of Sexuality* 20, no. 1 (2011): 28–61.

12. Edward Gibbon's clear distaste for monasticism and ecclesiastical authority is evident throughout his work. Edward Gibbon, *The Decline and Fall of the Roman Empire, vol. II (London: Frederick Warne and Co., 1872)*, 508–509. Almost two centuries later E. R. Dodds would link the popularity of monasticism to a profound response to the psychological crisis of the third century. E. R. Dodds, *Pagan and Christian in an Age of Anxiety: Some Aspects of Religious Experience from Marcus Aurelius to Constantine* (Cambridge: Cambridge University Press, 1965).

13. Brooks Hedstrom, "The Geography of the Monastic Cell," 774–76.

14. Tim Vivian, "Geographies of Early Coptic Monasticism," *Coptic Church Review* 12, no. 1 (1991): 15–21.

15. Bruce Trigger, *A History of Archaeological Thought* (Cambridge & New York: Cambridge University Press, 1989).

16. Lewis Binford, "Archaeological Systematics and the Study of Cultural Process," *American Antiquity* 32., no. 2, part 1 (1965): 203–10; Binford, "Archaeology as Anthropology," *American Antiquity* 28., no. 2 (1962): 217–25.

17. David Clarke, *Analytical Archaeology*, 2nd ed. (Routledge, New York: Columbia University Press, 2015), 468.

18. C. C. Walters, *Monastic Archaeology in Egypt* (Warminster, U.K.: Aris & Phillips, 1974), 7.

19. Elizabeth S. Bolman, ed., *Monastic Visions: Wall Paintings in the Monastery of St. Antony at the Red Sea* (New Haven: Yale University Press, 2002).

20. Philip Rousseau, *Pachomius: The Making of a Community in Fourth-Century Egypt* (Berkeley: University of California Press, 1999).

21. Peter Grossmann, Darlene Brooks Hedstrom et al., "Second Report on the Excavation of the Monastery of Apa Shenute (Dayr Anba Shinuda) at Suhag," *Dumbarton Oaks Papers*, 63 (2009): 167–220; Peter Grossmann, Darlene Brooks Hedstrom, and Elizabeth S. Bolman, "The Excavation in the Monastery of Apa Shenute (Dayr Anba Shinuda) at Suhag," *Dumbarton Oaks Papers* 58 (2004): 371–82; Rebecca S. Krawiec, *Shenoute and the Women of the White Monastery* (Oxford: Oxford University Press, 2002); Bentley Layton, "Social Structure and Food Consumption in an Early Christian Monastery: The Evidence of Shenoute's Canons and the White Monastery Federation A.D. 385–465," *Le Muséon* 115.1-2 (2002): 25–55.

22. Mariachiara Giorda, *Il regno di Dio in terra: Le fondazioni monastiche egiziane tra V e VII secolo* (Rome: Edizioni di Storia e Letteratura, 2011), 25–29.

23. Ian Hodder, *Theory and Practice in Archaeology* (London: Routledge, 1992), 11; Hodder, *The Archaeological Process: An Introduction* (London: Wiley-Blackwell, 1999).

24. Hayden White, *The Content of the Form* (Baltimore: John Hopkins University Press, 1987), 188–89.

25. Rebecca S. Krawiec, "From the Womb of the Church: Monastic Families," *Journal of Early Christian Studies* 11, no. 3 (2003): 283–307; Caroline T. Schroeder, "Child Sacrifice in Egyptian Monastic Culture: From Familial Renunciation to Jephthah's Lost Daughter," *Journal of Early Christian Studies* 20, no. 2 (2012): 269–30.

26. Mena of Nikiou, *The Life of Isaac of Alexandria*, trans. D. Bell (Kalamazoo: Cistercian Publications, 1988), 48–49.

27. Papyrological evidence in Greek, Coptic, and Arabic offers insight into the various economic and social interactions between the monastic communities and the urban periphery. Examples of this scholarship include Sarah Clackson, *It Is Our Father Who Writes: Orders from the Monastery of Apollo at Bawit* (Cincinnati: American Society of Papyrologists, 2008); Anne Boud'hors, *Ostraca grecs et coptes: Des fouilles de Jean Maspero à Baouit* (Cairo: IFAO, 2004).

28. Peter Brown, *Body and Society* (New York: Columbia University Press, 1988), 215.

29. For discussions and relevant bibliography of these sites, see Ewa Wipszycka, *Moines et communautés monastiques en Égypte (IVe–VIIIe siècles)* (Warsaw: Journal of Juristic Papyrology, 2009), 107–226, and Darlene L. Brooks Hedstrom, "Divine Architects: Designing the Monastic Dwelling Place," in *Egypt in the Byzantine World, 300–700*, ed. Roger Bagnall (Cambridge: Cambridge University Press, 2007), 368–89

30. Elizabeth S. Bolman, "Mimesis, Metamorphosis and Representation in Coptic Monastic Cells," *Bulletin of the American Society of Papyrologists* 35, no. ½ (1998): 65–77, plates 1–7; Bolman, "Depicting the Kingdom of Heaven: Paintings and Monastic Practice in Early Byzantine Egypt," in Bagnall, *Egypt in the Byzantine World*, 408–33.

31. Brooks Hedstrom, "Geography of the Monastic Cell," 785–90.

32. Jerome, *Letter 3.1* (to Rufinus), in *The Letters of St. Jerome*, trans. Charles C. Mieron (New York: Newman Press, 1963), 30.

33. Lewis Binford, *In Pursuit of the Past: Decoding the Archaeological Record* (Berkeley: University of California Press, 1983).

34. David Sibley, "Outsiders in Society and Space," in *Inventing Places: Studies in Cultural Geography*, ed. Kay Anderson and Fay Gale (Melbourne: Longman Cheshire, 1992), 107.

35. Ewa Wipszycka, "Resources and Economic Activities of the Egyptian Monastic Communities (4th-8th Century)," *Journal of Juristic Papyrology* 41 (2011): 159-263.

36. Sibley, "Outsiders in Society and Space," 112.

37. David Brakke, *Demons and the Making of the Monk Spiritual Combat in Early Christianity* (Cambridge: Harvard University Press, 2006).

38. Belden C. Lane, *The Solace of Fierce Landscapes: Exploring Desert and Mountain Spirituality* (New York: Oxford University Press, 1998).

39. Sibley, "Outsiders in Society and Space," 112.

40. Thomas F. X. Noble and Thomas Head, eds., *Soldiers of Christ: Saints and Saints' Lives from Late Antiquity and the Early Middle Ages* (University Park: Pennsylvania State University, 1995).

41. Sibley, "Outsiders in Society and Space," 113.

42. Ibid.

43. Vuk Trifkovic, "Persons and Landscapes: Shifting Scales of Landscape Archaeology," in *Confronting Scale in Archaeology: Issues of Theory and Practice*, ed. Gary Lock and Brian Leigh Molyneaux (New York: Springer, 2006), 258.

44. Ibid.

45. Ibid., 259.

46. Tim Ingold, *The Perception of the Environment* (London: Routledge, 2002).

47. Tim Ingold, "Materials against Materiality," *Archaeological Dialogues* 14, no. 1 (2007): 14.

48. Carol Meyer et al., *Bir Umm Fawakhir Survey Project 1993: A Byzantine Gold-Mining Town in Egypt* (Chicago: Oriental Institute of the University of Chicago, 2000). Steven Sidebotham, *Berenike and the Ancient Maritime Spice Route* (Berkeley: University of California Press, 2011).

49. Jennifer Dornan, "Beyond Belief: Religious Experience, Ritual, and Cultural Neuro-Phenomenology in the Interpretation of Past Religious Systems," *Cambridge Archaeological Journal* 14, no. 1 (2004): 25-36; Ian Hodder, ed., *Religion in the Emergence of Civilization: Çatalhöyük as a Case Study* (Cambridge: Cambridge University Press, 2010); Timothy Insoll, *Archaeology, Ritual, Religion* (London: Routledge, 2004); S. R. Steadman, *The Archaeology of Religion: Cultures and Their Beliefs in Worldwide Context* (Walnut Creek, Calif.: Left Coast Press, 2009).

50. Harvey Whitehouse, *Modes of Religiosity: A Cognitive Theory of Religious Transmission* (Walnut Creek, Calif.: Altamira Press, 2004), 74.

51. Insoll, *Archaeology, Ritual, and Religion*, 1-3.

52. Colin Renfrew, "The Archaeology of Religion," in *The Ancient Mind: Elements of Cognitive Archaeology*, ed. Colin Renfrew and Ezra B. W. Zubrow (Cambridge: Cambridge University Press, 1994), 47-54. He argues that we can seek to investigate the archaeology of religion by the indicators or physical evidence for four central activities linked to the archaeology of religion. These indicators include features that focus the attention of practitioners; establish boundaries between public/sacred space and private/profane space; encourage engagement with the presence of the deity and represent acts of participation and offering.

53. Elizabeth E. Oram, "In the Footsteps of the Saints: The Monastery of St. Antony, Pilgrimage, and Modern Coptic Identity," in Bolman, *Monastic Visions*, 203-13.

54. Joyce Marcus, "Rethinking Ritual," in *The Archaeology of Ritual*, ed. Evangelos Kyriakidis (Los Angeles: Costen Institute of Archaeology, University of California, 2007), 43-76.

55. S. Sauneron and J. Jacquet, *Les ermitages du désert d'Esna*, 4 vols. (Cairo: Institut Français d'Archéologie Orientale, 1972).

56. P. Grossmann, "Die Unterkunftsbauten des Koinobitenklosters 'Dair al-Balayza' im Vergleich mit den Eremitagen der mönche von Kellia," in *Le site monastique copte des Kellia*, ed. Philippe Bridel (Geneva: Mission Suisse d'Archaeologie Copte de l'Université de Genève, 1986), 33–40; P. Grossmann, "Ruinen des Klosters Dair al-Balaiza in Oberägypten," *Jahrbuck für Antike und Christenum* 36 (1993): 171–205.

57. Bill Hillier and Julienne Hanson, *The Social Logic of Space* (Cambridge: Cambridge University Press, 1984), 9.

58. Leslie S. B. MacCoull, trans., *Coptic Legal Documents: Law as Vernacular Text and Experience in Late Antique Egypt* (Tempe: Arizona Center for Medieval and Renaissance Studies, 2009), 2.

59. M. Martin, "La province d'Asmunayn, historique de sa configuration religieuse," *Annales Islamologiques* 23 (1987): 1–29.

60. Darlene L. Brooks Hedstrom and Hendrik Dey, "The Archaeology of the Earliest Monasteries," in *Cambridge History of Medieval Western Monasticism*, eds. Alison I. Beach and Isabelle Cochelin (Cambridge: Cambridge University Press, forthcoming); Joseph Patrich, "Monastic Landscapes," in *Recent Research on the Late Antique Countryside*, ed. W. Bowden, L. Lavan, and C. Machardo (Leiden: Brill, 2004), 413–46.

61. Catherine Saliou, *Les lois des bâtiments: Voisinage et habitat urbain dans l'empire romain: Recherches sur les rapports entre le droit et la construction privée, du siècle d'Auguste au siècle de Justinien* (Beirut: Institut Français d'Archéologie du Proche-Orient, 1994).

62. Aneta Skalec, "Private Buildings and Their Juridical Context in the Byzantine Near East," *Revista da Faculdade de Direito da Universidade de São Paulo* 106–107 (2011–2012): 67–83.

63. For a representation of the richness of the sources see Anne Boud'hors et al., eds., *Monastic Estates in Late Antique and Early Islamic Egypt: Ostraca, Papyri, and Essays in Memory of Sarah Clackson* (Cincinnati: American Society of Papyrologists, 2009).

64. Stephen J. Davis, Darlene Brooks Hedstrom, Salima Ikram et al., "New Archaeology at Ancient Scetis: Surveys and Initial Excavations at the Monastery of St. John the Little in Wadi al-Natrun: Yale Monastic Archaeology Project," *Dumbarton Oaks Papers* 64 (2010): 217–28; Gawdat Gabra, ed., *Christianity and Monasticism in the Fayoum Oasis* (Cairo: American University in Cairo Press, 2008); Alain Delattre, *Papyrus coptes et grecs du monastère d'apa Apollô de Baouît conservés aux Musées royaux d'Art et d'Histoire de Bruxelles* (Brussels: Académie Royale de Belgique, Classe des Lettres, 2007).

65. Darlene Brooks Hedstrom, "Models of Seeing and Reading Monastic Archaeology," *Cistercian Studies Quarterly* 48, no. 3 (2013): 299–315; Robin A. E. Coningham, "Monks, Caves, and Kings: Reassessment of the Nature of Early Buddhism," *World Archaeology* 27, no. 2 (1995): 222–42; Senake Bandaranayake, "Monastery Plan and Social Formation: The Spatial Organization of the Buddhist Monastic Complexes of the Early and Middle Historical Period in Sri Lanka and Changing Patterns of Political Power," in *Domination and Resistance*, ed. Daniel Miller, Michael Rowlands, and Christopher Tilley (London: Unwin Hyman, 1989), 179–95; B. R. Mani and S. C. Saran, *Purabharati: Studies in Early Historical Archaeology and Buddhism* (Delhi: Sharada Publishing House, 2006).

SELECTED BIBLIOGRAPHY

Books

Armanios, Febe. *Coptic Christianity in Ottoman Egypt.* New York: Oxford University Press, 2011.

———. "'The 'Virtuous Women': Images of Gender in Modern Coptic Society." *Middle Eastern Studies* 38, no.1 (2002): 110–30.

Armanios, Febe, and Andrew Amstutz. "Emerging Christian Media in Egypt: Clerical Authority and the Visualization of Women in Coptic Video Films." *International Journal of Middle East Studies* 45, no. 3 (2013): 513–33.

Atiya, Aziz S., ed. *The Coptic Encyclopedia,* 8 vols. (New York & Toronto: Macmillan, 1991).

———. "The Copts and Christian Civilization." *Coptologia* 1 (1981): 10–46.

———. *A History of Eastern Christianity.* London: Methuen, 1968.

Ayad, Mariam F., ed. *Coptic Culture: Past, Present, and Future.* Stevenage, U.K.: Coptic Orthodox Church Center, 2012.

Bagnall, Roger, ed. *Egypt in the Byzantine World, 300–700.* Cambridge: Cambridge University Press, 2007.

Berger, Maurits. "Public Policy and Islamic Law: The Modern Dhimmi in Contemporary Egyptian Family Law." *Islamic Law and Society* 8, no. 1 (2001): 88–136.

Bernard-Maugiron, Nathalie "Les amendements à la loi du statut personnel des coptes orthodoxies: Vers la fin du projet du code unifié de la famille en Égypt?" In *Chroniques Egyptiennes 2008,* edited by Iman Farag, 124–49. Cairo: Cedej, 2008.

Bingham-Kolenkow, Anitra. "The Copts in the United States of America." In *Between Desert and City: The Coptic Orthodox Church Today,* edited by Nelly van Doorn-Harder and Kari Vogt, 265–72. Oslo: Novus, 1997.

Bolman, Elizabeth S., ed. *Monastic Visions: Wall Paintings in the Monastery of St. Antony at the Red Sea.* New Haven: Yale University Press, 2002.

Botros, Ghada Barsoum. "Competing for the Future: Adaptation and the Accommodation of Difference in Coptic Orthodox Immigrant Churches." Ph.D. diss., University of Toronto, 2005.

———. "Religious Identity as a Historical Narrative: Coptic Orthodox Immigrant Churches and the Representation of History." *Journal of Historical Sociology* 19, no. 2 (2006): 174–201.

Boud'hors, Anne, et al., eds. *Monastic Estates in Late Antique and Early Islamic Egypt: Ostraca, Papyri, and Essays in Memory of Sarah Clackson.* Cincinnati: American Society of Papyrologists, 2009.

Bradshaw, P. F. ed., and C. Bebawi, trans. *The Canons of Hippolytus.* Nottingham: Grove Books, 1987.

Bradshaw, P. F., and M. E. Johnson. *The Origins of Feasts, Fasts and Seasons in Early Christianity.* Collegeville, Minn.: Liturgical Press, 2011.

Brakke, David. *Athanasius and Asceticism.* Baltimore & London: John Hopkins University Press, 1995.

———. *Demons and the Making of the Monk: Spiritual Combat in Early Christianity.* Cambridge: Harvard University Press, 2006.

Breydy, M., ed. *Das Annalenwerk des Eutychios von Alexandrien.* Corpus Scriptorum Christianorum Orientalium 471, 472. Louvain: Peeters, 1985.

Brooks Hedstrom, Darlene. "The Geography of the Monastic Cell in Early Egyptian Monastic Literature." *Church History* 78, no. 4 (2009): 756–91.

———. "Models of Seeing and Reading Monastic Archaeology." *Cistercian Studies Quarterly* 48, no. 3 (2013): 299–315.

Bostros. "Treading on Antiquity: Anglo-American Missionaries and the Religious Landscape of Nineteenth Century Coptic Egypt." *Material Religion* 8, no. 2 (2012): 127–52.

Buchinger, H. "On the Early History of the Quadragesima: A New Look at an Old Problem and Some Proposed Solutions." In *Liturgies in East and West: Ecumenical Relevance of Early Liturgical Development,* edited by Hans-Jürgen Feulner, 99–117. Berlin: Lit, 2013.

Burmester, O. H. E. *The Egyptian or Coptic Church: A Detailed Description of Her Liturgical Services and the Rites and Ceremonies Observed in the Administration of Her Sacraments.* Cairo: Societé d'Archéologie Copte, 1967.

Caner, Daniel. *Wandering, Begging Monks: Spiritual Authority and the Promotion of Monasticism in Late Antiquity.* Berkeley, Los Angeles & London: University of California Press, 2002.

Chitham, E. J. *The Coptic Community in Egypt: Spatial and Social Change.* Durham, N.C.: Center for Middle Eastern and Islamic Studies, 1986.

Chitty, Derwas. *The Desert a City.* Crestwood, N.Y.: St. Vladimir's Seminary Press, 1999.

Comings, J. B. *Aspects of the Liturgical Year in Cappadocia (325–430).* New York & Berlin: Peter Lang, 2005.

Connolly, R. H. *Didascalia Apostolorum.* Oxford: Clarendon Press, 1929.

Courbage, Youssef, and Philippe Fargues. *Chrétiens et juifs dans l'Islam arabe et turc.* Paris: Fayard, 1992.

Davis, Stephen, J. *Coptic Christology in Practice: Incarnation and Divine Participation in Late Antique and Medieval Egypt.* Oxford Early Christian Studies. Oxford: Oxford University Press, 2008.

———. *The Early Coptic Papacy: The Egyptian Church and Its Leadership in Late Antiquity.* The Popes of Egypt 1. Cairo & New York: American University in Cairo Press, 2004.

Davis, Stephen J., Darlene Brooks Hedstrom, Salima Ikram, et al. "New Archaeology at Ancient Scetis: Surveys and Initial Excavations at the Monastery of St. John the Little in Wadi al-Natrun: Yale Monastic Archaeology Project." *Dumbarton Oaks Papers* 64 (2010): 217–28.

Den Heijer, Johannes. "Considerations sur les communautés chrétiennes en Égypte fatimide: l'État et l'Église sous le vizirat de Badr al-Jamālī (1074–1094)." In *L'Égypte fatimide, son art et son histoire,* edited by Marianne Barrucand, 569–78. Paris: Presses de l'Université Paris-Sorbonne, 1999.

———. *Mawhub ibn Mansur ibn Mafarrig et l'historiographie copto-arabe: Étude sur la composition de l'Histoire des Patriarches d'Alexandrie.* Corpus Scriptorum Christianorum Orientalium 13 = subsidia 83. Louvain: Peeters, 1989.

Du Roy, Gaétan. "Le miracle de la montagne et les chiffonniers du Moqattam." In *Figures contemporaines de la transmission*, edited by Nathalie Burnay and Annabelle Klein, 201–16. Namur: Presses Universitaires de Namur, 2009.

Du Roy, Gaétan, and Jamie Furniss. "Sœur Emmanuelle et les chiffonniers : Partage de vie et développement : 1971–1982." In *Mission et engagement politique après 1945: Afrique, Amérique Latine, Europe*, edited by Caroline Sappia and Olivier Servais, 87–101. Paris: Karthala, 2010.

El-Khawaga, Dina. "The Laity at the Heart of the Coptic Clerical Reform." In *Between Desert and City: The Coptic Orthodox Church Today*, edited by Nelly van Doorn-Harder and Kari Vogt, 142–66. Oslo: Novus,1997.

———. "Le renouveau copte: La communauté comme acteur politique." Ph.D. diss., Institut d'Étude Politique de Paris, 1993.

El-Leithy, Tamer. "Coptic Culture and Conversion in Medieval Cairo, 1293–1524 A.D." Ph.D. diss., Princeton University, 2005.

Ellli, Alberto. *Storia della chiesa copta*, 3 vols. Studia Orientalia Christiana Monographiae 12–14. Cairo & Jerusalem: Franciscan Printing Press, 2003.

Elm, Susanna. *"Virgins of God": The Making of Asceticism in Late Antiquity*. Oxford: Clarendon Press, 1994.

Elsässer, Sebastian. *The Coptic Question in the Mubarak Era*. New York: Oxford University Press, 2014.

———. "Press Liberalization, the New Media, and the 'Coptic Question': Muslim-Coptic Relations in Egypt in a Changing Media Landscape." *Middle Eastern Studies* 46, no. 1 (2010): 131–50.

———. "La 'question copte' entre crispations confessionnelles et overtures civiques." In *Chroniques Egyptiennes 2008*, edited by Imam Farag, 101–21. Cairo: CEDEJ, 2008.

Emmel, Stephen. "Shenoute the Monk: The Early Monastic Career of Shenoute the Archimandrite." In *Il monachesimo tra eredità e aperture: Atti del simposio "Testi e temi nella tradizione del monachesimo cristiano" per il 50e anniversario dell'istituto monastico di Sant'Anselmo, Roma, 28 maggio-1e giugno 2002*, edited by Maciej Bielawski and Daniël Hombergen, 151–74. Rome: Pontificio Ateneo S. Anselmo, 2004.

Evetts, B. T. A. *History of the Patriarchs of the Coptic Church of Alexandria*, 4 vols. Paris: Firmin-Didot, 1904–1915.

Farag, Lois M., ed. *The Coptic Christian Heritage: History, Faith, and Culture*. Abingdon, U.K. & New York: Routledge, 2014.

Farah, Nadia Ramsis. *Religious Strife in Egypt: Crisis and Ideological Conflict in the Seventies*. New York: Gordon and Breach 1986.

Finn, Richard. *Asceticism in the Graeco-Roman World*. Cambridge: Cambridge University Press, 2009.

Gabra, Gawdat, ed. *Christianity and Monasticism in the Fayoum Oasis*. Cairo: American University in Cairo Press, 2008.

———, ed. "Claremont Coptic Encyclopedia," http://ccdl.libraries.claremont.edu/cdm/landingpage/collection/cce. Accessed April 29, 2015.

———, ed. *Coptic Civilization: Two Thousand Years of Christianity in Egypt*. Cairo & New York: American University in Cairo Press, 2014.

———. *Coptic Monasteries*. Cairo: American University in Cairo Press, 2002.

Gabra, Gawdat, and Hany N. Takla, eds. *Christianity and Monasticism in Upper Egypt: Akhmim and Sohag*. Cairo & New York: American University in Cairo Press, 2007.

Gabry-Thienpoint, Séverine. "Anthropologie des musiques coptes en Égypte contemporaine." Ph.d. diss, Université Nanterre-Paris X, 2013.

———. "*Tarânîm* et *madîh:* Chants liturgiques coptes ou chansons populaires égyptiennes?" *Cahiers Rémois de Musicologie* 7 (December 2013): 87–99.
Gingras, G. E. trans. *Egeria: Diary of a Pilgrimage.* New York: Newman Press, 1970.
Giorda, Mariachiara. *Il regno di Dio in terra: Le fondazioni monastiche egiziane tra V e VII secolo.* Rome: Edizioni di Storia e Letteratura, 2011.
Goehring, James E. *Ascetics, Society and the Desert: Studies in Egyptian Monasticism.* Harrisburg: Trinity Press, 1999.
———. "The Dark Side of Landscape: Ideology and Power in the Christian Myth of the Desert." *Journal of Medieval and Early Modern Studies* 33, no. 3 (2003): 437–51.
Griffith, S. H. "Apologetics and Historiography in the Annals of Eutychius of Alexandria: Christian Self-Definition in the World of Islam." In *Studies on the Christian Arabic Heritage,* edited by Rifaat Ebied and Herman Teule. Louvain: Peeters, 2004.
Guirgis, Magdi, and Nelly van Doorn-Harder. *The Emergence of the Modern Coptic Papacy.* The Popes of Egypt 3. Cairo & New York: American University in Cairo Press, 2011.
Guirguis, Laure, ed. *Conversions religieuses et mutations politiques en Egypte.* Paris: Non Lieu, 2008.
———. *Les coptes d'Egypte: Violences communautaires et transformations politiques.* Paris: Karthala, 2012.
Hasan, S. S. *Christians versus Muslims in Modern Egypt.* Oxford: Oxford University Press, 2003.
Ibn Sabbaᶜ, Yuhanna ibn Abi Zakariyya. *Pretiosa Margarita de scientiis ecclesiasticis (al-Jawharah al-nafisah),* edited by V. P. Mistrih. Cairo: Éditions du Centre Franciscain d'Études Orientales Chrétiennes, 1966.
Iskander, Elizabeth. *Sectarian Conflict in Egypt: Coptic Media, Identity and Representation.* London & New York: Routledge, 2012.
Johnson, M. E., ed. *Between Memory and Hope: Readings on the Liturgical Year.* Collegeville, Minn.: Liturgical Press, 2000.
Krawiec, Rebecca S. "The Role of the Female Elder in Shenoute's White Monastery." In *Christianity and Monasticism in Upper Egypt: Akhmim and Sohag,* edited by Gawdat Gabra and Hany N. Takla, 59–71. Cairo & New York: American University in Cairo Press, 2007.
———. *Shenoute and the Women of the White Monastery.* New York: Oxford University Press, 2002.
Leeder, S. H. *Modern Sons of the Pharaohs.* London: Stoughton, 1918.
Lyster, William. *The Cave Church of Paul the Hermit: At the Monastery of St. Paul in Egypt.* New Haven: Yale University Press, 2008.
MacCoull, Leslie S. B., trans. *Coptic Legal Documents: Law as Vernacular Text and Experience in Late Antique Egypt.* Tempe: Arizona Center for Medieval and Renaissance Studies, 2009.
———. "The Paschal Letter of Alexander II, Patriarch of Alexandria: Greek Defense of Coptic Theology under Arab Rule." *Dumbarton Oaks Papers* 44 (1990): 27–40.
Malaty, Tadros. *Introduction to the Coptic Orthdox Church.* Alexandria: St. George's Coptic Orthodox Church, Sporting, 1993.
Mango, C., and R. Scott, trans. *The Chronicle of Theophanes Confessor.* Oxford: Clarendon Press, 1999.
Matthew the Poor, *Orthodox Prayer Life: The Interior Way.* Crestwood, NY: St. Vladimir's Seminary Press, 2003.
Mayeur-Jaouen, Catherine. *Pèlerinages d'Égypte: Histoire de la piété copte et musulmane, XVe–XXe siècles.* Paris: EHESS, 2005.

Meinardus, Otto. *Monks and Monasteries of the Egyptian Deserts.* Cairo & New York: American University in Cairo Press, 1992.
Mikhail, Maged S. A. *From Byzantine to Islamic Egypt: Religion, Identity and Politics after the Arab Conquest.* London & New York: Tauris, 2014.
Mina, A. A., ed. *Le nomocanon du patriarche copte Gabriel II ibn Turayk,* 2 vols. Beirut: CEDRAC, 1993.
Moftah, Ragheb, Martha Roy, and Margit Toth. *The Coptic Orthodox Liturgy of St. Basil; With Complete Musical Transcription.* Cairo: American University in Cairo Press, 1998.
Moussa, Mark. "*I Have Been Reading the Holy Gospels* by Shenoute of Atripe (Discourses 8, Work 1): Coptic Text, Translation, and Commentary." Ph.D. diss., Catholic University of America, 2010.
Oram, Elizabeth E. "Constructing Modern Copts: The Production of Coptic Christian Identity in Contemporary Egypt." Ph.D. diss., Princeton University, 2004.
Patrich, Joseph. "Monastic Landscapes." In *Recent Research on the Late Antique Countryside,* edited by W. Bowden, L. Lavan, and C. Machardo, 413–46. Leiden: Brill, 2004.
Patrick, Theodore Hall. *Traditional Egyptian Christianity: A History of the Coptic Orthodox Church.* Greensboro, N.C.: Fisher Park Press, 1996.
Ramzy, Carolyn. "Music: Performing Coptic Expressive Culture." In *The Coptic Christian Heritage: History, Faith, and Culture,* edited by Lois M. Farag, 160–77. Abingdon, U.K. & New York: Routledge, 2014.
———."The Politics of (Dis) Engagement: Coptic Christian Revival and the Performative Politics of Song." Ph.D. diss., University of Toronto, 2014.
———. "*Taratil:* Songs of Praise and the Musical Discourse of Nostalgia among Coptic Immigrants in Toronto, Canada." M.A. thesis, Florida State University, 2006.
Reid, Donald Malcolm. *Whose Pharaohs? Archaeology, Museums, and Egyptian National Identity from Napoleon to World War I.* Cairo: American University in Cairo Press, 2002.
Reiss, Wolfram. *Erneuerung in der Koptisch-Orthodoxen Kirche: Die Geschichte der koptischorthodoxen Sonntagsschulbewegung und die Aufnahme ihrer Reformansätze in den Erneuerungsbewegungen der Koptisch-Orthodoxen Kirche der Gegenwart.* Hamburg: Lit, 1998.
Rousseau, Philip. *Pachomius: The Making of a Community in Fourth-Century Egypt.* Berkeley: University of California Press, 1999.
Russell, Norman, trans. *Historia monachorum in Aegypto 1: The Lives of the Desert Fathers.* London: Mobray, 1980.
Salama, Pishoy. "Of All Nations: Exploring Intercultural Marriages in the Coptic Orthodox Church of the GTA." D. Min. diss., University of St. Michael's College and University of Toronto, 2012.
Saleh, Malis J. "Government Relations with the Coptic Community in Egypt during the Fatimid Period (358–567 A.H. / 969–1171 C.E.)." PhD Diss., University of Chicago, 1995.
Saliou, Catherine. *Les lois des bâtiments: Voisinage et habitat urbain dans l'empire romain; Recherches sur les rapports entre le droit et la construction privée, du siècle d'Auguste au siècle de Justinien.* Beirut: Institut Français d'Archéologie du Proche-Orient, 1994.
Samir, Khalil Samir, and Jørgen S. Nielsen, eds. *Christian Arabic Apologetics during the Abbasid Period (750–1258).* Leiden & New York: Brill, 1994.
Satoshi, Toda. *Vie de S. Macaire l'Égyptien: Édition et traduction des texts copte et syriaque.* Gorgias Eastern Christian Studies 31. Piscataway, N.J.: Gorgias Press, 2012.
Schroeder, Caroline T. *Monastic Bodies: Discipline and Salvation in Shenoute of Atripe.* Philadelphia: University of Pennsylvania Press, 2007.

———. "Prophecy and Porneia in Shenoute's Letters: The Rhetoric of Sexuality in a Late Antique Egyptian Monastery." *Journal of Near Eastern Studies* 65, number 2, (April 2006):81–97.

Sedra, Paul. "Class Cleavages and Ethnic Conflict: Coptic Christian Communities in Modern Egyptian Politics." *Islam and Christian-Muslim Relations* 10, no. 2 (1999): 219–35.

———. *From Mission to Modernity: Evangelicals, Reformers, and Education in Nineteenth-Century Egypt.* London & New York: Tauris, 2011.

———. "John Lieder and His Mission in Egypt: The Evangelical Ethos at Work among the Nineteenth-Century Copts." *Journal of Religious History* 28 (October 2004): 219–39.

Seybold, Christian Friedrich. *Severus ibn al-Muqaffaʿ: Historia Patriarcharum Alexandrinorum,* 2 vols. Corpus Scriptorum Christianorum Orientalium 52 and 59 = ar. 8–9. Beirut & Paris, 1904, 1910.

Shenoda, Anthony. "Cultivating Mystery: Miracles and a Coptic Miracle Imaginary." Ph.D. diss., Harvard University, 2010.

———."Reflections on the (In)Visibility of Copts in Egypt," *Jadaliyya.com,* May 18, 2011, http://www.jadaliyya.com/pages/index/1624/. Accessed May 13, 2013.

Shenoda, Maryann M. "Displacing Dhimmī, Maintaining Hope: Unthinkable Coptic Representations of Fatimid Egypt." *International Journal of Middle East Studies* 39, no 4, (November 2007): 587–606.

———. "Lamenting Islam, Imagining Persecution: Copto-Arabic Opposition to Islamization and Arabization in Fatimid Egypt (969–1171 C.E.)." Ph.D. diss., Harvard University, 2010.

Stene, Nora. "Becoming a Copt." In *Between Desert and City: The Coptic Orthodox Church Today,* edited by Nelly van Doorn–Harder and Kari Vogt, 190–211. Oslo: Novus, 1997.

Shenoda, Maryann M., Johannes den Heijer, Yaacov Lev, and Mark N. Swanson, *Non-Muslim Communities in Fatimid Egypt (10th–12th Centuries CE),* ed. Maryann M. Shenoda, Johannes den Heijer, Yaacov Lev, and Mark N. Swanson, Special Issue of *Medieval Encounters* 21, nos. 4–5 (2015)

———."The Challenge of the Diaspora as Reflected in a Coptic Sunday School." *Journal of Eastern Christian Studies* 54, nos. 1–2 (2002): 77–90.

———. "Into the Lands of Immigration." In *Between Desert and City: The Coptic Orthodox Church Today,* edited by Nelly van Doorn–Harder and Kari Vogt, 254–64. Oslo: Novus, 1997.

———. "Multiple Choices? Language Usage and Transmission of Religious Tradition in the Coptic Orthodox Community in London." *British Journal of Religious Education* 20, no. 2 (1998): 90–101.

Swan, Laura. *The Forgotten Desert Mothers: Sayings, Lives and Stories of Early Christian Women.* Mahwah, N.J.: Paulist Press, 2001.

Swanson, Mark. *The Coptic Papacy in Islamic Egypt 641–1517.* The Popes of Egypt 2. Cairo & New York: American University in Cairo Press, 2010.

———. "Sainthood Achieved: Coptic Patriarch Zacharias according to *The History of the Patriarchs.*" In *Writing 'True Stories': Historians and Hagiographers in the Late-Antique and Medieval Near East,* edited by Arietta Papaconstantinou et al. Cultural Encounters in Late Antiquity and the Middle Ages 9. Turnhout, Belgium: Brepols, 2010.

Tadros, Mariz. "Behind Egypt's Deep Red Lines." *Middle East Report Online,* October 13, 2010, http://merip.org/mero/mero101310. Accessed May 4, 2015.

———. *Copts at the Crossroads: The Challenges of Building Inclusive Democracy in Egypt.* Cairo & New York: American University in Cairo Press, 2013.

———. "The Non-Muslim 'Other'; Gender and Contestation of Hierarchy of Rights." *Hawwa: Journal of Women of the Middle East and the Islamic World* 7, issue 2 (2009): 111–43.

———. "Vicissitudes in the Entente between Church and the State." *International Journal of Middle East Studies* 41, no. 2 (2009): 269–87.

Talley, T. J. *The Origins of the Liturgical Year*, 2nd ed. Collegeville, Minn.: Liturgical Press, 1991.

Thorbjørnsrud, Berit. *Controlling the Body to Liberate the Soul: Towards an Analysis of the Coptic Orthodox Concept of the Body.* Oslo: Unipub, 1999.

Trombley, Frank R. "Sawirus ibn al-Muqaffaʿ and the Christians of Umayyad Egypt: War and Society in Documentary Context." In *Papyrology and the History of Early Islamic Egypt*, , edited by Petra M. Sijpesteijn and Lennart Sundelin, 199–226. Leiden & Boston: Brill, 2004.

van Doorn-Harder, Nelly. *Contemporary Coptic Nuns.* Columbia: University of South Carolina Press, 1995.

———. "Copts: Fully Egyptian, but for a Tattoo?" In *Nationalism and Minority Identities in Islamic Societies*, edited by Maya Shatzmiller, 22–57. Montreal & Kingston: McGill-Queens University Press, 2005.

———."Recreating Saintly Women: Gender and Coptic Spirituality." In *Coptic Culture: Past, Present, and Future*, edited by Mariam F. Ayad, 201–214. Stevenage, U.K.: Coptic Orthodox Church Center, 2012.

van Doorn-Harder, Nelly, and Kari Vogt. *Between Desert and City. The Coptic Orthodox Church Today.* Oslo: Novus, 1997.

Viaud, Gerard. *La liturgie des coptes d'Égypt.* Paris: Librairie d'Amerique et d'Orient, 1978.

Vivian, T. *St. Peter of Alexandria: Bishop and Martyr.* Philadelphia: Fortress Press, 1988.

Vivier, Anne-Sophie. "Quand Le Caire se révèle copte: Traits et enjeux des pratiques de sociabilité des coptes orthodoxies dans Le Caire contemporain." *Revue des Mondes Musulmans et de la Mediterranée* (September 2005): 107–10, 205–27.

Voile, Brigitte. *Les coptes d'Égypte sous Nasser: Sainteté miracle, apparitions.* Paris: CNRS, 2004.

Wakin, Edward. *A Lonely Minority: The Modern Story of Egypt's Copts.* New York: William Morrow, 1963.

Ward, Benedicta. *The Sayings of the Desert Fathers: The Alphabetic Collection.* New York: Macmillan, 1975.

Watson, Johan. *Among the Copts.* Brighton: Sussex Academic Press, 2002.

Wilfong, Terry G. *Women of Jeme: Lives in a Coptic Town in Late Antique Egypt.* Ann Arbor: University of Michigan Press, 2002.

Wipszycka, Ewa. *Moines et communautés monastiques en Égypte (IVe–VIIIe siècles).* Warsaw: Journal of Juristic Papyrology, 2009.

———. "Resources and Economic Activities of the Egyptian Monastic Communities (4th–8th Century)." *Journal of Juristic Papyrology* 41 (2011): 159–263.

Wortley, John. *The Anonymous Sayings of the Desert Fathers.* Cambridge: Cambridge University Press, 2013.

Yassa, ʿAbd al-Masih, O. H. E. Burmester, Aziz S. Atiya, and Antoine Khater, *History of the Patriarchs of the Egyptian Church, Known as the History of the Holy Church, by Sawîrus ibn al-Mukaffaʿ, Bishop of al-Ašmûnîn*, vols. 2 (3 parts) and 4 (2 parts). Cairo: Société d'Archéologie Copte, 1943–1974.

Zaborowski, J. R. "From Coptic to Arabic in Medieval Egypt." *Medieval Encounters*, volume 14, Issue 1 (2008): 15–40.

Selected Journals

al-Kiraza, http://alkirazamagazine.com/Archive.aspx?IssueID=12&LanguageID=1. Accessed May 18, 2015.

Coptica, http://www.stshenouda.org/society/coptica.htm. Accessed May 18, 2015.

Coptologia Journal. http://www.coptologia.com/presta/category.php?id_category=5. Accessed April 29, 2015.

Journal of the Canadian Society for Coptic Studies, http://www.lockwoodpressjournals.com/loi/cscs. Accessed April 29, 2015.

Journal of Coptic Studies, http://www.peeters-leuven.be/journoverz.asp?nr=11. Accessed May 18, 2015.

Le Monde Copte, http://www.lemondecopte.com/. Accessed May 18, 2015).

Watani, http://en.wataninet.com/. Accessed May 18, 2015.

CONTRIBUTORS

GHADA BOTROS is assistant professor at the American University in Cairo. She wrote a dissertation on Coptic immigrant churches in North America at the University of Toronto, Department of Sociology.

DARLENE L. BROOKS HEDSTROM is professor and chair of history at Wittenberg University (Springfield, Ohio). She is also director of archaeology at Wittenberg, where she trains students in field archaeology. She directed excavation work for the Yale Monastic Archaeology Project at the White Monastery (2006–2008) in Sohag and at the Monastery of John the Little in Wadi Natrun (2006–2010).

GAÉTAN DU ROY teaches and works as a researcher at the Laboratoire de Recherches Historiques (LaRHis) at the Université Catholique de Louvain (Belgium). He is also an associate researcher at the Centre d'Études et de Documentation Économiques, Juridiques et Sociales (CEDEJ) in Cairo. His Ph.D. dissertation is entitled "Le prêtre des chiffonniers ou la construction d'une autorité religieuse au Caire, entre charisme, tradition et clientélisme (1974–2014)."

SEBASTIAN ELSÄSSER is assistant professor at the Institute of Oriental and Islamic Studies at Christian-Albrechts-Universität Kiel, Germany. He received his M.A. and Ph.D. degrees in Islamic studies from the Freie Universität Berlin and was an associated researcher at the Centre d'Études et de Documentation Économiques, Juridiques et Sociales (CEDEJ) in Cairo (2008 – 2011). In 2014 his book *The Coptic Question in the Mubarak Era* was published.

SÉVERINE GABRY-THIENPONT is an ethnomusicologist and a researcher at the French Institute for Oriental Archaeology (IFAO) in Cairo. She also is an associate researcher at the Research Center in Ethnomusicology (CREM-LESC-UMR 7186) in Paris. In 2010 she won the Michel Seurat Prize, awarded by the French National Scientific Research Centre (CNRS), for her fieldwork on Coptic music in Egypt.

ANGIE HEO teaches at the University of Chicago Divinity School. She was a research fellow at the Max Planck Institute for the Study of Religious and Ethnic Diversity in Göttingen, Germany, where she wrote her book on the material politics of Coptic Orthodox imagination in Egypt.

KAREL C. INNEMÉE taught early Christian art at Leiden University and served as visiting professor of Coptic studies at the American University in Cairo. At present he is assistant professor of Near Eastern Archaeology at Leiden University and director of various survey, excavation and conservation projects in Wadi Natrun, Egypt.

RACHEL LOEWEN obtained her master's in religious studies from McMaster University. Her current interests concentrate on the Coptic diaspora in North America, specifically, on the present-day activities in the Coptic communities in Toronto, Jersey City, and New York City.

MAGED S.A. MIKHAIL is professor of history at the California State University, Fullerton. Among other works, he is the author of *From Byzantine to Islamic Egypt: Religion, Identity and Politics after the Arab Conquest* (2014) and "A Lost Chapter in the History of Wadi al-Natrun (Scetis): The Coptic *Lives* and Monastery of Abba John Khame" (2014).

HIROKO MIYOKAWA is a visiting fellow at the Institute of the Asian, African, and Middle Eastern Studies, Sophia University, in Tokyo and a post doctoral fellow at School of Interdisciplinary Area Studies, University of Oxford. She conducted field work in Egypt from 2007 to 2011 and she obtained her Ph. D. in area studies from Sophia University in 2016.

CAROLYN M. RAMZY is an assistant professor of ethnomusicology at Carleton University. She specializes in music of the Middle East and specifically studies the performative politics of belonging among Egypt's Coptic Christians. Her work has been published in *Ethnos: Journal of Anthropology*, the *Journal of the Canadian Society for Coptic Studies*, *The Performing Arts Encyclopedia: Explore Music, Theater, and Dance at the Library of Congress*. Her article "Performing Coptic Expressive Culture" was published in Farag, *The Coptic Christian Heritage*, 2014.

CAROLINE T. SCHROEDER is associate professor of religious and classical studies at the University of the Pacific. She is the author of *Monastic Bodies: Discipline and Salvation in Shenoute of Atripe* (2007) and numerous articles in, among others, the *Journal of the American Academy of Religion*, the *Journal of Early Christian Studies*, *Church History*, the *Journal of Ancient Near Eastern Studies*. She has also contributed to various collected volumes. She co-directs the Coptic Digital Humanities project Coptic SCRIPTORIUM and is currently completing a monograph on children in early Egyptian monasteries.

NORA STENE is associate professor of religious studies at Oslo University, Norway. She has written about Copts both in Egypt and in diaspora, using perspectives from childhood- and minority studies. She is currently part of a research group at Oslo University studying present-day Christians in the Middle East.

MARK SWANSON teaches Christian-Muslim studies, interfaith relations, and global Christian history at the Lutheran School of Theology at Chicago; previously he taught at Luther Seminary (St. Paul, Minnesota) and at the Evangelical Theological Seminary in Cairo, Egypt. He is the author of *The Coptic Papacy in Islamic Egypt (641–1517)* (2010) and was the Christian Arabic section editor for *Christian-Muslim Relations: A Bibliographical History*, vols. 1–5 (600–1500 C.E.) (2009–2013).

MARIZ TADROS is a fellow at the Institute of Development Studies, University of Sussex, U.K., where she co-leads the Power and Popular Politics cluster. She is the author of several publications on Copts, religious pluralism in the Arab world, Islamist political parties, civil society and democratization, as well as on the politics of gender and development.

NELLY (PIETERNELLA) VAN DOORN-HARDER is professor of religious studies at Wake Forest University. She is the co-author of *The Egyptian Church and Its Leadership from the Ottoman Period to the Present: Part III, The Modern Coptic Papacy (1798–2010)* (2011), co-editor of *Between Desert and City. The Coptic Orthodox Church Today* (1997), and author of *Contemporary Coptic Nuns* (University of South Carolina Press, 1995).

INDEX

'Abd al-'Aziz ibn Marwan, governor of Egypt (r. 685–705 C.E.), 163–65, 167
Abd el-Kodous, 40
Abraham, Patriarch (r. 975– 978 C.E.), in Arabic: Afrahām ibn Zur'ah), 8, 73, 157, 187, 232
Abu al-Barakat, 173, 175–78
Abu Nofer, see: Onouphrios, Saint
Adel, Maged, 48, 49
Afrahām ibn Zur'ah, see: Abraham, Patriarch
Agbeyya (book of the hours), 85
Al-Hakim bin Amr Allah, Fatimid caliph, (r. 996–1020), 165–66
Al-Makin the Younger, 177–79
Al-Marinab, 30–31, 64
Al-Mu'iz, Fatimid Caliph, 73,
Al-Sha'er, Akram, 40
Al-Sisi, Abd al-Fattah, President, 33, 97
Alexandria, 1, 7, 13, 24, 27, 29, 38, 47, 54, 56, 62, 63, 94, 100, 161, 163, 169–77, 179, 183, 195, 200; Catechetical School of, 83, 118; Cyril of, 17; *History of the Patriarchs of*, 16, 157–59, 167, 199, 200; Demetrius of, 173; Isaac of, 210; Macarius of, 206; Patriarch of, 100, 151; Theophilus of, 197
Alhan, liturgical hymnody, 11, 85, 93–97, 99, 101, 103, 106, 236
Allam, Magdy, 40
'Amr ibn al-'As, 161–63
Angelos Saad, 102, 104, 105
Anthony, Saint (ca. 251–356 C.E.), 7, 16, 183, 188, 195, 197, 206, 208
apatheia, 195
Apophthegmata Patrum, 183, 194, 196–98, 206

Arab, conquest, 7, 8, 109, 151, 163, 172, 200, 217; identity, 4; invasion, 1, 3, 13, 155, 161, 223; nationalism, 22; spring 2, 14
Arabic (language), 3, 4, 16, 56, 88, 93–95, 97, 99, 103, 116, 119–21, 123, 126–27, 130, 136, 142, 147–48, 152–54, 157–58, 170–72, 174–76, 178–80
Ard el Lewa, 36–38, 43–44, 46
Asceticism, 181, 183, 188, 193–95, 206–7, 254
Assaad, Marie, 36, 42
Aswan, 4, 30, 64, 225
Asyut, 54–55, 83, 152
Athanasius, of Alexandria, Patriarch (r. 326–272 C.E.), 7, 170, 174, 195, 197
Atiya, Aziz, S. (1898–1988), 11, 157
Australia, 6, 56, 61, 107, 117
Awad, Father Rueiss, 104

Badr al-Jamali, governor (r. 1074–1094 CE), 167
Baptism, 52, 73, 97, 127–28, 136–37, 143, 169, 175, 198; baptize, 3
Bassily, Tharwat, 55
belonging, Coptic, 3–4, 6, 13, 52–53, 57, 65, 67, 76, 83, 101, 134–35, 141–43, 147–48
Benjamin I, Patriarch (623–662 C.E.), 161–63, 165–67, 200
Bishoy al-Antony, Father, 56
Bishoy, Bishop, 56, 73–74
Boutros, Zakareya, Father, 55, 69–70, 74–75, 230
Byzantine, 116, 160–61, 172, 210, 217; Empire, 3; era 84, 170

Cairo, 6, 10–11, 13–15, 17, 25, 27, 29–30, 35–38, 46–47, 50–51, 53–55, 57–59, 66,

Cairo (*continued*)
 70, 81–83, 86, 100–101, 104, 107, 111, 115, 134–36, 138, 141, 143, 146, 151–53, 158, 160, 165, 195
Canada, 4, 14, 56, 61, 94–99, 101–4, 106, 110–11, 114, 118, 121–22, 124–28, 132
Canons of Hippolytus, 174
Cassian, John (ca. 360–435 C.E.), 183, 197, 206
Cathedral, 96; St. Mark's, 1, 11, 14, 17, 27, 55, 77, 134
Catholic, Roman, 1, 5, 9, 59, 67–68, 76, 82, 87, 112, 143, 219
Catholicos, 169, 177
Chalcedon, Council of, 7–8, 130, 179, 199
Chalcedonian, 161, 163, 178; anti-, 161, 199, 200; pro-, 9, 171–72
charismatic, 13, 15, 66–69, 71, 73–77, 79, 105, 208
child, children, 6, 9, 13, 16, 41, 43, 46, 56, 70, 72, 78, 83, 88, 97, 108–9, 114, 116, 120–21, 126, 129–30, 134–48, 183, 185–89, 196, 198
Christodolous, Patriarch (r. 1046–1077), 167
Clement (ca. 150–215 C.E.), 7, 167
Clerical College (*al-Kulliya al-Iklirikiya*), 54, 228
collective memory, 8, 57, 59
Conference of the Council of Coptic Churches, 104
convent, of Abu Saifein, 13, 60; Amir Tadrus, 59
Coptic Canadian, 15, 93, 95, 98, 100–106; Center 96–98, 105; churches 99; identity 95; St. Mark's Village, 96
Coptic Encyclopedia, 11, 81, 158; file (al-milaff al-qibti), 4, 52; identity, 3–5, 8–9, 11–12, 14, 16–17, 21, 28, 32, 68, 80, 89, 107, 124, 142, 151, 154, 181; language, 8–9, 11, 16, 85, 95, 122, 126, 151–56, 158, 184; museum, 9, 81, 151; music, 80–83, 85, 87–89, 97, 111; question, 21, 24, 33; Youth Movement, 26–27, 30
Copticness, 3–4, 6, 12
Council of Nicea (325 C.E.), 176–79; of Chalcedon (451 C.E.), 7–8, 130, 161, 163, 179, 199; of Ephesus (431 C.E.), 17, 198
Cyril of Alexandria, 17
Cyril II, Patriarch (r. 1078–1092 C.E.), 167
Cyrus, al-Muqawqas, 161, 200

David Ensemble, 12
deacon, (*shammas*), 68, 70, 80, 84, 86–87, 94, 104, 111, 116, 118, 121, 137, 140, 144; Archdeacon, 9, 159–61, 163, 164; deaconess, 53
Dechert, Bob, 102, 105, 236
Deir el-Moharraq, see Monastery, 83, 85–87, 152
Demetrius, Patriarch, the Vinedresser (r. 189–232 CE), 16, 169–70, 173–79
diaspora, 3, 6, 10, 12–15, 39, 41, 53, 56, 61, 64, 87, 91, 96–99, 124–27, 129–30, 133, 136, 181
Didascalia, 170, 178–79
Didymus Institute (for Blind Cantors), 83–86, 88–89
Didymus the Blind, Saint, 85
Dimyana, Saint, 4
Diocletian, Emperor (r. 284–305 C.E.), 7, 154
Dioscorus, Patriarch (r. 444– 454 C.E.), 7
Dokki, 36, 50

ecumenical, 2, 13, 68–70, 76, 103, 176; bishop of ecumenical and social affairs, 67; councils, 84, 130; organization, 70
El-Gabbaly, Hatem, 42
El-Khawaga, Dina, 54, 68
Ephesus, Council of, 17, 198
Eucharist, 84, 127, 136–45, 175, 198
Europe, European, 56, 103, 107, 109, 158, 184
Eutychius, Melkite Patriarch (d. 940 C.E.), 172–73, 175–78, 199–200
Evangelical, 5, 66–67, 69, 71, 74–78, 100, 102, 163
exorcism, 62, 67, 70, 73–75, 77, 132
Ezbet el Nakhl, 28, 36–38, 43–46

Fanous, Father, 132
Fanous, Isaac (1919–2007), 12
Fatimid Dynasty (969– 1171 C.E.), 8, 165
Fayezz, Mahir, 74, 232

George the Archdeacon, 158–59, 161, 163–64
George, Saint, 4, 60, 62, 96' Church of, 96, 101, 104

Index

gender, 13–14, 16, 46, 135–42, 145, 148, 182–84, 186, 193; roles, 121–22
Giza, 26, 29, 36, 38, 47, 59–60
Greek, 3, 7, 81, 152, 154–55, 172, 174–75, 179–81, 185, 209, 215; Christians/Church, 104, 113, 126–27, 219
Guirguis, Habib (1876–1951), 9, 54, 83, 222, 230

Habib, Ibtessam, 40
hagiographic, 61, 66, 101, 168, 194, 204, 211
hagiography, 62, 73, 160, 176, 183, 196, 204
Heraclius, Emperor, 170–72, 177–78, 200
Higher Institute of Coptic Studies (ICS), 11–12
history of the Patriarchs of Alexandria, the, 16, 157–59, 167, 199, 200
Holy Family, 1, 78, 84
Holy Virgin, see Saint Mary
Holy Week, 163, 169–70, 174–76, 180

Ibrahim, Hussein, 40
icon, 5, 12–13, 29, 52, 57–62, 76, 116, 195–96
iconography, 9, 11–13, 52, 112, 204
identity, see: Coptic
Imbaba, 27–31, 36–37
Irini, Mother (1936–2006), Abbess of the Convent of Abu Saifein, 13, 60
Iskander, Andrawus, Father, 77, 78
Iskander, Elizabeth, 9, 62
Iskander, Laila, 46, 50
Islam/Islamic, 3–4, 6, 8, 15, 22–23, 26–27, 31–32, 38, 41, 55–56, 59, 69–70, 75, 85, 95–97, 103, 110, 113, 154, 158–60, 165, 170–71, 176–78, 217
Islamist, 21, 23, 25–26, 32–33, 40, 43, 49, 104
Issa, Ibrahim, 41

Jerusalem, 3, 84, 170–72, 176
John I, Patriarch (r. 496– 505 C.E.), 199
John II, Patriarch (r. 505–516 C.E.), 199
John III, Patriarch. 158, 163, 166

Kaleeny, Georgette, 40
Karygiannis, Jim, 104–5, 240
Khalas al-Nufus, (Society for the Salvation of the Souls), 70, 74
Kyrillos IV, Patriarch (1854–1861), 9, 16, 54, 57, 82, 151–52

Kyrillos V, Patriarch (1874–1927), 83
Kyrillos VI, Patriarch (1959–1971), 5, 9–11, 53, 68, 107
Kyrillos, George, 81

Labib, Iqladiyus (1868–1918), 9, 16, 151–56
Labib, Maher, Samuel, 70
London, 6, 14, 135–36, 138–39, 141, 143, 146–47

Mairoun, 136–37
Magued Tawfik, 60–61
Mamluk period (1250– 1517 C.E.), 1, 8
Mansheyet Nasser, 27, 36, 44, 47–48, 51, 62, 72
Maqrizi, 199–201
Marcos, Marcos, Father, 99–101, 104, 111, 114, 129, 237
Mark, Saint, the Apostle, 1, 9, 84, 100, 111, 130, 200
martyr(s), martyrdom, 1–2, 6–8, 11, 28, 59–63, 97, 130, 132, 154, 160–61, 163, 165, 172, 175, 195, 204; era of, 7; Alexandrian, 56; of the revolution, 48–49
Mary the Egyptian, Saint, 16
Mary, Virgin, 8, 10, 59–60, 68, 76, 83, 152, 154
Maspero (also see: youth, Coptic), 4, 27, 29–31, 47–49, 53, 56, 63–64, 95, 102, 104–5; Youth Movement, 4, 27
Matta el-Miskin (1919–2006), see: Matthew the Poor
Matthew the Poor, 14, 57, 67–68
Maurice, Sameh, Pastor, 78
Mawhub ibn Mansur ibn Mufarrij, 158, 167
media technologies, 14, 53, 56–57,64
Melkites, 7, 171–73, 176–79, 199–200
Menas, Saint, 57
Messalianism, 198
Meunier, Michael, 28
Michael of Damru, Bishop, 165–67
minority, 3, 8, 14, 17, 34, 36, 38, 41, 51, 79, 103, 116, 125, 135, 144, 147, 156, 212
miracles, 54, 62, 66, 68, 75–77, 132, 200
Misa'il, Father, 84–86
Mississauga, 96–98, 102, 118, 125
Mityas Nasr (Minqarius), 28
Moawad, Samuel, 8

Moftah, Ragheb (1898–2001), 11, 81, 85
monastery, 165, 206, 216; Abu Fana, 104; Anthony, St., 183; al-Baramus, 200–201; Muharraq, 83–84, 87, 152; Saint Macarius, 14, 57, 68, 195–96, 199–204, 206; Saint Paul, 183;Saint Samaan, 71–74, 76, 79; Shahran, 165; Saint Shenoute, 181–82, 184–86, 191; White, 17, 208
monasticism, 11, 14, 16, 118, 130, 181–83, 193–99, 201, 204–7, 211–12, 214–17
Morsi, Mohamed, President, 1, 33, 35, 49–50, 52, 56, 97, 113
Moses, Saint, 196
Mubarak, Hosni, President (1981– 2011), 14, 21, 23–26, 29–30, 32–34, 50–52, 62, 72, 78, 97, 101, 105, 110, 113
Mu'izz, al, Caliph, 73
Muqattam Mountain, 2, 8, 13, 15, 36–38, 44, 46–48, 55, 66–67, 70–79, 101 157
museum, Coptic, 9, 81; Canadian Coptic, 96, 151
Muslim Brotherhood, 1, 21, 25, 32–33, 40–41, 49–50, 52, 97

Nag Hammadi, 29, 63, 93–94, 102, 235
Nagib Sawiris, 32
Nakhlah, Kamil Salih, 157–59
Nasser, Gamal Abdel, President (1956–1970), 11, 15, 23, 36, 96, 100, 109–10
national unity (al-wihda al-wataniya), 23–24, 100–101, 106, 156
North America, 16, 96, 98–100, 107–11, 114–22, 125–26, 130, 181, 184

Onouphrios, Saint, 195, 200, 204
Origen (ca. 185–234/235 C.E.), 7, 174–75
Ottoman Empire (in Egypt, 1517–1867 C.E.), 9, 104

Pachomius, Saint (292–346 C.E.), 84, 155, 183, 197, 206, 208–9
Palladius (ca. 363–420 C.E.), 206
Pambo, Saint, 206
Paphnoutios, St., 195, 200
patriarchate, 56, 63, 69, 96, 100, 112, 167, 199, 200
Pentecostal (-ism), 67, 74, 103, 116
Peter of Alexandria, Archbishop, 174–75

Peter, Father (Toronto), 125, 128–33; of Rome, 175
pharaoh,. 9, 15, 17, 99, 103, 130, 154
pharaonic, 7, 9, 10, 12–13, 28, 81–82, 151–52, 156, 205–6
Poimen, Saint, 196, 198, 204
Pontius Pilate, 164–65
Protestant, 1, 5, 9, 13, 32, 66–70, 72, 74–77, 79, 83, 103, 132–33, 219
Pseudo-George of Arbela, 176–77
Pseudo-Macarius, 199

Qalyubiya, 36, 47, 54
Qasr al-Dubbara church, 74, 76–78

Rabia al-Adawiya Square, 1, 2
Rafiq Habib, 32
relics, 52, 61–62, 73, 169, 196
Renaissance (al-nahda), 11, 53
Rueiss, Saint, 96; Church of, 101–4

sacraments, 3, 5, 16, 127, 136–37, 142–43, 146, 148, 198
Sadat, Anwar, President, 23, 97, 100–101, 110, 113
Salafi (Muslims), 14, 27, 30, 32, 49, 225
Samaan, Father, 15, 47, 66–69, 71–79, 101
Samaan, Saint (Simon the Tanner), 8, 101, 157
Samuel, Bishop (1962–1981), 67, 70
satellite TV, 39, 53, 55, 64, 67, 69–70, 74, 98, 102; Aghapy TV, 55–56.; al-Haya TV, 55, 69–70.; CTV (Coptic TV), 55–56, 69.; CYC, 55.; meSAT, 55.; SAT 7, 55
sectarian, 22–24, 32, 39, 40–42, 62, 64, 173; conflicts, 21; incidents, 26–30, 101; strife, 24, 110, 113; violence, 4, 14, 31, 33, 93–97, 100–104
Shafiq, Ahad, 32, 33
Shari'a, 23, 41
Sharaf, Essam Abdel Aziz, 31
Shenouda III, Patriarch (r. 1971–2012 C.E.), 3, 6, 12–13, 17, 23, 27, 33, 41, 51, 53–56, 60, 67–71, 73, 77, 79, 84, 89, 100–101, 105, 107–8, 111–13, 125, 131
Shenoute the Archimandrite, or of Atribe, Saint, 8, 16–17, 155, 161–62, 181–93, 197, 208

Shubra, 29, 54, 63, 71, 86–87
Sketis, 165, 196–200, 204, 210
Society for the Salvation of the Souls, see: Khalas al-Nufus
Stoicism, Stoics, 188–92
Sul, 26–27, 30–31
Sunday school, 9, 11, 16, 76–77, 80, 88–89, 98, 103, 114, 117, 122, 126–27, 136, 141, 146–48; movement, 54, 67, 83, 147–48
Synaxarium, 62, 175–176/

Tahrir (square), 4, 24–25, 29–30, 53, 62–63
Taranim, 25, 80, 83
Taratil (singular, tartila), 95–101, 103, 106
Tawadros II, patriarch, 1–2, 33, 79, 125
Theodore, Abba, 198
Theodosius of Alexandria, patriarch, 199
Theofilus of Alexandria, patriarch (r. 384–412 C.E.), 197
Toronto, 16, 93–96, 98, 100–102, 104, 107–8, 111, 113, 116–17, 124

United State, USA, 2, 28, 38, 56, 61, 67, 97–98, 100–101, 110–11, 113, 115–17, 121

Wadi Natrun, 57, 196, 201, 210–11, 216–17
Wafd Party, 32

youth, Coptic, 9–10, 14, 16, 25, 33, 44, 47, 49, 53–54, 56, 64, 77–78, 83–84, 89, 94, 102–3, 108, 112–19, 121–23, 126–28; Coptic Youth Movement, 25–31

Zabbalin, 14, 34–51, 69, 71–73, 78–79
Zacharias, Patriarch (1004–1032 C.E.), 165, 167

CPSIA information can be obtained
at www.ICGtesting.com
Printed in the USA
BVOW03*2052060917
493616BV00003B/3/P

9 781611 177848